LANGUAGE IN SOCIETY 7

The Language of Children and Adol

Language in Society

GENERAL EDITOR
Peter Trudgill, Professor of Linguistic Science
University of Reading

ADVISORY EDITORS
Ralph Fasold, Professor of Linguistics
Georgetown University
William Labov, Professor of Linguistics
University of Pennsylvania

The Language of Children and Adolescents

The Acquisition of Communicative Competence

SUZANNE ROMAINE

BASIL BLACKWELL

P
118
.R65
1986

© Suzanne Romaine 1984

First published 1984
Reprinted 1986

Basil Blackwell Ltd
108 Cowley Road, Oxford OX4 1JF, UK

Basil Blackwell Inc.
432 Park Avenue South, Suite 1505,
New York, NY 10016, USA

All rights reserved. Except for the quotation of short passages for the purposes of criticism and review, no part of this publication may be reproduced, stored in a retrieval system, or transmitted, in any form or by any means, electronic, mechanical, photocopying, recording or otherwise, without the prior permission of the publisher.

Except in the United States of America, this book is sold subject to the condition that it shall not, by way of trade or otherwise, be lent, re-sold, hired out, or otherwise circulated without the publisher's prior consent in any form of binding or cover other than that in which it is published and without a similar condition including this condition being imposed on the subsequent purchaser.

British Library Cataloguing in Publication Data

Romaine, Suzanne
   The language of children and adolescents.
   1. Children–Language
   I. Title
   401'.9   B1139.L3
   ISBN 0-631-12927-8
   ISBN 0-631-12928-6 Pbk

DABNEY LANCASTER LIBRARY
LONGWOOD COLLEGE
FARMVILLE, VIRGINIA 23901

Library of Congress Cataloging in Publication Data

Romaine, Suzanne, 1951–
   The language of children and adolescents.

   (Language in society; 7)
   Bibliography: p. 272
   Includes index.
   1. Language acquisition. 2.Sociolinguistics.
   3. Communicative competence. I. Title. II. Series:
   Language in society (Oxford, Oxfordshire); 7.
   P118.R65 1984   401'.9   84-12471
   ISBN 0-631-12927-8
   ISBN 0-631-12928-6 (pbk.)

Typeset by Cambrian Typesetters, Frimley, Surrey.
Printed in Great Britain by Page Brothers, Norwich.

This book is affectionately dedicated to my parents, in fond remembrance of Woburn, in the time that I lived there so successfully disguised to myself as a child.

DABNEY LANCASTER LIBRARY

1000122111

Contents

Editor's preface

The notion of 'communicative competence' is now very well established in sociolinguistics, and beyond, as an important sociolinguistic complement to the more purely linguistic notion of 'competence'. As has often been pointed out, it is not sufficient for an adult learning a foreign language simply to learn the phonology, grammar and vocabulary of that language. He or she also has to learn how to use the language in an appropriate manner: how to be polite, how to be rude, when to speak, when to remain silent, how (and whether) to say hello, how (and whether) to say good-bye – and so on. The learner also has, ideally, to discover which words and pronunciations, if there are alternatives, to use on which occasions. Without these kinds of knowledge, no one can function completely successfully in the community where the language in question is spoken. The same, of course, is equally true of children acquiring their native language or languages. They, too, have to learn the norms of usage of the language as well as its words and grammatical rules. In recent years there has been a growth of interest in this aspect of child language acquisition, with an increasing number of publications on the subject of children acquiring English and other languages. Much of this work has been carried out from a psychological and psycholinguistic perspective. In this book, Suzanne Romaine, as one would expect from her well-known work in many different areas of sociolinguistics, emphasizes the more sociolinguistic aspects of children's language acquisition. She does not, however, ignore the more psycholinguistic points of view, and the result is a pleasing and original synthesis which will be of considerable interest not only for sociolinguists and other theoretical linguists but also for teachers and educationists. Romaine's use of, and concern for, real-live language data, and her concentration on the variable aspects of language use and development, combine here to provide an account that is both vivid and convincing, and that will surely prove to be of both practical and theoretical relevance.

Peter Trudgill

Foreword

This book is about children's acquisition of communicative competence. In adopting this perspective on the child's linguistic development, I have focused on the kinds of sociolinguistic skills children must learn in order to be able to interpret and produce utterances, which are not only grammatical but also appropriate within particular contexts.

I would characterize my approach as primarily sociolinguistic, rather than psycholinguistic, although these research traditions are by no means mutually exclusive in their methods and aims. Psycholinguists have, however, tended to look for universals in child language development, while sociolinguists have been more interested in the variable aspects of language which are related to features of social context, e.g. social class, age, sex, style, etc. Neither innate universals nor social environment is alone sufficient to account for the child's linguistic system. The development of communicative competence involves a continuing interaction between them.

Since language development is an ongoing process, which begins (arguably) even before the child starts to speak, and is never complete, my decision to place more emphasis in this book on the language development of school-age children is to some extent arbitrary. And in many cases I backtrack to take into account developments which have their origin in the pre-school period. It is probably fair to say, however, that much more is known about children's pre-school linguistic skills than about what happens in the so-called 'later stages of acquisition'; that is, what happens to the child's linguistic structure upon entering school and in subsequent years. The latter is thus an important, but nonetheless neglected, aspect of development from a linguistic and social point of view. As a sociolinguist, I have long had a special interest in this stage of language development.

Much of the data I discuss in the early chapters come from research I conducted with schoolchildren in Edinburgh. I have tried to integrate my own findings with those obtained by psycholinguists and sociolinguists. Although most of the discussion throughout is based on the acquisition of

English, I have included comparative data where they are available. The data contained in chapter 4 compare sociolinguistic patterns in the language of schoolchildren in Britain, the United States and Sweden, and relate these to the findings of the major urban sociolinguistic studies of adult populations.

In writing this book I have a number of potential audiences in mind. It should be useful as a general text for students of sociolinguistics and psycholinguistics. Only an elementary knowledge of linguistics is assumed. I hope, however, that it will be of interest to teachers. In the later chapters (5–8) I address the issue of how communicative competence can be affected by variations in setting and the problem of measuring language proficiency. These chapters can be easily read by those with no knowledge of linguistics. Chapter 3, which treats the development of syntactic structure, is technically the most difficult, and probably of particular interest to a more specialist audience. The second and fourth chapters should be relevant to those with interests in dialectology, language change and sociolinguistic research methods. I have given a more detailed overview of the structure of the book in chapter 1.

I am especially grateful to Peter Trudgill for encouraging me to write this book for the Language in Society series, and for his many helpful suggestions throughout the preparation of the manuscript. Since the work draws heavily on sociolinguistic research I carried out in Edinburgh, I would like to acknowledge my thanks to a number of persons who helped me at various stages. First of all, I am grateful to the Rotary International Foundation for awarding me a fellowship, which made the study possible; to Dr William Gatherer, who kindly allowed me access to the schools where I carried out my research; to the classroom teachers who let me disrupt their classes; and, of course, to the Edinburgh schoolchildren who took part in the research and who are no longer schoolchildren.

I would also like to thank Claudine Dannequin for discussing various aspects of the language of schoolchildren with me. In the preparation of the manuscript I was fortunate enough to benefit from the cheerful and efficient typing services of Jenny Saxby, Edith Sjoerdsma and Katie Wilde, and the advice and assistance of Urmi Chana.

The final stages of this manuscript were completed while I was at the Max-Planck-Institut für Psycholinguistik in Nijmegen. I was greatly aided there by the general support and encouragement I received from the directors of the Institute, W.J.M. Levelt and Wolfgang Klein, and the intellectual stimulus of the discussions I had with various members of the research group on language acquisition.

I owe a very special debt, however, to Roger Wales, who very generously undertook statistical analysis of some of the data in chapters 3 and 4. He also went through the manuscript with me, and thereby, I hope, has rescued me from my worst sins of omission and ignorance of the psycholinguistic literature on child language development.

Suzanne Romaine

1

Introduction to the study of children's acquisition of communicative competence

All normal children learn to use at least one variety of a language made available by their parents and/or care-takers and peers. This seemingly simple but nevertheless universal accomplishment is generally taken for granted. Upon reflection, however, it is not hard to see why language acquisition (both first and second) has come to receive increasing attention over the past 30 years or so. Indeed, the explicitly stated goal of Chomsky's theory of universal grammar, one of the most influential schools of linguistic thought in this century (cf. Smith and Wilson 1979) is to explain 'the logical problem of language acquisition'. Hornstein and Lightfoot (1981: 9) define it as: 'the problem of how a child masters a rich and highly structured system on the basis of deficient and degenerate data'.

I will show in this book that the competence underlying language use emerges early. Children acquire language by using it. Matthews (1979: 87) observes that the data from which the child constructs his grammar are not divided into data for the construction of communicative rules and data for the construction of cognitive or grammatical rules. Despite this, however, a great many studies of child language acquisition have tended to see the development of language in terms of the emergence of grammatical structures which are innately determined as part of a so-called Language Acquisition Device (LAD). The development of communicative skills has often been seen as a separate strand of development and of less interest to theoretical linguists. Within the past decade or so, there has been a shift in focus in child language research to a study of the functions of grammatical structures and a growing interest in the uses to which children put their language system (cf. Campbell and Wales 1970). In the next section I will sketch out what an approach to child language acquisition entails when seen within the context of the notion of communicative competence.

1.1 *On the notion of communicative competence in relation to child language acquisition*

The fundamental assumption of the sociolinguistic approach to language is the concept of communicative competence, which is most fully characterized by Hymes (1974: 277). He defines it as:

> the knowledge of sentences, not only as grammatical but also as appropriate. [The child] acquires the competence as to when to speak, when not, and as to what to talk about with whom, when, where and in what manner. In short, a child becomes able to accomplish a repertoire of speech acts, to take part in speech events, and to evaluate their accomplishment by others.

By contrast to Chomsky's purely grammatical competence of the ideal speaker–hearer, which is understood as an innate, biological function of mind, communicative competence is acquired through socialization into a particular language-using community. The uses of language which a child acquires will be determined by the functions which a language serves in a culture. Hymes stresses that language does not always and everywhere play the same role. What is a matter of language in one community may not be in another. Among the Athabaskans, for example, children learn to do things by observing their elders rather than by explicit verbal instruction (Scollon and Scollon 1981). Some implications of this pattern of socialization are discussed in later chapters.

When seen in its broadest possible sense as part of the sociocultural matrix in which people learn to do things and interact with each other, the notion of communicative competence threatens to become rather unwieldy. In so far as communicative competence can involve the whole of a person's knowledge base underlying not only specifically communicative behaviour but also more general social action, which is meaningful, its investigation is not the sole province of sociolinguistics, but impinges on sociology, anthropology, psychology and philosophy (cf. the essays in Brenner 1980). The insight that language, action and knowledge are inseparable, and that utterances can be understood as actions, is central to speech act theory as developed by Austin (1962) and others. Austin argued that an utterance such as *I now pronounce you man and wife*, said in the right circumstances, e.g. in a church, by a minister or other official who has the power to perform a marriage ceremony, counts as doing or performing the act of marriage. Speech act theory is a major concern of pragmatics; and in so far as pragmatics deals with the appropriateness of utterances in contexts, then it is difficult to draw a line between it and a sociolinguistic theory whose goal is to characterize communicative competence. Some studies of child language acquisition have taken a pragmatic perspective (e.g. Bates 1976a and Ochs and Schieffelin 1979 and 1983) to the child's emerging communicative system and have focused on the learning of discourse skills as part of developmental pragmatics. Some of this research will be discussed in chapter 5.

Another reason for the dissatisfaction with the restriction of the study of language to grammatical competence is that sentences seen in the abstract as the output of a generative grammar do not express definite propositions or statements. This means that the truth or falsity of a proposition, i.e. its truth value, can only be assessed when a sentence is uttered in a specific context, where context can include the social and psychological world in which the language user operates at any given time (cf. Levinson 1983: chapter 1). The following example of a note found in a bottle at sea, cited by Levinson (1983: 55) illustrates the importance of context in interpreting utterances:

Meet me here a week from now with a stick about this big.

In its decontextualized state, we do not know who to meet, where or when to meet him or her and how big a stick to bring.

Even though communicative competence cannot be strictly separated from general intellectual and social knowledge, it is evident that there are some aspects of linguistic knowledge which are distinguishable from knowledge about the world. Some things can be interpreted from language itself, while others have to be interpreted on the basis of real-world knowledge. A statement like the sentence below is interpretable with reference to knowledge about language, or what some have referred to as 'metalinguistic knowledge' (cf. Lyons 1977, and Levinson 1983 on token reflexive utterances):

This sentence has five words.

There is a great deal of cultural variability in terms of the aspects of language which are subject to metalinguistic comment and introspection. There is also evidence that the acquisition of written language in school develops children's metalinguistic awareness in interesting ways, which will be discussed in chapter 7 (cf. Gleitman et al. 1972).

Another example of language which makes no reference to real-world knowledge, but is no less a part of a speaker's competence, can be taken from Stubbs (1983). He says that an English speaker's knowledge that /nd/ is a permissible sequence word finally (e.g. *hand*), but not word initially, or similarly, that adjectives are placed before nouns (e.g. *the black dog*), is not related to any knowledge about the real physical world. It is purely linguistic.

Since there are some aspects of competence which are more purely linguistic than others, it is important not to conflate a sociolinguistic theory of communicative competence and a more general sociopsychological theory of action or human behaviour, of which the former is a part. Saville-Troike (1982: 25–6) outlines a wide range of linguistic, interactional and cultural phenomena which must be accounted for in an adequate model of communicative competence.

1 *Linguistic knowledge*
  (a) verbal elements
  (b) non-verbal elements
  (c) patterns or elements in particular speech events
  (d) range of possible variants (in all elements and their organization)
  (e) meaning of variants in particular situations
2 *Interaction skills*
  (a) perception of salient features in communicative situations
  (b) selection and interpretation of forms appropriate to specific situations, roles and relationships (rules for the use of speech)
  (c) norms of interaction and interpretation
  (d) strategies for achieving goals
3 *Cultural knowledge*
  (a) social structure
  (b) values and attitudes
  (c) cognitive maps and schemas
  (d) enculturation processes (transmission of knowledge and skills)

She stresses (1982: 213) the integral role which language learning plays in the enculturation of children. She notes that language is: (1) part of the cultural body of knowledge, attitudes and skills which are transmitted from one generation to the next; (2) a primary (though not the only) medium through which other aspects of culture are transmitted; and (3) a tool which children use to explore and manipulate the social environment and establish their status and role relationships within it.

It is evident that communicative competence continues to develop well into adulthood as one learns how to do new things with language. For many people, the ability to use language in specific ways is part of one's apprenticeship to a profession, e.g. learning how to write academic papers. There are substantial differences in individual language ability and behaviour, which are only beginning to be understood (cf. the papers in Fillmore, Kempler and Wang 1979).

From a cross-linguistic perspective, any adequate theory of communicative competence must make provision for the fact that most of the speech communities in the world are multilingual rather than monolingual; even monolingual communities are not homogeneous since there are often regional, social and stylistic varieties within what is thought of as one language. Competence may therefore encompass a range of skills (some of which may not be equally developed) in a number of languages and

varieties. A foreigner who manages to learn a variety of Telegu sufficient
to get by on the streets of Hyderabad will soon find out that that particular
variety of Telegu cannot be used for all purposes which an English
monolingual might use English for. The average educated person in
Hyderabad may use Telegu at home, Sanskrit at the temple, English at the
university, Urdu in business, etc., and may also know other varieties of
Telegu, or Tamil, Kannada or Malayalam for reading, dealing with
servants or other specific purposes. Many South Asians have active control
over what amounts to complex linguistic repertoires drawn from different
languages and varieties. In societies such as these, multilingualism is not an
incidental feature of language use, but a central factor and an organizing
force in everyday life. The sociolinguist faces the problem of describing
verbal repertoires such as these, where competence not only may span
more than one language, but the speaker's competence in each language or
variety is different.

The fact that speakers select different languages or varieties of a
language for use in different situations shows that not all languages are
equal or regarded as equally appropriate or adequate for use in all speech
events. While Chomsky assumes that grammatical competence is invariant,
the sociolinguist has to deal with problems of inequality in language use,
which arise on the one hand from the unequal distribution of languages,
and on the other from the individual's differential competence. Little is
known about the extremes of communicative competence; that is, what are
the minimal requirements for competence in a language, and what are the
outer limits of competence? Some aspects of these questions are
encountered in trying to measure notions like 'verbal ability', which will be
discussed in chapter 8.

Fillmore's (1979) discussion of the notion of 'fluency' recognizes the
need for distinguishing between *how* people speak their language and *how
well* they speak it. He says there are at least four ways in which speakers
are generally judged to be fluent. The maximally gifted speaker is someone
who has the following four abilities (Fillmore 1979: 93):

1 to talk at length, fill time with talk, e.g. disc jockeys;
2 to talk in coherent, reasoned and semantically dense sentences,
   mastering the syntactic/semantic resources of the language;
3 to have the appropriate things to say in a wide range of contexts;
4 to be creative and imaginative in language use.

It would be beyond the scope of this book to discuss the development of
communicative competence in its widest possible sense. In the next section
I will outline the structure of this book in summary form to give an
indication of the kinds of sociolinguistic phenomena I have included under
the heading of communicative competence. In doing so, I will suggest

briefly why some of these are of importance and interest for developmental theories of language, and why I have selected some of these particular areas for special attention.

1.2 *The structure of this book*

I have decided to begin the book with a discussion of methodology, since the procedures and techniques which are used in order to investigate some phenomenon are arguably at the foundation of understanding what any discipline is all about and what it is trying to achieve. Methodology impinges on all stages of research from the very beginning, e.g. formulation of hypotheses, data collection, analysis of results, theoretical interpretation, etc. For example, if one makes the assumption, as I have done here, that certain features of social context are crucial in shaping the child's linguistic development, then one must have some methodological procedures for taking context into account.

A great deal of research on child language acquisition has been done from the perspective of experimental psychology and psycholinguistics. It has relied heavily on the findings of data elicited in the context of carefully designed experimental tasks, which are often not easily relatable to the kinds of behaviour one observes children engaging in within spontaneous ordinary interaction. It is also the case that more emphasis has been placed on tracing the emergence of syntactic structure (rather than, say, discourse), partly in response to the significance attached to this component of language by Chomsky. However, most of the methods used by Chomsky and generative grammarians in investigating syntactic structures, such as consulting the intuitions of native speakers about the grammaticality of sentences in their language, are not so readily usable with young children. This is not to say that work in semantics has been neglected. Particularly in the late 1960s, many studies investigated the nature of lexical representation in relation to conceptual structure and cognitive development.

I have biased most of my methodological discussion towards those techniques of elicitation, which have been developed primarily within the context of recent sociolinguistic research on urban social dialects, and I have tried to indicate the insights which I think some of these procedures give us into children's developing sociolinguistic competence. Within the framework of sociolinguistic research on the study of language in its social context as elaborated in particular by Labov, there have been a number of important changes in linguists' ideas about what constitutes data. These will have repercussions in formulating a (socio)-linguistic theory. At the heart of Labov's approach lies his commitment to investigating language spoken in everyday life and accounting for the distribution of features which vary regularly in accordance with factors such as age, sex, social class, style, etc.

Although most of these techniques have been devised for investigating adult populations, it is clear that some of them are relevant in understanding the behaviour of young children. I have described in some detail my own attempt to adapt some of these methods of data collection in a study which I made of some sociolinguistic variables in the speech of Edinburgh schoolchildren. The results of this study are discussed in various places throughout the book, especially in chapters 3, 4 and 5, in relation to the more general issues and findings of research on the development of communicative competence.

It has been found, for example, that formal settings tend to skew data towards more formal styles of speech. The interesting question from a developmental perspective is how and when children begin to attune to some of these contextual features and shift their behaviour in a similar way to adults. Another finding to emerge from sociolinguistic research is that speakers are often unreliable in reporting out of context those aspects of language which vary according to social or situational context. This has obvious theoretical implications for the working methods of generative grammarians referred to above; but again the interesting question to ask as far as children are concerned is when and how their evaluative skills develop in relation to their productive skills. That is, when do children make judgements about what is appropriate to say and modify their behaviour in ways which take their assessments of the situational variables into account? I have tried to indicate too how the ethnographic methods used by anthropologists to investigate naturally occurring speech events can be of use to sociolinguistic research on children's language, in particular, in investigating the uses of language in the classroom.

In chapter 3 I talk about the development of syntactic structure with particular reference to two features of complex syntax; namely, the acquisition of strategies of relative-clause formation and passives. This may seem an odd point of departure, given my already implicit criticism of research on child language acquisition which has focused on the development of syntactic structure at the expense of neglecting the communicative functions to which syntax is put. I feel that my inclusion of this topic at the outset of the book can be justified on several grounds.

Firstly, it has been fashionable to say that the bulk of language acquisition takes place between the ages of two and five. There is a great deal of truth in this, in as much as by the time the child comes to school, he has a richly differentiated linguistic system. However, there are still some difficulties in certain areas of English syntax and the uses of complex syntactic structures which remain to be mastered. The fact that children acquire properties of grammar at different rates reflects a number of things about the process of acquisition, from both a cognitive and a social perspective, and tells us something of the nature of the child's emergent grammar. For example, the complexity of the construction types which are late has been discussed in terms of the processing and perceptual difficulties they pose for the child's developing cognitive system. However, one must not ignore other 'external' factors such as the frequency of complex syntactic structures in the input to which the child is exposed.

Secondly, the acquisition of certain formal structural features of language has been seen as a crucial index of cognitive maturity. Researchers have looked at features such as number of words in a child's vocabulary, variety in the syntactic categories he uses (nouns, verbs, etc.), particularly, however, MLU (mean length of utterance), mean T-unit length (i.e. a main clause + all the subordinate clauses attached to it). Some of these measures have been used by van der Geest (1975) in his study of the child's communicative competence.

While it has been argued that some of the hallmarks of language development for children have to do with things like having more to say on a topic and using longer sentences, the notion of syntactic complexity embodied in a measure like the T-unit is that having strategies for subordinating clauses and embedding sentences within each other is indicative of greater verbal ability and cognitive skill. Since embedding often involves a reduction in overall sentence length, however, this means that the relationship between length and complexity is not an absolute or straightforward one. Nor does it make much sense to apply measures of this type based solely on length to children's development beyond the very early stages.

Measures such as MLU and mean T-unit length are nevertheless useful measures in some sense, if only as crude indicators of surface structure. The mean T-unit lengths for the six-, eight- and ten-year old children with whom I worked in Edinburgh (cf. Romaine 1975 and 1979), for example, were respectively 6.7, 7.2 and 8.1. While there is nothing in these figures to suggest that syntactic complexity (in so far as this is what is being measured by mean T-unit length) is developing in any other than a normal way for these children, this measure does not take into account semantic complexity and meaning. Nor is it sensitive to the demands of various tasks in which these children are required to use and display their syntax. I show in chapter 3 that there is a great deal of variability in individual linguistic behaviour, and that it is a mistake to look at the evolution of children's grammars as a unilinear progression from more primitive to more complex syntax.

This brings me to my third reason for my inclusion of a discussion of this aspect of language development; and that is that there is often a large gap between production and perception, and/or alternatively between competence and performance as far as the use of certain syntactic constructions is concerned. Young children may be able to interpret and produce a syntactic construction in an experimental situation at an early age, but not use it spontaneously until much later, if indeed at all. This suggests that alternative constructions may serve at least some of the same functions in discourse. If, however, this is not the case, then the question arises how such communicative functions are realized, if at all, in the absence of any formal linguistic marking of them. The two features I discuss in chapter 3 touch on these issues and illustrate some of the discrepancies between knowledge and use.

Another important aspect of learning a language is the acquisition of more than one variety of it, or learning alternative ways of saying the same thing. The norms of language as an abstract system are different from those of language in use. Not all of the constructions which are formally possible occur with the same frequency. It has become evident from sociolinguistic research on adult populations that one of the most salient sociolinguistic facts about the way in which speech communities are organized is the unequal distribution and use of certain variable features of language among different social groups, e.g. men vs. women, working vs. middle class, older vs. younger, etc.

Thanks to the work of sociolinguists like Labov, a great deal is now known about these kinds of correlations between language use and social structure, particularly in the English-speaking world. These have been referred to as 'sociolinguistic patterns'. We can think of these as comprising part of the variable component of communicative competence. These patterns are, however, generally seen as synchronic and static with little emphasis given to their historical genesis or developmental progression.

Chapter 4 deals with the acquisition and development of sociolinguistic rules for the use of linguistic variables and the manipulation of their social meaning. The data which are discussed come to a certain extent from my own work with schoolchildren in Edinburgh, but I try throughout to integrate these findings more generally with those obtained by others who have studied the language of school-age children, particularly from a sociolinguistic perspective. I hope this will allow some synthesis of the accumulating body of research which deals with the later stages of acquisition, i.e. what happens to linguistic structure after the child enters school. Sociolinguistic patterns of social class, stylistic, sex and age differentiation are discussed and compared with those found in the adult population.

There is also a discussion of the evaluative component of communicatve competence; that is, how children learn to make judgements about their own and others' performance. From a very early age children monitor and correct their own and others' linguistic production 'errors'. Oksaar (1981: 282), for example, reports an instance where a child corrects her younger brother's attempt to produce the Swedish word *katt* (cat): 'Säg inte "datt", säg "katt" ' ('Don't say /dat/, say /kat/'). Even at a stage where children's productions do not match those of adults, they can discriminate between 'correct' adult productions and adult imitations of their own 'incorrect' productions (Smith 1973). This is just one instance in which there is an asymmetry between production and perception.

Another dimension of evaluation is metalinguistic awareness, i.e. knowledge about oneself as a language user and about language as language. Oksaar (1981: 282–3) notes a young child putting a handkerchief in her pocket and making the observation to her mother that the reason why they are referred to as *Taschentücher* in German (literally: 'pocket cloths') is because 'Taschentücher gehören in die Taschen' ('handkerchiefs belong in pockets'). This comment presupposes that the child has made a linguistic analysis of the component constituents of the compound *Taschentuch*.

These examples involve the more purely linguistic aspects of evaluation, but it is clear that along with this, children develop notions of social appropriateness and make judgements about who uses what kind(s) of language in certain situations.

In chapter 5 I look at the way in which children learn how to use language in socially appropriate ways to get things done within the context of certain speech events, e.g. by taking roles in conversations, using forms of address, performing politeness routines and telling narratives. Some of these aspects of the child's development of communicative competence have been discussed under the heading of 'developmental pragmatics' (cf. the papers in Ochs and Schieffelin 1979) or 'conversational/discourse competence' (cf. Ochs and Schieffelin 1983).

Some of these kinds of communicative skills are learned very early before children go to school, for example in conversing with parents. Play with other children in which adult roles such as father and mother are acted out also allow children to gain experience in coping with the communicative demands of particular settings and social relationships. In other cases, the 'ground rules' for certain speech events are explicitly taught. Heath (1983: 123–4) describes one such scene in which two girls (aged 2.8 and 3) were setting up a tea party while their mothers were drinking tea and conversing nearby. The girls prepared their own tea and handed each other cups and things to eat. One child handed the other a biscuit saying, 'Here'. At this point her mother interrupted and said, 'Wendy, that's no way to talk. "Have a cookie [biscuit]". Now say it right.' Wendy then repeated her mother's prompt, and the other child accepted the cookie and began to eat it. The latter's mother then intervened and said, 'Kim, what do you say?' Kim replied, 'It's good, good.' Her mother said, 'No, uh, yes, it's good, but how about "Thank you"?'. Kim then said, 'Thank you, good.'

A large part of chapter 5 is spent discussing the development of children's spoken narrative skills outside the classroom setting. This sets the scene for later chapters, 6, 7 and 8, in which the production of spoken and written narratives in school is examined. Some narratives told by the Edinburgh schoolchildren are analysed in detail, with particular attention paid to the way in which syntactic structure is used to produce connected narrative.

Social interaction is an important prerequisite for the development of sociolinguistic skills. Chapter 6 looks at three main influences on children's language: family, school and peer group. These three contexts constitute primary spheres of interaction in which very different ways of using language can be developed, maintained and reproduced.

All normal children learn to talk; yet the social and linguistic environments which surround young children as they acquire competence differ in striking ways cross-culturally. If, however, the Language Acquisition Device is innate, then the quality and/or quantity of input which children receive should not matter. Nevertheless, a number of studies have found that children learn to talk faster if their mothers (and/or other care-takers) provide a large proportion of conversational responses that are syntactically and semantically contingent on the child's own utterances, and that fall within the child's limits of complexity. It has been argued that the mother's simplification of input establishes an affective bond and serves as a teaching style which aids and promotes the child's acquisition.

These findings, however, derive largely from research done in white, middle-class English-speaking homes, where it is often assumed that children's language learning is an apprenticeship to the skills and practices of adult language. Hymes (1974: 97–8) says that this view of children as possessors of a language, albeit in yet undeveloped form, which is learned, processed and used in the same way as adult language, is peculiar to our own culture. We tend to de-emphasize the differences between the adult and child with regard to language. In other cultures, however, the differences are strongly emphasized. I discuss in this chapter some of the ways in which beliefs and expectations about children as language users affect care-taking styles cross-culturally. Hymes, for example, describes a number of cultures in which children's language is treated as if it were of a basically different order and derived from a different source compared to adult language. Both Chinookans and the Ashanti believe that infants share a first language, which is not the same as the adult one. For Chinookans, the baby's talk is shared with certain spirits, and shamans who are able to communicate with these spirits interpret it. The Ashanti traditionally exclude infants from a room in which a woman is giving birth. They fear that an infant would talk to the baby in the womb in the special language they share, and by warning it of the difficult life ahead would make it reluctant to emerge, thereby causing a hard delivery.

The differences in children's early experiences of linguistic interaction are not neatly associated with social class (as Bernstein's 1973 work would suggest) and/or ethnicity. Heath's work emphasizes the very different ways of speaking and using language which can co-exist within the same community. There has been much discussion of the question of discontinuity between the uses of language at home and school. Some have suggested that the traditional classroom is an extension of the mainstream, middle-class home and value system. This view again promotes the idea that some children (i.e. those of middle-class background) are in some sense 'mini-adults'. The transition between the communicative skills used at home in speaking and those required for school involves socialization into ways of speaking which rely heavily on the written language. I show that many of the same notions about what counts as appropriate classroom discourse from the teacher's point of view apply in both France and the United States.

Linguistic input from peers is also important in shaping emergent communicative competence. Socialization in sex-specific peer groups exerts pressure towards conformity in linguistic and other behaviour. This is particularly true for young adolescents. I discuss the membership-marking functions of non-standard English and the ways in which children adapt their speech to display allegiance to the values associated with the groups they identify with.

Chapter 7 extends the discussion begun in section 6.2. I argue that the factors related to school success involve more than just differences in formal structures of language and amount of parent–child interaction, etc. I discuss the acquisition of literacy and its role in the child's communicative competence. The emphasis here is on the development of reading and writing as social skills; and the concept of literacy is treated within a sociohistorical and cross-cultural perspective.

It has been argued that literacy is an independent variable in the make-up of a community, which has autonomous cognitive effects. For example, it is often claimed that writing is a prerequisite for the development of abstract, decontextualized modes of thought. Learning to write requires different strategies of using language from learning to speak; and furthermore, some difficulties in acquiring reading and writing arise from 'dialect interference'. However, differences in the way in which children have been socialized to use language and assimilate and display knowledge are even more fundamentally problematic when seen in terms of their educational implications.

There is a range of possibilities for realizing language, which range from more literate to oral. This continuum is not, however, to be confused with that between spoken and written language. Oral modes of expression (whether realized in speech or writing) focus on contextualized, participant interaction. By contrast, literate modes emphasize decontextualized non-participant presentation of material organized according to logical sequence. Students are given little guidance from teachers about the conventions which are implicit in the uses of language sanctioned by the school.

Chapter 8 takes up the problem of how one measures proficiency in language. I look at how standards are set and examine the kinds of notions about language which underlie the assumptions made by testers.

It is a matter of objective fact that, whatever knowledge of language the school tests appear to be measuring, it is unevenly distributed amongst schoolchildren. Current definitions of success in school rely heavily on the measurement of reading and writing ability. However, it appears that some of the features, e.g. spelling and punctuation, which have become established measures of language proficiency are only indirectly related to common-sense notions of what it means to be a competent language user.

I argue that the kinds of tests which children take in schools are tailored to a special kind of consciousness about language, which is deeply conditioned by western modes of literacy. Testers have often assumed that cognitive skills can be tapped 'objectively' apart from the social context in which they were acquired and habitually used. In these tests meaning is taken to be given and not negotiated. Standardized tests tap the child's familiarity with testing situations and measure his degree of conformity to the dominant mainstream cultural tradition. Children from minority backgrounds, who may have different learning and behavioural styles, are at a disadvantage.

The apparent 'crisis' over declining standards of language proficiency is thus in some respects an academic problem which arises because definitions of literacy, competence, etc., have been narrowed to such an extent that they make children's experience with language at school discontinuous with everyday communicative competence. I also suggest some guidelines for a more realistic assessment of prevailing ideas about and attitudes towards language, literacy and the testing of language proficiency. In measuring communicative competence we are attempting to assess a potential not a product. And there is always the question of the relationship between what is possible and what actually occurs.

Finally, in chapter 9 I summarize some of the main arguments of the book and consider the relationship between linguistic theory and the study of child language acquisition from a sociolinguistic perspective.

2

Methodology for studying the language of children

In the most general terms it can be said that methodology concerns the problem of sampling; namely, what to sample and how to sample it. In the case of linguistic research one must make choices about the speakers to be included, the settings in which to collect data and the kinds of linguistic phenomena to study. If, for instance, we assume (as many sociolinguists do) that one of the most important influences on a person's speech is his social class membership, i.e. that a person's linguistic behaviour is explained partly by, or is a reflection of, his status in society, then we are immediately involved in a number of methodological problems. For example, how do we find persons who differ in terms of social class? How many do we need to look at? How do we assign social class membership to them? What kinds and quantity of data do we need? How do we collect the data, and what methods are appropriate to their analysis? I will not discuss all these problems in detail here (cf. Romaine 1980c for an overview of the methodology of sociolinguistics).

As far as the problem of choosing speakers is concerned, there are statistical procedures which allow one to make informed decisions about the number of speakers of a particular type (e.g. women between the ages of 35 and 40), which need to be selected in order to make valid claims about the representativeness of the behaviour of the sample for a larger population sharing the same characteristics. Similarly, there are tests of statistical significance which can be applied to the results of experiments, etc. (cf. Moser and Kalton 1958). The crucial question in any discussion of methodology concerns the nature of the claims one is entitled to make in relation to the choices made in these areas.

As far as the question of setting is concerned, a basic premise for anyone wishing to do research on some aspect of human behaviour (linguistic or otherwise) is that human action is context-dependent. Context itself cannot be defined in terms of a fixed set of properties, but comprises a set of variables that are constantly being re-evaluated by the participants during the course of interaction. The fact that human behaviour can only be studied within the context of a situation, which will have various effects on the behaviour being studied, poses a great many methodological problems. Whether we investigate behaviour in so-called 'naturalistic' settings or in the experimental laboratory, we must always take context into account. Although it is often not mentioned by those who favour experimental research, the laboratory constitutes a special type of ecological context, and findings which emerge from experimental settings have no privileged status as context-free or objective.

Those who have worked on children's language from the perspective of psychology or psycholinguistics have often focused more attention on experimental research, using carefully constructed, artificial tasks, which are designed to assess the development of referential skills and the acquisition of linguistic forms, especially syntactic structures. Children's performance on these tasks has sometimes been explained in terms of underlying cognitive abilities, especially within the Piagetian model of development. The research tradition which has been developed within sociolinguistics over the past two decades has sought, by contrast, to explain children's communicative behaviour in terms of social and contextual variables, and has accordingly concentrated on investigating communicative competence in 'natural' settings. In this respect sociolinguistics has benefited from the ethnographic tradition of anthropology, to be discussed in section 2.5.

In deciding to adopt one methodological strategy rather than another, there can be no question of choosing one method which will be universally the 'right' one. Methodology can be evaluated only within the context of some question which one wants to answer, i.e. in relation to what one wants to know and the possible ways there are of finding out about it. One cannot therefore dismiss, say, experimental methods out of hand as a way of investigating some aspects of linguistic development. Ideally, a research programme should incorporate complementarity of methods in order to look at the same phenomena from different perspectives. In addition, there are some important aspects of any phenomenon to be investigated which may affect the possible means of studying it. From studies of language in various contexts, sociolinguists have identified a number of special factors which have to be taken into account in studying linguistic behaviour. Since a great many of these are relevant to the study of children's language, I will discuss them in detail from a general perspective before turning specifically to their relevance for doing sociolinguistic research.

2.1 *The Observer's Paradox*

The Observer's Paradox has been much discussed by sociolinguists, particularly Labov, who has made a major methodological contribution in devising ways to overcome it. The Observer's Paradox is not peculiar to linguistics, or for that matter to the behavioural sciences. It is a fundamental philosophical problem in the natural sciences, such as physics, where it has been extensively considered by physicists within the context of quantum mechanics, and also by philosophers of science. Very simply, the Observer's Paradox refers to the effect of the researcher on the phenomenon being investigated. Labov (1972a: 113) has formulated it with specific reference to the problem of collecting natural speech data in the community: 'To obtain the data most important for linguistic theory, we have to observe how people speak when they are not being observed.'

The effects of observation on behaviour are many and varied; perhaps the most important ones to be noted in conjunction with linguistic research are a decrease or increase in the behaviour one is trying to observe, e.g. people talk less, too much, or not at all in certain situations for a variety of sociopsychological reasons. People may be suspicious of being observed and behaviour which is highly stigmatized socially may be avoided, e.g. swearing and local linguistic stereotypes. Conversely, people may display or show off other abilities.

Labov (1969) gives the striking example of an interview between a black child and a white interviewer, who puts an object on the table in front of the child and says: 'Tell me everything you can about this.' The result is a series of long pauses between utterances of one or two words, all extracted by the interviewer only after considerable prompting. Of course there are a variety of factors in this particular situation which impose constraints on speech, e.g. race, age and power. The asymmetries between child and adult with respect to each of these dimensions act as powerful determinants of social behaviour (cf. also Giles and Smith 1979 on the dynamics of dyadic interaction and also Erikson 1982 on inter-ethnic communication). I shall have more to say in chapter 7 about the reasons why this type of encounter was unsuccessful.

Many sociolinguists have put great emphasis on obtaining samples of so-called 'vernacular' speech, following Labov's claims (1972a et passim) that the best (i.e. most consistent and natural) data for sociolinguistic analysis are the types of speech used by the working class in their most informal casual styles. (Cf. section 2.3 on the problem of 'naturalness'.) Attempts to elicit the vernacular in formal settings, such as in a face-to-face interview between strangers, are subject to what Labov (1972a: 111–2) refers to as the Principle of Subordinate Shift. Elicitations reflect normative data influenced by considerations of social prestige and stigma and may diverge from actual behavioural norms in more intimate in-group settings. When speakers of a subordinate group (e.g. children in relation to adults, lower-class speakers of a non-standard in relation to middle-class speakers of a standard variety or minority language users in relation to speakers of a majority language) are asked questions about their language, or are put into situations where they must interact with the superordinate group, they will shift towards the norms of that group. This phenomenon has been referred to recently by Giles as 'upward convergence'. Formal settings skew data towards more formal styles. Labov (1966) found in New York City that lower-middle-class informants typically exceeded the norm of the middle-class in their use of socially sensitive linguistic variables in their more formal styles. He refers to this pattern as 'hypercorrection by the lower middle class' (cf. section 4.2).

The divergence between overtly recognized prestige norms and behaviour also has consequences for relying on informants' judgements and intuitions about their language. While this method has been widely relied upon as the foundation of Chomskyan linguistics, it is open to rather substantial criticisms. Sociolinguistic research shows that speakers are unreliable in reporting out of context those aspects of language which vary according to situation. New York City speakers who are normally non-rhotic (i.e. do not pronounce post-vocalic /r/ in words like *car*) consistently report themselves as using post-vocalic /r/. Young lower-middle-class women, who are affected most by the external prestige norms, are the most frequent 'over-reporters'. The self-reports of most speakers are regularly shifted towards the norm that they aim at rather than the form they use in actual speech. This means not only that some speakers will over-report their usage of some features, but also that they will under-report others, not necessarily stigmatized features. Trudgill (1972), for example, found in Norwich that men typically under-reported their use of more standard forms, presumably because they wished to identify with the covert norms of local working-class speech rather than with the overt prestige standard. The occurrence of under- and over-reporting is not to be taken as an indication of people's dishonesty, or conscious deceit, but merely as a reminder that there are important asymmetries between production and perception which are linked to social factors.

It also appears that self-awareness of language is more difficult in certain areas of performance, e.g. intuitions about syntactic constructions. Speakers can often be seen to report that they never use a particular construction, only to be observed later using it. And it is now evident from sociolinguistic and psycholinguistic work that intuitions about grammaticality may vary significantly according to context (cf. Labov 1972a and Carroll et al. 1981). Speakers who have had extensive contact with the standard language no longer have access to intuitions about their vernacular (Labov 1972b: 186). In Labov's terms they become 'lames', or marginal members of their former group.

Labov (1972a: 214n.) comments that one cannot ask young children whether a non-standard sentence is well formed or adults to reconstruct their childhood grammars, thus pointing to the limited usefulness of using intuitions in the study of children's language. Brown (1970: 79) describes his attempt to elicit grammatical judgements from a young child, Adam. In asking the child to distinguish between correct and incorrect forms of the plural, he said, 'Adam, which is right, two shoes or two shoe?' Adam replied, 'Pop goes the weasel.' Nevertheless, methods of this type have been used with children, asking for their judgements about their own and others' utterances. While it may be the case, as Labov (1972a: 111–12) says, that the elicitation of data from children is not easily related to their linguistic productions, it is evident that at an early age children are aware of the social significance and appropriateness of language and can offer judgements in this area, which with increasing age approach adult norms. (Cf. section 4.5 on the development of the 'evaluative' dimension of communicative competence.) It is important to note, however, that in formal and/or experimental settings children have often shown a linguistic competence which is below that displayed in spontaneous performance; but the reverse is sometimes true too. I will return to this in the discussion of the use of standardized tests and experiments to assess children's linguistic abilities in chapter 8.

2.2 *The use of the interview for obtaining data*

These considerations can all be used to make a strong case for not using interviews to obtain sociolinguistic data from either adults or children; but in fact a great deal of sociolinguistic work (if not the majority of work on urban social dialects) has relied on this technique of data collection. Labov (1972a: 181), in particular, argues: 'No matter what other methods may be used to obtain samples of speech (group sessions, anonymous observation), the only way to obtain sufficient good data on the speech of any one person is through an individual tape-recorded interview: that is, through the most obvious kind of systematic observation.'[1]

A significant part of Labov's contribution to sociolinguistic methodology consists in devising procedures to overcome the Observer's Paradox while using the linguistic interview. Since the interview setting defines a situation in which formal rather than casual speech is likely to occur, Labov tried to vary certain factors in the interview in order to produce samples of more spontaneous speech. One of these techniques was to elicit narratives on various subjects. Labov identified a number of themes which appeared to reduce the amount of attention people paid to their speech, and hence produced less formal styles. These had to do with: danger of death, childhood games and moral indignation. Labov found that when informants were asked about these areas of their personal experience, they became very involved in relating narratives, and there was a marked difference in their use of certain variables.

In order to produce more careful speech, Labov gave his informants various reading tasks, which were designed to focus awareness on speech. He asked informants to read a text, to read word lists and to read lists of minimal pairs. Labov has postulated the existence of a stylistic continuum (shown in figure 2.1) ranging from formal or careful to informal or casual speech, in which the degree of formality of the style is contingent upon the amount of attention paid to speech. Although there have been a number of criticisms of this view of style (cf. Romaine 1975, Macaulay 1977, Milroy 1980, Romaine and Traugott 1981), Labov found in his study of New York City speech that these five styles contrasted with each other in terms of the frequency of occurrence of certain linguistic variables (e.g. post-vocalic /r/), not only in the different styles of one speaker, but also between different groups of speakers, e.g. middle vs. working class. The finding that both 'styles' and 'social dialects' can be defined in terms of regularly contrasting patterns of the same linguistic variables indicates that in many English-speaking communities stylistic variation is linked to social dialect variation in a systematic way. Thus, if a feature is found to be more frequent in the speech of the working class, it will also be found in the most informal styles of the middle class. Figure 2.2 illustrates such a pattern of social and stylistic differentiation obtained by Labov in New York City for the variable (ing), i.e. the realization of the final sound in words like *working* as [n], or [ŋ]. We can see that the higher a person's social class and the more formal the style the greater tendency there is to use the more standard forms, i.e. [ŋ].

Given Labov's two-fold claim to the effect (1) that the most informal speech of the working class is the most systematic, natural or closest to the 'vernacular' of the community and therefore the most interesting for sociolinguistic research, and (2) that the tape-recorded interview is the best means of obtaining it, we need to address two questions: first, what is the nature of the sociolinguistic interview as a speech event? In other words, where does it fit into the stylistic repertoire of the individual and the speech community? And what relationship does the so-called casual speech of the

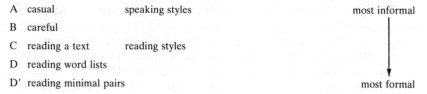

A   casual   speaking styles   most informal

B   careful

C   reading a text   reading styles

D   reading word lists

D' reading minimal pairs   most formal

Figure 2.1 Labov's stylistic continuum
Source: Labov 1972a

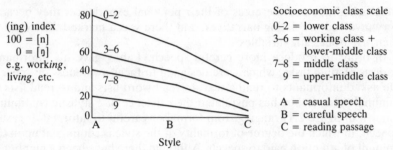

Figure 2.2 Social and stylistic stratification of a linguistic variable: (ing) in New York City
Source: Labov 1972a

interview have to 'natural speech', i.e. the ordinary everyday speech people use when they are not being observed? Second, how suitable a technique is it for obtaining data from children? I will consider the problem of 'naturalness' first.

2.3 The problem of 'naturalness' and the nature of the sociolinguistic interview as a speech event

It follows logically from what I said at the beginning of this chapter about the context-dependence of human activity that linguistic behaviour can only be natural in relation to some setting. I think there is a dangerous trend within sociolinguistics to pursue an elusive 'vernacular' or casual speech in the belief that it is somehow more authentic than the speech used by other members in the community (e.g. the more formal styles of the middle class) or indeed, by the same speakers in their more formal styles. Sociolinguists appear to be championing working-class speech in much the same way as dialectologists romanticized the allegedly 'pure' dialect of rural male farmers.

Part of the problem here arises through Labov's overuse of the term 'vernacular' to refer to speech varieties which are coincident with social groups, styles and age groups. Some have called attention to these conflicting senses of the term (cf. Romaine 1980c, Cheshire 1982a, Romaine and Traugott 1981, and Macaulay, forthcoming). At times, it refers to the most localized forms of speech associated with the lowest socioeconomic group (e.g. Milroy's 1980 'Belfast vernacular') or ethnic group (e.g. Labov's BEV or Black English Vernacular), while at others it has been used to refer to the most informal speech style of an individual (cf. Labov 1972a). And elsewhere, Labov (1981: 3) refers to the vernacular as that mode of speech that is acquired in pre-adolescent years; those between the ages of 9 and 18 are said to speak the most consistent vernacular. Using

Labov's argument, Cheshire (1982a: 7) based her analysis of Reading teenage peer groups on 'the vernacular style of the vernacular', i.e. the most informal style of working-class adolescent. Given this definition of the vernacular, most adults would probably be characterized as inconsistent users. And not everyone will have an individual vernacular which coincides with the vernacular of the speech community; in other words, an individual's casual style may contain none of the features associated with the group lowest in the social hierarchy. It is evident from Cheshire's work (and others) that some forms are used both by adolescent and adults, but with different meanings.

I share Wolfson's criticisms (1976) of Labov's use of audio-monitoring, i.e. the amount of attention paid to speech, as a criterion for defining a stylistic continuum, and his assumption that all speakers share the same evaluative norms (cf. Romaine and Traugott 1981 for further discussion). One can tell a narrative about being in danger of death in a relatively casual style or render it as a formal report. It is reasonable to expect that if some people monitor their speech in order to produce what they regard as formal speech on certain occasions, others may attend most carefully to their speech when making an effort to be colloquial. In many situations, middle-class speakers may use certain marked forms (e.g. regionalisms) which are used outside their defining context, i.e. working-class speech. In doing so they use these forms 'strategically' to create the context and to achieve a special effect. This happens frequently in Scotland, e.g. at readings of Burns's poetry.

If speech style reflects choices which an individual makes in a given situation, it is difficult to accept Cheshire's (1982a: 113) claim that 'the most "natural" speech style occurs in spontaneous everyday interactions . . . in other situations speakers modify the way that they speak to produce the style that they consider appropriate for the occasion.' This implies the paradoxical conclusion that other styles are somehow not natural, even though they are produced by the speaker in response to his own subjective evaluation of what is appropriate to the situation, just as presumably casual speech is seen as appropriate to an informal or spontaneous situation. It also relies on the assumption that 'everyday spontaneous interactions' are casual; Goffman's (1981) analysis of conversation would suggest otherwise. The fact that there appear to be major differences in the assumptions which different individuals and groups make about the appropriateness of language in certain settings will be of major concern later in chapters 6 and 8. There are strong constraints on speaking casually when there is little solidarity between participants.

If no particular speech style has the special status of being natural, except in relation to a context, then 'naturalness' is a chimera. This does not mean that the sociolinguistic interview is useless as a means of collecting data. However, it does entail a consideration of the nature of the claims which have been made about the use of the interview to elicit spontaneous speech and informal narratives of personal experience. The only way to assess where the style of speech obtained within the context of the interview stands in relation to the type of speech people use elsewhere is to observe them speaking elsewhere, e.g. through anonymous observation or surreptitious recording. A number of linguists have used the ploy of removing themselves from recording situations, so that the constraints of peer-group interaction will take precedence over the tape-recorder and speakers will respond naturally to one another. Labov, for example, on occasion brought a rabbit with him when he wanted to make recordings of children's speech. He would leave a group of children to mind the rabbit for him while he went away to do something else. He left a tape-recorder running and told the children that the rabbit liked to be talked to.

Reid (1978) also used this technique in his study of Edinburgh schoolchildren by employing a radio microphone so that he could monitor performance from a distance. It does not appear to be the case, however, that we can conclude that informants forget the presence of the tape-recorder as observer. Wolfson (1982: 57f.) discusses cases where subjects are very much aware of the tape-recorder so that the tape-recorder in effect functions as a participant in the speech event: speech is addressed to it and it is often the topic of conversation. Fortunately, awareness of the tape-recorder is less of a constraint in working with adolescents than with adults. Most children nowadays have had experience with cassette recorders, and indeed many have their own and are less inhibited by recording equipment. Still, Wolfson is easily justified in saying (1982: 59) that we have no right to assume that the speech forms informants use when being recorded are those they would have used had they not been recorded.

Wolfson is also critical of the nature of the linguistic interview as a speech event within which spontaneous speech can be collected. Each society has its own class of what Hymes (1974) and others refer to as speech events, i.e. activities or aspects of activities that are directly governed by rules or norms for the use of speech. The notion of an interview as a speech event governed by rules for speaking is well recognized within English-speaking societies, at least among the adult population. Wolfson (1982: 60) says that speakers of English are aware of the rule which gives one of the participants in the event the unilateral right to ask questions and the other the obligation to answer them. Distribution of power is clearly delimited and free conversation is not expected. Attempts to elicit narratives and spontaneous speech by breaking out of the question/answer format violate the norms governing the event. According to Wolfson, the informant's reaction to this may be surprise, confusion, suspicion or even resentment. By comparing the structure of narratives elicited within the context of the interview with that of those told spontaneously, she shows that there are important differences. For one thing, in everyday life it is usually the teller who introduces the narrative and thus chooses the topic, and his audience. In the interview they occur in response to questions asked by the interviewer and often require a lot of successive prompting. Narratives within the interview are usually in the form of a summary, short and to the point with little elaboration. Conversational narratives by contrast are often 'performed' and show a number of grammatical, phonological and stylistic features which may be absent from elicited narratives. Some of these aspects of children's narrative structure will be discussed in chapter 5. Wolfson (1982: 60) emphasizes the paradox in the fact that the interview is a speech event which makes it legitimate to ask personal questions of a total stranger but at the same time limits severely the kind of interaction which can take place within it, and consequently, the type of data one can collect. The contrast between narratives told in two different settings was indeed a crucial one as far as the feature which Wolfson studied was concerned; namely, the use of the conversational historical present. This variable appears rarely outside naturally occurring narratives in spontaneous conversation.

Wolfson (1982: 66) concludes that there is nothing artificial or unnatural about being interviewed, even though most people probably have no direct experience of it. Thus there is no reason to believe that the speech produced in it is anything but 'natural' relative to the context of the interview. But the so-called sociolinguistic interview which attempts to elicit spontaneous speech is not a speech event since it goes by 'no name recognisable to members of the speech community and it has no rules of speaking'. She further observes (1982: 70):

> there is no such absolute entity as natural/casual speech. If speech is appropriate to the situation and the goal, then it is natural, whether it takes place within an interview or outside it. It is only when rules of speaking are violated that we get inappropriate or unnatural speech . . . people do not speak in a social or situational vacuum. They speak in specific places, on specific occasions about specific topics and to specific others.

It is obvious from what I have said so far that I endorse Wolfson's view. Nevertheless, that does not mean that we cannot use interviews in sociolinguistic research. The problem hinges on how we interpret the data obtained from interviews and the claims we are entitled to make on the basis of them. As Wolfson (1982: 70) puts it,

> If we are interested in learning how men and women of differing ages, social and educational backgrounds respond in a tape-recorded interview situation with a particular investigator of a given age, sex

and background, we should of course use just this method. But to claim that the same subjects would use just these forms in just this way in other speech situations with other participants is obviously not possible.

The solution to this methodological problem, as I hinted earlier, lies in obtaining as broad a data base as possible by collecting data and making observations in as many situations as possible. Although 'natural speech' is all around us, in many cases it is not possible to observe precisely the features we are interested in merely by waiting for them to turn up spontaneously. Some variables, as we shall see, have rather strict co-occurrence relations with particular contexts, and the only way to obtain instances of them is to elicit them directly. It is also often the case that naturalistic situations do not permit one to separate the effects of different variables which may interact with one another (a case in point is discussed in section 3.6). Often, what is not mentioned is the simple fact that researchers work under severe constraints of time, money and other practical resources. One cannot always spend a great deal of time observing people.

2.4 *The use of the interview with children*

A number of studies of the sociolinguistic patterns of adolescents to be discussed in chapter 4 have been based on data collected mostly or partly in interviews both within school and outside. In my research on the speech of Edinburgh primary school children between the ages of six and ten, I relied on the use of face-to-face tape-recorded interviews in which I tried to elicit as much speech from each child on a variety of topics likely to be of interest to children. With each child I asked questions about the following broad topic headings: personal background, games and activities, peer groups, and fights. The questions about personal background were necessary in order to obtain a profile of the informant. I introduced the questions wherever I could at various points in the interview rather than placing them at the beginning to avoid the possibility of setting the tone for a formal interrogation. Some of the questions I asked under the other topic headings are as follows:

Games/activities
1 What do you like to do best when you're not in school?
2 What TV programmes do you like to watch? Can you tell me about one you saw this week?
3 What games do you play in the playground?
4 What pictures have you been to see? What was the scariest/funniest one you ever saw?

5 How much pocket money do you get? What do you buy with it? Has anybody ever pinched it from you?

Peer groups and friends
1 Who are your best friends?
2 What sorts of things do you do together?

Fights
1 What kinds of things do fights usually start about?
2 Have you seen any good/bad fights?
3 Have you been in any? With someone bigger than you?
4 Are there any rules about fair/unfair fights? What would you do if somebody came up to you and called you a name? Kicked you? Pulled your hair?
5 Have you ever been blamed for something you didn't do?
6 Have you ever been badly hurt? In hospital?
7 What's the worst thing that ever happened to you?

Some of these are similar to the themes Labov used with adults.

For the interviewer who wants to overcome certain asymmetries between himself and children, the problem is how to ask questions to which children can relate. However, an adult outsider may not be aware of the indigenous interests and activities of the group he wishes to work with. This deficiency can of course be remedied by participant observation and/ or by familiarizing oneself with child culture by looking at comic books, annuals, toy shops and listening to children's programmes on TV and to pop music on the radio. It is often easier to elicit speech by asking a question which shows some knowledge of what the child's interests are rather than general questions which may seem vague to the child. A certain amount of background information can be gleaned indirectly from books such as Opie and Opie (1959), which contains information on children's games and activities. The Opies claim that the language of schoolchildren plays an important role in the creation of a separate childhood culture. In my work in Edinburgh I was able to consult Ritchie (1964), which contains some of the traditional 'street culture' of Edinburgh children. Although some of the material was outdated, it served a useful starting point. But by and large the most important skill in successful interviewing is to pick up cues about the informants' interests as these crop up and to pursue them to their fullest extent.

Ultimately, I think that as an outsider to the Edinburgh linguistic situation in many respects I had the advantage of 'positive stranger-value' (cf. Moser and Kalton 1958: 250). I was able to ask legitimately certain questions which a member of the community would not normally be expected to ask. I explained to the children at the outset that I was an American,[2] and that I wanted to find out about all the games, activities, etc., which went on in Scotland. I asked the children if they would help. On the whole most were very receptive to this idea and volunteered information to 'help' me. Labov (1966: 140) commented that he gauged the success of his interviews by whether he was offered anything to eat. He maintains that the best informants bake the best apple pies. Schoolchildren are not of course in a position to offer such tangible tokens of exchange. However, the corresponding guiding principle which emerged from my study of schoolchildren was that the best informants showed the most battlescars and tattoos.

Like Labov, I found that the introduction of certain topics provoked stylistic shifts in the direction of more casual speech as indicated by the increased use of marked linguistic variables. Under the heading of the topic games and activities, the questions about horror films, scary TV programmes and events were the best for overcoming the constraints of formality. The following extract from an interview with an eight-year-old Edinburgh girl illustrates such a shift in style.

Interviewer: What scary pictures have you seen?
Informant: I'm not allowed to (gs-1) see them cause my wee sister she
             always has nightmares about (au-0) them. She always wakes
             up in the night (gs-1).
Interviewer: What's the scariest thing you've ever seen?
Informant: . . . You went through this big tunnel. This big fluffy man,
             he's dressed up in fur and I bumped into (gs-1) him and
             I screamed and I nearly jumped out (au-1) my skin
             (i-1).

(gs-1) indicates [ʔ], as opposed to (gs-0), which indicates /t/. (au-1) indicates /u/, and (au-0) indicates /au/; (i-3) indicates a vowel of the quality [ɛ] (cf. Romaine 1975: 70). These variables are socially significant ones in Edinburgh. In each case the child used the realization closest to lower-class urban Scots speech. The variables are discussed in greater detail in chapter 4.

In other cases stylistic shifts appeared to occur as part of the more general process of familiarization between the child and interviewer. This process can be seen to operate in this extract from the first few minutes of an interview with a six-year-old girl. (ing-0) indicates /ŋ/; (ing-1) indicates /n/. (th-0) indicates /θ/; (th-1) indicates /h/.

Informant: I think (th-0) it's scared. He's getting (gs-0) (ing-1) scared of
             the elephant now (au-0) . . . it moves itself /ɪtsɛl/.

This utterance refers to a comic strip which the child is looking at on a viewmaster projector. In the next she begins to relate an incident about herself and her brother unprompted by the interviewer. In this extract there is a dramatic shift toward the more characteristic local Edinburgh Scots speech:

Informant: This was my wee brother, your toy's been moving (ing-1), your toy's been moving (ing-1) itself /ɪtsɛl/. I says they dinnae move, its your imagination. He didnae move again.

The rest of the interview continued more or less in this less formal style that the informant adopted after the first five minutes. There are several noteworthy remarks to be made about this particular sequence. Firstly, it demonstrates that there is a great deal of variability in children's speech and that young children are not monostylistic, as has been suggested by some (cf. section 4.2 on the development of stylistic variation and register). Secondly, but more problematically, this extract raises questions about some issues discussed in the last section in relation to the status of the interview as a speech event. There are presumably some important differences between children's and adults' assessment of the situation, which will be reflected in the linguistic behaviour they choose as appropriate to it. The youngest age groups in my sample certainly have a less clear idea of what an interview is; the two older groups (aged eight and ten) were no doubt familiar with this routine from listening to television and radio. However, it is unlikely that any of my informants had ever *participated* in an event like the interview. By comparison with the adult interviews discussed by Wolfson (1982), children generated more spontaneous narratives, perhaps because they did not consider the event to be as strictly governed by the adult rule: the interviewer asks the questions and defines the topic (cf. chapter 5). The six-year-old girl generates a narrative which is in some sense, at least from an adult perspective, a non-sequitur to her previous utterance (cf., however, the discussion of Michaels's work in section 6.2).

It is not clear at what age very young children are able to control the participation structure of certain events involving adult–child interaction, i.e. the overall pattern of allocation of communicative rights and obligations among partners. Some research which has been done from a developmental sociolinguistic perspective shows that even pre-school children can vary their language in role-playing situations and have good skills across a range of interactive settings (cf. chapter 5). It now appears that there may be important social class and ethnic group differences in interaction styles which emerge in different settings. Some of these will be discussed in connection with the assessment of children's abilities in test situations in chapter 8.

In addition to eliciting conversation from children on various topics, I also got them to do various tasks in an attempt to vary the style of speech. I decided to ask the oldest group (ten year olds) to read a text in order to get some idea of the contrast in style they might produce in this situation, which could then be compared with a style from the more casual end, the rest of the interview. Reading represents, according to Labov (1966), a context in which a great deal of attention is paid to speech. I would say that the degree of attention probably varies with the degree of difficulty which the child has in reading (cf. also Milroy's 1980 comments on the reading styles of some of her semi-literate working-class Belfast speakers). Degree of ability ranged from those who were fairly 'fluent' (whom teachers would probably refer to as 'expressive readers') to those who took quite a while to get through the passage.

Since I was aware that reading out loud was likely to be a very intimidating task if a child was a poor reader, I attempted to introduce this part of the interview as naturally as possible within the context of topics related to the content of the story in order not to make the child feel that he was being tested. This was done again under the pretext of asking the children if they would help me by reading a story I had written and giving me their opinion of its suitability. The relative success of this approach in reducing possible anxiety about reading aloud was evidenced by a number of requests from the children for more stories of that type. The style of speech which occurred in the reading passage could hardly be called 'natural' speech for all speakers. But then reading has its own characteristic prosodic structure. Some passages were characterized by stretches of syllable-timed speech. For this reason the reading passage does not, I think, yield very interesting data in itself. Nevertheless, it is an example of the speech of ten year olds in a carefully defined and controlled context which can be compared with the style of the interview.

As far as the younger children were concerned, I gave them slightly different tasks in order to vary the setting. They were given some comic strips to look at on a viewmaster projector and a book which contained pages which were each divided into three parts which the children could flip through and piece together in different ways so as to create their own composite pictures, e.g. one page might have the top portion of a picture of a giraffe and the bottom half of a picture of an elephant. In each of these tasks I tried to get the children engaged in discussion of the pictures they were looking at. In the case of the viewmaster comic strips, I pretended I had not seen them yet, and asked them to tell me what was happening.

2.5 The use of the ethnographic method

A number of sociolinguists have relied on the ethnographic method developed by anthropologists as a means of understanding the ways of living of an unfamiliar social group or culture (cf. Blom and Gumperz 1972). More often than not, the ethnographic method has been used among poor, rural, minority groups in natural situations rather than in mainstream urban populations or in institutional settings. This method has, however, recently been applied to the study of an urban social dialect by Milroy (1980). The essence of the ethnographic method is participant observation. In other words, the fieldworker attempts to become a participant in a group in order to describe the behaviour of it and to understand it in terms of the conceptual framework the members themselves use to order their own subjective experience instead of in terms of a predetermined system of categories brought to the field and imposed by the fieldworker. We might say that participant observation differs from ordinary 'anonymous' observation by being characterized as observation from the inside out rather than outside in (cf. Geertz 1976, and also the notion of 'bottom up' in ethnomethodology in Grimshaw 1982).

Within anthropology as it is traditionally practised, the ethnographer uses a range of techniques such as charting kinship, collecting life histories and recording narratives, songs, myths, etc. If used at all, survey data, questionnaires and experimental methods play a much less significant role. It is a holistic approach which attempts to produce a 'cultural grammar', a set of rules which one would have to know in order to be a competent member of the group.

Hymes (1968) has developed a model which specifically relates to my discussion of communicative competence called 'the ethnography of speaking'. The goal of the ethnography of speaking (1968: 101) concerns 'what a child internalises about speaking, beyond rules of grammar and a dictionary, while becoming a full-fledged member of its speech community'.

The research programme which Hymes outlines for an ethnography of speaking has not received the attention it deserves, although now there is a small body of studies within this framework (cf. especially the papers in Bauman and Sherzer 1974). Most of the work concentrates on adult speech events, and even in the anthropological literature there is little enough work which looks specifically at children as a subculture. Most of the work in the area of so-called 'child acquisition' speaks as if there were only one route of acquisition, that defined by the norms of middle-class Anglo society. As I pointed out in chapter 1, Hymes (1968: 126–9) raises a number of questions about the differences in social norms for using language cross-culturally and how cultural attitudes and beliefs about communication between care-givers and children affect the form and content of the child's grammar and the order of acquisition (cf. also Schieffelin, 1979). It has become increasingly clear from Heath's work (1983) on socialization in rural lower- and middle-class black and white communities in the southern United States that we need not look to 'exotic' cultures to find examples where different norms lead to rather dramatically different outcomes than one would expect from having read the standard literature. I shall return to the findings of ethnographic studies of communicative competence in chapter 6.

The early work of Labov et al. 1968 on Black English Vernacular was based partly on participant observation of 'vernacular' culture. In his research on black teenage gangs Labov engaged young black fieldworkers to follow the groups' activities and to make observations and recordings. Among the activities included in 'vernacular culture' was a rich repertoire of speech events typical of many Afro-American communities, e.g. rules for ritual insults, rapping, playing the dozens, etc.

Labov's work was among the first to demonstrate the importance of peer-group membership in influencing norms of speech. Those who were most firmly integrated into local street gangs were also those most firmly entrenched in vernacular culture. Outsiders or marginals were, by contrast, 'linguistic lames', i.e. they did not know the rules for behaviour in the vernacular culture and were more receptive to influence from outside. Labov was able to show that there was a correlation between membership in a peer group and success vs. failure in reading. In effect, the peer group which revolved around the vernacular activities had created a 'counter-culture' with an opposing set of norms to those of the school (cf. also Edwards 1979 and Sutcliffe 1982 for a discussion of British Black English). A number of studies of teen-age groups by sociolinguists have revealed the existence of distinctive in-group ways of talking as important markers of group identity and solidarity.

Cheshire's (1982a) study of adolescent speech in Reading is based on long-term participant observation of single-sex peer groups. Her study is closely modelled on Labov's and her findings are similar. Adherence to vernacular cultures acts as a powerful influence on group behaviour (cf. section 6.3).

The ethnographic method has also recently been introduced into the classroom. This may at first blush seem at odds with my characterization of it as a method which takes a holistic approach and avoids formal institutionalized settings. Strictly speaking, of course, no such thing as a holistic description exists: all theories and observations deal only with an aspect of the total phenomenon. This cannot therefore be considered a major weakness of the ethnographic method; it is merely a consequence of methodology. Recently, however, ethnographic methods have been applied to research in education. This has come about partly through dissatisfaction with large-scale surveys, quantitative (especially correla-tional) studies which do not provide a qualitative assessment of events in the classroom or the interactions between teachers and student. Yet these studies are often used to stereotype children as achievers or failures. Hymes, again, has been the forerunner in arguing for the use of 'ethnographic monitoring'[3] in educational settings (cf. in particular Hymes

1979, Heath 1982a and the papers in Gilmore and Glatthorn 1982 and Spindler 1982).

Spindler (1982: 6–7) outlines the criteria for good 'ethnography of schooling'[4] as follows:

1 Observations are contextualized and the process of observation and inquiry must disturb the process of interaction as little as possible. Observation is prolonged and repetitive.
2 The instruments for eliciting data are generated in the field; hypotheses and questions emerge as the study proceeds. Any form of technical device which allows the ethnographer to collect the data, videotapes, and which permits the cultural knowledge of participants to unfold naturally should be used.
3 The native view of reality is brought out by inferences from observed behaviour and various forms of ethnographic inquiry, e.g. interviews and other eliciting procedures. A major task is to understand what sociocultural knowledge participants bring to and generate in social settings. Ethnography thus makes explicit what is often known only implicitly.

It is clear from this sketch of what constitutes the research programme of the ethnography of schooling that it is just as demanding methodologically as any experimental design or correlational research strategy. Yet Heath notes that the introduction of ethnographic methods into education has met with resistance for a number of reasons. She observes (1982a: 23):

Ethnographic research does not lend itself to being categorised, tabulated, or correlated, and it will not necessarily identify specific indicators which predict success of either programs or students. In short, ethnographic research does not meet the criterion of traditional research in education in either methodology, format or results. It cannot be carried out in a brief time period. It does not generalise the findings from one setting to another without comparable work elsewhere. It does not fit neatly into current calls for efficient, business-like approaches to education, and it will not specify discrete non-contextualised factors which may lead to improving either schools or students.

She adds that these alleged weaknesses are from the perspective of the anthropologist the advantage of the method. Heath's own contribution to this enterprise has lain in co-ordinating ethnographic research in the community with what goes on in the school. She sees the socialization process which takes place in the home both pre-school and during formal school education as crucial in understanding children's performance in schools. Studies which have relied on formal assessment in classroom settings, e.g. standardized testing, have revealed the static correlation between socioeconomic class and reading ability. Heath demonstrates that in order to understand the significance of such correlations one has to look at the degree to which reading is relevant to group membership, status, achievement, work opportunities and retention of cultural values in the community. Information about these aspects of literacy can only be uncovered by ethnographic monitoring. In order to understand the process of mutual transmission one must view socialization of children taking place on a continuum between community and school where each environment influences the other. Heath (1982b) outlines a methodology for community/ school-based research on literacy skills.

Those who advocate the ethnographic approach to the study of the language of education do so in the belief that research outside schools uncovers evidence of abilities in community situations that puts the display of abilities in schools and test situations into perspective. I have already discussed a number of ways in which display of abilities may be tied to situations. Observation of children in school, at play and home can reveal quite contradictory stereotypes of talkative vs. shy children (cf. Philips 1974). Characterization of the verbal repertoires which the child brings from home to school is a first step in understanding where the school fits into the child's modes of learning so far. Research in this area (which I will look at in more detail in chapters 6 and 7) indicates that children may be excluded from equality of access and opportunity if they do not fit into the classroom management style and the communicative expectations of schools (cf. Michaels 1981).

Ethnographic methods have also proved to be useful in evaluating educational curricula and programmes. Heath (1982b: 39) reports a case where reading scores rose in one school and not in another despite the fact that the teaching methods, in-service practice, access to audiovisual materials and the sociodemographic characteristics of the two schools were ostensibly the same. Researchers did a content analysis of the reading materials and collected ethnographic data from the communities served by the two schools in order to check the degree of match between items and behaviour which occurred in the materials and in the communities. They found that, in the communities attending the school with increased reading scores, at least 90 per cent of the items (e.g. apartment buildings) and cultural behaviour (e.g. riding a bus) used in the text were familiar. In communities where scores had not improved, only 60 per cent of the items and behaviour were familiar.

2.6 Some advantages and disadvantages of conducting sociolinguistic research with children

Some of the advantages and disadvantages of working with young children and adolescents are discussed by Bowerman (1981), Labov et al. (1968) and Cheshire (1982a). Among the most important factors which Cheshire mentions in connection with the study of the speech of adolescents is the relative ease of access to this age group by comparison with adults. Adolescents can be easier to approach in some cases because they may be less suspicious of researchers than adults, and the constraints on the kinds of tasks one can legitimately ask them to do are fewer. Children at school and in the street and playground are a 'captive' population; one need not gain access to people's homes in order to work with children in naturalistic settings, although, in order to obtain a full profile of children's linguistic development, one would want to observe them in as many different settings as possible.

Cheshire says that adolescents can give up more time than adults, who have more structured lives. Children are often quite happy to serve as the subjects of linguistic research over long periods of time, especially when it involves taking time from school lessons, as was the case in my research with schoolchildren in Edinburgh. Pupils begged the teacher to be allowed to participate in an interview. Attention shown by adults to children can sometimes be positively welcomed. While this may mean that some children may have few inhibitions, it may also lead to 'showing off', as noted earlier. I also gave some examples of how formal settings, such as the school or an interview, may create an unfavourable context for eliciting data from some children. Cheshire says she found it easy to contact and establish rapport with adolescents by doing participant observation in adventure playgrounds in Reading. They could be approached there on 'neutral territory', where neither the fieldworker nor adolescents have the clearly defined social roles of, for example, teacher vs. pupil, as they might in the school setting. By dressing informally and acting somewhat unconventionally, e.g. arriving on a motorbike, she was able to get accepted by these groups. Corsaro (1981) describes how he was able to join young children's play groups and participate in their games; he also notes some of the problems adults face as 'outsiders' to children's cultures.

The extent to which one can establish rapport with informants, whether children or adults, is of course in some respects a matter of individual personality. Some sociolinguists may not be good fieldworkers for a variety of reasons. Furthermore, one can be genuinely interested in people and still not be able to break down whatever constraints of formality and so on there may be, governing interactions with strangers. Hymes (1971) has said that the difficulties fieldworkers encounter in collecting data are often a good indicator of what the ground rules for speaking are in a particular community. Eades (1982), for example, talks about why the strategy of direct questioning is inappropriate in Australian Aboriginal communities in South-East Queensland, and therefore not likely to be a productive technique for eliciting data. The relative success which Cheshire and I had in collecting data reflects partly the fact that we did not have to override substantial cultural constraints.

By contrast, Bowerman (1981: 109) discusses the difficulty which Blount had in studying the language development of Luo children in East Africa. Despite the fact that he visited homes repeatedly and provided props for stimulating speech, he was able to collect fewer than 200 spontaneous utterances from a total of six children. While a great many middle-class English-speaking children can be talkative and relaxed across a wide range of familiar and unfamiliar settings, this is not everywhere the case. The Luo teach their children to be silent in the presence of adult strangers and to speak to adults only in certain respectful ways. Blount found that even when the children were encouraged by their parents to talk to him, they found it difficult to 'violate' the local rules of language use. In cases such as these, the traditional western technique of taping mother–child interactions in the home is unsuitable. Bowerman observes that in order to obtain maximally informative speech samples, one would have to follow children to the settings in which their most representative and varied speech takes place. Schieffelin (1979) describes in detail how she managed to identify situations which were likely to be productive for collecting data from Kaluli children in Papua New Guinea.

2.7 Evaluating methodology

I will conclude this chapter by summarizing some of the main points I have made about the advantages and disadvantages of some of the methods used by sociolinguists in collecting data. The most important point I want to stress is that in evaluating the suitability of a research methodology no one research method or context has any privileged status as the 'right' or 'best' one. No methodology is intelligible, or determines what shall be observed and recorded, how it shall be interpreted and what its significance is, except in relation to some theoretical framework, model or set of hypotheses, which shows how the observations relate to one another.

Language behaviour, like other forms of cultural behaviour, is a construct of the researcher rather than a directly observable phenomenon. One does not describe a language or a culture, but constructs and reconstructs it out of what has been observed. This is just another way of saying that as researchers, we never work on 'raw' data; we always work on transcripts of it.

Since different methods of observation give us different perspectives on a phenomenon, and are therefore complementary, it is important to evaluate research findings in terms of the methodology or theory which generated them. One would want to ask at least the following questions: How was the research perspective arrived at? What details were left out and which included? What do we know about the constraints of the setting in which the observation was carried out? I claimed in section 2.3 that one cannot define a priori some settings as natural and others as unnatural without some knowledge of the typical range of behaviours to be found in them. One cannot say then without further qualification that the classroom is an unnatural setting for doing research on children's language. It is of course an unnatural setting if one wants to make claims primarily about the language children use in casual interaction with their friends. Some aspects of behaviour in some cultures can probably be approached only through ethnographic monitoring, while others only through direct elicitation and experimentation. It is also probably true that all levels of language (i.e. phonology, syntax, semantics, pragmatics) are susceptible to culturally and socially conditioned variability in performance. The next two chapters look at variation in children's syntax and phonology.

It is worth mentioning another possible disadvantage of working with children and adolescents as the subjects of sociolinguistic research, which has to do with the goals of the research. Most of the major urban sociolinguistic studies to be discussed in chapter 4 surveyed adult populations. Although some of these included subsamples of children of various age groups, the main objective was to obtain a sociolinguistic description of the norms of the adult speech community. One would not be able to make claims about the usage of a whole community on the basis of the investigation of the language of schoolchildren or teenage peer groups, since they may be out of step linguistically with trends in the adult community (cf. section 6.3 and chapter 9 for further discussion). This may be particularly the case with minority groups, such as those of West Indian origin in Britain, who deliberately adopt a set of forms for group identification which are markedly deviant from the mainstream ones. One cannot really address the question of where children fit into the overall communicative structure of the speech community without comparing samples of speech from both children and adults.

3

The development of syntactic structure

In this chapter I will talk about children's acquisition of two features of complex syntax: namely, relative clauses and passives. There are a number of reasons for choosing these particular syntactic constructions. For one thing, both have received extensive discussion in the psycholinguistic and child development literature; but the focus there has generally not been on the communicative functions which these syntactic structures serve in social context. Furthermore, although both passives and relatives have been widely studied cross-linguistically (cf. the typological framework employed by Comrie 1981, in particular chapter 7), it is usually the standard written varieties which are taken as representative of the languages in question. As far as children's acquisition is concerned, there has generally been little attempt to distinguish structural and developmental effects from non-standard aspects of these construction types. In general, not much attention has been paid to the often great divergence between the syntax of standard and non-standard varieties. This is no less true of English than of other languages.

It has been fashionable to say that the bulk of language acquisition takes place between the ages of two and five (cf. Chomsky 1969 and, more recently, Maclure and French 1981: 207, and Cummins 1981: 8). There is a great deal of truth in this, in as much as by the time the child comes to school, he has a richly differentiated linguistic system. Chomsky (1969) was among the first to show that there are still some basic difficulties in the use of complex syntactic structures like passives and relatives, which remain to be mastered after the child has entered school.

Another reason for looking at complex syntactic constructions is that children's language development has often been assessed in terms of measures which rely on the assumption that having strategies for subordinating and embedding sentences within each other is indicative of greater cognitive skill and verbal ability. I will offer a treatment of relativization and passivization from the perspective of universal grammar and linguistic typology. I will discuss in particular Keenan and Comrie's accessibility hierarchy with reference to developmental data, drawing on my own work with schoolchildren in Edinburgh in order to compare their course of acquisition with that of other children. I will argue that the hierarchy suggests some basic inequalities with respect to the kinds of strategies of relativization and passivization which different languages make available to their speakers.

A final reason for looking at children's acquisition of passives and relatives is that there is often a large gap between production and perception, and/or, alternatively, between competence and performance, as far as the use of these (and other) constructions is concerned. Young children may be able to produce and interpret a syntactic construction in an experimental situation at an early age, but not use it spontaneously until much later, if indeed at all. There is also a great deal of individual variability among children of the same age. This suggests that for some children alternative constructions may serve at least some of the same functions in discourse. If, however, this is not the case, then the question arises of how such communicative functions are realized, if at all, in the absence of any formal linguistic marking of them. I will also offer an integrative account of the acquisition of passives and relatives within a functionalist, pragmatic view of discourse and syntax. I will argue, in particular, that it is a mistake to look at the evolution of children's grammars as a unilinear progression from more primitive to more complex syntax, and that there is ontogenetic and diachronic continuity between relative clauses and passives, and early topic/comment structures. Thus the highly codified canonical structures which go by the name of relative clauses and passives in the formal theoretical (and also less formal prescriptive) grammars of standard English are the products of a chain of grammaticalization, which has brought about a transition from pragmatically to syntactically defined surface structure.

By way of introduction, I will make a few remarks about the background of the Edinburgh study (cf. Romaine 1975 for full details). The data to be discussed come from a corpus I collected from 24 Edinburgh primary school children in 1975. The children were all Edinburgh-born and -bred speakers from working-class families (chosen on the basis of father's occupation using the Registrar General's Classification of Occupations). Four males and four females were selected from three age groups: six, eight and ten year olds. The sample was non-random and judgemental. All speakers were recorded in a face-to-face interview with me, using the methods described in chapter 2.

3.1 Psycholinguistic perspectives on the acquisition of relative clauses

The late development of relative clauses in child acquisition has been attributed, among other things, to the alleged processing difficulties posed by their syntactic complexity.[1] I will assume in the following discussion one of the views of relative-clause formation current in generative grammar: namely, that relativization is a syntactic process whereby a sentence becomes embedded as a modifier in an NP (noun phrase), where the embedded sentence and main (or matrix) sentence share an identical nominal constituent, which is realized as a relative marker or pronoun (e.g. *who*, *which*, *that*, etc.).[2] The following example, taken from my study of Edinburgh schoolchildren, was produced by a ten-year-old boy:

(1) The lassie was remembering about things [that had happened]

The matrix sentence or main clause is: *The lassie was remembering about things* and the relative clause, enclosed in brackets, is: *that had happened*. The relative clause is considered to be a modifier of or embedded within the noun phrase *things*, which is coreferential with the relative marker *that*. I will refer to *that* as a *marker* to distinguish it from what traditional grammarians call relative *pronouns*, e.g. *who*, *whom*, *whose*, *which*. The choice among these in English relative clauses is determined by whether or not the antecedent or coreferential noun phrase in the matrix sentence is human, and the function of the relative in the relative clause, e.g. subject, object, etc. The marker *that* is invariant and not sensitive to these features of the antecedent, while the WH forms of the relative are. A good descriptive account of relative clauses in English can be found in Quirk et al. (1972). We will see, however, when we look at their observations, that some modifications to these generalizations will be necessary to account for some of the relative-clause constructions which children use.

   If we return to example (1), we can identify two factors which have been cited as contributory to the complexity of these constructions. The first of these is what is referred to as *embeddedness*; that is, distance of the relative clause from the syntactic position occupied by the antecedent in the main clause. In this particular sentence there is 'no distance'; in other words, the relative clause immediately follows the noun phrase in the matrix sentence which serves as the direct object. We can break it down into its constituents as follows:

(2) The lassie was remembering about things [that had happened]
    NP1   V   [NP2] [NP3]   V   (OS)
                                     object subject

The second factor to be considered has been called *focus*; that is, the grammatical function or syntactic position of the relativized noun phrase in the relative clause. In this sentence the relative occupies subject position. I will use the notation OS to refer to this type of relative clause, where O represents object and S subject position. By varying these two parameters, embeddedness and focus, we can also have relative clauses of the type SS, OO and SO. The first member of each of these pairs stands for the syntactic position occupied by the head NP in the matrix S, and the second for the syntactic position occupied by the relativized NP in the relative clause. Examples from the Edinburgh data illustrating each type are given below, each with its constituent structure:

(3) That person [that hasnae scored] goes out   (SS)
    [NP1]   [NP2] V   V
    subject subject

(4) Ken they carties [that you pull behind you]?   (OO)
   V   [NP1] [NP2]   V
       object object

(5) The one [that I like best] is kick the can   (SO)
   [NP1]   NP2 V   V   [NP4]
    subject   object

    It has been proposed that there is a relation between ease of processing and the order in which children acquire these four types of relative clauses. It is not hard to imagine why researchers have claimed that relativization on the object NP of the matrix sentence is easier than relativization on the subject because the former still entails (in terms of surface structure) only paratactic conjunction of sentences rather than the insertion of one within the other (i.e. embedding), as in the case of relativization on the subject. We should expect then to find that children are able to process the OO and OS types earlier and with greater accuracy than the SS and SO types. This would follow from the hypothesis that children are using a parsing strategy of the type proposed by Slobin, where sequences of NVN are interpreted as subject verb object (SVO). More specifically, Slobin's developmental universal is (1973: 198) 'Sentences deviating from standard word order [SVO] will be interpreted at early stages of development as if they were examples of standard word order.' This strategy would yield the correct interpretation for an OS relative clause, but not for the other types. The problem posed by subject-embedded relative clauses is that the relative clause interrupts the linear processing of constituents, i.e. it is embedded in a sequence like NP1 [NP3 V NP4] V NP2 where either NP3 or NP4 is the position relativized within the relative clause.

    A number of experiments have been conducted to test children's ability to understand relative clauses. In most of these, children were asked either to repeat various types of relative clauses or to manipulate toys. For example, Tavakolian (1977) and de Villiers et al. (1979) asked children to make toys act out the sequence of events in sentences such as:

(6) The dog stands on the house [that the giraffe jumps over]   (OO)

In order to score a correct interpretation the child must be able to comprehend the roles of agent and patient correctly. This type of experiment was also used by Chomsky in her study of children's acquisition of complex sentences. In the case of the relative-clause experiments, children have to be able to decode two agent–action–patient sequences.

The experimental literature has produced conflicting findings. Sheldon (1974) and Tavakolian (1977) studied three to five year olds and found the following hierarchy:

SS > OO > OS > SO

This means that children produced the most correct responses for SS relative clauses and the fewest for SO. Sheldon explained her results in terms of what she called the Parallel Function Hypothesis.[3] She argued that the SS and OO types were easier than the OS and SO ones because in the former the head NP of the relative clause plays the same grammatical role in both the matrix and relative clause, i.e. subject or object. In the OS and SO types the NPs in the relative and matrix clauses do not have parallel grammatical functions.[4] De Villiers et al. (1979) challenged the Parallel Function Hypothesis with their findings, which showed that children did not respond to SS and OO sentences more accurately than to OS and SO. They found the following hierarchy of difficulty:

OS > SS > OO ⩾ SO

The OO and SO types were found to be roughly equally difficult, which is more in line with what we would expect if children were using an NVN type parsing strategy. This is the explanation de Villiers et al. favour.[5]

Before discussing some of the reasons why there seems to be disagreement in the experimental results, let us look at the relative clauses produced by the Edinburgh schoolchildren. There was a total of 201 relative clauses. There appear to be only slight differences in the number of relative clauses produced by each age group, the numbers being 73, 59 and 69 for the ten, eight and six year olds respectively. The oldest group uses the most, but it is interesting that the youngest speakers use a greater number than the eight year olds. There is a great deal of individual variability, however; the largest number produced by any one child was 24 (a six-year-old boy) and the least was one (an eight-year-old boy). The differences here are, however, not large enough to support age-related claims.

Using the factors of focus and embeddedness, the data can be grouped under the four possible types for each age group, as in table 3.1. The number of relative clauses is slightly less ($N = 183$) since certain types, which will be discussed later, have been omitted for the moment. We can see that, if we take the total for the whole sample without regard to age group, we obtain the following hierarchy for the production of relative clauses. Age in itself is not statistically significant here, although the factor of age in relation to variable type, i.e. SS, SO etc., is.[6]

Table 3.1 Relative clause types in relation to embeddedness and focus

	SS	SO	OS	OO	Total	%
Age 10	15	5	26	25	71	39
Age 8	5	4	22	18	49	27
Age 6	11	13	15	24	63	34
Total N	31	22	63	67	183	
%	17	12	34	37		100

Note: Figures for SO and OO include direct objects and obliques.

OO > OS > SS > SO

This trend is not operative, however, within the individual age groups. The ranking of OO and OS is reversed for the ten and eight year olds, and the ranking of SS and SO for the six year olds. Table 3.2 breaks the data down further to look at the effects of the two factors, focus and embeddedness, for each age group. The factor of embeddedness is clearly the one which carries the most weight, with object relative clauses being greatly preferred over subject ones. The effect of focus, which is a much weaker factor in these data, results in fewer relative clauses being produced on NPs which serve as the object of their clauses. The interaction between age and focus is statistically significant. As far as the factor of embeddedness is concerned however, age is not significant.

The results for all the data we have examined so far are summarized in table 3.3. There are at least two major findings which need to be explained: Why are there differences between the oldest and youngest age groups of Edinburgh schoolchildren? And why are there discrepancies between the production and perception data? It is perhaps easier to try and answer the second question first by noting that there are often asymmetries between production and perception (others are discussed in chapter 4). What is difficult to perceive may be easy to produce or vice versa; one must be

Table 3.2 Effects of focus and embeddedness on relative-clause production

	Focus S > O				Embeddedness O > S			
	subject focus		object focus		Subject embedded		Object embedded	
	(SS + OS)		(SO + OO)		(SS + SO)		(OS + OO)	
	N	%	N	%	N	%	N	%
Age 10	41	22	30	16	20	11	51	28
Age 8	27	15	22	12	9	5	40	22
Age 6	26	14	37	20	24	13	39	21
Total	94	51	89	49	53	29	130	71

Table 3.3 Hierarchies for relative-clause types

Perception experiments						
Sheldon	SS	> OO	> OS	> SO
Tavakolian	SS	> OO	> OS	> SO
De Villiers et al.	OS	> SS	> OO	> SO
Production (Edinburgh children)						
Age 10	OS	> OO	> SS	> SO
Age 8	OS	> OO	> SS	> SO
Age 6	OO	> OS	> SO	> SS
Average	OO	> OS	> SS	> SO

careful to distinguish between what is difficult/easy for the speaker and hearer respectively. Most of the research on the acquisition of relative clauses has focused on perception rather than production in order to investigate processing or decoding strategies used by learners. Further-more, most of the data have been obtained in highly controlled experimental situations rather than in naturalistic settings, and as I pointed out in chapter 2 data have to be interpreted in the light of the context in which they were elicited. Children of different sociocultural backgrounds respond differently to context-independent situations, where knowledge of linguistic constructions is abstracted from the context in which the rules are applied and learned. The functions in which syntactic constructions like relative clauses are used must play an important role in their processing and production. This would follow from Hymes's (1974) view that there is an interplay between the use of grammar in context to accomplish particular goals and the linguistic knowledge of the rules abstracted from their use.

The earliest experiences which children have with language are highly dependent upon social context for their meaning; only later are more abstract demands made which rely more on linguistic rather than social knowledge (cf. chapters 6 and 7). The disjunction between these two uses of language is particularly salient when the child enters school, where processing depends increasingly more on abstract linguistic relations and the context of the utterance does not support the meaning. What the experiments on processing overwhelmingly demonstrate is that until the age of six and older it is not easy for children to parse relative clauses correctly in situations where comprehension is tested outside a social context. It may also be the case that the experimental tasks, i.e. toy manipulation or sentence repetition, did not test the children's knowledge adequately. Factors such as short-term memory, expectations about what meanings are likely to be expressed, and the ability to respond to sentences as stimuli to perform actions with real-world objects may affect children's performance and obscure the knowledge they might be able to demonstrate under other circumstances. It may be the case that children tend to perform the actions in the order in which they are mentioned rather than in terms of structural relations or meaning. An 'order of mention' operating strategy appears to be at work in learning how to use adverbial clauses containing *before* and *after* (cf. chapter 5). Some evidence that strategies may be a function of the task comes from Johnson (1975), who found that tasks which require the child to act out two events tend to elicit an order-of-mention response strategy, while other tasks do not (cf. Munro and Wales 1982 for more recent experimental evidence and discussion). In interpreting the results of experiments, we have to be careful to avoid what Karmiloff-Smith (1979b) calls the experimental dilemma: that is, how to distinguish between ad-hoc experiment-generated behaviour and normal language usage. Bowerman (1979: 304) sums up the state of the art as far as our understanding of the results of this type of psycholinguistic experimentation is concerned when she says:

> It is unclear whether the response patterns detected in children's performance on psycholinguists' tests of comprehension actually play any role at all in acquisition. Different children appear to use different strategies for the same sentence structures, and some children seem to use no consistent strategies at all.
>
> Yet . . . they all end up learning the constructions . . . Once [children] can process these sentences, they no longer need the strategies and begin instead to interpret them on the basis of structural knowledge.

3.2 *Relative-clause formation strategies in universal grammar*

I will consider now to what extent the production data shed light on children's operating principles, and in particular what answer they suggest to my first question above: namely, why are there differences between the age groups? Once we recognize that children may have more than one strategy for parsing a syntactic construction and that a strategy may be a function of the task, we can see that the data show the evolution of relative-clause formation rules. In order to trace the development from the child to adult system, we will need to take a brief look at adult relative-clause formation strategies. The most detailed work in this area comes from cross-linguistic research done by Keenan and Comrie (1977, 1979) who have made some interesting predictions about the types of relative-clause formation strategies possible in languages. After examining a wide cross-section of different types of languages, they found that they did not vary randomly with respect to the syntactic positions of the NP which could be relativized. They postulated the existence of an accessibility hierarchy which predicted constraints on the positions in which relative clauses could appear:

Subject > Direct > Object > Indirect Object > Oblique > Genitive > Object of comparison

The two most important predictions made by Keenan and Comrie to be considered here are:

1 The frequency with which NPs in certain syntactic positions are relativized in a language is in accordance with their ordering in the case hierarchy; i.e. subject NPs are most frequently and objects of comparison least frequently relativized.
2 The order of cases in the hierarchy is correlated with ease of relativization, i.e. subject is the easiest position to relativize.

The first of Keenan and Comrie's predictions about accessibility relates to my previous discussion of the factor of focus, i.e. the position occupied by the relative in the relative clause. According to their hypothesis, subject relatives (i.e. OS and SS) should be more frequent than object relatives (i.e. OO and SO cf. the results of de Villiers et al. 1979). This prediction is supported when we consider the total relative clauses produced by the Edinburgh children. This can be seen in Table 3.4. A few comments are necessary. There were no indirect object relatives in the sample; that is, a relative clause in which the syntactic function of the relative is that of indirect object, e.g.

Table 3.4 Relatives clauses according to syntactic position of the relativized NP (N = 201)

	Subject	Object	Oblique	[Locative	Temporal]	Genitive
N	94	73	16	9	8	1
%	47	36	8	4	4	0.4

(7a)   The man [*that* I gave the book to]
(7b)   [*to whom* I gave the book]

The term *oblique* is used to refer to relatives in whose underlying structure the coreferential NP functions as the object of a preposition, e.g. the house [*that* I used to live in].[7] There are two types of oblique relative constructions: stranded and shifted. These terms refer to the placement of the preposition in relation to its object. If the preposition is separated from its relative marker or pronoun, as it is in (7a), then it is stranded. The term 'shifted' refers to a relative clause in which the preposition has been fronted along with the coreferential NP to the beginning of the relative clause, e.g. the house [*in which* I live]. The fact that WH relatives behave differently to *that* in oblique constructions is one of the arguments used by syntacticians to justify the treatment of *that* as a non-pronominal relativizer. Oblique relatives marked by *that* cannot undergo stranding. Sentences like (8) are ungrammatical:

(8) The house in that he lived

WH pronouns on the other hand can occur in both stranded and shifted constructions as in (9) and (10):

(9) The house in which he lived
(10) The house which he lived in

If *that* had the same syntactic status as the WH pronouns, we would expect them to behave similarly. We will see further evidence of the different nature of *that* later.

The categories of temporal and locative were included here, although they are not strictly speaking syntactic positions on a par with the others in the case hierarchy. There seems to be no general agreement among syntacticians with regard to the status of adverbs of time and place when used in a relativizing function. Examples of what I will refer to as temporal and locative relatives are:

(11) locative: I've watched a horror film [where's there's a big giant]
(12) temporal: The first time [that I tried it] I liked it

I have included clauses of this type in the category of relative clauses because they participate in a pattern of variation similar to the other types of relative clauses; that is, they may be introduced by WH forms like *where, when*, by *that* or by no marker at all. Only cases in which there is a nominal element which can be understood as coreferential with the temporal or locative marker are included here. In some cases locative relatives can be thought of as having some similarity to oblique relatives, as in the example:

(13) That's the place [*where* I got my fishtank frae]

Locative and temporal relatives are also sometimes paraphrasable by oblique relatives, e.g.:

(14) I like the one [*what* Tom plays a trick on Jerry]

This sentence might be paraphrased as:

(15) I like the one [*where* Tom plays a trick on Jerry]
(16) I like the one [*in which* Tom plays a trick on Jerry]

The Edinburgh children use *what, where* and *that* in relatives of this type.

There was only one example of a genitive relative construction in the Edinburgh data, produced by a ten-year-old boy:

(17) The person [*that's* foot is touched]

In modern standard English the only permissible construction in this case would be *whose*, which is marked for genitive case, and is used with personal human antecedents.[8] The fact that Scots uses a form of *that* to mark relativization on a genitive NP reflects its historical development (cf. Romaine 1980b and 1981). Although Scots possesses the option of using *whose* to relativize genitive NPs, it tends to favour the alternative strategy of using *that's*, which is otherwise invariant in other varieties of English, or it uses a pronoun-retaining strategy, e.g. the person [that his foot is touched]. These two alternative strategies permit case marking on the lower positions of the case hierarchy. In general the use of WH pronouns as relatives is very infrequent in Scots; the most commonly used one is *that*, or often no marker appears at all.

I have already noted some of the constraints which affect the choice of relatives according to features of the antecedent in particular syntactic positions. In a very useful diagram shown in figure 3.1 Quirk et al. (1972: 867) give a synopsis of the options which are available for relativizing on different types of antecedents in different syntactic positions. The notation ø indicates absence of a relative. The diagram does not, of course, give any idea of the choices people make when using relative clauses. Quirk (1957), who studied a corpus of relative clauses produced by 50 university-educated speakers, found that the WH forms were in the majority. From this he concluded that the WH strategy of relativization was the primary one.[9] The primacy of the WH strategy over the option of using *that* or ø is also noted by Keenan and Comrie, although they intend the term *primary* in a more technical sense. They argue that WH is primary because all the

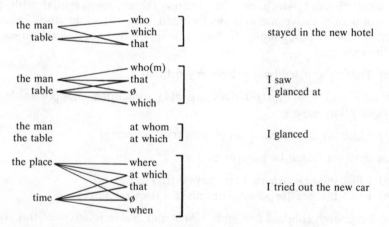

Figure 3.1   The relative system in modern English
Source: Quirk et al. 1972

positions in the case hierarchy are accessible to relativization by means of this strategy. However, we have already seen that since Scots has the option of relativizing genitive relatives by means of a strategy using *that*, we could easily argue for the primacy of *that*. Although Quirk's findings are probably valid for a large proportion of educated speakers of standard English, they run counter to observations made by a number of grammarians over the last century such as Sweet (1900), who observed that in spoken English *that* and ø are preferred to WH. Empirical data from varieties of British and American English support this claim (cf. Hackenberg 1972, Romaine 1980b and Brown, forthcoming).

The data from the Edinburgh schoolchildren also substantiate the view that in spoken English *that* and ø are more frequent than WH forms. Table 3.5 shows the results by age group.

Table 3.5 WH forms, *that* and ø in Edinburgh schoolchildren's relative clauses

	WH forms		that		ø		Total
	N	%	N	%	N	%	
Age 10	16	22	39	53	18	27	73
Age 8	11	19	24	41	24	41	59
Age 6	6	9	25	36	38	55	69
Total	33	16	88	43	80	42	

The Edinburgh schoolchildren on the whole tend to use *that* and ø roughly equally in preference to WH. Although neither age nor type of relative marker is statistically significant, there are some important developmental trends in evidence here, and there is a clear trend for interaction between type and age. Limber (1973), who studied the development of complex sentences in pre-school children, found that the first relative clauses involved no relative pronouns; later *that* is used. Menyuk (1969) reports 'errors' in relative selection at later stages in development, such as the use of *what* for *who*, *which* or *that*. Similar findings are reported for French by Kail (1975). She says that the most common error made by children between five and six is the omission of the relativizers *que* and *qui*. It is more frequently absent in sentences where the embedding factor is present,

(18) La fille [qui pousse le garçon] renverse le bol
      NP1 NP3   NP4   NP2
      The girl [who pushes the boy] knocks over the bowl

Kail also found the substitution of *qui* by *que* (and vice versa though less frequently) was a frequent error made by French-speaking children. Both these errors decreased with age; the first was not found after 7.6 years and the second not after 9.6.

We must be careful here not to confuse the term 'error' with notions of correctness based on the norms prescribed by the standard language. French does not allow deletion of relatives in the way that English does; therefore, acquisition of adult norms involves losing a primitive rule or strategy which juxtaposes clauses without any formal mark of their relation. English allows relativization by deletion and this strategy is commonly used by adults. Acquiring the adult norm in English then involves not a wholesale qualitative shift from one strategy to another, but adding other strategies (i.e. WH and *that*). This involves a decrease in the frequency with which the ø strategy is employed. We can see a clear progression from the six to ten year olds, which is characterized by increasingly less reliance on the ø strategy and a correspondingly greater increase in the use of WH and *that*. Overall, however, even in the ten-year-old group, the WH strategy is not very frequent; *that* is the preferred relativizer. These findings are well in line with the local adult Edinburgh norms.

A similar warning about the use of the term 'error' applies to the finding that children sometimes select the 'incorrect' relative. Again, we must be careful to view the choices which children make in relation to the adult (and other) norms they are exposed to, and not in terms of some idealized prescriptive grammar. Some non-standard varieties of English allow the use of *what* as a relativizer (cf. Cheshire's 1982a discussion of adolescents in Reading and also section 4.4). I have already noted its use among the Edinburgh children to relativize locatives. It is also used in subject, object and oblique relatives, as indicated in the following examples:

(19) Subject: The boy [*what* was staying with us] jumped out the window   (eight-year-old girl)
(20) Object: I forget all the other things [*what* he says]   (six-year-old boy)
(21) Oblique: Things [*what* you sit on] they go   (six-year-old boy)

It may, however, be reasonable to view the use of *what* as a developmental error (i.e. an error related to immaturity common to all speakers acquiring a language) since I have not encountered the use of *what* as a relativizer among Scottish adults in Edinburgh. Even though it accounts for 13 of the 29 WH forms, its use as a relativizer is rather infrequent overall (i.e. 6 per cent). Table 3.6 gives a breakdown of the choice of relatives made by the Edinburgh children in relation to syntactic positions in the accessibility hierarchy.

As far as the use of WH relatives is concerned, only the subject form *who* is used; the inflected forms *whom* and *whose* never appear. The form *who* appears more in object position, but the most favoured relative in this position is ø. Table 3.7 shows the preference for each of the three types of

Table 3.6 Relative markers used by Edinburgh schoolchildren

		Subject	Object	Oblique	Locative	Temporal	Genitive	Total
	WH[a]	13	2		1			16
Age 10	*that*	25	10	3			1	39
	ø	3	11	4				18
Sub-total		41	23	7	1		1	73
	WH[b]	5			6			11
Age 8	*that*	21	1	1	1			24
	ø	1	16	4		3		24
Sub-total		27	17	5	7	3		59
	WH[c]	2	2	1	1			6
Age 6	*that*	21	3	1				25
	ø	3	28	2		5		38
Sub-total		26	33	4	1	5		69
Total		94	72	16	9	8	1	200

Notes:
(a) WH forms include: *who* = 11; *which* = 1; *what* = 1 in subject position; *what* = 2 in object position; *where* = 1 in locative position.
(b) WH forms include: *who* = 2; *what* = 3 in subject position; *where* = 4 and *what* in locative position.
(c) WH forms include: *who* = 2 in subject position; *who* = 1, *what* = 1 in object position; *where* = 1 in locative position; *what* = 1 in oblique position.

strategy, WH, *that* and ø, in relation to syntactic position in the case hierarchy. We can compare these results with Quirk's system of options shown in figure 3.1.

The form *that* is strongly preferred in subject position, followed by WH and ø. Quirk's diagram does not show ø as a possibility in subject position. This reflects the fact that Quirk is describing standard English. In many varieties of non-standard English (and probably in most kinds of casual colloquial English), deletion of subject relatives can be found. Examples from the Edinburgh children are given below.

(22) I've got quite a few friends [ø stay up the street] (ten-year-old girl)
(23) There's lots of people [ø got killed] (eight-year-old boy)

Table 3.7 Choice of WH, *that* and ø strategies in relation to the case hierarchy

	Subject	Object	Oblique	Locative	Temporal	Genitive
WH	20	4	1	8	0	0
that	67	14	5	1	0	1
ø	7	53	10	0	8	0

Since adult speakers also delete subject relatives under some circumstances, there is no reason to treat this as a purely developmental error. There is no evidence in the data to indicate that its use is increasing or decreasing.

In object position the ø strategy is the most frequently and WH the least frequently used. This is also true for oblique relatives. The ø strategy is the only one used in temporal relatives while *that* is the only option in genitive relatives. The only case where WH relatives are used in preference to *that* and ø is in locative relatives.

There is one further comment to make about the kinds of relative-clause formation strategies used by these Edinburgh children. One of the examples I cited previously does not fit neatly into the typology established so far in the discussion. Earlier, I defined relativization as a process of embedding in which a relative clause is embedded in a matrix clause and there is a relation of coreference between an NP in the matrix and an NP in the relative clause. The example which I used to illustrate oblique relativization is repeated again for ease of reference (cf. (21)):

(24) Things [what you sit on] they go

It can be seen that the relationship between these two clauses is not quite the same as in the other examples I have cited so far. The use of the pronoun *they* to mark the subject slot is in a sense redundant because *things* already serves this function. The NPs *things* and *they* are coreferential, just as the relative marker *what* is also coreferential with *things*. The term resumptive, shadow or copy pronoun is used to refer to a pronoun like *they*.[10] Another example of a genitive relative which I gave previously (but which did not actually occur in the data) illustrates a similar phenomenon:

(25) The person [*that his* foot is touched]

This time the resumptive pronoun is marked for genitive or possessive case since this is the function it serves in the relative clause. Furthermore, it sometimes happens that the resumptive element is a full NP and not a pronoun, as in (26):

(26) Then whoever *the person* [*that's* he] catches first *that person's* he in the next game ˙(ten-year-old boy)

In this sentence *that person* is coreferential with the NP *the person*, as is the relative marker *that*. There were 15 instances in which shadows or resumptives were used by the Edinburgh children. Most of these cases (N = 13) were like the two sentences above, (25) and (26), where a resumptive pronoun occurs in subject position of the matrix clause immediately following a relative clause in subject position. The other two cases were like (27), where the resumptive appears within the relative clause itself to mark the position of the relativized NP:

(27) but the ones [ø you can put pounds and notes on *it*]   (eight-year-old
      boy)
(28) That man [who Mickey Mouse was putting] Mickey Mouse [who was
      putting *him* upside down]   (six-year-old girl)

The first of these has a resumptive pronoun as the object of a preposition,
or in other words, it appears in the slot which would have been occupied by
a relative pronoun or marker. The prototypical relative clause in this
syntactic position would have been either (29), (30) or (31):

(29) but the ones on which you can put pounds and notes
(30) but the ones which you can put pounds and notes on
(31) but the ones that you can put pounds and notes on

Since the child has used a zero strategy of relativization in which there is no
overt relativizer to indicate the case relation of the relativized NP, the
pronoun *it* marks its slot. The second example is slightly more complicated
to explain. The girl appears to be hesitating between two constructions,
e.g.

The man [who Mickey Mouse was putting upside down]
Mickey Mouse was putting the man upside down

What results is a conflation of the two, with a resumptive pronoun
appearing in direct object slot, which is the syntactic position she was
trying to relativize initially.

We can think of these two additional types of relative clauses as
alternative strategies to the ones we have already discussed. It remains to
be seen, however, what role they play in the child's syntactic development,
and what implication they have when seen in terms of the Keenan–Comrie
accessibility hierarchy and the perceptual hierarchy based on focus and
embeddedness.

There is evidence from a variety of sources which can be used to argue
that these alternative strategies serve an important syntactic and pragmatic
function and represent intermediate developmental stages in the child's
acquisition of the fully syntacticized adult prototype construction. Children
seem to be using these alternatives in cases which involve some degree of
perceptual difficulty. For example, in the case of the use of resumptive
pronouns to mark the case relation of relativized genitive and oblique NPs
in the relative clause, I would claim that the pronouns help make the case
of the relativized NP recoverable, particularly when a zero strategy of
relativization is used. Resumptive pronouns aid the relativization of NPs
which are in less accessible positions of the Keenan–Comrie case
hierarchy. From a universal perspective Keenan and Comrie (1979) have
noted a tendency for languages to use pronoun-retaining strategies on the
lower positions of the hierarchy. The use of these alternative strategies is

no doubt also connected with the fact that these children do not seem to use the pronominalizing or case-coding WH strategy with great frequency. The alternative strategies take up the slack in the system at the lower end of the hierarchy in particular. One could also argue that perceptual difficulties are at work in the other type of alternative relativization strategy in which the copy appears in the matrix clause. In this case the syntactic position is easily accessible to relativization, i.e. most of these copy pronouns appear in object position. However, as we have seen, subject relatives on subject antecedents interrupt the matrix clause, and in terms of deep structure the two NPs are maximally distant. Here the copying of the subject after the relative clause may serve to minimize the effects of interruptibility and act as a place holder for the referent introduced initially by the speaker.[11]

Although perceptual factors probably go a long way towards accounting for the appearance of these two types of resumptive pronoun strategies, they do not completely explain the developmental changes. For one thing adults use these alternative strategies too (cf. Romaine 1980b), and it may be that children are not exposed to the fully syntacticized strategies in any great frequency until they reach school. Thus the difference between these two modes of relativization reflects in part a dichotomy between written and spoken language on the one hand, and formal and informal language on the other. Secondly, resumptive pronouns can occur when the relativized NP occupies one of the more accessible syntactic positions in the case hierarchy,[12] e.g. subject and direct object. There are no examples of these in the Edinburgh children's data, but Wald (1982), who studied relativization in the discourse of 11–12 year olds in Los Angeles, found cases in which subject shadows appeared in the speech of 11–12 year olds,

(32) It was about some lady *that she* was asleep and *that they* told her to read the Bible

In fact, Wald reports that subject shadows were more common than shadows in other relations in embedded clauses. This appears to be at odds with what we would expect the case hierarchy to predict if perceptual factors were the most important; namely, that the least accessible positions would be most likely to retain pronouns. His result indicates a need for examining the functions relative clauses serve in actual discourse. From a functional perspective relative clauses do the work of providing further information about an NP which has been introduced into discourse. In this respect, they are like comments on topics. For a sentence like (33):

(33) That lassie [ø I go to school with]   (eight-year-old boy)

the relative clause identifies the NP, *that lassie*, as one of a potential group of lassies and singles one particular one out for further comment. Along with various other syntactic devices (e.g. definiteness/indefiniteness, cf.

chapter 5, and Bates and MacWhinney 1979 for a list of devices which act like topics or comments), it provides some necessary background information which the speaker may assume the listener does not have. One reason why we found that children produced more object- than subject-embedded relative clauses (cf. table 3.2) is that new information nouns tend to be located in object position.[13] Thus the high percentage of object relatives may merely reflect this fact.[14] During the course of acquisition it may be that speakers switch from a primarily discourse-oriented system to a more purely syntactically motivated one. Bickerton (1977), for example, found in Hawaiian English creole, in which relativization is being introduced as a new syntactic construction where none existed previously, that object relativization was more frequent than subject relativization. In the data from the Edinburgh children we can see an indication of this switch from object to subject relativization between the ages of six and eight. This is apparent in table 3.2, where subject focus relatives do not become more frequent than object focus relatives before the child is eight.

Another parallel can be drawn from Bickerton's work on the development of relative clauses in Hawaiian English creole. He gives the following examples:

(34) Da boi jas wawk aut from hia, hiz a fishamæn
      The boy [(who) just walked out of here] (he's) a fisherman

Bickerton argues that we can see the beginnings of a rudimentary strategy of relativization. In the earliest stages of the development of this construction, it is difficult to tell whether 'true' embedding or merely a conjoining process has taken place. The surface marker which eventually becomes used in a relativizing function is not a specialized relative pronoun like *who* in English, but a simple pronoun. Bickerton (1977: 274) suggests that the use of pronouns represents an intermediate stage between zero forms and the full range of English relative pronouns. Thus the route to fully syntacticized relativization in Hawaiian English creole can be illustrated in the three sentences (35–37):

(35) You fain Hawaiian [ø spik English]   (zero strategy)
      You found Hawaiians who could speak English
(36) Sam [dei jrink] meik chrabol   (pronoun strategy)
      Some who drink make trouble
(37) Evri filipino [hu kud aford it] bai wan   (English relative pronoun)
      Every Filipino who could afford it bought one

The fully syntacticized stage is reached when zero marking in subject position gives way to overt relativization (either by WH pronominalization or *that*), and the copy pronoun in the subject slot of the matrix following the relative clause is deleted.

A similar progression can be traced in children's acquisition of relative clauses. In the earliest stages of syntactic development children do not use embedded sentences at all; and indeed, even in the casual spoken language of adults, simple conjunction of clauses or the use of independent sentences may be a preferred discourse alternative to relativization.[15] We can see the close relationship between these alternatives in examples like (38) where two independent clauses occur side by side with no formal mark of connection (either subordination or co-ordination) between them:

(38) He met toothless. *That* was this big lion   (eight-year-old boy)

Another possible way of presenting the same information or introducing the referent 'toothless' would be a fully syntacticized relative clause, as in (39):

(39) He met toothless, who was a big lion

Another example attesting the close relationship between relative clauses and conjoined sentences is given in (40):

(40) There's a big alarm bell and that goes off   (eight-year-old girl)

A possible alternative again would be a relative clause, as in (41):

(41) There's a big alarm bell that goes off

The existence of sentences like (38) and (40) as possible alternatives to relativization and their earlier emergence than relatives indicates that in the initial stages of syntactic development children do not possess strategies for the syntactic incorporation of one clause within another. Two propositions simply occur side by side or in a co-ordinate construction as shown in the diagram in figure 3.2. Only later do they acquire the syntactic means for making the relation between propositions and clauses explicit. In the case of OS relatives there is little in the way of formal marking to distinguish them from two independent clauses which occur side by side; and it is therefore not surprising that these are among the first types to be perceived and produced by children. Later the child is able to produce true embedded constructions. In stage (1) the interpretation of such a construction as relative as opposed to two distinct clauses where no connector appears is largely a pragmatic and prosodic matter.[16] The transition from stage (1) to (2) illustrates a change-over from discourse-pragmatic to grammatical-syntactic constraints on relativization. In this way loose paratactic structures become condensed or syntacticized into tight hypotactic structures. The distinction between hypotaxis and parataxis is commonly made by traditional grammarians; it corresponds roughly to the dichotomy I have drawn here between embedding and conjunction. It was frequently argued by these traditional grammarians, and even by more modern scholars like Bernstein (1973), that hypotaxis is the more sophisticated syntactic structure and is indicative of a higher level of

Stage (1) Conjunction of independent clauses Stage (2) Embedding

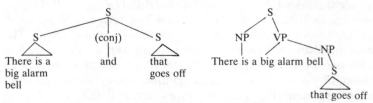

Figure 3.2   Stages in the syntacticization of relative clauses

evolution on both the linguistic and cognitive level. And it was largely under the influence of Greek and Latin grammar teaching that the use of complex syntactic structures has come to be taken as an important, if not indeed the most significant, means by which ability in language is displayed and evaluated. Wald (1982) underlines this point when he says that the command of highly syntacticized language is a principal goal of education and the means by which the literacy achievement of students is constantly judged. This view of syntactic development fails to recognize, however, that the acquisition of syntax is not merely a unilinear progression from a primitive mode of syntactic expression to a more complicated one; an important part of acquisition is the learning of alternative ways of saying the same thing. The use of independent clauses and conjoined clauses as alternatives to relative clauses is an option which exists well into adulthood and is exploited for stylistic purposes. It is not the case that one entirely replaces the other.

Although Labov (1972a) may be right in claiming that all rules begin as variable rules, they do not necessarily become categorical over time; and the competition between two or more rules for the same territory may persist over long periods of time. In order to obtain a more complete picture of the child's syntactic development we have to view the acquisition of particular linguistic structures like relative clauses from the perspective of the other options with a different syntactic status which the child has in his system at a particular time for use in discourse. It is apparent from the Edinburgh data that children at the age of ten are choosing the option of relativization more frequently than eight year olds, but other alternatives are still available.

Following Wald (1982), we can draw together some of the phenomena we have looked at by sketching out the following developmental scheme from independent clauses with overt subjects to the fully syntacticized pattern of subject relativization on a subject matrix (SS):

(42) This guy he owns the hotel he went to B
     This guy that he owns the hotel he went to B
     This guy that owns the hotel he went to B
     This guy that owns the hotel went to B

The first stage consists of the introduction of a new referent, *this guy*; two independent clauses follow, *he owns the hotel* and *he went to B*. The use of the sequence of NPs, *this guy*, *he 1* and *he 2* all referring to the same referent, establishes what Wald refers to as an *overt subject chain*. The second stage involves the use of a relative clause with a subject shadow which forms part of a subject chain. The third consists of a full relative clause followed by a subject copy in the matrix. These second and third constructions represent intermediate stages between the sequence of independent clauses linked by the subject chain and the fully syntacticized construction illustrated in the last stage.

3.3 *The acquisition of passives from a psycholinguistic perspective*

The passive is another construction which displays features associated with so-called complex syntax and is acquired relatively late. As in the case of relativization previously discussed, the difficulties children encounter with passives are apparently partly maturational. Evidence for 'delayed acquisition' comes from languages such as English (cf. Horgan 1978, Bever 1970, Turner and Rommetveit 1967 and 1968 and Strohmer and Nelson 1974) and French (cf. Sinclair and Ferreiro 1970). The 'errors' made by children cross-linguistically are similar, thus indicating that there are some common syntactic, semantic and pragmatic difficulties inherent in passives, e.g. understanding that the grammatical subject is necessarily the agent.

In her study of children's acquisition of various complex sentence types, Chomsky (1969) found that sentences such as (43) and (44) are often misinterpreted until the child is eight years or older.

(43) The duck is hard to bite
(44) John is easy to please

The problem here, as Chomsky puts it, is that children begin by assuming that all verb complements work in the same way. They interpret *The duck* and *John* as subjects or agents, when in fact they are objects or patients. We can compare a sentence like *John is easy to please* with *John is eager to please*. Although the sentences are superficially the same, they express different relations between the agent and patient (or subject vs. object). In the case of *John is eager to please*, *John* is the agent; the patient is left unexpressed. However, in the sentences *John is easy to please*, *John* is the patient of the verb *to please*. We might paraphrase this sentence as: (*Someone pleases John*) and (*it is easy to please John*). English combines these two sentences into one surface form: *John is easy to please* by transforming an underlying patient into an agent. Syntactically speaking, this involves movement of the object into subject position. In earlier models of transformational generative grammar, this operation was referred to as 'Tough movement' (cf. Smith and Wilson 1979) since the class of adjectives to which it applied included *tough* (e.g. *The brick is tough to move*), *hard*, *difficult*, *easy*, etc. In fact, adjectives which behave in this way are fewer than those of the *eager* type, which present no problem of interpretation. In English there is a tendency for nouns which function as agents to occur in sentence-initial position; by and large, this principle works as an interpretive strategy except where surface order does not correspond to the underlying semantic relations.

Chomsky used experiments which were similar to those used by Tavakolian (1977) and de Villiers et al. (1979) in their study of relative clauses. For example, to test whether children had acquired the rule of Tough Movement, she presented them with a blindfolded doll and asked: 'Is this doll easy to see or hard to see?' In order to score a correct interpretation, the child must be able to comprehend the roles of agent and patient correctly. She found that almost all the five year olds answered incorrectly that the doll was hard to see. This response indicated that these children had taken *doll* to be the logical subject of the verb *to see*. The answers of the six to eight year olds were not completely correct; only by the age of nine could children interpret this type of sentence correctly.[17]

Most of the evidence on children's acquisition of passives comes from comprehension and imitation tasks of this type. Sinclair and Ferreiro (1970) found that sentences such as (47) are understood later than those of type (46), while sentences such as (45) are the earliest to be understood correctly:

(45) The car is knocked down by the lorry
(46) The car is pushed by the lorry
(47) The car is followed by the lorry

Other experiments have shown that passives of the type in (48) are earlier and more easily understood than the type illustrated in (49):

(48) The plate was broken by the girl / with a hammer
(49) The girl was hit by the boy

The difference between these two types lies in their semantic reversibility or non-reversibility. In sentence (48) the hearer does not need to pay attention to syntactic or other linguistic cues such as the morphology of the verb in order to assign the correct semantic role to the NPs *the plate* and *the girl* or *a hammer*. 'Common-sense' knowledge tells us that only the plate could be the recipient of the action, even though from its syntactic position the 'normal' tendency would be to assign it the role of agent. Passives of this type are non-reversible since the nature of the NPs does not allow the roles of agent and patient to be exchanged. Sentence (49), on the other hand, illustrates a reversible passive, where either *the boy* or *the girl* could be agent or patient. The only way to be sure is to pay attention to the order of constituents, the morphology of the verb and the agent phrase beginning with *by*. Horgan (1978: 72–3) found that when children begin using passives, some use only reversible and others non-reversible ones initially. The non-reversible passives however are of the instrumental (e.g. *the plate was broken with a hammer*) rather than of the agentive type. The agentive non-reversible type (e.g. *the plate was broken by the girl*) did not appear until after age nine, and until age eleven no child in her study produced both reversible and non-reversible passives. Baldie (1976) studied production, comprehension as well as imitation, of various types of passive constructions by children between the ages of three and seven. He found that all the age groups showed a higher rate of comprehension for non-reversible than reversible passives (with the exception of the six year olds, who comprehended both equally well). There was, however, an asymmetry in the production results; non-reversible passives were less often produced than reversible ones.

Before the significance of these findings can be fully appreciated, we must first discuss the concept of passivization and define the types of constructions which grammarians refer to as passives. This is unfortunately much easier said than done; the notion of passive and the rules necessary for its description within a grammar of English have been among the most controversial and hotly debated issues within syntactic theory (cf. Chomsky 1981b: 120–38). There is no general agreement on how best to treat this problem. Let us begin, however, with an attempt to define some of the types of structures which go by the name of 'passives'.

3.4 *The notion of 'passive' in universal grammar*

The most general definition that can be offered would be to describe the passive as a syntactic means for encoding the same semantic role in a different way. If we compare (50) and (51), we can see how they might be thought of as alternatives for expressing the same proposition.

(50) Mary hit John   (active)
(51) John was hit by Mary   (passive)

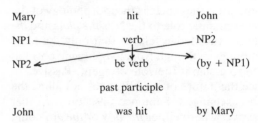

Figure 3.3 The relationship between active and passive

The structural relationship between the two is indicated in the diagram in figure 3.3. More specifically, we can say that passivization is a syntactic process which allows the direct object of an active verb to appear as the subject. The original subject is deleted or demoted to an agentive phrase, e.g. *by Mary*, and the object *John* advanced to subject position. This movement and reordering of noun phrases within the sentence, however, does not entail a change in semantic roles. In the formation of the passive, English makes use of the auxiliary BE (or GET as in *John got hit by Mary*); and a prepositional phrase (usually with *by* at its head) is used to mark the agent. I have already noted that in English word order and grammatical relations correlate very closely; passivization destroys the correspondence between semantic roles and grammatical relations in that subjects are generally agents and patients do not usually appear in subject (i.e. sentence-initial) position. It is partially due to this factor that passives pose comprehension problems for children. Although they can produce well-formed passives spontaneously at age two, their full productive and receptive skills do not match those of adults until as late as thirteen years. Baldie (1976: 338), for example, reports that by age eight all children can comprehend and imitate passives, but the rate of production is 80 per cent.

It is important at this stage to make it clear that not all languages have passives in the specific sense in which I have defined them above, e.g. Hungarian and Finnish. However, probably all languages have a number of syntactic processes which either put the same semantic role in different grammatical relations or make use of the same grammatical relation to serve a number of semantic roles. Languages which do have passives or passive-like constructions differ in the extent to which the semantic transformation of roles is marked syntactically (e.g. by movement of a patient into a position normally reserved for the object) and/or morphologically (e.g. by marking the 'voice change' on the verb and/or in case endings on noun phrases).[18] I have already discussed a similar syntactic process in English which serves essentially the same function as the passive, but bears no formal marks of the alteration in agent–patient relations, namely the rule of Tough Movement, as in (52) and (53):

(52) It is easy to see the doll
(53) The doll is easy to see

This rule of subject to object raising enables the object of an embedded construction to appear as the subject of the main clause. From a universal perspective then, we can say that the point of passivization is to demote the agent when it is not a topic (Givón 1979a: 21); and that the category of voice has to do with variation in the semantic role of the subject. The essence of passivization lies in the choice between constructions in which the subject as opposed to the predicate can be either agent or patient

(Matthews 1981: 106–10). Thus, given an agent, verb and patient, many languages allow either noun to be selected as the subject, e.g.

boy hit girl
NP1 predicate NP2

In English and other languages the choice is even wider since the subject may be an indirect rather than a direct object. In sentences where a verb has two objects,

(54) John gave the children the money
     (Indirect Object) (Direct Object)

either NP may be promoted to subject position. Thus,

(55) The children were given the money by John
(56) The money was given to the children by John

Not all languages allow an indirect object NP to be the subject of a passive sentence, and according to Matthews (1981), some speakers do not produce this type. In terms of the Keenan–Comrie hierarchy I discussed in connection with relativization, it would appear that direct objects are more accessible to passivization than case relations further down the hierarchy. Some languages allow passivization an even wider scope than English (cf. Keenan's 1974 discussion of circumstantial 'voice' in Malagasy). In her study of the comprehension of passives, Wright (forthcoming) found that young West Indian males between the ages of 13 and 15 had some difficulty in producing a passive version of a stimulus sentence like (57):

(57) A farmer gave the boy this puppy

Some children produced sentences which were not true passives:

(58) The boy took the dog by the farmer
(59) I had a puppy off the farmer
(60) Puppy a farmer gave a boy

There are, of course, particular problems which children of West Indian origin face in the production and comprehension of the full English passive due to the differences between passivization in English and varieties of West Indian creole. However, amongst a white adult control group, Wright found that more informants chose the direct rather than indirect object as the subject of the passive version. She also found that oblique NPs (e.g. *John took advantage of Jane*) were least frequently advanced to subject position (i.e. *Advantage was taken of Jane by John*) in accordance with the predictions of the accessibility hierarchy. In English, however, most cases of oblique NPs involve idioms of this type, which tend to be taken as chunks.[19]

From the errors which the West Indian children produced on other types of active sentences which they had to convert into passives, it appears to be the case that they had a rough idea of the semantic and syntactic rudiments, e.g. moving a topic into semantic focus by putting it in subject position, although they did not have control over the morphological coding properties of the passive. For example, when asked to passivize a sentence like (61) or (62):

(61) We ate a big meal
(62) I offended the milkman

they produced topicalized versions like (63) and (64), where the object NP is left-dislocated:

(63) A big meal we ate
(64) The milkman offended I

At an early stage children also omit the copula BE:

(65) The cat licked by the dog

(see Maratsos and Abraovitch 1975) and the past tense morpheme:

(66) She's got lift up by the boys

(see Whitehurst, Ironsmith, and Goldfein 1974). Turner and Rommetveit (1968) argue that uncertainties about irregular past participal forms make passive production difficult for young children. This may be true for all children in the early stages of acquisition; for some speakers of non-standard English, however, the use of 'incorrect' past participles or the absence of the past tense morpheme cannot be seen as errors. Amongst Edinburgh speakers, for example, passive verbs like *get took* instead of *get taken* can be heard from both children and adults (cf. chapter 4). The form *tooken* (e.g. *A girl got her bus fare tooken*) appears to be a developmental error since it does not occur in the adult community. It is also clear from many of Wright's results that children are able to infer what the semantic focus of a passive should entail because they produce alternative syntactic constructions which paraphrase the passive, e.g.:

(67) It was a big meal we ate

This so-called cleft construction is functionally equivalent to a passive in that it moves an NP into focus. Similarly,

(68) A big meal was what we ate

Others paraphrased the passive by using two sentences or clauses:

(69) People drink lemonade
(70) Lemonade is nice and people drink it
(71) One can hear birds singing
(72) The birds were singing and one can hear them

Wright's findings suggest that there are a number of options to full passivization which children draw on in an experimental situation. This suggests one reason why researchers have often found passives to be infrequent; apparently other constructions serve as the functional equivalents of passives in discourse (cf. also Dannequin 1977 for a discussion of some of the options to full passivization used by French children).

The examples given in (51) and (55–6) are generally referred to as *full or agented passives*; they contain at least two NPs, one of which is expressed by an agentive phrase, and a passive verb form consisting of a form of BE or GET plus the past participle. Since the role of agent correlating with subjecthood tends to be thought of as a more basic semantic role than that of patient (cf. Comrie 1981), syntacticians have generally favoured treating the active as the more basic syntactic structure. As Givón (1979a: 64) puts it, humans tend to talk more about human agents and to put them into subject/topic position.[20]

Another factor which has been cited in favour of taking the passive as the more complex structure is the verb form, which in English at any rate bears the marks of passive verb morphology (cf. also Matthews 1981: 106–7, and Huddleston 1984). In early models of transformational generative grammar the full passive was regarded as related to its active equivalent by means of the so-called passive-transformation (cf. Chomsky 1957, 1965). Some analyses postulated the existence of a further optional rule which allowed the deletion of the agent phrase to produce what has been called the *truncated or agentless passive*, e.g.:

(73) Mary was hit
(74) The plate got broken

In both these sentences the logical subject is not expressed.

As Horgan (1978: 68) points out, this derivational history is suspect when seen from the perspective of child language acquisition. Truncated passives are frequently used by children, whereas full passives are rare. For those who believe that the order of acquisition is dictated either fully or partly by grammatical complexity (cf. Brown and Hanlon 1970 and Slobin 1980), and that the latter in turn corresponds to derivational depth (cf. Yngve 1972), it is hard to explain why children should acquire the seemingly more complex construction first.

Fodor, Bever and Garrett (1974) conclude that the derivational theory of complexity is not supported by experimental evidence. In its earliest version, it states that the complexity of a sentence is a function of the number of rules involved in its derivation. Their conclusion must, however, be seen in relation to the theory of grammar which the experiments claim to be testing. The derivation of the active and passive from the same abstract underlying representation has been increasingly questioned by generativists; indeed, some have argued that passivization need not be handled by a transformational rule at all (cf. Bresnan 1976 and Wasow 1980). In the most recent versions of generative grammar passives arise via a movement rule which preposes an NP. Since the agentive phrase is no longer base-generated, there is no need to delete it at a later stage. Thus, in this particular version of generative grammar, an agentless passive would not be more complex than an agented one. Deletions are no longer formulated as transformational operations anyway (cf. Chomsky 1981b).

There is, however, another issue in the nature of the claims often made in connection with the derivational theory of complexity, which must be distinguished. This is the question of the psychological reality of linguists' theories of grammars and the kinds of claims one should expect to follow from them if they are psychologically real for children (cf. the discussion in White 1982 and also chapter 9). Watt (1970), for instance, holds the view that 'grammar' may be psychologically real, but that a speaker's mental representation may not necessarily coincide with the formal grammars which linguists write, relying on methodological requirements of simplicity, etc. He observes that young children produce truncated passives early, and this therefore suggests that in the mental grammars of these children agentless passives are analysed as adjectival. The optimal grammar for the linguist, however, is one in which truncated passives are best derived by deletion from full passives; all passives are thus seen to be transformation-ally related to their active forms. He considers it furthermore implausible that children should later alter their mental grammar when they become aware of the full passive. If, however, the agentless passives that children produce are adjectival, then there is no difference between their mental grammar and the optimal grammar of the linguist. One could assume that all agentless passives would be analysed adjectivally in all the stages the child passes through. Maratsos (1978), however, argues that truncated passives are not first acquired and later restructured in accordance with the rules necessary for full passives, because this sort of reanalysis would involve the child in extensive restructuring (cf. section 6.3 for a more detailed consideration of whether children are capable of restructuring).

Watt is assuming here of course one of the earlier versions of generative grammar. Under the analysis proposed by Wasow (1977), which distin-guishes between adjectival and verbal passives, only the latter are transformationally derived. White (1982: 23) notes that the examples of agentless passives cited in the child language literature would seem to count as lexical passives; that is, in Wasow's terms, they would be derived by lexical redundancy and not transformational rules. One would assume that children acquired the transformational passive later.[21] The distinction between lexical and verbal passives may help to clarify some of the contradictory results obtained in the early experiments. As in the case with the conflicting findings reported by those who studied relative clauses, it is important to bear in mind that the evidence from processing and production may be consistent with a number of possible grammars, and that non-production of a structure does not necessarily entail any claims about it complexity.

There is still another issue in this argument which must be considered separately, and that is the question of complexity. There is no reason to expect that complexity is solely a matter of syntax.[22] Givón (1979a: 59) argues that passive sentences are more marked in terms of their presuppositionality. By this he means the degree to which the identity of the underlying agent is predictable or recoverable from the context. If the speaker presupposes something which the hearer does not know, the hearer may be expected to have difficulty in identifying the referent. Givón therefore distinguishes semantic, syntactic and presuppositional complexity.

In a study of passives in a variety of texts, Givón found that agents tended to be definite and presupposed. Nearly 80 per cent of the passives involved a presupposed agent; and nearly half of the agents were recoverable from the immediate discourse context. If most agents turn out to be predictable from the immediate discourse context or common-sense knowledge, there is no need for them to be mentioned. It is partly for this reason that most passives are agentless (90 per cent in Givón's sample). The small proportion (10 per cent) of passives with overtly expressed agents are mostly indefinite and all express agents as the focus of new information. The full agented passive is used mostly then when the agent is new information (cf. also Johnson-Laird 1968a and b; Grieve and Wales 1973, who find that in children's passives those NPs which were more definite also tended to be more focused; and also Kirsner 1976 on focus and passivization).

It would appear to be the case then that the syntactic and semantic relationship between the agented and agentless passive may not be as close as generative grammarians have maintained (cf. also the discussion in Weiner and Labov 1983). In early transformational grammars it was a requirement that sentences which stood in a transformational relationship should preserve semantic equivalence. Agentless passives do not always strictly entail their agented counterparts. Compare the three sentences below.

(75) Max was killed
(76) Max was killed by someone
(77) Max was killed by an explosion

Without a supporting context the agent is not recoverable and clearly the meaning is different if Max is killed by an explosion as opposed to a person. The question of semantic equivalence is even more problematic in the case of the relationship between agented passives and their active counterparts. In a sentence like (78), we get an argument reversal in the corresponding passive sentence (79).

(78) Each student admires no teacher
(79) No teacher is admired by each student

The fact that there are a number of semantically related constructions which serve as alternatives to passivization creates additional problems for a transformational analysis. Topicalized, cleft and relative constructions cannot be easily derived from basic active sentences by means of the syntactic operations I have described, even though they bear some relation to them. Chomsky (1981b: 120–1) observes that the category commonly called 'passive' may not constitute a natural class, either within or across languages.

Alternative analyses, such as that of generative semantics, capture more readily the semantic relationship between some of these passive-like structures. One could derive sentences like those in (80) from an underlying abstract representation such as that in (81):

(80) The morning sun dried the sweet raisins   (inchoative)
     The sweet raisins were dried by the morning sun   (passive)
     The sweet raisins dried in the morning sun   (inchoative)
     The sweet raisins were dried in the morning sun   (passive)
     The morning sun caused the sweet raisins to dry   (causative)
     The sweet raisins dried because of the morning sun   (causative)
(81) (CAUSE SUN (DRY RAISINS))

Speakers apparently have different intuitions about the extent of relatedness among sentences like these (Carroll et al. 1981). Markey and Fodale (1983) propose a scale of passivization which includes causatives, inchoatives and passives. Hakes (1982: 164) says that it is not until some time after children give evidence of understanding passive sentences that they begin to judge passives and actives to be synonymous. Judgements of this type presuppose a certain level of development of children's metalinguistic awareness (cf. chapter 7). One could argue that the productive use of transformational rules assumes a knowledge of the relatedness of the structures concerned.

In some languages there is no separation between passivization and topic shift rules. In others there is a close relation between causatives, reflexives and passives. Horgan (1978: 75–6) argues that reflexives and passives are more closely related in child than adult language. The so-called passive transformation in generative grammar accounts only for a central core of constructions, even in English. I will return to some of these points later.

I have already cited one piece of evidence in support of the view that agentless passives are more basic than agented ones; namely, the fact that they appear earlier in child acquisition. Another argument in favour of their basicness can be put forward from the claim that cross-linguistically agentless passives seem to be more frequent. Not all languages have agented passives. Many more have agentless ones. In fact Keenan (1975) predicts that the existence of an agented passive in a language implies the presence of an agentless one. And Lyons (1968) states that the primary function of passivization in languages of the world is to make the agentless construction possible. In other words, it allows the deletion of an agent, whereas the subject of an active sentence cannot ordinarily be deleted.

In her study of the acquisition of passives Horgan (1978) argues that for children the agented and agentless passive are grammatically distinct and do not share the same privileges of occurrence. Almost all the agentless passives produced by children between the ages of two and four had inanimate logical objects; that is, they were of the type, *the plate got broken*. The majority of full passives, however, had animate logical objects as in *John got hit*. Furthermore, most agentless passives used familiar verbs such as *break*, which were also used in a stative sense. For example, *the cup was broken* can refer to the action which broke the cup or to the cup's state of being broken. The notion 'stative' refers to a state of affairs by contrast to the notion 'dynamic', which refers to an active event or process. Some passives can have both a stative and a dynamic interpretation. The process of causing the state and the resultant state itself are not always clearly distinguishable. Grammatical descriptions of English generally treat this difference in discussions of so-called verbal as opposed to adjectival passives, a distinction referred to previously (cf. Huddleston 1984). In example (82) there are two possible syntactic analyses of *broken*:

(82) The vase was broken
(a) NP verb Adjective
(b) NP Aux. + Past participle

Under one interpretation, (a), *broken* functions as an adjective to refer to the state of the vase, i.e. its brokenness. In (b) the interpretation is dynamic and verbal; *broken* is analysed as the past participle of the verb *break* and part of the verb. Most adjectival passives are obligatorily agentless. A sentence like (83) can only be verbal (unless the phrase *by John* is construed as a locative complement):

(83) The vase was broken by John

Perhaps one reason why children have less difficulty in comprehending agentless passives is that these can be interpreted as a basic sentence type (compare: *The house was pretty*) and the problem of assignment of a semantic role to an agent does not arise. The agented passive, however, is structurally (though not semantically) related to a basic sentence type, e.g. *John was standing by Mary*, when *by Mary* is a locative rather than adjectival complement to the verb. Indeed, it is partly due to the structural similarities between these two types of constructions on the one hand, and to the less direct relationshp between adjectival and verbal passives, and their active counterparts on the other, that the notion of a generalized passive transformation has come into dispute.

Both GET and BE can occur with verbal and adjectival passives, but GET passives are almost always dynamic. There are also informal stylistic connotations to GET. It tends to be avoided in formal contexts (cf. the discussion in Svartvik 1966). This may explain another reason why children acquire GET passives earlier; namely, because they acquire language largely through informal interaction in the first instance. It may also be the case that the notion 'dynamic' is functionally more salient. There is more ambiguity in BE passives since they are more likely to have both stative and dynamic interpretations; the verb *break* supports the distinction between adjectival and verbal passives more readily than others. Svartvik (1966) has proposed a scale of passivization which ranges from agented passives which have a close relation to their corresponding active sentences to those agented passives which have closer affinity with adjectives and a more tenuous relation with actives.

Horgan believes that the category of stative may be the more inclusive one for young children, and that many of the verbs which for adults would receive a dynamic interpretation are treated statively by children. In sentences like *John got hit*, *get* should be treated as the main verb and *hit* as an adjective, as in a sentence like *I am tired*. Agented passives, by contrast, make use of a wide variety of verbs. Thus the two construction types differ in terms of the animacy of the NPs and the verbs with which they co-occurred. Her analysis requires some modification in the light of the data on passives produced by Edinburgh schoolchildren which I will look at next.

3.5 *Some comparative data on children's acquisition of passives*

Horgan presents longitudinal data from children aged two to thirteen, which shows the separate route of development of agentless and agented passives. The use of the full passive begins at age two, but is very infrequent; approximately 10 per cent of the children in the sample use it. There is a slight drop at age six in the percentage of children using it, but thereafter a steady increase until age eleven, at which point the construction is used by about 30 per cent of the children. By comparison, the use of the agentless passive is more frequent at earlier and later stages. At age two, nearly 60 per cent of the children use it, and by age thirteen 100 per cent do. Similarly, Baldie (1976) reports that the agentless passive is both produced and comprehended earlier than either the reversible or non-reversible types discussed in section 3.3.

We can compare her results with the passives produced by Edinburgh schoolchildren. There is a total of 144 passives. Table 3.8 shows the rate of production of agented and agentless passives for each age group. There is a progressive increase in the number of passives produced as children grow older, with the greatest difference occurring between the six and eight year olds. Most of these passives are agentless, 90 per cent (N = 130), and most of them are produced by the ten year olds, although the relative proportion of agentless to agented passives remains about the same throughout all the age groups. Horgan (1978) managed to elicit 81 agented passives from the five- to thirteen-year-old groups and 32 from the two to four year olds. Although the rate of occurrence is higher than that of the Edinburgh children, this probably reflects the nature of the task. Otherwise, Horgan's findings and mine are similar: the younger the child, the less tendency there is to produce agented passives. Three of the examples which I have included under the heading of agented passives are cases in which the agent is not expressed in a preposition phrase with *by*.

(84) I got battered *off* my big brother   (eight-year-old girl)
(85) I never got hurt, just my arm that got hurt *on* the chair   (eight-year-old boy)
(86) Josie got hit *with* a cricket bat   (ten-year-old girl)

It is arguable whether the second of these is really an agentive phrase. In the first of these examples the agent is animate, and in the second and third, inanimate. All of the other agented passives involved the use of *by*; of these 13 per cent (N = 8) were animate and 27 per cent (N = 3) inanimate.

Table 3.9 shows the agented and agentless passives produced by the children in relation to the animacy of the logical objects (i.e. patients) and subjects (i.e. agents). As far as the agentless passives are concerned, we can see that most of the logical objects are also animate, i.e. 87 per cent (N = 130). All the logical objects in agented passives are animate (N = 14). Thus the results confirm a close correlation between animacy and agentivity as well as animacy and patienthood. This finding is not in agreement with Horgan's observation that agentless passives produced by

Table 3.8 Agented and agentless passives produced by Edinburgh schoolchildren

	Age 10		Age 8		Age 6		Total	
	N	%	N	%	N	%	N	%
Agented	8	11	4	8	2	10	14	10
Agentless	63	89	49	92	18	90	130	90
Total	71	49	53	37	20	14	144	100

Table 3.9 Animacy of logical objects and subjects in agented and agentless passives

	Age 10		Age 8		Age 6		Total	
	Agented	*Agentless*	*Agented*	*Agentless*	*Agented*	*Agentless*		
Animate object	8	53	4	45	2	15	14	113
Animate subject	8	53	2	–	2	–	9	–
Sub-total	13	53	6	45	4	15	23	113
Inanimate object	0	10	0	4	0	3	0	17
Inanimate subject	3	–	2	–	0	–	5	–
Sub-total	3	10	2	4	0	3	5	17
Total	8	63	4	49	2	18	14	130

younger children tend to have inanimate logical objects. Thus one major difference between the agentless and agented passive with respect to animacy of object is not supported by my data.[23]

This discrepancy could of course reflect the nature of the context in which her and my data were elicited. She asked children to describe pictures which presented a wide range of situations with both animate and inanimate potential agents. It could be the case that, since most agents tend to be animate, the children selected only those agents which were inanimate in the pictures for special attention. In other words, her data may reflect the tendency of speakers to encode deliberately what they think the hearer is unlikely to assume. This would follow from the more general principles mentioned earlier; namely, the higher presupposition-ality of agents in general, and the tendency for agents to be animate and human (cf. also note 20). By contrast, my data were more spontaneous, but less controlled, since the children had a wider range of topics to draw on when answering my questions in the interview (cf. chapter 2 for a list of the topics). I also did not try to solicit information regarding inanimate topics.

Another possible reason for the difference in our results may be due to age. The youngest children in Horgan's sample were two to four years of age. She did not study the development of the agentless passive through to adulthood; however, it could be the case that there is a shift with increasing age to favour animate logical subjects. She found a shift from inanimate logical subjects to animate ones in full passives, which was age-related. The youngest children used 75 per cent inanimate logical subjects in agented passives, while children aged five to thirteen had only 39.5 per cent. This is quite closely paralleled by the Edinburgh data, where 36 per cent of the agented passives had inanimate logical subjects. Two of the inanimate logical subjects have appeared in the examples (85) and (86) above. The other three are:

(87) The horse got scraped by a bad wire   (ten-year-old girl)
(88) He's been knocked by a car   (ten-year-old girl)
(89) He's getting banged by the pram   (eight-year-old girl)

Given the way in which Horgan and I obtained our data, neither of us is able to separate the effects of animacy from those of agenthood vs. patienthood. Experiments conducted by Angiolillo and Goldin-Meadow (1982), however, controlled for the fact that agents tend to be animate and patients inanimate, in order to see whether children could separate the notion of animacy from that of agentivity.

They asked children between the ages of two and three to describe actions involving animate and inanimate entities, which played both agent and patient roles. They found that eight out of nine children differentially placed agents and patients in their utterances. Patients, whether animate or inanimate, were placed post-verbally, while agents, animate or inanimate, seldom occupied this position.[24] Thus the children were using word order systematically to mark agents differentially from patients, independently of animacy. Angiolillo and Goldin-Meadow (1982: 641) claim that their findings constitute evidence for the psychological reality of semantic categories like agent and patient in young children's language. I will return to the question of children's ordering strategies in relation to the problem of deciding what kinds of categories children can be assumed to have internalized in section 3.6.

As far as the choice of verbs made in agentless and agented passives is concerned, it does not appear to be the case that a wider variety of verbs is used with agented than agentless passives, although this is what Horgan found in her data. This is difficult to assess, however, since the agentless passives far outnumber the agented ones. Of the fourteen verb forms which appeared in the agented passives in my data, only four do not appear in agentless passives (i.e. *got scraped*, *got called up*, *got splattered*, *has been stopped*). There appears to be nothing unusual about the semantics of these verbs. All of the other verbs (ten) appear in both types of passives; two of these, *got beat* and *got caught*, are very frequently used. Horgan suggests that in her data the difference in the verb types found with each of the passive constructions reflects a semantic opposition between stative and dynamic. I do not think this interpretation is correct for my data; another factor, which Horgan does not take into account in her discussion, may be responsible. That is the difference between passives formed with GET or BE as the auxiliary discussed earlier. The two types are illustrated in (90) to (92) with examples from the Edinburgh data:

(89) BE passive: Everybody was captured   (ten-year-old boy)
(90) GET passive: I got knocked down   (eight-year-old boy)
(91) BE/GET passive: The leader wasn't pleased at all of them getting shot because he wasn't shot   (ten-year-old boy)

Most of the passives produced by the Edinburgh children were GET passives, as can be seen in table 3.10, which shows the occurrence of both types in each age group. Overall, BE passives are produced with a frequency of 22 per cent (N = 31).

We can see that the youngest group uses almost exclusively GET passives; this is also true for the eight year olds. Only in the oldest group do the BE passives amount to a sizeable proportion of the passives, i.e. 35 per cent (N = 25). This finding is in agreement with a number of studies of both adults and children. Turner and Rommetveit (1968), for example, say not only that BE passives are infrequent in everyday language but also that children probably do not acquire them until they are at school.

Two conclusions emerge from the literature on child acquisition of passives: first, agentless passives are more basic than agented passives; second, GET passives are more basic than BE passives. The evidence for the first conclusion has already been discussed. A few more points can be added about adult usage to strengthen the argument. Brown (1973) claims that one reason why children produce so few agented passives is that they hear so few as input from adults. He found that in a sample of 713 utterances used by three sets of parents to their children no agented passives appeared. Harwood (1959) reports that in a sample of 12,000 utterances of five year olds there were no full passives. Slobin's (1968) observation that agentless passives account for all occurrences of passives is well in line with Svartvik's (1966), Jespersen's (1924) and Stein's (1979) estimates of its frequency among adults, i.e. 75–80 per cent of passives are agentless. A number of sociolinguists have commented on the difficulty in obtaining instances of agented passives in spontaneous speech (e.g. Van den Broeck 1977 and Weiner and Labov 1983). In his study of texts Givón (1979a: 51) found that the frequency of actives and passives varied according to genre. Passives occurred most frequently in non-fiction texts, but even there they amounted only to 18 per cent. The average for all the texts was 8 per cent. Passives, and in particular, agentless passives occur very frequently in written narratives, bureaucratic language and scientific texts to avoid self-reference and attribution of blame.

(93) The forms should have seen sent (by us to you)
(94) No responsibility is taken for lost articles (by the management)

Table 3.10 GET and BE passives

	Age 10	Age 8	Age 6	Total
GET	46	48	19	113
BE	25	5	1	31
Total	71	53	20	144

Although these findings appear to be evidence that there is a close correlation between input and output vis-à-vis parent and child, the divergence between production and perception seems considerable. Although children as young as two can provide syntactically well-formed passives, even in young adulthood the passive is not well understood. Horgan compared the results for the children in her sample with those of college-age students. The students had a slightly different task to perform in addition to the picture description task given to the children. They were given pictures with an appropriate sentence frame such as: the window was broken – the boy. They were asked to describe the pictures using a passive sentence in both types of task. Horgan found that 36 per cent of the sentences produced in the spontaneous condition were not passives and there were a number of errors in the choice of prepositions used in the agentive phrase. There were cases in which *from* and *with* were used instead of *by*. I have already noted some examples of variability in choice of prepositions by the Edinburgh children. Horgan found that the youngest children did not use *with*, but for older children it was the second most frequent preposition. She hypothesized that children were using only the instrumental passive, e.g. the lamp was broken *with* the ball (where *with* expresses an instrumental rather than agentive type of causality). Children used only *by* with instruments while adults used *by* and *with*. Children's passives until age nine tended to have the instrument rather than the agent as logical subject.

This finding suggests that children may be treating passivization as a syntactic strategy for expressing non-agent causation, i.e. a state of affairs which is due to an unknown cause or brought about by some means other than a causal agent. This may be an important link with the finding that the most frequent and earliest passives produced by children are agentless GET passives. The GET passive can be used in certain constructions which express reflexiveness and emphasize the involvement of the patient, where the BE passive cannot.[25] Lakoff (1971) claims there is a universal semantic link between reflexiveness and passivization with GET. She (1971: 157) uses the examples (95) and (96) to illustrate two different senses associated with the verb GET, which underlie the ambiguity of (97).

(95) John got a present for his mother   (agent)
(96) John got a present from his mother   (patient)
(97) John got his dishes washed[26]

In the last of this set of sentences the different possible meanings of GET give rise to three possible interpretations:

(98) Someone washed John's dishes for him   (John is patient, non-agentive causation)
(99) John managed to wash his own dishes   (John is agent)

(100) John got someone to wash the dishes   (John is the agent of the action of getting someone to wash the dishes, but is the beneficiary of the action he instigates, which someone else performs)

In terms of its underlying syntactic representation we might think of the third interpretation as one which consists of two separate propositions: *John got X*, and *someone washed the dishes*. *John* is the agent of the main clause predicate and the object is the agentless passive *his dishes (were) washed (by someone)*. There are only a few examples in the Edinburgh data, where the agentive interpretation of GET passives is possible:

(101) We got the roof repaired   (eight-year-old boy)
(102) I went and got my finger stuck in there

In the second case, the use of the construction *went and* suggests a notion of deliberateness, cf. *I went and bought a car*. Otherwise, all the passives imply agentless causation. And it may be that *get* passivization serves an important discourse function in allowing the speaker the option of absolving the agent of responsibility for causing an action. Woehr et al. (1974: 156) suggest that inchoative constructions and *get* passives do not convey the same agentive force as the full agented BE passive: 'The one who is speaking makes the action more impersonal and makes himself less responsible.' Wright (forthcoming) illustrates the different connotations of the two constructions, when seen as replies to the question: 'What happened to the cup?'

(103) It got broken   (reflexive passive)
(104) It broke (inchoative)

The implication of the first is that the cup got *itself* broken. The interpretation of the logical object as reflexive removes the responsibility from the agent. From a cross-linguistic perspective, it is interesting that these reflexive uses of the GET passive in English often have translation equivalents in other languages which are active and reflexive.[27] Berk-Seligson (1981), for example, compares three similar construction types in Spanish:

(105) Juan perdio la carta   (active)
      John lost the letter
(106) Se perdio la carta   (reflexive)
      Itself lost the letter
(107) Se le perdio la carta   ('reflexive passive')
      Itself on him lost the letter

She says that the two reflexive constructions are used by children to avoid attributing blame, particularly to oneself. Agented passives in spoken Spanish are regarded as extremely formal and normally occur only in the written language. They are morphosyntactically similar to English agented passives, e.g.:

(108) La pelota fue tirada por Juan
      The ball was thrown by John

The infrequentness of passives then (particularly the full agented BE passive) is due partly to the existence of other available syntactic alternatives which put a non-agentive NP into topic/subject position and semantic focus, and partly due to the fact that passives tend to presuppose causative agents. If most agents are predictable from discourse, then it is in unusual or pragmatically marked circumstances that agents will be specified. Thus the basic choice appears to be between the active and the agentless passive.

To summarize briefly then, I have looked at two syntactic constructions which are acquired relatively late. I have suggested that both passivization and relativization are sensitive to a case hierarchy which makes certain claims about the degree of accessibility of various grammatical relations, such as subject, to these (transformational) rules. The two constructions can be thought of as complex from a syntactic point of view, since they involve movement rules which give rise to an ordering of constituents deviating from the more frequent *agent verb patient* analysis strategy. This disruption creates a recoverability problem. In the case of the passive, this means that when the non-agent is advanced into the role of subject-topic, its semantic function cannot be recovered from the word order or the morphology of the passive sentence. There were similar recoverability problems in the case of relative clauses when relativization on NPs in certain syntactic positions creates a word order which 'violates' the expected NVN. Speakers resort to a number of remedial strategies and to paraphrase to repair the non-transparency. Some of these involve the use of syntactic alternatives which apparently serve the same function in discourse. Both passives and relatives share some similarities with topicalization, a process which selects an NP and puts it into semantic and syntactic prominence. It is a short step from topicalization to passivization and/or relativization. I have discussed the link most fully for relativization, where a topic chain may become syntacticized as a relative clause. Givón (1979a: 196) sees a similarity between a topicalized sentence like (109) and a passive.

(109) John, they saw him → John was seen by them

And we have seen that constructions of this type appear when children are asked to produce passives from actives. Both constructions present potential difficulties to children when they learn to read and write; the written language is the most highly syntacticized register the child will encounter and it is in this context that these types of constructions appear in their greatest frequency. By adopting a more pragmatic, rather than syntactic and semantic, perspective, we can trace these syntactic structures even further back in the child's grammatical development to much earlier topic/comment ordering principles.

3.6 A pragmatic account of relativization and passivization

As early as 1967 Gruber (reprinted 1971) argued for a topic/comment analysis in early child language. Although his study is based on the speech of one English-speaking child at the age of just over two years (recorded from birth onwards), he claims more generally that a child learning a language for the first time produces sentences without subjects first. Then he uses the innate topic/comment construction.[28] Gruber stresses the formal rather than functional aspects of topicalization, and does not explicitly make the link between early topic/comment structures and later 'full-blown' syntactic structures like the relative clause and passive, which are, as we have seen, generally assumed to be transformationally derived in many of the models of autonomous syntax used to describe adult grammars. Even so, a number of his ideas foreshadow a perspective on child language which has become increasingly fashionable; namely, one which assumes the basically pragmatic nature of children's early speech.[29]

Gruber speculates, for example, that the stage preceding these early topic/comment structures is probably one in which neither subjects nor topics are generated. This amounts to a claim that the child's earliest utterances are both topicless and subjectless. Bates and MacWhinney (1979: 190–1) see the origins of topic/comment structures in the gesture stage, even before the onset of speech, which reflects the natural tendencies of the human attentional system.

Among the properties of the linguistic entities which children place in utterance-initial position are: animacy, agency, subjecthood, topicality and newness. I noted earlier in discussing the importance children appear to attach to word order that there is psycholinguistic evidence from a variety of languages (among them Russian, French and English) which shows that children in general tend to interpret utterances consisting of the sequence noun + verb + noun as Subject Verb Object, even if case marking shows them to be Object Verb Subject (which is a possibility in a language like Russian). Children apparently ignore morphological clues in assigning surface grammatical relations and place greater reliance on word order. This is in accordance with one of the general operating principles proposed by Slobin (1973), which says: 'Pay attention to the order of words and morphemes.' Much of the evidence for this principle comes from children's acquisition of relative clauses and passives (Ervin-Tripp 1978a and others have noted, however, that this principle is operative in adult and child second-language acquisition).

There has been a great deal of dispute over the validity of Slobin's principle. Bowerman (1981: 129), for example, notes that children learning highly inflected, flexible languages do not necessarily preserve word order in imitating the utterances of others or in their own spontaneous speech before they acquire the inflections which mark case relations (cf. also Sinclair and Bronckhart 1972). I have already discussed the evidence underlying Angiolillo and Goldin-Meadow's conclusion (1982) that semantic factors, in particular notions like the role of agent and patient (rather than syntactic ones such as subject and object), determine word order. The primary evidence that children talk about entities as agents and patients is their consistent placement of them in pre-verbal and post-verbal position respectively.

There is also considerable cross-linguistic evidence supporting the view that children's early word-order tendencies are based on the pragmatic distinction of topic/comment rather than purely syntactic categories like subject/predicate or semantic roles like agent/patient. The transition to the syntactically based subject/predicate type of constructions characteristic of the adult English speaker's system occurs later. Gruber's analysis assumes that the subject/predicate distinction is merely a special case of the topic/comment construction, and that the latter is logically the more fundamental. This is consistent with more recent statements by Li and Thompson (1976), and others, that subjects are grammaticalized topics.[30]

The fact that children end up with an arbitrarily defined surface structure does not entail the claim that they start out with it initially. It is not clear at what age the transition into syntactically defined surface structure occurs. Bowerman (1973) has argued that unless the data require us to assign syntactic categories to the child's language (for example, data suggesting that the child has a passive transformation which operates identically on sentence constituents differing in their semantic functions), we should be content to attribute to the child only the less abstract semantically based categories.[31]

Bates and MacWhinney (1979: 193) also claim that the English category 'subject' may have no psychological reality for children until the age of four or five. Until that time, subjects could be based on a category that is derivative of semantic-pragmatic notions such as agency and topicality. In their view, subject and predicate are surface sentence-level configurations which have evolved in language to reflect the fact that topics are generally agents, or other ego-related entities, while comments are likely to be dynamic. A range of relatively 'nouny' and 'verby' surface devices reflect prototypical selections for each. In order to have firm evidence for a category of subject that is distinct from both topic and agent, we would need instances in which the child uses alternative word orders like the passive, where the surface topic is clearly distinguished from the agent. Since these alternative surface forms are late developments in English speech, and non-agentive subjects are rather infrequent, we cannot be certain at what point English-speaking children have derived a notion of surface subject that is something more than the category of agent.

The amount and type of topic specification required on any given occasion will be a function of the amount of shared information speaker and hearer can assume. Givón (1979a) suggests that there is a continuum from presupposed background to proposed foreground information, with elements varying in their degree of presuppositionality. In human languages there is a wide variety of grammatical devices associated with the topic/comment function. The minimal surface form for indicating a topic is 'zero' or 'ellipsis'. For example, within a given context, where it is assumed to be clear to the speaker that the hearer will know the referent to which he is drawing attention, the speaker may comment: 'terrific'. If the topic is lexicalized, it can be encoded by such devices as a noun phrase like 'the meal', with various degrees of modification, e.g. 'my last meal in that restaurant', or a relative clause, e.g. 'the last meal I ate in that restaurant was terrific'. A restrictive relative clause in this case serves the pragmatic function of topic specification at the sentential level.

Given the basicness of both topics and comments in communication, both compete for sentence-initial position. According to Bates and MacWhinney, this has a decisive effect on the early word orders used by children. They say (1979: 180) that the earliest pragmatic ordering will reflect the child's own view; thus the child may order a comment before the topic. Later, when he becomes aware of the need to specify topics for the listener, he may switch to a 'topic first, comment second' order. So the shift from comment fronting to topic fronting could be related to a shift away from the egocentric perspective (cf. Piaget 1926, and chapter 5).

There are a number of ways one might generate these constructions in a formal model of grammar, which I will not elaborate here. Bates and MacWhinney (1982: 197) observe that 'The semantic-pragmatic meanings that constitute topic and comment have proven elusive and frustrating to linguists who want to incorporate them within a formal grammar. There is very little agreement about the internal structure of this system, and every investigator who studies it feels the need to add new terms and distinctions.' They stress (1979: 178) the 'process' aspect of topicalization, rather than attempt to define it formally. They claim that there is a single pragmatic function involved in setting up topics/referents in discourse (i.e. topic selection) and making comments about them.

Gruber (1971: 370–1), on the other hand, defines topicalization as a construction in which some major constituent of a sentence, which is identical with (or has the same referent as) a constituent in the given sentence, may be generated before or after this sentence. The constituent is represented in this sentence by a pronoun or as nothing at all. The co-generated constituent is called the topic and the given sentence the comment. The tree diagrams in figure 3.4 illustrate the structures of the two basic sentence types, which occur with more or less equal frequency in Gruber's data.

Gruber rejects various other possibilities for incorporating topicalization in the child's grammar.[32] One possibility which he rules out is extraposition; that is, an analysis in which some NP of a sentence is extraposed either before or after the sentence. This would mean that nouns would have to be generated in subject position and be potentially extraposable. In Gruber's view, it is counter-intuitive to generate subjects under S at all and then delete them, because in the child's grammar at this stage subject position is restricted to morphemes categorized as Pro. Since the element Pro in the child's grammar is not a subject in the same sense as in the adult's grammar, and there is no evidence for the prior stage of subject generation, Gruber opts for a single conjunction analysis in which two types of sentences are juxtaposed, the free NP and a sentence of any other type. The co-generation of NP and S in the base makes the child's grammar simpler than the adult's; whereas, with the extraposition analysis, it would have been at least as, if not more, complex.[33]

I will conclude this chapter by highlighting some of the main points in my argument within the context of more general methodological and theoretical issues relating to children's syntactic development.

Firstly, language acquisition is an ongoing process, and continues well beyond the age of five. Within the dynamic, developmental model I have tried to sketch out here, it does not make sense to try to establish discrete and precise points in time when children can be assumed to have 'acquired' a rule. This has been a much discussed issue in the psycholinguistic literature, where there has been a tendency to plot children's linguistic and cognitive development against the acquisition of certain syntactic constructions at specific stages (cf. Brown 1973 and Berko 1958 for discussion of the problem of how to decide when children have productive mastery over rules). Rule acquisition is not an all or nothing affair; and presumably 'complete' mastery involves both comprehension and production. There may be a number of aspects to the internal workings of a rule, some of

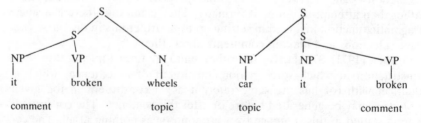

Figure 3.4 The structure of topic/comment sentences

which may be acquired before others. There are also social dimensions of a rule relating to its use, which will be dealt with more fully in the next chapter.

Secondly, I would like to stress again that it is a mistake to see the development of syntactic structure as a unilinear progression from simple to more complex structures and to view children's grammars as merely more primitive versions of those of adults. This is another issue which has been debated by child language researchers. The idea that the child proceeds through a series of grammars on his way to mastery of the adult system raises a number of theoretical issues, e.g. what is the status of the child's grammar at each stage, and how does the child make the transition from one to another (cf. White 1982, and chapter 9 for discussion)? I have already noted my dissatisfaction with Chomsky's (1969) claim that the rate of acquisition of syntactic structure decreases markedly by age five. I am also in disagreement with her further statement that the differences between the child's and adult's grammar at this stage are no longer so readily discernible.

This view is to some extent an artefact of the assumption that superficially similar structures have the same source in child and adult grammars. I have already indicated the problems entailed in assuming that children's agentless passives are derived from agented passives by means of transformational rules, in view of Horgan's and my own finding that the agented passive is rare in children's speech. Similarly, Ingram (1975), who studied the relative clauses produced by children when telling stories, found that children younger than five produce a very limited variety of relative clauses that do not seem to require transformational rules, but could result from phrase structure rules. Clark (1974) also argues for the non-transformational nature of some early child language structures, which are the result of 'performance' rather than a manifestation of underlying linguistic competence. For example, when a child produces a clause with no overt relative marker, we could assume that this utterance has the same internal syntactic structure of one produced by an adult. However, my own view would be that it is implausible that children's early use of the zero strategy is a result of the type of derivational processes which have been postulated for the generation of the comparable prototype adult construction, e.g. WH movement and deletion in situ, etc. (cf. Chomsky 1977). Indeed, it is not clear that one would wish to postulate such a derivational history for all speakers of English as part of some shared panlectal grammar (cf. Romaine 1982a).

I suggested above that a rule can have external as well as internal components. In English (both standard and non-standard), there are several strategies available for relativization, which are conditioned by internal linguistic factors, such as the syntactic position of the head NP etc., and social factors, such as style and regional dialect (to be discussed in chapter 4). From an educational perspective, problems may arise when not all children have equal access and/or exposure to the highly syntacticized strategies sanctioned by prescriptive grammars. Take, for instance, the case of the Scots child who may not have *whose* as an option for relativizing on genitive NPs, or the West Indian child who may be behind his white peers in producing the morphological and syntactic hallmarks of the full passive (cf. section 6.3 and chapter 7 for further discussion of the educational implications of these findings).

Since some constructions may be acquired and used only in certain contexts, such as school, it is important to look at the communicative functions which syntactic structures serve, not only for certain groups of speakers, but also in particular languages. I have already alluded to the inequality of languages with respect to the kinds of strategies of relativization and passivization they make available to their speakers (cf. also note 1). Slobin (forthcoming) observes that Turkish children paraphrase relative clauses by discourse particles, which are used in adult discourse to emphasize or remind the listener of an item of shared information or common knowledge. Their early use of relativizers is found in contexts where appeals are made to shared knowledge to identify referents. These discourse particles can be seen as having similar functions to other devices such as demonstratives, pronouns, deictics, which are often used as relativizers. The common unity of these linguistic elements is probably best accommodated within a deictic theory of discourse reference; that is, they can all be used to alert the listener to a referent. This view is in sympathy with the perspective of Givón (1976b) and Sankoff and Brown (1976), who have argued for the origins of syntax in discourse.

My concluding remark pertains to diachrony and the contribution it makes to our understanding of child language. Chains of grammaticalization repeat themselves developmentally and diachronically. A number of emergent solutions may compete for accomplishing the same discourse functions in face-to-face interaction. Some may eventually come to be grammaticalized and, as such, serve as highly conventionalized and often efficient strategies for dealing with recurrent communicative problems. One can look at the evolution of relative-clause formation strategies and passives from this perspective. Deuchar (1983), for example, has suggested that relative clauses develop as explicit syntactic structures for the identification of referents in non-interactive situations. They are thus well suited for written communication and autonomous discourse. Certain seemingly arbitrary syntactic structures may have their diachronic and developmental origin in a few basic universal communicative functions. Within a highly standardized language such as English, the codified norms of the written language create pressure to enforce the canonical, fully syntacticized strategy of referring to referents, which grammarians call the relative clause. Similarly, in the case of passives, undue emphasis has been placed on the highly idiosyncratic and formal syntactic aspects of the English agented passive, which can be seen as a strategy developed by subject-prominent languages to put a non-subject NP into focus. The agented passive is from this standpoint only one of a number of constructions which are functionally equivalent; that is, like topicalization, it serves to put referents into focus (cf. Grieve and Wales 1973). Attempts to trace rules, either diachronically or developmentally in terms of the changes in formal manifestation they have undergone, without regard for their communicative function are fundamentally misguided. Most studies on the acquisition of relative clauses and passives have emphasized control of the more purely syntactic rather than the pragmatic and semantic aspects of these constructions.

I have tried here to stress the continuity in development from early topic/comment structures to fully syntacticized structures like relative clauses and passives. I have argued that this is possible once it is recognized that a key part of the common semantic-pragmatic function of passives and relatives is their use as strategies which single out an NP for semantic prominence (i.e. set it up as a topic by putting it into focus), and make a comment on it.

4

The acquisition and development of sociolinguistic patterns

It would be very surprising to come across a textbook on English grammar which reported the finding that a speaker should omit the final consonant more often in words like *trust* than in words like *passed*, or that he should sometimes omit relative pronouns when they occur in subject position, e.g. 'There's a man wants to see you.' Textbooks of course codify prescriptive and not descriptive norms. However, it is a fact that native speakers know these rules and use them spontaneously, in spite of what grammar books say is 'correct'.

Given the rather significant increase in sociolinguistic research over the past two decades, it seems reasonably safe to say that a great deal is now known about many kinds of correlations between language and social structure, particularly in the English-speaking world. These correlations give rise to so-called 'sociolinguistic patterns' in the adult community. These patterns, however, are generally seen as static or synchronic with little emphasis being given to their historical or developmental genesis. Thus not much is known about the role and place of children in the overall communicative structure of the adult speech community. In this chapter I will examine one particular aspect of the development of communicative competence; namely, the acquisition of sociolinguistic rules for the usage of linguistic variables. We will look at how children acquire and what control they have over the patterns of sociolinguistic variation observed in the adult population. Most of the data I will discuss here, from a variety of sociolinguistic studies of adults and children, show that there are important trends towards interaction between certain types of social and linguistic variables. Labov identifies four major external variables in the study of sociolinguistic patterns: social class, style, age, and sex, all of which will be discussed here. One has to be careful, however, in interpreting the kind of aggregated data, which is typically presented in sociolinguistic studies, where individual variability has been averaged out (cf. the discussion in Romaine 1980c). The failure to carry out tests of statistical significance is in general a weakness of sociolinguistic research of this kind. In reporting the results of others I have not always had access to the raw data; nor have I always been able to look independently at the effects of the major social variables. However, I have tried to note throughout where such difficulties of interpretation arise. Finally, I will consider the evaluative aspect of sociolinguistic competence and look at evidence which suggests that very young children are aware of the social significance of linguistic variation.

4.1 Social class differentiation

In an important paper discussing the process of acquisition of standard English, Labov (1970a) says that the kinds of sociolinguistic patterns found in adult speech communities are acquired during adolescence. His view then is that pre-adolescent children do not control the full resources of sociolinguistic variability. He (1970a: 275) observes that 'there are many stages in the learning of spoken English which cannot be reached until much later in life, and there are skills in the speaking of English which the grade school child knows nothing about.' Labov's conclusions are based largely on the findings of urban social dialectology in the United States. In these studies the major focus of the investigation has been on the adult population, rather than on younger speakers. Many of these studies have, however, included for comparative purposes a subsample of school-aged children, e.g. Labov's (1966) study of New York City, Trudgill's (1974a) in Norwich, Wolfram's (1969) in Detroit, and Macaulay's (1977) in Glasgow, just to name a few whose findings I will look at in this chapter. Nevertheless, there have been a few studies within this social dialectological framework which have concentrated exclusively on adolescents, e.g. Romaine 1975, Reid 1976, Aniansson 1979, Mees 1977, Cheshire 1982a. These latter studies have shown that one can observe a number of sociolinguistic patterns among very young children – in some cases these are similar to those reported for adults.

In order to understand the reasons for these divergent findings, let us look first at what Labov has to say about stages in the acquisition of standard English in relation to the findings of some of the major urban sociolinguistic studies in the US. Labov postulates six stages (1970a: 288–9):

1. Basic grammar (three to four years): At this stage the main body of grammatical rules and lexicon of spoken English are learned, normally under the influence of the parents. This is the language which the child brings to school.

2. The vernacular (five to twelve years): Labov sees this level as the most crucial from the standpoint of linguistic evolution. During this stage a child learns a local dialect which is that of his immediate peer group. This peer

influence cannot be underestimated since it is at this stage that local neighbourhood dialect features become established in the everyday speech patterns of the child and the previously dominant parental influence is submerged under that of the peer group. Payne (1980) has found evidence that many of the features of the language which a child has learned from his parents can be radically transformed under the influence of his peers, e.g. when families move from one dialect region to another. I will look at this stage in more detail in chapter 6. Labov further notes that it is during this transitional stage from parental to peer-group influence the child learns to read in school and hence is exposed to the process of socialization into the norms and uses of school language.

3. Social perception: This stage begins with early adolescence, when the child starts to come into wider contact with adults. The increasing exposure to a wider range of social classes and the linguistic patterns of the adult population begin to make the significance of the vernacular pattern apaprent. It is at this stage, Labov says, that we can notice a movement from the vernacular pattern of speaking towards a more prestigious form of speech. By the age of 14 or 15 children begin to respond to subjective reaction tests in conformity with the adult norm.

4. Stylistic variation: In this phase the child learns what Ervin-Tripp (1972) has referred to as 'co-occurrence rules', which relate linguistic forms to contexts. The child learns how to modify his speech in the direction of the prestige standard, especially in formal situations. The crucial transition is exposure to a group outside the neighbourhood, which occurs during the first year of high school (i.e. 13–14 years). Labov cites his finding that the number of stops and affricates used for (th) (e.g. *thin, tin*) differs greatly between those speakers who have never been to high school and those who have had at least one year.

5. Consistent standard: This stage is not acquired by all speakers. It involves the ability to maintain standard styles of speech. Labov says that some New Yorkers may be able to add a few corrected forms to their speech patterns, but the ability to maintain a consistent standard is a skill acquired mainly by the middle class.

6. Full range: Similarly the final stage is not reached by all speakers, i.e. the acquisition of a wide range of styles appropriate to a wide range of speech events. Labov notes that most of those who do attain this level are college-educated people with special interest in speech. It is also interesting that consistent mastery of the standard is accompanied by the loss of the ability to switch downwards to the vernacular.

To support his view of acquisition Labov (1970a: 287) compared the patterns he found among some of the children of his New York City informants with the adult ones. He looked at their use of the linguistic variables (i.e. production), their subjective reaction and self-evaluation tests (i.e. perception). This comparison revealed a steady progression towards the norms of the adult community, as can be seen in table 4.1.

Table 4.1 Conformity with adult norms amongst children in New York City

Age	%
8–11	52
12–13	50
14–15	57
16–17	62
18–19	64
(20–39	84)

Since social class is seen as one of the most important four major external variables which influence a person's speech, I will begin by looking at some of the sociolinguistic studies which have found correlations between social class/status and the speech of children. To talk of social class differences being reflected in children's speech requires some clarification of the notion social class and the effect it has been observed to have on the speech of the adult population. Simplistically speaking, the findings of many of the major urban surveys of speech in the US, Britain and elsewhere, e.g. Sweden, have shown that there is a bipolarization of norms between middle- and working-class speech. The middle-class adhere more closely to the norms of the overt prestige standard, while the working-class are closer to the norms of local non-standard speech, or what Labov and others refer to as the vernacular. This bipolarization is particularly clearly seen in the use of certain grammatical variables, which characteristically show *sharp stratification*. This can be seen in table 4.2, which compares the use of verbs without /s/ amongst two groups of adults who are representative of different social class groups in Norwich and Detroit. The data come from Trudgill's (1974a) study of Norwich and Wolfram's (1969) study of Detroit.

In these results we can see that usage is very sharply divided between middle and working class; this is particularly true in Norwich where the use of the non-standard suffixless present tense is almost never used by middle-class speakers, and the lowest speakers in the social hierarchy use it almost categorically. The division between these two social class groups is no less clear in Detroit, although not as decisive as in Norwich, presumably reflecting the greater openness and mobility in the American social class hierarchy, compared to the British class system. The notion 'social class', however, is problematic for both sociologists and linguists, and in these

Table 4.2 Percentage of verbs without /s/ in Norwich and Detroit (e.g. *he go*)

Social class[a]	Norwich	Detroit
UMC	–	1
MMC	0	–
LMC	2	10
UWC	70	57
MWC	87	–
LWC	97	71

Note:
(a) UMC = upper-middle class;
MMC = middle-middle class; LMC = lower-middle class; UWC = upper-working class;
MWC = middle-working class; LWC = lower-working class.

studies it is generally assumed that social class membership can be assessed in terms of criteria such as occupation, income, etc. (cf. Romaine 1980c for discussion).

Phonological variables, by contrast, show patterns of fine stratification, as can be seen in table 4.3. This shows the correlation between social class and the pronunciation of post-vocalic /r/ amongst two groups of adults in New York City (cf. Labov 1966) and Reading, England (cf. Trudgill 1974a).

The findings show that the use of post-vocalic /r/ is socially diagnostic, i.e. indicative of social class membership, but in different ways in the two cities. In New York City the lower one's social status the fewer /r/s one uses, while in Reading the reverse is true. This pattern reflects the historical fact that in Britain accents which have lost post-vocalic /r/ generally have more social prestige than those which preserve it. In many

Table 4.3 Percentage of post-vocalic /r/ pronounced in New York City and Reading (e.g. *car, farm*)

Social class[a]	New York City	Reading
UMC	32	0
LMC	20	28
UWC	12	44
LWC	0	49

Note:
(a) UMC = upper-middle class; LMC = lower-middle class; UMC = upper-working class;
LWC = lower-working class.

parts of the United States it has become increasingly prestigious to use rhotic speech (i.e. to pronounce post-vocalic /r/), although this has not always been the case. In New York City there has been a trend in recent years to move away from non-rhotic to rhotic speech, which is now establishing itself as a new prestige norm in many parts of the US (cf. Levine and Crockett 1967). Unlike the social distribution of the grammatical variable we have just looked at, however, this one shows fine rather than sharp stratification. That is, post-vocalic /r/ (and many other phonological variables) show continuous, gradient variation along a linguistic dimension (i.e. in this case phonetic) as well as a social one. The indices show a regular, monotonic relationship with the social class hierarchy, but there are no sharp breaks between each group. Although there is a great deal of difference between the norms of the highest and lowest groups, it is not as sharply polarized as in the case of grammatical variables. It is worth pointing out that the non-discreteness of social dialect boundaries is a major finding of urban sociolinguistics. In other words, dialects can be defined quantitatively in terms of relatively different levels of usage of the same linguistic features which serve to characterize different groups of users. To summarize briefly then the connection between social class and linguistic variables which has been observed for adults we can say that the higher a person's position and status in the social class hierarchy, the more likely he is to use standard forms, and the lower he is, the less likely. I will now look at what evidence there is to indicate that similar patterns of social class stratification are to be found in the speech of younger speakers.

I will begin by looking at the findings of some of the American surveys which have compared patterns of social class stratification between children and adults. I will examine first some of the major phonological variables, before looking at cases which involve grammatical and syntactic variation. Table 4.4 shows the results for four of the phonological variables in the Detroit urban dialect study (Wolfram 1969), which included children in two age groups, 10–12 and 12–14. It is evident that the four variables show correlations with social class stratification which are in accordance with the general principle cited earlier; namely, the most frequent use of standard forms appears in the speech of those higher up in the hierarchy. The variable (t/d) refers to the deletion of final /t/ and /d/ in consonant clusters in words like *walked*, *mist*, *grabbed*, etc. As indicated at the beginning of the chapter this is a fairly regular variable rule affecting the phonology and morphology of English. All speakers of English simplify some consonant clusters, regardless of their social class, age, sex, etc. This is especially the case when they occur in monomorphemic forms such as *mist* rather than in bimorphemic forms such as *grabbed* and *walked*, where the final /t/ and /d/ is an inflectional suffix marking the past tense of the verb. Simplification is also more frequent when the t/d occurs in an environment

Table 4.4 A comparison of patterns of social class stratification for 10–12, 14–17 year olds and adults in Detroit

		Age 10–12				Age 14–17				Adult			
		(t/d)[a]	(θ)[b]	(d)[c]	(r)	(t/d)[a]	(θ)[b]	(d)[c]	(r)	(t/d)[a]	(θ)[b]	(d)[c]	(r)
Class[d]	UMW	6.7				4.7				8.6			
	UMN	18	16.9	13.6	11.3	15.9	10.2	16.6	41.3	10.2	9.2	3.6	8.8
	LMN	33	34	28.1	40	27.4	7	20.7	45	23.5	11.2	10.4	33.7
	UWN	47.2	73.2	25.9	51.3	50	66	31.7	71.3	48.5	73.2	19	61.3
	LWN	58.4	75	38.7	80	46.7	84.2	32.5	61.3	53.4	54.7	26.7	73.8

Notes:
(a) These scores collapse two environments, monomorphemic words, e.g. *past*, and bimorphemic ones, e.g. *passed*.
(b) These scores indicate the use of all non-standard realizations, i.e. /f/, /t/ and ø.
(c) These scores indicate the use of both /t/ and ø in non-vocalic environments.
(d) UMW = upper-middle white; UMN = upper-middle negro; LMN = lower-middle negro; UMN = upper-working negro; LWN = lower-working negro.

where the following word begins with a consonant rather than a vowel, e.g. *fast train* as opposed to *passed away*. Thus there is a hierarchy of internal constaints, phonetic and morphological, which affect the realization of final t/d. Deletion is most likely in cases where a monomorphemic form is followed by a word beginning with a consonant, i.e. *fast train* and least likely in cases where a bimorphemic form is followed by a word beginning with a vowel, i.e. *passed away*. The latter environment is more socially diagnostic than the former, but the rule appears to be a stable and equally binding one for most native speakers of English.[1] In the Detroit data for black and white adults we can see that there is a regular relationship between the social class of the speaker and frequency with which he deletes t/d. When we look at the two younger age groups, we see the same tendency, especially for the 10–12 year olds. There are some irregularities in the 14–17 year olds. Generally, scores (which represent percentage of use of the variables) are higher for the younger age groups, though there does not seem to be a clear progression of the type Labov's views might lead us to expect.

The variable (θ) shows much the same trend. The variable concerns the realization of morpheme medial and final /θ/ as /f/, /t/ or ø, e.g. *tooth*, *nothing*. There is a pattern of social class stratification in the adult sample as well as in the two younger age groups (note, however, the exceptional behaviour of the 14–17 year olds in the LMN). There is also a tendency for the youngest age group to be greater users of the non-standard realizations.

Similar results obtained for the variable (d), which refers to the realization of syllable final /d/ as /t/ or ø, e.g. *hood*. This variable does not serve to distinguish the social classes to the same extent as the other variables. The two youngest age groups show the same type of pattern of stratification as the adults (but note the scores for the 10–12 year olds in the LMN). However, there is no clear evidence that the youngest speakers use the non-standard realization more frequently than others.

As far as post-vocalic /r/ is concerned, we can see a clear pattern of social stratification in all three age groups (note, however, the behaviour of 14–17 year olds in the UWN), although there is no general progression towards the adult norms. Both younger groups are deviant with respect to the adults, though in different ways.

I will look next at some of the results obtained in sociolinguistic work in Britain. The first of these is Macaulay's (1977) survey of five phonological variables in Glasgow among four social class groups and three age groups, ten and fifteen year olds and adults. The results are shown in table 4.5.

Macaulay found similar patterns for all four variables; low scores in each of the variables indicate in each case a usage which is closest to the standard. Looking first of all at the adults, we can see that there the variables correlate very closely with the social class hierarchy and each serves to stratify the population finely (note, however, the anomaly in the score for (i) in Class IIb). In remarking on the great consistency of his results, Macaulay concluded that Glasgow appears to be a relatively stable, socially stratified speech community. He has argued on the basis of both

Table 4.5 A comparison of social class stratification patterns in 10 and 15 year olds and adults in Glasgow

	Age 10					Age 15					Adults				
	(i)[a]	(u)[b]	(a)[c]	(gs)[d]	(au)[e]	(i)[a]	(u)[b]	(a)[c]	(gs)[d]	(au)[e]	(i)[a]	(u)[b]	(a)[c]	(gs)[d]	(au)[e]
Class[f] I	235	200	176	66	244	199	192	165	43.5	242	174	145	133	35.9	152
IIa	261	261	169	85.7	272	249	237	200	78.3	286	238	212	201	54.4	247
IIb	270	306	247	84.4	322	294	298	234	84.3	349	287	284	261	84.4	334
III	291	304	236	88.2	343	308	314	264	95.6	342	283	321	260	91.6	362

Notes:
(a) (i) refers to the vowel in *hit, will*, etc. Scores range from 100 for a vowel of [I] quality to 500 for a vowel of [ʌ] quality
(b) (u) refers to the vowel in *school, book*, etc. Scores range from 100 for a vowel of [u] quality to 400 for a vowel of [I] quality
(c) (a) refers to the vowel in *cap, bag*, etc. Scores range from 100 for a vowel of [a] quality to 300 for a vowel of [ɑ] quality
(d) (gs) refers to the use of a glottal stop word medially and finally as in *butter, bet*, etc. Scores are given in percentages from 0–100
(e) (au) refers to the diphthong in *now, house*, etc. Scores range from 100 for a vowel of [au] quality to 400 for a vowel of [u] quality
(f) The social class groupings are based on the Registrar General's Classification: Class I = professional and managerial; Class IIa = white collar; Class IIb = skilled manual; Class III = semi-skilled and unskilled manual

linguistic data as well as comments from informants that there seem to be three major social class dialects in Glasgow. The differences between Classes IIb and III are not as great as those between the other classes.

As far as patterns of class stratification in the two younger age groups are concerned, it can be seen that there are some regularities as well as some irregularities. For example, if we look at the scores for the variables (i), (u), (gs) and (au) we can see patterns of social class stratification similar to those in the adult population (with only relatively minor deviations, e.g. in the ten-year-old Class IIa scores for (gs) and Class III scores for (u); in the fifteen-year-old Class IIb scores for (au)). The results for (a), however, do not show a clear pattern for the youngest age group. Some of the variables confirm Labov's view that the process of acquisition of adult norms is one of gradual increasing approximation to the patterns of adult speech, e.g. (i), and (u) with the exception of Class III, which involves movement away from non-standard to standard speech. Others, however, show nearly the reverse; that is, the younger age groups show less evidence of non-standard forms than the adults, e.g. (a) (note, however, the anomaly in Class I and Class IIb and II 15 year olds). The use of glottal stops increases with age for Class III speakers while it decreases for others. The variable (au) shows evidence of these two competing tendencies, i.e. movement towards and away from the most local norms of Glasgow speech.

The presence of these conflicting tendencies in the data prompted Macaulay (1977) to comment that the sociolinguistic patterning which he found to be characteristically related to social class and sex in the adult community was 'by no means clear at the age of ten, although fairly well established at fifteen'. Thus Macaulay endorses Labov's notion that the acquisition of adult norms takes place mainly between the ages of ten and fifteen.

Just as there is no reason to expect that every instance of linguistic variation will have correlates with aspects of social structure, there are also no grounds for expecting the process of acquisition to proceed at the same rate and in the same way across all social groups in a society, let alone across the English-speaking world or cross-culturally. The next few studies I will look at show clear patterns of social class stratification amongst primary school children.

The first of these is a study of language and social class among Cardiff schoolchildren (Mees 1977). The purpose of this study was to examine the extent to which social class had an effect on the pronunciation of certain vowels, which have a range of realizations from local Cardiff speech to more RP variants. The results for variables can be seen in table 4.6. The eighty children who took part are between the ages of nine and eleven and were recorded reading a text. The social class membership of the children was assessed on the basis of their father's occupations, as in Macaulay's study, using the Registrar General's classification.

Table 4.6 Patterns of social class stratification in the speech of Cardiff schoolchildren

		(ng)[a]	*(a)*[b]	*(h)*[c]	*(ai)*[d]	*(au)*[e]	*(o:)*[f]
Class	I	006	032	000	110	060	007
	II	043	068	000	142	110	063
	III	083	316	020	163	170	096

Notes:
(a) The scores for (ng) range from 0–100, where 100 = [n], e.g. *reading*.
(b) The scores for (a) range from 0–400 where 0 = a vowel of [a] quality and 400 a vowel of [æ] quality, e.g. *after*, *carpet*.
(c) The scores for (h) range from 0–100, where 100 = ø, e.g. *hang*.
(d) The scores for (ai) range from 0–200, where 0 = a non-centralized diphthong of [aɪ] quality and 200 a centralized diphthong of [əɪ] quality, e.g. *night*.
(e) The scores for (au) range from 0–200, where 100 = a vowel of [aʊ] quality and 200 a centralized diphthong of [aʊ] quality, e.g. *house*.
(f) The scores for (o:) range from 0–100, where 0 = diphthong of [aʊ] quality, to 100 for a diphthong having a more retracted starting point [öö] or a monophthong of [ö:] quality.

Mees's results establish that there is a very close correlation between linguistic variation and social class differences. They are striking for at least two reasons; firstly, for every variable there is a steady increase from one social class to the next, with the lowest social group being closest to local Cardiff speech and the highest the furthest away from it; and secondly, these findings challenge Labov's view that patterns of class stratification of an adult-type emerge only at the beginning of the child's entry into secondary school. The speakers here are all primary school children.

Although there has been no detailed sociolinguistic investigation of the adult population in Cardiff (cf., however, Coupland 1980), the nature of the interaction between social factors and some of the variables in this study is known to us from other studies in various parts of the English-speaking world. Thus we are able to make some inferences about the position of these children in the Cardiff speech community on the basis of their usage of these variables.

In a very early sociolinguistic study of schoolchildren in New England, Fischer (1958) linked the use of the variable (ing) (i.e. the pronunciation of the *-ing* ending in words like *reading* as either [n] or [ŋ]) to a number of social factors. Among these were sex, formality of the situation, orientation towards school, and social status. Fischer says that the variable is a sociosymbolic variant used to signal the relative status of participants in conversational interaction. Other studies of this variable, e.g. Labov (1966) in New York City, have found that the presence or absence of a final velar nasal, [ŋ], for (ing) is one of the most general and stable sociolinguistic markers (cf. Labov 1972a: 238). Generally speaking, the most standard variant is the velar nasal, but there are some interesting exceptions to this in parts of the English-speaking world (cf. the discussion in Cullum 1981 on (ing) in Birmingham speech).

Another of Mees's variables, (h), has been studied in various parts of Britain, where it has been found to correlate with social class and other factors. Unlike RP, most accents in England do not have initial /h/ in words like *heart*, *ham*, etc. Speakers in the northeast of England, Scotland and Ireland tend to retain /h/. Trudgill's (1974a) study of (h) in Norwich demonstrated that middle-class speakers tended to be closer to the norms of the standard than the working class. What is particularly interesting about Mees's results is the almost consistent use of [h]. This, in Mees's view, reflects the fact that she recorded the children in a formal style where their speech was more likely to reflect the prestige standard. This is a factor to bear in mind particularly with consonantal variables since in reading styles informants' attention is drawn to the orthographic presence of *h* and *ing*, which are indicators of their pronunciation. By comparison, the orthographic symbols used for vowels do not provide unambiguous cues as to their standard realizations.

As for the vocalic variables in Mees's study, we have already seen that (au), e.g. *house*, showed a correlation with social class in Glasgow and similarly (a), although the precise variant realizations are of course different in Glasgow and Cardiff. The variable (ai), e.g. *might*, is interesting in that there are no scores under 100 for any social class group. The variable (o:) on the other hand shows a pattern similar to that of (ing). Not all the variables stratify the children in the same way or to the same extent. In some cases the biggest differences emerge between Classes II and III, e.g. (ing), (a), (h), (au), but in others they appear between I and II, e.g. (o:) and (ai).

Other studies done in Britain and Sweden support Mees's finding that some sociolinguistic variables can be firmly established in the speech of very young schoolchildren to such an extent that they show patterns of social class stratification of a type characteristic of adult populations. A study done by Beaken (1971) on the acquisition of cockney phonology by London schoolchildren showed that by the age of eight children were using language in social significant ways. Reid (1976) looked at the incidence of two variables, (ing) and (gs) in the speech of some 11-year-old Edinburgh schoolboys. The boys were ranked in terms of social status on the basis of their father's occupation using the Registrar General's Classification. They attended three schools in Edinburgh which contrasted in terms of the demographic characteristics of the catchment areas they served, e.g. housing conditions, employment, etc. School 1 ranks among the bottom schools and School 2 among the top; School 3 is a fee-paying school which attracts a very high proportion of the sons of social class I. Reid found that the school which an individual attended was also an important indication of social position and a relevant factor in determining accent. In table 4.7,

Table 4.7 Some phonological variables in the speech of 11-year-old Edinburgh schoolboys

	$(gs)^a$	$(ing)^a$		$(gs)^a$	$(ing)^a$
Social class			*School*		
I	55	18	3	48	5
II	74	66	2	64	34
III	78	74	1	77	78

Note:
(a) Scores for both variables are given in percentages, where 100 indicates the non-standard variant.

where the results for the two variables are given, it can be seen that whether the boys are grouped by father's occupation or by school affiliation the basic relationship between high indices (i.e. non-standard pronunciation) and low social status, low indices (i.e. standard realizations) and high social status is confirmed (cf. Reid 1976: 61–2). The biggest difference is between Classes I and II. The data are based on recordings made of the boys in four different contexts. I will look more closely at Reid's evidence on stylistic variation in section 4.2. Reid's findings also challenge Labov's views on the age of emergence of patterns of social class stratification in relation to age in that boys in their last year of primary school (i.e. at the age of ten to eleven years) use linguistic variables in a systematic way which relates to their social status, or more precisely, to the social status of their families assessed on the basis of father's occupation.

I will look at one more study which supports the British findings. It was done in Sweden as part of a project on the child's linguistic identity (cf. Aniansson 1981), which investigated the development of children's sociolinguistic competence in spoken language. The research hypothesized that the children brought with them to the school their home variety of speech, but that under the influence of school and friends their speech changed. They looked at certain variables in the speech of children from three to eighteen.[2] Their results for (t) can be seen in table 4.8.

In general, Aniansson found that schoolchildren aged seven to sixteen used more standard forms than young adults aged sixteen to twenty. The variable has to do with the realization of final /t/, which is an inflectional suffix indicating either the neuter singular definite article (e.g. *huset* – '*the* house') or the past participle of certain verb classes (e.g. *kastat* – 'thrown'). In its latter realization it is similar to the English (t/d) variable discussed earlier (cf. Romaine 1984 for further discussion and a comparison of the sociolinguistic status of this variable in Swedish and English). The use of forms with /t/ is in general increasing throughout Sweden under the influence of the norms of the written language (cf. Nordberg 1972). Thanks to the extensive sociolinguistic research done in various parts of Sweden by

Table 4.8 Percentage of /t/ forms in the speech of Eskilstuna schoolchildren in relation to social class

	Age 7–16	Age 16–20	Adults
Social group[a] I	39.5	15.7	78
II	31.3	12.9	52
III	20.5	2.8	37

Note:
(a) The groups are ranked from highest (I) to lowest (III). Cf. Nordberg 1969 for further details of the criteria used to assess social class membership

Nordberg and his colleagues we are able to establish a clear profile of this variable in relation to a number of social factors. As can be seen from the adult scores from Nordberg's survey of Eskilstuna, (t) is a marker of social class membership, with the highest group (I) using the most standard forms. This pattern also appears in the youngest group included in the study, namely sixteen to twenty year olds, and in Aniansson's school-children aged seven to sixteen. Aniansson's findings again challenge Labov's idea that regular patterns of social class stratification tend to emerge relatively late in adolescence. I will have more to say about the pattern of age grading in section 4.3.

In this section I have looked at phonological variables which show patterns of variation correlated with social class, and we have found that regular social differentiation is no less characteristic of children's than adult's speech. However, it is important to bear in mind that we have examined a fairly superficial level of oral language skills; and for the moment I have not tried to define the notion of social class, or indeed to separate it into components such as class, status, solidarity and power (cf. Weber 1964) and to examine these concepts in relation to situation. I have, however, laid the groundwork for a more detailed discussion of some of these questions in chapter 6. Systematic studies of the association between the use of language and socioeconomic status have a long history, beginning at the turn of the century, and have been very influential in educational circles. A great many of the established correlations between high achievement in certain types of linguistic skills believed to be essential to success in school and higher social status rely on syntactic measures. A variety of explanations have been proposed; perhaps the most influential and controversial are the ideas of Bernstein on the relationship between language and social class. Most of what Bernstein has to say on this subject deals with the syntactic and semantic organization of language rather than phonology. I will be looking at his theory and the influence of school on the language use of children in the next chapter.

4.2 *Stylistic variation*

In the discussion of methodology in chapter 2 I examined Labov's view of style and his notion of a stylistic continuum based on the amount of attention paid to speech during the linguistic interview. I have already argued that this one-dimensional concept of style tied to a continuum of formality/informality is over-simplistic. Style in its broadest sense is multi-dimensional and thus related to many components of a speech event; it depends, for example, not only on factors such as topic, participants and channel, but also things like motivation, role relations, intention, etc. (cf. Traugott and Romaine 1983 for discussion). I have also pointed to the difficulty in maintaining that speaking and reading styles are governed by the same constraints. Despite these limitations, however, the fact remains that a great deal of sociolinguistic work has been based on Labov's assumptions and many have followed his approach to tackling the problem of stylistic variation. Regardless of Labov's claims about the connection between amount of attention paid to speech, its relationship with style and formality, his methods do yield interesting findings about the ways in which people adjust certain features of their speech to 'context' defined in this way. In this chapter I will look at some investigations of the speech of schoolchildren which have relied on Labov's methods to see what evidence there is for stylistic variation. Later, in chapter 7, I will take a different perspective on the question of style and context.

In order to understand the development of stylistic variation in children's speech we need to review briefly some of the major findings of sociolinguistic research on style in adults. In his New York study Labov found that he could isolate five styles, which contrasted with each other in terms of the frequency of occurrence of certain linguistic variables (e.g. post-vocalic /r/) not only in the different styles of one speaker, but also between groups of speakers, e.g. middle vs. working class. To the extent that both 'styles' and 'social dialects' appeared to be definable in terms of regularly contrasting patterns of the same linguistic variables, then stylistic variation is not different in kind from social dialect variation. In other words, the identification of styles in Labov's sense can be undertaken in much the same way as the identification of different dialects of the same language, in that the boundaries of both may be established on the basis of quantitative patterns or recurrent selections of certain optional features of the linguistic code. If the same markers may serve to distinguish both social groups and style, then there is a sense in which styles are dialects. The connection between the social and stylistic continuum has already been illustrated neatly in chapter 2 (figure 2.2), which showed Labov's results for the variable (ing).

The parallel behaviour of certain socially significant variables along both social and stylistic continua is one of the major findings to emerge from sociolinguistic research. This pattern of social and stylistic stratification indicates that if a feature is found to be more common in the lower than in the upper classes, it will also be more common in less formal than in more formal styles.

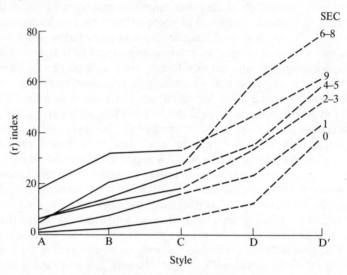

Figure 4.1   Social and stylistic stratification of post-vocalic /r/ in New York City Class stratification of a linguistic variable in process of change: /r/ in guard, car, beer, beard, board, etc. SEC (Socioeconomic class) scale: 0–1, lower class: 2–4, working class: 5–6, 7–8, lower-middle class: 9, upper-middle class. A, casual speech: B, careful speech: C, reading style: D, word lists: D', minimal pairs.

Source: Labov 1966

There is one seeming exception to this pattern which turns out to be of great significance. If we look at the diagram in figure 4.1 we can see what looks like a deviation; namely, the production of the lower-middle class exceeds that of the highest social group in the most formal style. This 'cross-over pattern' has been explained by Labov as a manifestation of hypercorrection (by the lower-middle class). This deviation from the expected sociolinguistic structure is an indication of the upward social aspirations of a group in society, who aim at the norm of the next highest – in this case, to such an extent that the result is a style shift exceeding that of the middle class in their most formal styles. Labov found that younger lower-middle-class women showed the greatest tendency towards hypercorrection. It is this group, at least in New York City, who recognize most strongly the external standard of correctness.[3]

Labov also found that this pattern of stylistic variation had important implications for change. Hypercorrection acted as a feedback mechanism to increase the use of prestige variants in the community. Another important point to observe is the depth of the slope and the tendency for the spread between the classes to be greater in casual than in formal speech (at least for phonological variables). In the most formal style the style vectors for each class tend to converge (apart from the hypercorrect pattern). Generally the slopes for the working class are higher than those for the middle class, indicating greater style shifting in the former.

We have already seen that Labov identifies late adolescence as the turning point in the child's development of the social significance of speech. It is at this stage that we should expect the onset of style shifting patterns similar to those we have examined for adults. But is there evidence that children show style shifting at an earlier age?

Table 4.9 Percentage of despirantized interdental fricatives in three styles

		Speaking	Reading	
		Casual	Narrative	Minimal pairs
Grade 1	(6 year olds)	84.2	75.3	–
Grade 4	(10 year olds)	92.9	80.3	75.7
Grade 8	(13 year olds)	74.8	72.8	73.1

There is some support for the idea that they do. Biondi's (1975) study of Italian–American children investigated style shifting using Labov's method of comparing speech in the interview with reading styles (narrative reading and reading of minimal pairs). In table 4.9 we can see his results for the despirantization of fricatives, i.e. the percentage of /t/ and /d/ forms produced for /θ/ and /ð/ in words like *both, thin, they*, etc. It is clear that only the two youngest age groups show style shifting. In the more formal reading styles the six and ten year olds use the standard forms more frequently. The ten year olds show the greatest style shifting. Biondi (1975: 612) says he does not have an explanation for the absence of any tendency to style shift among the oldest groups. This is the group who are just about to enter secondary school; and if Labov is right about the significance of this phase of an adolescent's life as being crucial in the development of sociolinguistic patterns, we would expect there to be some style shifting. The eighth grade did, however, show style shifting for another variable, consonant cluster simplification. Their scores decreased from 34.8 per cent in the casual style to 17.2 per cent in narrative reading.[4]

Let us look at some evidence from Edinburgh schoolchildren. We have already looked at some of the results of Reid's study (1976) of 11-year-old schoolboys and found that the two phonological variables he investigated, (ing) and (gs), showed patterns of social class stratification. There were also clear patterns of stylistic variation, as can be seen in table 4.10. The results are based on recordings which Reid made in four different contexts:

Table 4.10 Percentage of non-standard variants in the speech of
Edinburgh schoolboys in four styles

	Reading	Interview	Peer group	Playground
(ing)	14	45	54	59
(gs)	25	71	84	79

(1) reading a text, (2) face-to-face interview (3) peer-group speech, and (4)
playground interaction. He hypothesized that these four contexts would
form a stylistic continuum ranging from the most formal to most casual and
that this would be reflected in the boys' shifts towards more or less
standard speech. Apart from the deviation in the playground situation for
the variable (gs)[5] we can see that there is a progressive increase in the
frequency of use of non-standard variants of both variables. The slope is
somewhat steeper for (gs) than (ing), which perhaps indicates the greater
social significance of this variable. The greatest shift occurs between the
reading and speaking styles.

Tables 4.11 and 4.12 show the effect of social class membership/school in
relation to three styles (the playground style has been excluded).
Regardless of whether social class membership or school attended is taken

Table 4.11 Percentage of non-standard variants of (ng) and (gs)
in relation to social class and style

		Reading	Interview	Group
	Class 1	5	12	18
(ng)	2	24	74	88
	3	20	90	100
	Class 1	21	50	70
(gs)	2	22	91	98
	3	48	97	100

Table 4.12 Percentage of non-standard variants of (ng) and (gs) in
relation to school attended and style

		Reading	Interview	Group
	School 3	0	5	0
(ing)	2	7	21	45
	1	30	96	100
	School 3	20	37	58
(gs)	2	22	68	85
	1	31	98	100

as the relevant social grouping, the same trend obtains; namely, the social and stylistic continua run parallel to one another, thus offering support for the view that young children are able to produce speech in conformity with the social and stylistic constraints governing that of more mature speakers. The patterns of social and stylistic variation in the speech of these boys is strikingly adultlike in other respects too. We can see for example the same tendency for the scores to converge in the most formal style; i.e. the differences between the social groups/schools is greater in the more casual styles. There is also a tendency for the slopes of the highest social group and the most prestigious school to be shallower than those of the lower groups and less prestigious schools. Reid (1978: 169) observes that 'It is as true of the eleven year old Edinburgh boys as of older informants investigated previously in a similar way in the United States and in Britain that there are features of their speech which relate in a systematic way to their social status and to the social context in which their speech is produced.'

Further support for Reid's findings can be found in my study of Edinburgh schoolchildren. I examined the use of three phonological variables in relation to style for the ten year olds in my sample of informants. Table 4.13 compares the scores for these three variables in the interview style and reading passage. The variables (gs) and (ing) are the same as those we have looked at in Reid's and Macaulay's work; and (i) represents the same variable as in Macaulay's study, i.e. the vowel of *bit*, *kill*, etc. The scores for the latter range here from 100 to 400. The scores for (ng) and (gs) indicate the percentage of non-standard forms. It can be seen that there are quite dramatic downward shifts in the reading passage style for (gs) and (ing), but less so for (i). This indicates that ten year olds are able to vary their speech in response to the demands of the situation, presumably because they are aware that the use of the more stigmatized variants is not appropriate when reading aloud.

Both my study and Reid's challenge the opinion put forward by Labov and Wolfram and Fasold (1974: 92) that in pre-adolescence there is generally little stylistic variation and that during these years a child may still be close to being a 'monostylistic' speaker. Although I did not attempt to elicit reading styles from the two younger age groups (i.e. six and eight

Table 4.13 Stylistic variation in the speech of ten-year-old Edinburgh schoolchildren

	Interview	Reading
(gs)	81	8
(ing)	96	12
(i)	194	148

year olds), I do not think there is any basis for concluding that they were monostylistic. If I had applied a measure of style which relied on the frequency of particular linguistic variables at various points during the course of the interview, I could have isolated instances of 'style–switching'. However, I chose not to subdivide the interview into casual and more careful conversation and to treat instead the interview as one style. The following two extracts from an interview with the same six–year–old girl illustrate this switching (Romaine 1975: 204–5):

> I fall out (au–1) the bed. She falls out (au–1) the bed and we pull off the covers. I fell out (au–1) the bed so D. says, 'Where are you J?' I says, 'I'm down (au–1) here'. She says, 'Come up'. Babies *dinnae* do that. They should be in their cot' (gs–1). So she gets out (au–1) the bed. She falls out (au–1) cause she bumps her head on the wall and she says, 'Oh, this is a hard bed too.' So she says, 'Oh, I'm on the *floor*' (e).

> It's a house (au–o), my house (au–0) that I live in now (au–0), cause I flitted (i–2) (gs–1). The house (au–0) is still in a mess anyway. It's still got plaster and I've no fireplace now (au–0), all blocked up. Working (ing–1) men plastered where they used to be, there and there, and they did (i–1) the same to (gs–0) the fireplace. They just knocked it all out (au–0) (gs–1).

The first passage is much closer to the Scots end of this girl's repertoire than the second. In the first one we can see that all of the variables studied have non–standard realizations, e.g. (au–1) indicates a pronunciation with /u/ instead of (au) in words like *down*; (gs–1) indicates the use of a glottal stop; (ing–1) indicates the use of [n]. There are also other marked Scots forms in the first passage such as the pronunciation /fler/ for 'floor' and the use of the Scots negative form *dinnae* instead of English *don't*. The second sample of speech is by comparison much nearer standard Scottish English.

If we take the term monostylistic to mean that there is little or no variation we would certainly not be justified in applying it to the speech of these children. If we examine any of the speakers we can see that there is a great deal of inherent variability, i.e. variation that takes place while the linguistic and extra–linguistic context remain the same. There are many examples of the following type, where the speaker displays great variation in the use of one feature, e.g. (neg) while other features remain more or less constant, e.g. (gs) and (ing). At this stage there is much more work to be done on the co–occurrence restrictions on choice of variants of different variables in the same context. This passage is from an interview with an eight-year–old girl (Romaine 1975: 205–6): 'I says, I feel like getting (gs–1) (ing–1) her back, but *I cannae* do /e/ that. I *don't* like doing (ing–1) that, feel like I want to (gs–1), but I *can't*. I *dinnae* do it.' Similar behaviour can be seen in this extract from an interview with a six–year–old boy (Romaine 1975: 15): 'I *dinnae* play with them at home /e/, cause they're not allowed in my house (au-1). I stay just down (au-1) that road. They *dinnae* like me. I don't know. They *dinnae* play with me. I *dinna ken* why they *dinnae* play with me, just because I *dinnae* give /gi/ them my play piece.'

These samples are illustrative of some of the types and range of variation a sociolinguist will encounter in urban varieties of speech. This behaviour is reminiscent of Labov's (1970b: 189) examples of switching in the speech of a Black American adolescent or indeed of the switching between two languages in situations where they are in contact (cf. for example some of the studies by Gumperz 1976 on code-switching). In cases like these, index scores which average all the instances of a particular variable over all the speech in a single context, e.g. the interview, cover up some of this inherent variability. The somewhat misleading assumption behind the notion of the index is that if we took a slice out of the interview and counted tokens of each variable it would correspond more or less to that index score. This may not be the case in practice depending on the range and degree of variability displayed by each informant. What we do not have here is evidence of what the speakers do elsewhere, i.e. outside the context of the interview. It may be that some of this inherent variability of the younger age groups later becomes associated with different contexts. In fact, this is one conclusion I would draw from the results for the variable (au) in my study. If we look at the pattern of age and sex differentiation together, as in figure 4.2, we can see that younger children are likely to use

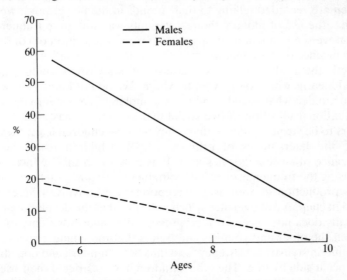

Figure 4.2 Usage of variable (au) = percentage of monophthongs for boys and girls in three age groups

the monophthongal variants more frequently than older children and there are also differences in the boys and girls in each age group. The greatest difference in the use of the variable occurs in the youngest age group, the six year olds. The change in the pattern of usage is greatest for the males and the difference between males and females levels out as the children become older (see table 4.14).

Table 4.14 Indices for variable (au)

Age 10		Age 8		Age 6	
Males	Females	Males	Females	Males	Females
11	12	31	6	53	10

We will see in section 4.4 how familiar these findings are to sociolinguists who have studied adult populations. That is, it has generally been the case that males on the whole use more non-standard forms than females. Here younger speakers also use more non-standard forms than older ones. This pattern indicates, in my opinion, that acquisition is taking place. This might at first seem paradoxical, since it appears that the use of the more stigmatized dialect pronunciations, e.g. *hoos*, are disappearing as the child gets older, and this is certainly one conclusion that might be reached on the basis of recording children in a face-to-face interview. Yet if these same children are recorded talking to their friends in the playground, we would find that the use of monophthongal variants was still quite frequent.

What we see happening in this pattern is the acquisition of control over the occurrence of these features in response to changes in context. It shows indirectly the gradual process of acquisition of stylistic variation, i.e. how the child learns when to say what to whom. We do not know precisely how early or under what social conditions completely consistent control over the situational selection of two social dialects can be mastered, but there appears to be strong evidence that many Scottish children learn these skills during the later stages of primary school. Children learn the social significance of switching styles as well as how to do this by increasing or decreasing the frequency of certain variables in certain situations. There is thus a production as well as a perception aspect involved here; I have looked in chapter 3 at evidence which indicates that the development of the two skills does not necessarily progress at the same rate. The difference between the older and younger children is that the younger speaker does not maintain stylistic consistency, and thus both standard and non-standard forms occur side by side. The older children have restricted their use of the Scots forms to more casual domains while the younger children have not yet acquired this ability to contextualize the variants they use.

Table 4.15 Percentage of /t/ (standard forms) in four situations for Swedish
schoolchildren

	Most formal			Least formal
	Reading	Board game	Discussion	Card game
% of /t/	77.3	60.6	29.3	23.6

There is further support from Sweden for the conclusion that situational
and stylistic variation is established in the primary school years. Aniansson
(1981) examined children's speech in different situations which she
hypothesized would form a stylistic continuum from most to least formal.
She recorded children in the following situations: (1) reading a text; (2) a
board game in which one child had to instruct another how to play without
visual contact between the two; (3) group discussion, and (4) a card game
with friends. Her results are shown in table 4.15, where it can be seen that
the children produce more /t/ forms, the standard ones, in each of the
situations which she assumed could be ranked in numerical order according
to formality. There is not much difference in the scores in the discussion
session and card game, but the other styles appear well demarcated. In
particular, there is a big gap between reading a text and speaking in a
discussion group.

The ability to switch styles also varies depending on sex and age as can
be seen in tables 4.16 and 4.17. Table 4.16 shows that there is a tendency
for the older pupils to use more standard forms in all three styles than the
youngest group, and the girls use more standard forms than boys in all
three situations.[6] It is by no means the case, however, that the youngest
group is monostylistic.

Table 4.16 Percentage of /t/ (standard forms) in three
situations for Swedish schoolchildren of different ages

	Reading	Board game	Discussion/ card game
Age 7–9	–	59.3	25.4
Age 10–12	73.7	61.4	25.7
Age 13–16	78.2	61.2	29.5

Similar results were obtained by Aniansson and Hammermo (1981), who
looked at additional phonological variables. They found that in most cases
the reading passage produced the lowest scores for the variables and the
group discussion the highest.

Table 4.17 Sex differentiation in the use of /t/ in Swedish schoolchildren

	Reading	Board game	Discussion/ card game
Boys	75.3	54.6	25.0
Girls	79.2	66.6	28.7

4.3 *Age-grading*

Within the life history of an individual there are behavioural patterns that are considered appropriate for various stages. We are all accustomed to making both conscious and unconscious assessments of people by their physical appearance, the way they dress and behave. Speech is only one of the behavioural characteristics which reveals age-grading. In some cultures there are often elaborate initiation rites that mark a person's entrance into a new phase or transition from one phase to another, e.g. initiation or puberty rites. In most industrialized western societies there are generally no formal elaborate rites of passage which mark age. However, a person who does not dress 'appropriate' to his age group will be ridiculed, just as the adult who tries to use the slang terms of the younger generation will be laughed at.

In talking about linguistic patterns of age-grading then, I mean the characteristic linguistic behaviours which are appropriate to and typical of different stages in the speaker's life span. One of the most frequently observed differences between different age groups in the US and Britain, for example, is the existence of 'teenage slang'. This is a fairly superficial difference, but can serve to date groups very accurately. Slang terms have a rapid turn-over; *groovy*, for instance, seems to be out of vogue already. Some of these, however, do eventually make their way into the language permanently and are after a time not thought of as slang, e.g. *cop*. The use of special vocabulary by groups, whether these are age groups or occupational groups (e.g. linguists), serves a similar function: it indicates in-group membership and facilitates communication among groups who share common interests and a common vocabulary for talking about them. I will be looking at some of the ways in which peer groups enforce ways of speaking in section 6.3.

In a number of sociolinguistic studies significant correlations between age and some of the major phonological and grammatical variables we have been looking at in this chapter have been found. I will look first at patterns of phonological variation in relation to age. Generally speaking, it appears to be the case that during the adolescent years the use of socially stigmatized forms is at its maximum. In my study of Edinburgh schoolchildren some of the variables showed the pattern: the younger the speaker, the greater the use of the more stigmatized feature (and the males in each age group generally use more stigmatized forms than females).

The clearest illustration of this pattern of age-grading can be seen in the results for the variables (au), (th), (neg) and (i) in table 4.18. In each case (except for the variable (th)) there is a distinction between each age group and a progression from higher to lower use of the variable with increasing age. In some cases the greatest increase occurs between the ages of eight and ten, e.g. (th), (i), (neg), while in others (au) it is between the ages of six and ten. This indicates that at least for some variables age differences of only two years are not sufficiently large to show clear age-grading. And there is no a priori reason to believe that two-year intervals provide the best time scale for looking at the longitudinal development of sociolinguistic varibles. Within sociolinguistic surveys of the adult population it is often even less clear what the relevant age categories are.

Table 4.18 Age-grading of some linguistic variables in Edinburgh schoolchildren

	Age 6	Age 8	Age 10
(au)	31	18	6
(th)	18	19	10
(neg)	38	35	22
(i)	211	204	194

Other variables in the Edinburgh study did not show age-grading of this type, although there were differences in the behaviour between some of the age groups; and others showed no real differences. This can be seen in table 4.19. The use of glottal stops does not vary much from one age group to another, although there is a slight tendency for the two older age groups to use glottal stops more frequently than the youngest group. There are virtually no differences related to age in the use of the variable (ing); the use of [n] forms is consistently high for all speakers. This was also the case in Wolfram and Christian's (1976) study of Appalachian English. The range of [n] realizations for the variable ranged from 80 to 100 per cent

Table 4.19 Some variables with mixed or no patterns of age-grading in Edinburgh schoolchildren

	Age 6	Age 8	Age 10
(gs)	75	81	81
(ing)	97	97	96
(a)	227	264	236

with no appreciable differences between younger and older speakers. Although there was some degree of differentiation related to class and style factors (just as there was in Reid's 1976 study of this variable among Edinburgh schoolboys), the differences do not appear to be as extensive as in other varieties of English in which the variable has been studied.[7] In the case of the variable (a) there is age-grading, although the pattern is not a consistent one. The youngest and the oldest groups show the lowest scores, while the eight year olds have the highest.

We can compare Macaulay's (1978a) results for the younger and adult Glasgow informants with those of some of the Edinburgh variables. In table 4.20 I have shown Macaulay's results for the Glasgow variables for

Table 4.20 Age-grading in Glasgow

	Age 10	Age 15	Adults
(i)	264	263	246
(u)	268	262	241
(au)	295	305	274
(a)	207	216	214
(gs)	81	75	67

ten and fifteen year olds and adults. Some trends similar to those observed in the Edinburgh data can be noted. Firstly, there are some variables which show the pattern: the younger the speaker, the greater the use of the variable. This is true in the case of (au), just as it was in the case of (au) for Edinburgh children's speech. This is also the case for the use of glottal stops in Glasgow, though not in Edinburgh. It is interesting that Macaulay's ten year olds show the same score for this variable as the eight and ten year olds in my Edinburgh sample. The scores of the fifteen year olds and adults appear to indicate that clear age-grading emerges later, i.e. after the age of ten, for this particular variable. In the case of the variable (i), there is a difference between the younger informants and the adults, although there is no pattern of age-grading for the two young groups. The variables (a) and (au) are unclear. In this respect, the variable (a) seems to be similar in Glasgow and Edinburgh (for further discussion of this variable in Scots, cf. Romaine 1983b). The variable (au) on the other hand shows a difference between the younger age groups and adults, but not the clear progression with age which obtained in the Edinburgh sample.[8]

Other studies of phonological variables which are socially diagnostic have revealed similar findings. Biondi (1975), for example, found that the oldest children in his sample (8th graders, 12–13 year olds) showed the least tendency towards despirantization of fricatives. There was not, however, a clear decrease with age in the use of this socially stigmatized feature. The first graders (six year olds) showed a lesser degree of despirantization than the 4th graders (nine to ten year olds).

Aniansson (1981) found very clear evidence of age-grading in the use of the variable (t), which is a well-developed sociolinguistic marker in Swedish showing patterns of social class, stylistic and sex differentiation (cf. Nordberg 1972). Table 4.21 gives the scores for the retention of the standard form (i.e. those with /t/) for the different age groups in Aniansson's sample of seven to sixteen year olds with Nordberg's youngest groups (sixteen to twenty) in the Eskilstuna adult survey. The younger informants use the more standard forms with /t/ overall about 25 per cent of the time, while the 16–20 year olds use it with a frequency of only 10 per cent. The average for all the informants in Nordberg's survey was 55 per cent use of the standard form. Thus the younger informants on the whole appear to be further away from the norm of standard Swedish than the adult population, with young adults the closest to dialect norms.

Table 4.21 Age-grading in the use of /t/ in Eskilstuna, Sweden

	Age 7–9	Age 10–12	Age 13–16	Age 16–20
% of /t/	25.4	25.7	29.5	10.9 ⁻

Wolfram (1969) studied a number of phonological variables among black speakers in Detroit, which show patterns of age-grading. Some of his results are given in table 4.22. The realization of morpheme medial and final /θ/ as /f/, /t/ and ø shows a regular progression with age with the youngest speakers using the non-standard realizations most frequently. A similar pattern obtains in the case of consonant cluster simplification, although the effect is clear only in the phonetically conditioned environment (i.e. monomorphemic words). There is also a difference in the pattern of age-grading which emerges with respect to the two main non-standard realizations of syllable final /d/; the /t/ realizations show a regular pattern of age-grading with the youngest speakers using the most non-

Table 4.22 Some phonological variables in Detroit in relation to age

	Age 10–12	Age 14–17	Adults
Consonant cluster simplification			
Monomorphemic	45	43	38
Bimorphemic	13	15	14
/ø/	50	42	28
/d/:/t/ realizations	38	36	12
ø realizations	14	17	11
Post-vocalic /r/	46	55	44

standard realizations. The ø realizations, however, do not show a regular progression, although the younger speakers use them more frequently than older speakers. No clear pattern of age-grading arises for the absence of post-vocalic /r/. Wolfram (1969: 117–8) notes, however, that the majority of adults have migrated to Detroit from non-rhotic regions of the south, while all the younger informants were born in Detroit, where the white norm at any rate is rhotic. This does not really clarify why younger speakers, especially the teenage group, exceed the adults in their use of non-rhotic speech, unless it is a case of deliberate adoption of the norms of black speech in opposition to those of the surrounding white majority community (cf. section 6.3).

There is also evidence from the study of morphological and syntactic variables to support the claim that the use of socially stigmatized forms is at its maximum in a speaker's adolescent years. In their study of Appalachian English Wolfram and Christian (1976: 115) found that younger informants tended to use multiple negation with greater frequency than adults. Their results can be seen in table 4.23. An example of multiple negation is: *I don't like nothing*, in which a negative element is realized multiply in the sentence (further discussion of this variable appears in section 4.4).

Table 4.23 Percentage of multiple negation and use of *ain't* in relation to age in Appalachian English

	Multiple negation	ain't
Age 7–11	72.8	94.4
Age 12–14	62.5	100.0
Age 15–18	61.8	90.0
Age 20–40	68.2	100.0
Age 40+	53.1	88.9

Table 4.23 also shows their results for the use of *ain't*. In the case of this variable, however, there do not appear to be any significant differences in the age groups. For most speakers of Appalachian English, *ain't* is used almost categorically instead of standard English *isn't* and *aren't*. Feagin's (1979: 214) study of *ain't* in Anniston, Alabama revealed a widespread use of *ain't* amongst both young and older informants. Although she found major sex and social class differences, the differences between the younger and older informants were not great. Feagin's findings for multiple negation do not agree with Wolfram and Christian's. Both her groups of older informants (working-class urban and rural men and women) used multiple negation more frequently (80.3 per cent) than the teenage working-class informants (64 per cent). Wolfram's (1969: 163) study of black speakers in Detroit, however, revealed a pattern of age-grading

Table 4.24 Percentage of stigmatized grammatical
variables in relation to age among black speakers in
Detroit

	Age 10–12	Age 14–17	Adults
Multiple negation	49.1	40.9	25.1
Zero copula	35.6	27.8	18.9
Invariant BE	3.2	4.4	1.4
3rd person singular -Z	42	34	28
Possessive -Z	18.4	14.8	7.3
Plural -Z	7.8	3	3.7

more similar to the one found in Appalachian English; namely, that
younger speakers are likely to use socially stigmatized patterns of negation
more frequently than older speakers. The pattern of age-grading is regular
and clearer in the Detroit data as can be seen in table 4.24. Table 4.24 also
shows patterns of age-grading which Wolfram found for other grammatical
variables he examined. Examples of each of these variables with standard
English equivalents are as follows:

(1) Zero copula: John there in the house   (non-standard)
                   John is there in the house   (standard)
(2) Invariant BE: Sometime she be fighting in school   (non-standard)
                   Sometimes she fights in school   (standard)

This variable has received extensive discussion in the literature on black
English and creoles. Although it occurs in many of the same types of
syntactic environments as the inflected forms of the copula and auxiliary
BE in standard English (and in some cases preserves rough meaning
equivalence), it has some aspectual functions which are distinctly different.
It can be used in black English to mark the habitual and durative aspect (cf.
Wolfram 1969: 180–96).

(3) Third person singular –Z: He go   (non-standard)
                                He goes   (standard)

Wolfram's results can be compared with those of Trudgill for the suffixless
present tense in Norwich given in table 4.2, and with those of Cheshire in
table 4.32.

(4) Possessive –Z: John hat   (non-standard)
                     John's hat   (standard)
(5) Plural –Z: two black shoe   (non-standard)
                 two black shoes   (standard)

There is further discussion of the last three variables in relation to
children's written language in chapter 7 (cf. table 7.1).

The use of the zero copula, third person singular –Z and possessive –Z also show a progressive decrease in frequency with increasing age, like multiple negation. Other variables, however, like the use of plural –Z and invariant BE, show more general age-grading with younger speakers using the non-standard forms more frequently than adults, but no clear unidirectional decrease with increasing age.

So far we have looked at only one case where older speakers have much greater use of stigmatized variables than younger speakers, i.e. multiple negation in Anniston (Feagin 1979). There are other variables which show this pattern; in general, it appears to be an indication of the increasing influence of standardization on the younger population and the disappearance or restriction of some of the most local forms of regional speech to older, rural and uneducated speakers. This is the case with the use of perfective *done*, *a*-prefixing and possibly also double modals in Appalachian English (cf. Wolfram and Christian 1976: 89, 74). This pattern can be seen in table 4.25. The use of *a*-prefixing is even more recessive. The eight speakers with the highest frequency level are all over 50. Similarly, Feagin (1979: 103) found in her study of *a*-prefixing that the variable was very frequent only among working-class informants over 60. It did not occur at

Table 4.25 Percentage of perfective *done* and double modals (+ *liketa*, *supposeta*) in Appalachian English

	done	double modals(+ *liketa*, *supposeta*)
Age 8–11	6	8
Age 12–14	7	5
Age 15–18	5	11
Age 20–40	14	9
Age 40 +	33	23

Table 4.26 Percentage of *a*-prefixing, perfective *done* and double modals in relation to age, class and rural/urban residence in Anniston, Alabama

	a-*prefixing*	*done*	*double modals*
Urban upper-class			
teenagers	0	0	11
over 60	8	0	0
Urban working-class			
teenagers	27	47	13
over 60	74	62	42
Rural			
over 60	80	47	11

all in the speech of upper-class teenagers. The results for the use of perfective *done* also indicated a greater tendency for the variable to occur more frequently in the speech of older working-class informants over 60 than in teenagers. There were no occurrences in the upper-class informants of either age group. The pattern for the use of double modals in relation to age is not clear. Some of Feagin's results are given in table 4.26.

These are some examples of the variables, with standard English equivalents:

(6) Done: I done went yesterday   (non-standard)
            I went yesterday   (standard)
(7) *a*-prefixing: He's been a-workin' all day   (non-standard)
            He's been working all day   (standard)
(8) double modal: I might could do it   (non-standard)
            I might be able to do it   (standard)

In the case of the first two variables, *done* and *a*-prefixing, it has been suggested that aspectual differences not encoded in standard English may be realized in non-standard varieties which use these forms (cf. Wolfram and Christian 1976). There is further discussion of these variables in relation to patterns of sex differentiation in section 4.4.

4.4 *Sex differentiation*

The general lack of investigation of differences in male and female speech in western society has been seen by Hymes (1968: 132) as being tantamount to passive acceptance of the assumption that such fundamental properties of social life as sexual role and gender find no verbal expression in most of the world's languages. Before the availability of recent sociolinguistic surveys linguists seem to have been interested in distinguishable varieties of male and female speech only in a few exotic societies, and then only to the extent that a linguistic description could not have been carried out with reference to sex differences because verbal paradigms and canonical phonological shapes were affected. Haas (1964), for example, notes differences of this type in Koasati (an American Indian language) which are predictable by regular rules, e.g. men: /ka:s/ 'he is saying'; women: /kã:/. She points out that languages with major or minor differences between the speech of men and women are not as rare as might be supposed (cf. Bodine 1975 for a list of languages together with the types of differences to be found in them, and also Maccoby and Jacklin 1974).

Since very overt restructuring of grammatical paradigms does not occur in English as a marker of gender, it is perhaps not surprising that until recently there have been few studies that attempt to deal with the differences between male and female speech at any level more complex than vocabulary. And in fact most of the sex markers turn out to be phonological rather than grammatical in the largely English-based literature I will discuss here. With the advent of the women's liberation movement attention has been focused on 'women's language', in particular by Lakoff (1973), who argues that stereotypes about how women are expected to behave and their subordinate role in relation to men are reflected in women's use of language. The female register, according to Lakoff, consists of women's greater use than men of politeness formulas, hedges, and tag questions. The greater use of these by women is alleged to reflect the greater insecurity of women. There were also a number of vocabulary items which Lakoff believed women used more frequently than men, e.g. *divine, adorable, lovely*, etc. Lakoff relied mainly on her own intuitions and subsequent research has not substantiated her claims in all these areas (cf. in particular Brouwer et al. 1979).

Perhaps most importantly, however, other research has suggested that the features comprising women's language are not used solely by women, but more generally by those in subordinate positions and roles in society. This led to the view that women's language was the language of the 'powerless', thus supporting indirectly Lakoff's view that women are society's main examplars of the powerless role. Even more recent research indicates, however, that it is far from clear who speaks this language variety and there are many contradictory findings in the literature (cf. Rubin and Nelson, 1984, for some recent findings, and Smith 1979 for a review of the literature on sex markers). It is not clear in some of the studies whether the sex of the speaker is truly an independent variable, and whether the results reflect instead the effects of social status and situation and other psychological variables such as anxiety. The fact that some of the stigmatized style features occur in the speech of all members in the community in some contexts illustrates the complex nature of style. Whether sex markers exist is a separate question from the problem of stereotyping and its consequences (cf. Smith 1979 on the distinction between marker and stereotype). The fact that people apparently do react negatively to certain features and believe that women (or other groups) use them more so than others has nevertheless been well established.

The most detailed evidence of sex differences in western societies exists at the phonological level, and most of it comes from quantitative sociolinguistic studies of urban societies (and the latter largely focused on varieties of urban American English – cf. Levine and Crockett 1967, Shuy et al. 1968, Wolfram 1969 and Labov 1966). The study by Fischer (1958) of schoolchildren in a semi-rural New England village (mentioned earlier) showed that variation in the use (ing) was tied to sex (as well as social background context and various personality factors). We may summarize the basic findings of the research tradition by saying that women consistently produce forms which are nearer to the prestige norm more frequently than men. Trudgill (1974a) and Macaulay (1977) present data for Norwich and Glasgow speech respectively, which show that this pattern is not a linguistic idiosyncracy of the American social structure. Evidence from Nordberg's survey (1971, 1975) of Eskilstuna speech has confirmed the existence of the same trend in Sweden. Nordberg (1975: 596) in fact concludes that this pattern of sex differentiation seems to be so general in western societies today that one could look at women's speech to determine which forms carry prestige and at men's to see which are stigmatized in the community. I will look at the proposed explanations for this correlation after I have considered some of the evidence from sociolinguistic studies of children's speech.

The main question which will concern us here is at what age and in what way do various patterns of sex differentiation found in the adult population develop in children? How are sex-typed language differences learned? Lakoff (1973: 47) suggests that both boys and girls first learn 'women's language' from mothers and other female figures, e.g. nursery and primary school teachers who are usually female. As girls grow older they retain this way of talking, but boys begin to shift to male forms, largely under the influence of peer pressure (cf., however, Haas 1979 for some experimental data).

In my study of Edinburgh schoolchildren, I found some evidence for sex differentiation in the use of certain variables by children as young as six years old. Although all of the phonological variables I examined (with the exception of (ing)) showed a trend towards sex differentiation, the results are not statistically significant. Some of these are illustrated in table 4.27. We can however get some idea of the long-term significance of this pattern by comparing them with some of Macaulay's (1977) results from the adult population of Glasgow[9] (see table 4.28). To discuss first the variables which both studies have in common, namely, (gs), (au), (i) and (a), we can see that the frequency with which these features occur depends on the sex

Table 4.27 Variables correlated with sex of the speaker in Edinburgh school-children

	Males	Females
(gs)	91	63
(i)	218	187
(au)	31	6
(th)	36	8
(neg)	41	23
(a)	248	240

Table 4.28 Variation
correlated with sex of the
speaker in Glasgow

	Males	Females
(gs)	70	61
(i)	273	242
(au)	299	283
(u)	262	249
(a)	254	232

of the speaker. It is generally true for both these Edinburgh schoolchildren and Glasgow adults that males on the whole use more non-standard forms than females. The fact that Macaulay and I used somewhat different scoring procedures for these variables does not obscure this basic pattern, although different variables correlate with sex of the speaker to different degrees. For example, the use of glottal stops appears to be more of a sex marker for younger than older speakers, but less significant in the case of (a). In Macaulay's study (a) seems to be more strongly correlated with sex than for the younger speakers.

Table 4.29 Variation correlated with age and sex of the speaker in Glasgow

	Age 10		Age 15	
	Males	Females	Males	Females
(gs)	77	78	74	61
(i)	272	256	279	245
(au)	297	294	312	297
(u)	266	270	272	248
(a)	202	204	226	205

Macaulay also included in his study a sample of ten- and fifteen-year-old school pupils with the results shown in table 4.29. Apart from three deviations, there is a regular pattern of sex differentiation with males scoring higher than females. The exceptions occur in the ten year olds' scores for the variables (gs), (u) and (a), but the differences between the sexes is minimal for these variables in any case and not strong enough to support substantive claims. The 15 year olds show the regular patterns of sex differentiation found in the adult population. These results do not take into account social class differences. The subgroup which is most comparable to my sample of Edinburgh speakers are Macaulay's ten-year-old males and females of Class III. The scores are given in table 4.30. Again, taking into account the differences in Macaulay's and my scoring procedures, the results are strikingly similar. With the exception of Macaulay's results for (a), both sets of variables are clearly differentiated according to sex in Glasgow and Edinburgh ten year olds.

Table 4.30 Sex differentiation in Class III ten year olds in Glasgow and ten-year-old Edinburgh children

	Glasgow		Edinburgh	
	Males	Females	Males	Females
(gs)	92	79	84	78
(i)	302	280	210	177
(au)	359	326	11	2
(u)	305	303	–	–
(a)	238	233	246	224

Biondi's (1975) study of Italian–American children in Boston is one of the few sociolinguistic studies devoted entirely to examining the development of sociolinguistic patterns in schoolchildren following the Labovian methodology. He studied a number of phonological variables, which to differing degrees showed correlations with age, sex, style and ethnicity. Table 4.31 shows a trend of sex differentiation for two of his phonological variables. In both cases the boys use a greater number of non-standard forms than the girls. Although Biondi did not compare his results for the schoolchildren with adult speech, it is clear from other studies of American English that the despirantization of (th) and (dh) (e.g. /θɪn/ → /tɪn/, /ðɛn/ → /dɛn/) and the simplification of the consonant clusters (e.g. /nɛst/ → /nɛs/) are phonological processes which occur more frequently in working- than middle-class speech (cf. Labov 1966: 365f. on (th) (dh) and Wolfram 1969 on consonant cluster simplification).

Although there are a number of other major sociolinguistic surveys which contained members of the population under 20, it is often difficult to

Table 4.31 Percentage of non-standard forms: patterns of sex differentiation among Italian–American schoolchildren

	Males	Females
Variable (th)/(dh)	87.3	79.1
Word final consonant cluster simplification	44.2	36.6

find analyses of the data presented in a format which makes the isolation of patterns of sex differentiation possible for the younger informants. For example, in Labov's study (1966) the basic sample of New Yorkers included only adults over 20, although by interviewing some of the children of his adult informants Labov was able to form some impressions of the relationship between the variables and age-grading. However, since the number of children included is so small, it is impossible to separate the dimension of age from sex. The same is true for Wolfram's (1969) study of Detroit, which includes samples from two younger age groups (10–12, 14–17). There are two males and two females in each age group from four social classes. When patterns of sex differentiation are discussed, all the males and females of each social class have been grouped together. In his survey of Norwich, although Trudgill (1974a) looked at the patterns of sex differentiation in the adult population, he does not compare these with his findings from the subsample of schoolchildren. Nevertheless, it is clear from the Scottish evidence that sex differentiation of socially diagnostic variables in the adult community can emerge in the speech of speakers ten years old and younger. Before considering the reasons for this finding and discussing the correlation between age and sex differentiation, I want to examine some patterns of sex differentiation in the area of syntax and morphology.

Cheshire's study of the use of non-standard grammatical features in the speech of adolescents in Reading provides one of the most recent and thorough treatments of this subject. As indicated earlier in my discussion of methodology. Cheshire observed two groups of girls (ranging in age from nine to thirteen) and a group of boys (ranging in age from eleven to seventeen). The members of the peer groups were a homogeneous social group in that they were of similar ages and had similar social and regional backgrounds. Cheshire found (1982a: 86–7) that with the exception of two variables (i.e. the use of the non-standard past form *done* and the non-standard present tense form *do*), the girls used the non-standard forms less often than boys. Her results are given in table 4.32. The figures represent the percentage of non-standard variants used. Although the male/female differences are not statistically significant across all the variables, there is some support for the significance of *do*, *was*, *see*, *come*, *ain't*, negative concord, relative pronoun and demonstrative adjective.

The first four variables have to do with non-standard verb forms for the present tense of verbs including DO and HAVE. In standard English present tense verb forms require the suffix -s with third person singular subjects only, e.g. *he walks*, but in many varieties of non-standard English, the suffix also occurs with other subjects, e.g. *I walks*. The non-standard suffix can occur with most verbs, including irregular HAVE and DO.[10] However, it never occurs when HAVE and DO are auxiliaries, but only when they are used as main verbs as in the examples:

Table 4.32 Some non-standard features in the speech of Reading male and female peer groups

	Males	Females
Present tense -*s* (regular verbs)	53.16	52.04
Present tense *has*	54.76	51.61
Present tense *does* (full verb)	71.43	50.00
Present tense 3rd singular *do* (auxiliary)	57.69	78.95
Past tense *was*	88.15	73.58
Past tense *were*	5.36	2.64
Past tense *see*	85.71	44.44
Past tense *come*	100.00	75.33
Past tense *done*	100.00	100.00
ain't = auxiliary HAVE	92.00	64.58
ain't = copula BE	85.83	61.18
ain't = auxiliary BE	74.19	42.11
Negative concord	88.33	51.85
never	46.84	40.00
Relative pronoun	36.36	14.58
Demonstrative adjective	92.31	33.33

(9) We has a muck around in there (Cheshire 1982a: 32)
(10) That's what I does anyway (Cheshire 1982a: 34)

Cheshire says (1982a: 34) that the difference between the use of HAVE as an auxiliary and a main verb represents the state of affairs at an earlier stage in the development of this variety of English.

The situation with respect to the verb DO is more complex since there are three non-standard verb forms which occur variably along with the standard English form. There is a non-standard suffixed form (analogous to the non-standard forms of HAVE and regular verbs), which occurs with non-third person singular subjects, as we have seen in the example above. Secondly, there is a non-suffixed form, which occurs with third person singular subjects, e.g. *she do*. And thirdly, there is a form *dos* (/du:z/), which can occur with all subjects, though mostly with third person singular subjects, e.g. *we does*. Cheshire (1982a: 36) observes that the occurrence of the different forms of the verb DO is dependent on different factors in Reading English from those in standard English, where it depends only on the subject of the verb. In Reading it also depends on the syntactic function of the verb; namely, whether it is a full verb or an auxiliary. The present tense forms of DO and HAVE are marked differently according to syntactic function as they were earlier in the history of English. This is a case then where non-standard English makes a distinction which has since been lost in standard English.

The next five variables have to do with the variability in the formation of past tense forms of verbs. In Reading English *was* is used with first and third person singular subjects and *were* elsewhere. It is interesting that this non-standard variety of English shows alternation (though differently distributed) between two forms, just as standard English does. Other varieties of English have regularized the paradigm, though in different ways. In Bradford, for example, the form *were* can occur with all persons both singular and plural (cf. Hughes and Trudgill 1979: 60), while in other varieties (e.g. the Appalachian English described by Wolfram and Christian 1976), the form *was* is used throughout the paradigm.[11] In his study of the absence of /s/ suffixes in third person singular present tense forms among Boston schoolchildren, Biondi (1975: 97) also found that males used suffixless forms more frequently than females (i.e. M = 24.6, F = 17). The reduction of the verbal paradigm of irregular verbs is a well-known feature of many non-standard varieties of English. Where standard English has a three-way distribution among stem, past tense form and past participle, as in *see, saw, seen*, non-standard English sometimes has only two (i.e. *see, seen*). In addition, there are other cases where verbs which form their past tense by internal vowel change in standard English have regular t/d endings in non-standard varieties, e.g. *fighted/fought*. In cases where standard English has only a two-way distinction, (e.g. *run, ran, run*), non-standard English has only one form, e.g. *run*.

There are still other variants like *driv* (cf. *driven*) cited by Cheshire (1982a: 48) and *tooken* (cf. *taken*) in Edinburgh children.[12] In some cases, then, the productive suffix t/d is regularized or extended to irregular verbs; in others, the past tense form is used as a past participle, while in others a participle is used as the past. Among the Edinburgh schoolchildren I studied there is also a pattern of sex differentiation in the use of non-standard past tense forms with boys using more than girls.

In her study of Alabama English Feagin (1979) found little evidence of patterns of sex differentiation among her younger and older informants in the use of irregular past tense forms of the verbs. This can be seen in table 4.33, which shows the percentage of non-standard forms of the preterite and past participle used by teenage boys and girls. The participal forms as a group appear to have a greater degree of non-standard usage than the preterites and there is some sex differentiation in the use of non-standard

Table 4.33 Non-standard preterite and past participles for irregular finite verbs for teenagers in Anniston, Alabama

	Males	Females
Preterite	22	12.2
Past participle	34	32.5

between males and females. On the whole Feagin (1979: 89) concludes that age and sex do not have a significant effect on the use of non-standard irregular verbs.

The next five variables in Cheshire's study have to do with negation in non-standard English. Of these the first three involve the present tense negative forms of the auxiliaries BE and HAVE and the copula BE. Cheshire (1982a: 50) gives the following examples:

(11) Aux. BE + not: How come that ain't working?
(12) Cop. BE + not: You ain't no boss
(13) Aux. HAVE + not: You ain't been round here

In each case the girls use *ain't* less often than boys.[13]

These non-standard uses of negation can be found among Edinburgh schoolchildren as well, although this area of the grammar is complicated by the existence of Scots forms of the negative *not*, which is attached directly to the verb.[14] Phonetically the negative is realized as /ni, ne, nʌ/, usually represented orthographically by *nae, na* or *ny*. Not all verbs can be negated in this way, however. Among Edinburgh schoolchildren only the forms *do, does, did, is, are, were, can, could, have, has, had, would, should* can take the Scots form of the negative. According to Wilson (1926: 80), however, the class of verbs was formerly more extensive and included *must, ken, love, need* and *care*. Here are some examples from the Edinburgh children (cf. also Millar and Brown 1979, Brown and Miller 1975, and Brown and Millar 1980):

(14) That wasnae a goal
(15) They didnae ken that they had landed
(16) I cannae see the person
(17) My house isnae far away

The use of the Scots negative shows sex differentiation, as we have already seen earlier in the chapter, with boys using more of the Scots form than the girls (M = 41, F = 23).

The feature negative concord (also referred to as a multiple negation) is also a widespread syntactic variable in many varieties of non-standard English. Labov (1972b) has given the most extensive analysis of this variable in BEV.[15] Negative concord refers to the realization of a negative element at two or more places in the sentence, e.g. *I don't want nothing*. Its use in non-standard English serves an emphatic stylistic function. The negative can apparently be attracted to any number of indeterminates in the sentence, as indicated by Labov's (1972b: 773) by now famous example:

(18) It ain't no cat can't get in no coop
　　　There is no cat which can get into any coop

The variable *never* in Reading non-standard English refers to the use of *never* as a negative preterite verb with the meaning 'not on one specific occasion', where standard English uses it with the meaning 'not on any occasion', e.g. *I never went to school today*. This feature is common to a number of non-standard varieties of British (though apparently not American) English and to many English-based creoles, such as Hawaiian English creole (cf. Labov 1972b and Cheshire, forthcoming, for a more complete treatment of this variable).

The variable relative pronoun refers to the use of *who, whom, which, that* and zero to introduce relative clauses. The system for standard English is described in Quirk et al. (1972) and Quirk (1957). In many non-standard varieties of English *what* may be used as a relative marker, as in the following examples from Edinburgh schoolchildren:

(19) The new record what they've got out
(20) The boy what was staying with us

As can be seen from these examples, *what* can be used to introduce a relative clause when the antecedent is non-personal or personal, unlike standard English, which would require the use of *who* with personal antecedents. Cheshire (1982a: 72–3) found this to be the case in Reading, although overall the use of the standard English forms predominates. As I have shown, in Edinburgh (and more generally in Scottish) English, there is a tendency to avoid the use of WH relatives and to use *that* and zero more frequently. (Further details can be found in Romaine 1980b[16] and in Brown, forthcoming.) The use of zero relatives in subject position is also more widespread in non-standard English, as in the following example from an Edinburgh schoolboy.[17] (Further discussion of relative clauses may be found in chapter 3.)

(21) There was a lot of people (ø) died

The variable demonstrative adjective in Cheshire's study refers to the use of *them* as the plural deictic marker of distant reference, where standard English would have *those*. This feature is widespread in many non-standard varities of British and American English (cf. Wolfram and Fasold 1074: 175). It is used by Scots-speaking children, although it fits into a different system of deixis; as can be seen in table 4.34. Scots differs from other non-standard varieties and standard English in using *they* as a marker of distant plural reference and *thon* as a marker of more distant reference. Thus Scots has a potential three-way distinction in its deictic system unlike most varieties of English. It has been suggested that *thon* derives from *that* + *yon*.[18] The following examples are taken from Edinburgh schoolchildren:

(22) They thought they were *they* witches
(23) I get *they* wee spiders

Table 4.34 Demonstratives in standard English and Scottish English

	Standard English		Scottish English	
	sing.	plur.	sing.	plur.
'near' reference	this	these	this	they
'distant' reference	that	those	that	they
'more distant' reference	–	–	thon	thon

(24) Do you see *thon* man?

(25) I've not got *they* ones

Wolfram and Christian (1976) found evidence of sex differentiation for some grammatical variables among younger speakers of Appalachian English, although in general sex was less significant than other social dimensions in their study. Some of these have been mentioned briefly already in connection with patterns of age-grading in section 3.3. One of the variables they studied was the use of *done* as a perfective aspect marker, as in the example below (Wolfram and Christian 1976: 85):

(26) I done forgot when it opened

Like the use of non-standard multiple negation, it has an emphatic stylistic function and it is a stigmatized feature. Wolfram and Christian found (1976: 89) that males in their sample of younger speakrs (eight to thirteen year olds) were more likely to use perfective *done* than females (M = 12, F = 6: the numbers here indicate number of occurrences and not percentages). Feagin (1979: 124) also found a pattern of sex differentiation for the use of the perfective *done*. There were no instances of the variable at all for upper-class informants, either teenagers or adults, but among the working class there is a clear pattern of sex differentiation for young and older informants. Teenage girls score 5 and boys 10 (number of occurrences).

Wolfram and Christian (1976: 93–4) also found evidence of sex differentiation in the use of double modals, e.g. *might could, useto could*, etc. Generally speaking, in standard English there is a restriction on the co-occurrence of two modals.[19] They give the following example (1976: 90)

(27) He musta didn't hear me

Among the younger speakers female used more double modals and *liketa, supposeta* than males (M =8, F = 16: the numbers here indicate number of occurrences and not percentages). This is the second case we have looked at which shows females using more frequently than males a feature of local dialect. (Recall Cheshire's results for the present tense of DO in table 4.32.) It is not clear, however, whether there is any particular social stigma or prestige attached to the use of these double modals. It is just a syntactic idiosyncrasy of some varieties of southern American and regional varieties of British English (cf. also Butters 1973).[20] Feagin (1979: 154–5), for example, finds that most of the double modals are distributed throughout the social class structure, e.g. *might could* and *useta could*. Overall there were only 16 occurrences in her sample and 12 of these were used by women. This supports Wolfram and Christian's (1976) finding. Feagin (1979: 158) concludes that the use of double modals has no social evaluation. Thus it is unlike most of the other variables we have looked at so far which do show patterns of sex differentiation: namely, they have all been cases where the variants in question reflected opposing norms of social prestige. I will look at features which show sex differentiation, but are not markers of social status in chapter 6.

All the variables we have discussed so far have been taken from sociolinguistic research on varieties of English. It is worth noting that similar patterns of sex differentiation have been observed elsewhere for similar types of variables. In a study of Swedish schoolchildren Hallencreutz (1979) found that spoken language forms which have been making headway into standard written Swedish (e.g. *mej* instead of *mig* – 'me', *nån* instead of *någon* – 'nothing') are used more often in the essays written by boys than girls. Hallencreutz concentrated in particular on variation in the use of *de*, *dem* and *dom* to see if there was evidence that pupils were familiar with the standard Swedish norms of use. The variable has to do with the use of *dom* (a pronunciation form), where standard Swedish should have *de* (e.g. the definite article, and personal pronoun) or *dom* (e.g. a demonstrative pronoun or objective form of the personal pronoun). She found that *dom* was the most frequently used written form in the essays (i.e. 57.5 per cent), as in the following examples (1979: 11):

(28)   dom åker moped   They are riding a moped
    Standard Swedish: de åker moped
(29)   dom flesta   the most
    Standard Swedish: de flesta

Hallencreutz looked at two classes of pupils (the 7th and 9th year) and found sex differentiation in both with girls in each group closer to the norms of the written language than the boys. This was especially true for the older age group. Half of the essays written by ninth-year class which show the correct use of *de/dem* were written by girls. Of those who used *dom* 57 per cent were boys and 43 per cent were girls.

This particular feature also shows a social class stratification among both schoolchildren and the adult population (cf. Thelander 1982 for a discussion of the variable in regional and standard Swedish). Most of the children who use *dom* are in the lowest social class gorup, while the highest social group has the most *de/dem* users. This can be seen in table 4.35

Table 4.35 Use of de/dem/dom and social
class in Sweden

	Social class		
	I	II	III
% users of de/dom	60	36	20
% users of dom	40	64	80

(Hallencreutz 1979: 16). These results were based on a free writing task
which the children were asked to undertake after having seen a stimulus
picture. Hallencreutz also administered a forced choice test in which the
children had to fill in the blanks with either de or dom. In general the older
children did better (i.e. had scores closer to the norms of the standard
written language) and there were no apparent sex differences. This result is
not surprising since the only way to learn the distinction between de/dem is
through exposure to the education system. The variable is an interesting
one in the Swedish context, however, since it is generally the case that the
norms of the written language are exerting an important influence on the
norms of the spoken language. Spoken language forms are not making an
inroad into the written language. In both types of change, however, the
result is the same; namely, a narrowing of the differences between speech
and writing.

4.5 Evaluation

Thus far we have looked only at the productive aspect of sociolinguistic
competence, and we have found evidence that consistent control over the
use of certain linguistic variables which have social significance in adult
communities is mastered by many schoolchildren in the early (but more so
in the later) years of primary school. I will now turn to the evaluative
dimension of receptive competence and address the question of the extent
to which young children are aware of the social significance of various
kinds of speech and whether they share the normative evaluative reactions
of the adult community to linguistic variables.

First, let us summarize some of the findings of urban sociolinguists on
the question of attitudes and evaluative reactions to speech. Perhaps one of
the more seemingly paradoxical conclusions to emerge from research into
the attitudes of speakers towards non-standard speech is that those who
themselves use the most socially stigmatized forms of speech are the most
sensitive to these features in the speech of others and are quick to condemn
them for their use (Labov 1966: 441). However, despite the fact that

people may condemn others' (and indeed their own) speech they do not want to (or do not) change the way they speak themselves. In other words, there appear to be strong social pressures which work to maintain vernacular speech (cf. Milroy and Margrain 1980). On the basis of subjective reaction tests in which informants were asked to rate a series of speakers whose speech differed in terms of certain variables, and self-evaluation tests where informants were asked to report their own usage of the variables, Labov (1966) found that there was a striking asymmetry between production and perception. For various reasons New Yorkers were inaccurate judges of their own usage and tended to over-report their use of prestige variants. In other words, they report themselves as using the standard forms presumably because they would like to be perceived as belonging to the social group who speak in this way, i.e. the middle class. When asked about their attitudes towards New York City speech most people were very critical of it and had negative reactions; thus Labov concluded that New York City was a 'sink of negative prestige'. At the same time however, he remarks (1966: 108) that 'we must assume that people in New York want to talk the way they do.'

The acceptance of this conclusion as a basic sociolinguistic principle rests on the assumption that each variety has its own 'prestige' and is an important factor in creating and maintaining one's social identity. There is support for this principle from various sources. For example, Trudgill (1972) has produced evidence that working-class speech is, for male speakers at least, a highly valued attribute. His evidence comes from actual statements by informants who had initially said that they did not speak properly but would like to do so. When pressed on the subject, however, they admitted that they would probably not really like to do so because they would likely be considered foolish, arrogant or disloyal by their friends and family. Trudgill also obtained rather different results for Norwich speech in the self-evaluation test from those obtained by Labov for New York City. In the scores for under- and over-reporting of usage of particular forms Trudgill noticed the emergence of the hidden values that underlay patterns of sex differentiation. He found that males were notably more acccurate in reporting their linguistic behaviour than females. In each of the Norwich variables tested, Trudgill obtained the result that there were more speakers who claimed to use a less prestigious form than they actually did than there were males who over-reported. In fact, Trudgill noticed that Norwich informants had a tendency to under-report more than New York City informants; but, more importantly, male informants in Norwich were much more likely to under-report and female informants to over-report their linguistic usage.

From this Trudgill has concluded that male Norwich speakers are, at least at a subconscious level, very favourably disposed towards the non-standard speech forms. This observation was forcefully demonstrated by the fact that in one case as many as 54 per cent claimed to use stigmatized forms even when they did not actually do so. If we accept Labov's and Trudgill's conclusion that informants perceive their own speech in terms of the norms they aim at rather than the sounds they really use, then the norm at which a large number of Norwich males are aiming is non-standard speech. Moreover, recognition of this covert prestige is something common to a majority of males regardless of which social class they belong to.

It is not exactly clear why Trudgill obtained this result in Norwich and Labov did not in New York City. Trudgill has advanced the idea that working-class speakers in Britain have not accepted middle-class values so readily or as completely as their American working-class counterparts nor have they been 'embourgeoised' to the same extent. Trudgill cites Mayer's (1955: 67) belief that 'the conspicuous lack of corporate or militant class consciousness (in America) is one of the most important contrasts between American and European systems of stratification.' It should not of course be surprising that fundamentally different modes of organization in social systems should be reflected in different principles governing the norms of speech and evaluation in various speech communities (cf. Romaine 1982b for further discussion of the sociolinguistic differences between American and European speech communities).

Further support for recognizing the importance of the role that speech plays in one's social identity comes from Le Page's (1978) view of sociolinguistic processes, in particular the notion that every utterance of the individual is 'an act of identity, revealing the supposed properties of the various model groups with which the speaker wishes to associate himself or from which he wishes to distinguish himself'. I will discuss the factor of identity in connection with the influence of peer groups in language in section 6.3.

As Trudgill's work demonstrates, it can be very difficult sometimes to elicit good information concerning attitudes. Although informants have very strong opinions about language and are able to detect the presence/ absence of certain socially diagnostic features and evaluate these in social terms with great regularity, the reactions to many linguistic variables are inarticulate responses below the level of conscious awareness. Perceptions of language are mediated through a stereotyped view of a group which is believed to speak in a given way. Most informants if pressed as to which particular features they find offensive are able to mention only a few stigmatized and much-talked-about features, such as glottal stops, to take a Scottish example. These stereotypes have risen to the level of conscious awareness and become part of the accepted folklore about language. A basic problem in investigating linguistic attitudes is that most informants do not have a vocabulary of socially and linguistically meaningful precise terms with which they can evaluate speech. This is why Labov and others have gone to great lengths to devise experimental situations in which to elicit these reactions. Let us turn now to look at some of the attitudes which children express about language, which indicate an awareness of its social significance. We will also look at the findings of some experiments in which children's reactions to various kinds of speech have been elicited.

I will begin by discussing some findings of my own and those of Reid (1976) which show that Edinburgh schoolchildren have an awareness of the sociolinguistic significance of speech. The following extract from an interview with a ten-year-old schoolgirl is revealing (Romaine 1975: 94–5):[21]

Interviewer: Does your Mum ever tell you to speak polite?
Informant: If (i-3) there's somebody polite (gs-1) in. Like see, some
              people come in (i-3). There's new people in the stair we've
              moved up to (tae) and they come in and I'm always saying
              (ing-1) 'down' (au-1) Shep, cause it's my wee dog, so I say
              'down' (au-1). My mum says: 'That's not what (gs-1) you
              say'. She says, 'It's sit down (au-0)' Ken, cause she doesn't
              like me speaking (ing-1) rough.
Interviewer: Why do you think she doesn't like it?
Informant: Well, if I speak rough she doesn't like it when other people
              are in because they think that we're rough tatties (gs-1) in the
              stair.
Interviewer: Does your mum ever speak polite?
Informant: She doesnae really speak polite, but she corrects all her
              words.
Interviewer: How about your teachers, do they ever say anything to you
              about the way you speak?
Informant: I've never actually said 'down' (au-1) to the teacher.

It is clear from this passage that this child knows quite a bit of the social significance of speech, which she is able to evaluate in terms of the dimensions 'polite' and 'rough', which are widely used in the community. Moreover, she is aware that the way one speaks is an important part of the impression one conveys to others and that others make judgements about social character on the basis of speech. She has learned also that there are at least two contexts for 'polite' speech, i.e. in front of strangers and to the teacher in the classroom. However, if we examine the values of the variables, she is certainly not speaking in her most formal or polite style to me, even though I was a stranger and outsider. Not only does this child know that there is a way of speaking politely, but she can also identify the form /dun/ – 'down' as an inappropriate one for contexts requiring polite speech. This is the form she would most likely use consistently among family members at home and, as she says, when addressing her dog, or when 'speaking rough'. When used in the home and with in-group members 'speaking rough' is the normal unmarked mode of behaviour, similar in social significance to the use of familiar vs. polite forms of address in a language like French, where one marks the dimension of intimacy/solidarity by using *tu* rather than *vous*. Outside these domains however 'speaking rough' is negatively evaluated.[22]

I asked children if they could name some of the things which they had been corrected for and what things they wouldn't say when speaking polite (Romaine 1975: 97–8). One child said, 'Well, "ay" instead of "yes", "dinnae" instead of "don't", and "cannae" instead of "can't", and things like that'. A study done by Rosenthal (1973) in the United States supported the view that even many pre-school children have remarkably consistent notions of what is 'correct' and 'incorrect' in language. It is likely though that this awareness extends only to certain features, and children who are repeatedly corrected for the use of some feature may be aware only of the fact that there are 'two ways of saying something' and not be able to say which is 'right' or 'wrong'. One boy whom I interviewed told the following story about being corrected by his neighbours (Romaine 1975: 98):

My next door neighbours [correct me], cause see they've got a boy four called Andrew and they don't want him to learn the bad habits and they're always checking me for saying it cause I usually go there for my dinner in the holidays and they're always correcting me for that sort of thing. When I say – I don't know if it's right or wrong – I say like, if I done something today, they go: you *did* and they do it like that all the time.

When I asked if he really knew which one was right, he replied 'I just take pot luck.' Apparently the boy does take 'pot luck' in choosing between the two forms. Earlier in relating a television programme he saw, he says, 'The Mexican hired seven men to get rid of an army of bandits and they *did* – *done* it in the end – *done* it in the end.' His awareness of variation between *did* and *done* leads him to question his own choice and to 'hypercorrect' it, but he chooses the wrong form. Cheshire (1982a: 47) reports a similar case from a Reading youth who said, 'How much money have you hold, held, holded in your hand?'

These extracts from the interviews also provide insight into the process by which children learn the appropriate contexts for dialect and polite speech. Mothers and school teachers clearly play a large role in this aspect of socialization; a number of children mentioned being corrected by mothers and teachers.[23] Sandred (1983) reports a case where a woman vividly recalled being corrected as a child by her mother for using the word *ken*: her mother slapped her in the face so hard, she lost a tooth as a result.

This is perhaps an extreme example of the pressure even young children can be put under to conform to the overt prestige norms.

Reid's (1976) study of 11-year-old Edinburgh schoolboys also indicated the development of understanding of the social significance of variation in English. Reid asked the boys about their attitudes towards national and local variation as well as style shifting. The children noted differences between the speech of England (often referred to as 'posh') and Scotland but preferred Scots speech; they did not appear to recognize a distinctly Edinburgh accent. Most reported that they were quite happy with the way they spoke themselves. The boys were less clear, however, on the subject of major influences in their speech; there was little support for the notion that school played an important part. One boy however remarked on the contradiction in attitude towards the use of Scots in school (Reid 1976: 72): 'when it comes to Burns time you're told to speak like that when [i.e. in Scots] . . . when you're saying the poem . . . but I don't really see how you can speak like that then and then all the rest of the year speak differently.'

It is interesting that one of the influences noted by some of the children I spoke with came from older relatives, e.g. grandmothers. One boy for example commented that he had learned certain dialect words and expressions from older people. He said, 'It's just the way Scottish people talk, just learn them off old folk. I just learn them. My big sister speaks like that – to me anyway' (Romaine 1975: 93–4). A similarly revealing instance of the influence of older relatives on children's speech is cited in Saunders (1982: 99). In the following extract, Thomas, age six, is talking to a great-uncle, Georgie, and switches from standard English *those* to *them*, the form used by the uncle.

Georgie: By bloody oath, you're growin'.
Thomas: Georgie, in Sydney we went to this beach and saw these hang-gliders fly off these bloody cliffs.
Georgie: Yeah?
Thomas: Yeah. Remember you said we could go up to Scamander and practise flying on the sandhills?
Georgie: On them beaches, yeah, when we get up on them sandhills.
Thomas: Yeah, those beaches.
Georgie: We'll have bloody fun then.
Thomas: Yeah, it's bloody good at those beaches – them beaches.

Language attitudes in Scotland are very complex, as one might expect, given the long and intricate relationship between varieties of Scots and those of English, with which they have been in contact since the twelfth century. A further relevant factor is the changing status of Scots in relation to English. As a regional variety of English which has lost its former autonomy, it is now heteronymous (i.e. has a dependent relationship) with respect to standard English, yet it probably has more prestige than other regional accents of Britain (cf. the discussion of the terms *heteronomy* and *autonomy* in Chambers and Trudgill 1980: chapter 1). Today in Scotland it is easy to elicit conflicting attitudes towards urban and rural Scots. The reaction to rural speech is likely to be positive, and the middle-class reaction is often a slightly patronizing approval of 'good old Scots speech'. Working-class speech on the other hand, typical of the industrial areas of central Scotland, is no less Scots in that it shares many features in common not only with the rural dialects but also with Scottish Standard English, arouses great disapproval and is branded as 'slovenly and degenerate' speech (cf. Macaulay 1975 for a discussion of language attitudes in Glasgow, and Romaine and Dorian 1981 for a discussion of language attitudes in Scotland). Sandred's (1983) study of attitudes and social class in Edinburgh indicates that there are well-established folk notions among the middle class as to what constitutes acceptable Scottishness in speech. Some features which informants condemn as 'bad Scots' are really more generally features of non-standard English, e.g. *I seen* instead of *I have seen*.

Trudgill (1974b: 20) has commented on the tendency for people to rate the accents of urban areas much less favourably than those of rural parts of Britain. He says that it reflects the way in which rural and urban life are evaluated. Work done by Giles and his colleagues (see e.g. Giles 1970) has established that speakers with accents of industrial areas like Glasgow, Birmingham and Liverpool are consistently ranked unfavourably on a number of dimensions, e.g. personality characteristics, education, socio-economic success, etc. RP accented speech on the other hand has high prestige for many people in Britain. Cullum (1981) elicited reactions to Birmingham speech from two groups of 12–14-year-old girls and found that the girls did not have a favourable attitude towards it. Cullum's findings confirm those of an earlier study done by Wilkinson (1965) on the attitudes of secondary school children in Birmingham. He found that the prestige of RP was so high that many people imagined they spoke RP and even when they heard themselves on tape were unwilling to admit that they deviated much from a perceived RP prestige norm. Cullum also found that some of her girls did not think they had a Birmingham accent.

Despite the overriding influence of RP in Britain as an overt prestige accent, some groups of speakers do display 'accent loyalty'. In other words, some people express linguistic solidarity (rather than insecurity): in spite of any socioeconomic superiority of the dominant group or implied denigration of the subordinate group a speaker displays loyalty by affirming the linguistic norms of the community in which he lives. In subjective reaction and matched guise tests[24] of the type used by Giles and others, one can detect accent loyalty when there is a split between the evaluation of characteristics concerning personality and status. Cheyne

(1970) found, for example, that Scottish subjects rated their own group as more generous, friendly, humorous and likeable than English speakers, even though the latter were rated higher in terms of status, income, etc. Milroy and McClenaghan (1977) report a similar result in a study of evaluations of Belfast speech. Giles (1970) found that social class differences were an important correlate of accent loyalty, thus adding further support to Trudgill's (1972) notion of 'covert prestige'. He found that working-class 12-year-old males in rural and industrial areas rated a significant number of 'prestige' accents lower than their middle-class peers in terms of their aesthetic value. On the whole the working-class boys displayed greater accent loyalty than the middle class.

The children in Reid's and Cullum's study were well aware of the pressures to conform to group ways of speaking, as well as of the necessity of adapting one's speech to situations and the differences between male and female speech. One of Reid's (1976: 72) informants commented: 'if you're at a school where the children all round you speak rough . . . well then you've just got to fit in with it . . . I don't think you pay that much attention to the teachers.' Some mentioned being teased and ridiculed for using forms the others perceived as inappropriate or posh. One of Cullum's (1981: 101) girls said: 'If you was in a rough surrounding where there was a lot of rough people, you'd tend to talk more slangish and swear.' Another commented (1981: 108): 'You always try to be the same as everyone else. You don't sort of want to be made fun of . . . sort of posher than everybody else. Then you get sort of picked on. But then if you use a lot of slang and that, people don't think very much of you.' Another said (1981: 75): 'It's no good speaking in a posh voice if you live in a rough town or street . . . just wouldn't suit it.'

We have seen that young children are able to adapt their linguistic behaviour according to the situation and the participants in different types of interaction, e.g. talking to the teacher as opposed to adults one knows. My own research on the language of Edinburgh children as well as Reid's and Cullum's studies provide evidence that children are able to verbalize the kinds of constraints they perceive to be operative in different situations. Cullum, for example, asked some of the girls in her study if they put on posh voices. One replied (Cullum 1981: 101): 'Like when I go to my aunty's, she's a bit of a snob and I tend to talk nice, but I don't talk very much there.' Another said that she put on a posh voice if she went 'someplace posh or nice'. Some of the Edinburgh schoolchildren noticed that their mothers 'put on posh voices' on the telephone and offered imitations of posh speech.

Reid, Cullum and I also asked our informants if they thought there were any differences in the way girls and boys spoke. Reid's and my Edinburgh informants generally said that girls spoke more politely and boys more roughly, and that boys used more slang and swear words, thus reinforcing some of the stereotypes of genderlects we discussed earlier in this chapter. Some of Cullum's girls also commented on the rough speech of boys. One of my schoolgirls said: 'The boys just talk any old way. The girls take more care in talking' (Romaine 1975: 99). It has been noted that in many places boys and men retain more conservative dialect features than women: this is one reason why regional dialectologists always sought older male speakers as the ideal informants. This is not by any means a cross-cultural universal; it just reflects the different exposure to the norms of speech in a society at large, educational opportunities and community norms about how men and women should speak. Speitel (1975) in fact suggests that if women and girls do not develop an antipathy to Scots they often show a larger potential dialect reserve than their husbands and consequently preserve a large amount of conservative dialect forms. It is due to such 'resistant types' in Speitel's opinion (both men and women) that the dialect has survived at all in urban communities in Scotland.

Edelsky (1977) found that children showed a gradual progression in their acquisition of adult norms of interpretation linking language to sex roles. The youngest children's (six year olds) responses showed minimal resemblence to those of adults, while the oldest children (eleven year olds) showed adult-like competence in terms of the judgements they made about the sex-appropriateness of different features. Edelsky devised an experimental situation in which she gave the children pictures with sentences, e.g. 'Damn, the TV's broken,' and the children were asked whether a man or a woman would be more likely to say them. She then compared children's and adults' responses. The results are suggestive of a developmental change in the component of communicative competence related to knowledge of language stereotypes, but there are certain difficulties in the design of the experiment, some of which Edelsky (1977: 227, 235) herself notes. Adults and children had different tasks to perform: the adults were offering their own 'native-speaker' intuition, while children were making inferences about adult's behaviour. The youngest children seemed to link topic with sex and explained their choices in terms of relationships between topic and sex role, e.g. 'Daddy says "Damn the TV's broken" because Daddy watches TV.' This would appear to indicate that at different ages children use different strategies to make judgements about the sex-appropriateness of speech. At any rate, by the time children were eight or nine years old there was enough intersubjective agreement to provide consensus on all the adult-defined male items and many of the female items. For the oldest group the children defined all the variables except one in the same way that adults did. Edelsky did not, however, find that the girls were more sensitive to the sex-linkage of form than boys.

It seems then that children are aware of many different (often competing) sources of influence on their way of speaking, e.g. regional, social, gender-specific, situational variation, etc. It is not however always clear that these factors represent separate dimensions of evaluation, or indeed objectively separate aspects of variation. Mees (1977: 39), for example, observed that many of the Cardiff schoolchildren she spoke to were aware of the social rather than regional significance of local Cardiff accents. Some said 'I don't speak posh I know that' or 'In Cardiff they say ([kɛ:dIf).' This pronunciation of *Cardiff* with a very front and raised vowel is a well-known popular stereotype. In objective terms of course the social and regional dimensions of dialect differentiation are closely connected, at least in Britain. Trudgill (1974b), for instance, uses a triangle diagram to indicate the relationship between the two. Those who are lowest in social status are most likely to preserve the most regional forms of speech.

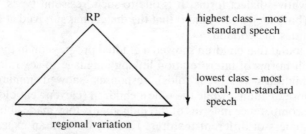

Figure 4.3   Relationship between social and regional variation in Britain
Source: Trudgill 1974b

One could argue that there is a common core of grammatical features shared by most non-standard varieties of English (cf. Cheshire 1982a) and that most people simply do not realize (unless they have a great deal of exposure to different kinds of regional speech) that these are not the sole province of any one particular regional dialect, as is often the case with certain features of accents. In the case of Scots, however, the situation is somewhat different since the ways in which Scots speech is different from English are spread throughout the system, e.g. accent, grammar, lexis, intonation, etc. In this respect, switching between Scots and English bears resemblance to cases where people switch between two separate languages, e.g. French and English. The Scottish situation is more similar to those described by Ferguson's (1959) term 'diglossia'. Ferguson intends diglossia to refer to a particular type of language standardization in which two distinct varieties of a language exist side by side throughout the speech community and where each of the two varieties is assigned a definite social function. One of Ferguson's examples is the relationship between Swiss German and standard German in Switzerland.

It may be the case that diglossic situations provide the speaker with a forceful representation of the social salience of linguistic forms and that awareness and control over them emerges at an earlier age than Labov suggests is the case for American children. Craig (1971: 375) writes about West Indian creole speakers that:

> the early age at which children learn to switch linguistic forms in the presence of elders, teachers and strangers in general, given the evidently vital social significance of language in the West Indies, seems to indicate that the stages of 'social perception' and 'stylistic variation' begin much earlier and at the same time are probably more prolonged for West Indian children than for the New York children described by Labov.

I have mentioned some of the results of regional accent evaluation studies done with adults. I will now look at some of the studies which have attempted to tap young children's perceptions of regional and social variation and their attitudes towards regional dialect. In the Swedish project on the development of the child's social identity, a series of evaluative tests were conducted to see at what age children were able to identify regional speech and to assess the social significance of certain variables. Aniansson (1981) administered the following listening tests in which children had to choose which of two Eskilstuna informants they thought spoke like themselves; a regional test to see if children were able to recognize Eskilstuna speech as a variety distinct from other regional varieties of speech in Sweden; a rank-ordering test to see if children ranked speakers in terms of status dimensions in the same way as adults (cf. especially Labov's 1966 subjective reaction test); and an occupational listening test to see if children could order speakers in a social hierarchy according to their occupation and the way they spoke. The purpose of the experiments was to find out not only what knowledge children had of the regional and social dimensions of dialect variation, but also to see if the child had an awareness of his own place with the sociolinguistic system, i.e. what groups he identified with.

Aniansson (1981: 11–12) found that the ability to recognize Eskilstuna speech from samples of speech of speakers of different regional dialects increased with age. There were no sex differences on judgement ability. There were, however, social class differences with the result that those from higher social groups made more correct identifications than those from lower social groups. Aniansson (1981: 13–17) attributes this finding to two factors. Firstly, she suggests that it is well known that children of higher social class background often perform better in test situations than lower-class children; and secondly, it is probably the case that the higher group have had more exposure to different kinds of speech and hence have more experience of making judgements of this kind. (I will discuss in chapter 5 the results of some Hungarian experiments which support Aniansson's latter argument.) It was interesting that the regional origin of the parents did not have a significant effect on the children's judgement ability. The most important factor in predicting the rate of correct guesses was simply age.

On the question of the child's identity vis-à-vis standard vs. regional speech, Aniansson (1981: 30–9) found that in general more children selected the more local variant of Eskilstuna speech as the one most similar to their own. There was a tendency for this association to increase with age (more so for boys than girls). And more boys than girls chose local over standard speech, especially in the oldest age group (14–15 year olds). There was also a tendency for children from the lower social groups to identify with the more local variety of speech.

In certain respects Aniansson's results are not surprising. They serve to reinforce some of the sociolinguistic patterns we have looked at already, e.g. that women and middle-class speakers align themselves more with the standard speech than men and working-class speakers. They do not, however, support Labov's view that children gradually move away from non-standard speech towards the standard as they grow older. A study done by Portz (1979) in Norwich also challenges Labov's assumption that there is a gradually increasing conformity with adult norms of production and evaluation. Portz found that there is an interval of significant 'regression' in the stages of acquisition in which 15–16 year olds strongly reject the standard both in production and evaluation of male/female speakers in a matched guise test. Part of the explanation behind this discrepancy between Labov's and Aniansson's findings reflects simply the differences between the social significance of standard and regional speech in the US and Sweden. Although in Sweden it is true that there is an increasing tendency for certain features of regional speech to give way to the norms of standard written Swedish, there is at the same time a great deal of pride in local speech. This has emerged quite clearly in a study of children's attitudes to dialect and standard done by Hammermo et al. (1981) in Gotland in the south of Sweden. The results of a questionnaire they administered to the children showed that there was a strong preference for local speech. Although only 17 per cent reported that everyone used dialect all the time at home, most of the children reported they used dialect in some situations. In fact 34 per cent said they used it all the time regardless of the topic or addressee while 15 per cent claimed to use standard. Nearly a quarter of the pupils said that their speech was a blend of local speech and the standard and that they shifted more towards one than the other depending on the situation. There were some interesting social class and sex differences. For example, the girls in every social group, but especially the lowest, preferred the dialect as opposed to the standard more so than boys, and more girls reported that they used the dialect all the time than did boys. This finding runs counter to Nordberg's (1969) study of the adult community in Eskilstuna and Pedersen's (1977) study of Danish schoolchildren. Nordberg observed that young Eskilstuna women preferred standard speech; and Pedersen found that nearly twice as many boys reported the use of dialect as girls. There are at least two reasons why Hammermo et al. obtained different results. One is simply that the speech of Gotland has positive prestige, or more so than Eskilstuna at any rate. Another may be that there is a revival of interest in and pride attached to speaking dialect on the part of the younger generation. As far as social class differences in the reported use of dialects are concerned, there was a tendency towards the 'bipolarization of norms' pattern we observed earlier: 31 per cent of the highest social group report they always use the standard and 44 per cent of the lowest group report they always use the dialect.

Hammermo et al. also asked the children about their use of dialect and its appropriateness in certain situations. There was a tendency for the use of dialect to correlate with the perceived informality of the situation. The most frequent choice, however, even in the most formal situation (e.g. a job interview in Stockholm) was the use of a blend between local dialect and standard. The most informal situation (i.e. when out with friends) prompted the highest percentage of claims of 'dialect only' usage. There were however no situations in which some use of dialect was regarded as inappropriate. Again it proved to be the case that girls opted for dialect more than boys. However, the difference between the sexes was less in informal situations requiring more personal contact than in formal situations. The greatest difference between males and females emerged in the situation described as a group discussion in class, where girls most frequently chose the dialect. Hammermo et al. (1981: 27) speculate that their findings may reflect the boys' greater concern with ambition and their desire for status and position in society (cf. Douglas-Cowie 1978 on the dimension of social ambition and the use of dialect vs. standard in Northern Ireland).

There was also a tendency for the higher social groups to report less use of dialect in all the situations and girls less so than boys. In the next to the highest social group, however, the girls appear to have a very strong preference for the use of dialect, just as much as the girls in the lowest social group. It is worth noting that this would be the group one would expect to *under-report* their use of dialect if Labov's ideas about women's tendencies toward hypercorrection were applicable here.

The children were also asked about their parents' use of dialect at home and whether they changed their speech in school. Most reported that their parents used just as much with them as in speaking to others. And a majority said they used just as much dialect in school lessons with teachers as in the break. Generally speaking, a majority (62 per cent) reported that they had not changed their speech since they had started school. There was, however, a tendency for more boys to say they had changed in the direction of the standard than girls and for more girls to report there had been no change. When asked if they had changed their speech upon entering higher study (i.e. Labov's turning point in the acquisition of the standard) more girls than boys (80 per cent) said they had not changed; but more girls also reported that they had switched to the standard. There were no major differences linked with social class and three-quarters reported that they had not changed their speech upon entering secondary school. In addition, 42 per cent said they thought the use of dialect ought to be encouraged and 47 per cent said there were no situations in which it was not 'polite' to speak dialect. There was a tendency on the part of lower-class informants to endorse the use of dialect more strongly than the middle class. The only situation in which a majority thought it would be improper to speak dialect was in talking to strangers who might not understand. Some of the comments made by the pupils are interesting. One said (Hammermo et al. 1981: 43): 'A person from Gotland should speak Gotland dialect. It sounds ridiculous if people from Gotland try to speak standard Swedish.'[24] Another commented: 'If you're from Gotland I think you should stick to your dialect and not be ashamed of it.' Still another said (Hammermo et al. 1981: 49): 'We don't want to talk bloody standard Swedish.'[25] These comments illustrate a very positive attitude towards the use of dialect as a marker of regional identity and solidarity. A majority also said that they thought that outsiders should not try to talk Gotland dialect because they sounded ridiculous. Giles and Smith too (1979) found that not all attempts at accommodation to local speech (i.e. downward convergence) were positively evaluated. The support of local speech was so great that 75 per cent said they would keep their dialect if they moved away. More girls than boys reported that they would not change, but there were also more girls than boys who said they would change to the standard. There were no major social differences.

Melchers is currently in the process of conducting a similar survey in Shetland.[26] In general, the reactions to Shetland dialect were positive, at least for those pupils who are from Shetland and want to remain there. (Nearly all those who want to leave have one or more parents who come from the south; compare Labov's 1963 study of attitudes towards Martha's Vineyard in terms of their correlation with the use of local speech forms.) Most of the pupils in Melchers's survey reported that they did not think they had changed their speech towards the standard when they entered secondary school, and that even if they moved to London, most would like to keep on speaking in the way they do at present.

5

The ontogenesis and development of children's speech events and discourse skills

Up to this point I have focused my discussion on those aspects of the child's language development and communicative competence which are fairly visible and to some extent easy to measure; namely, syntactic structures and sociolinguistic patterns. The use of quantitative methodology in these domains gives us a means of measuring growth by demonstrating either an increase or a decrease in features which are present in adult speech. It should probably be pointed out that there is no disjunction between the research traditions and methodological strategies employed by psycholinguists (see, for example, the papers in Wanner and Gleitman 1982, Brown 1973) and sociolinguists in that both are attempting to trace milestones of development by measuring certain phonological and syntactic variables. Psycholinguists have tended to pay less attention to social context and discourse, while sociolinguists have seen these aspects of language development as central to their investigations. It is also the case that psycholinguists have tended to be more concerned with uncovering the nature of the mechanism for acquisition (e.g. the Language Acquisition Device), in relating linguistic and cognitive development (see, for example, Slobin 1973), and in making claims about the pyschological reality of models of grammar (see, for example, Wexler and Culicover 1980 and White 1982). A crucial question to be raised is whether evidence from sociolinguistic studies provides a foundation for arguing that the nature of the Language Acquisition Device must be substantially altered in order to account for how language is used. I will return to this question in the final chapter.

The ability to use language to get things done is no less a fundamental component of communicative competence. We might think of this as the ability to put the pieces of language together in the right way at the right time in an effective way. It is this aspect of the child's communicative development that Hymes (1974: 75) refers to when he says:

> A child from whom any and all of the grammatical sequences of a language might come with equal likelihood would be, of course, a social monster. Within the social matrix in which it acquires a system of grammar, a child acquires also a system of use regarding persons, places, purposes, other modes of communication, etc, – all the components of communicative events, together with attitudes and beliefs regarding them. There also develop patterns of the sequential use of language in conversation, address, standard routines and the like. In such acquisition resides the child's sociolinguistic competence (or, more broadly, communicative competence), its ability to participate in its society as not only a speaking but also a communicating member.

In this chapter I will look at how children acquire the knowledge needed for certain speech acts and events, e.g. making requests and performing politeness routines, and how they learn to adopt different communicative and social roles in relation to other participants in speech events. I will also look in some detail at the development of narrative skills as exemplified by some of the Edinburgh schoolchildren I have referred to in previous chapters.

5.1 *The acquisition of rules for speech acts and events*

There are a number of ways in which one can approach the study of this aspect of communicative competence. We could think of the development of social communicative skills as the acquisition of a set of necessary and sufficient communicative rules, which once acquired are followed with increasing proficiency. In order to pursue this line of investigation, one would look at how children learn to cope with the communicative demands of particular speech acts and events in terms of some criteria for competence. The qualities of an effective language user across a range of speech events might seem difficult to define, let alone measure quantitatively (cf. also the discussion in chapter 8). Nevertheless, some quantitative work has been done. Read and Cherry (1978), for example, examined the development of the directive function of language, i.e. the use of request forms for actions and objects. To get someone to give a doll, a child might say any of the following:

(1) Give me a doll　(imperative)
(2) Can I have the doll?　(question/embedded imperative)

(3) I want the doll   (declarative expression of want or need)
(4) That doll sure looks nice   (declarative statement with directive force)

Although these might be thought of a equivalent 'alternative ways of saying the same thing', they do not all have the same effect on the hearer; and they differ not only in complexity, but also in directness.

Read and Cherry found that there was a developmental progression in the complexity of the linguistic expression of the children's requests with increasing age during the pre-school years. First-year primary school children knew a variety of forms and linguistic rules for making requests; but while most of their requests were successful, nearly half of their refusals were not accompanied by excuses, as they would tend to be in adult discourse. Even pre-school children were found to be capable of manipulating indirect request forms and using politeness markers and mitigated requests. Ervin-Tripp (1977: 176) reports a four year old saying: 'I'm sorry. My room's too messed up', in order to solicit help in cleaning it. And Shuy (1978: 272) relates how Joanna, a five year old, got herself invited to dinner by making three declarative statements which had the force of directives. The child first drew his attention to the fact that the family car was absent and her mother worried if she missed meals. She then remarked, 'You know, I eat almost anything.'

The fact that young school-age children use few direct need or want statements in a request function matches findings that Ervin-Tripp (1976) reports for adults; namely, statements of personal need or desire are primarily addressed to subordinates. Not surprisingly, given the dependence of very young children on their care-givers, need and want directives are the earliest and most frequent of request forms used. Lawson (1967) found that two- and three-year-old children had acquired rules for the systematic social distribution of requests according to age and rank. A two-year-old child gave almost entirely simple imperatives to her peers, but with adults she used desire statements, questions and permission requests. The child furthermore did not issue imperatives to older children, but used only questions or permission requests (cf. Mitchell-Kernan and Kernan 1977).

It appears that children are competent at a very early age in issuing directives in appropriate ways according to the addressee, but what evidence is there to support the idea that they can interpret correctly the social meaning of various kinds of directives?[1] Certain declarative statements and indirect questions may be ambiguous as to their intent, even for adults, and they are sometimes misinterpreted. Shatz (1978) reports that the comprehension dimension is difficult to investigate since the discourse context of directives contains redundant clues. Ervin-Tripp (1977: 182) has noted cases in which three year olds in conversation with their mothers responded appropriately to indirect directives. An example follows:

(5) Mother: I'm cold.
    Child: I already shut the window.

There is also evidence that mothers alter the forms of their directives to children so that as children get older, mothers' imperatives resemble directive conventional imperatives less and less in terms of certain properties of surface structure (cf. Bellinger 1979). When children fail to respond to an indirect directive, mothers often rephrase it in a more direct form. The effects of the mother's modifications when speaking to children are discussed more fully in the next chapter.

There is also an evaluative aspect of requests. In a study of Italian children Bates (1976b) asked children to request a piece of candy from a handpuppet, and then to 'ask more nicely' to get two pieces. Most of the children began with simple imperatives and need statements such as: *Give me a candy/I need a candy*. When asked to be polite, the youngest children (three years old) did not change their request forms; older children sometimes switched to interrogatives and used *please*. In another experiment she asked children to give a candy to the puppet which asked the most nicely. The use of *please* was the earliest discriminated marker of politeness; not until a later age did children recognize the greater politeness of conditionals and the use of T/V pronouns.[2] Bates concluded that children have a 'concept of politeness' by age three, but that politeness is probably directly taught.

In fact, there is evidence for direct teaching of politeness and other social routines at a very early age. Routines such as 'bye-bye', 'please' and 'thank you' are among the English-speaking child's earliest acquisitions (cf. Berko-Gleason and Weintraub 1976 and Greif and Berko-Gleason 1980). The ability to use greeting, farewell and politeness routines is an essential part of adult communicative competence, which is taught to children at an age when they have no understanding of the referential semantic basis of the routine. In other words, the child does not connect the routine of saying 'thank you' with the meaning of the verb 'to thank' or the statement 'I thank you.' Similarly, Ervin-Tripp (1971: 34) reports a child playing with a toy telephone and engaging in a rudimentary telephone conversation which consisted only of the formula: 'Hello, fine, goodbye.' The greeting ritual is what the child has perceived as salient to the conversation rather than the message which is embedded in it.

Berko-Gleason and Weintraub (1976), who studied children's use of the Halloween 'Trick-or-treat' routine, found that there was age-grading. The youngest children (two to three year olds) said nothing; four to five year olds said nothing but 'trick or treat'; older children said 'trick or treat' and 'thank you', but only children over ten tended to produce the whole routine ending with 'goodbye'. Berko-Gleason and Weintraub observed that although adults gave a great deal of explicit teaching or coaching either before the children set out on their rounds or while accompanying them, there was no attempt to embed the routine in an explanation of what its significance or meaning was.

These studies show that learning such routines is one of the earliest parts of the child's training in communicative competence. Greif and Berko-Gleason (1980) found that spontaneous production of routines like 'hi', 'bye' and 'thanks' was rare, but the parents' promptings were not. After prompting, the children performed the routine without elaborating the form given them by their parents. The learning of routines is particularly important, but performance rather than competence (in the sense of understanding their full meaning) is all that matters.[3] Berko-Gleason and Weintraub (1976: 134) point out that the acquisition of routines proceeds in the opposite direction to most other features of language where competence comes first, then performance. In the case of routines, it is long after a child learns to say 'trick or treat' that he learns what it means.[4]

It has been observed that the referential, as opposed to the social, expressive (or what Halliday 1976 has referred to as the interpersonal) use of language comes relatively late in the child's linguistic development. A bias in research on child language towards studying the development of referential communicative skills has led to the conclusion that even school-age children are 'incompetent' in transmitting information to listeners. Children's failure to take the listener's needs into account by providing background information is often attributed to Piaget's observation that early speech is egocentric. He (1926) claims that the utterances of children below the age of eight are communicatively inadequate because they are not successfully adapted to the needs of the listener. Communicative success, however, increases with age as the child moves beyond egocentric speech to consider the knowledge of the listener. There are a number of studies which claim to show that young children are relatively deficient in a number of skills relevant to performance in the listener role. Asher (1976), for example, asked second-, fourth- and sixth-grade children to judge the adequacy of a number of instructions given on how to play a game. Younger children were less successful in identifying adequate (i.e. unambiguous) messages produced by themselves and others.

Role-playing is an important part of the child's development of communicative competence because once the child realizes that differences exist in the roles participants play in speech events, he finds out that different ways of speaking are appropriate in relation to different addressees. It has been shown that quite young children are able to modify their speech by using simpler and shorter utterances when speaking to younger children (cf. Shatz and Gelman 1973 and Sachs and Devin 1976). Gleason (1973) has observed stylistic adaptation in children from four years old onwards (cf. also the discussion in chapter 4). And Garvey (1975: 46) cites the case of a three-year-old child producing deliberate syntactic errors in role-play baby talk.

Hollos (1977) studied the acquisition of the Hungarian pronominal address system, which encodes distinctions of politeness and formality in relation to addressees, by asking children to play various roles, e.g. a mother greeting a shopkeeper. The youngest children (seven year olds) distinguished between the use of T/V forms with familiar adults, but none of the children up to the age of nine was able to use consistently the reciprocal V form, which would be required between adult strangers. It was also the case that children were better in comprehension than production tasks, which indicates that a knowledge of the linguistic forms and social rules alone does not able the child to play different roles. The reciprocal V form is not used in the home by family members or other adults the child is familiar with; thus it is not until the child begins to socialize beyond his family network that he is exposed to this distinction.

The precise determinants of the developmental relationship between comprehension and production have not been well investigated cross-culturally. Although comprehension precedes production for many of the features we have looked at, the reverse is true for some forms (cf. Chapman 1978). Hollos's study suggests that a rural vs. urban environment may have an important effect. She found that both rural and urban children did better in comprehending the social distinctions encoded by the pronouns than in producing them in role-playing. The urban children, however, were more advanced than the rural ones in both production and comprehension. Hollos says that this reflects the urban child's greater opportunities for social interaction with a wider range of persons. The fact that the differences between the children were greater in production than comprehension deserves further study.

One way in which children learn to become competent in adult roles is by practising them with other children in play groups. With their peers children very often adopt a range of adult roles in playing school, house, etc. Vygotsky (1966), who argued that early speech is sociocentric, observes that in play a child is above his age in terms of his linguistic behaviour. Hymes (1971: 17) cites the remark made by a mother who watched her children at play: 'You know, I've noticed that when the children play school outside, they talk like they're supposed to in school; and when they stop playing school, they stop.' The switch in the children's language in this case involved adopting forms which were closer to standard English and less influenced by black English vernacular. Philips (1974) has noted similar code-switching among young Indian children playing school.

Ehimovich (1981) found that children as young as four years old used terms of address (real vs. pretend names) and changes in key to define frame shifts in interaction (cf. Goffman 1981 on the notion of 'frame' as the scaffolding or structuring of an event). Goffman and Hymes have used the term *key* in a metaphorical sense to refer to the manner or spirit in which an act is done, while Brazil (1975) uses it literally as an extension of the musical terminology to refer to shifts in pitch and tone. Ehimovich maintains that both senses of key were applicable to the children's framing of play activities. When they played house, not only did they speak in a higher key, but they shifted into another context where different roles and relationships were operative. The new context was marked paralinguistically, prosodically and linguistically; or, in Goffman's terms, it was bracketed as a new frame. The play itself was clearly childish, but the management of it was adultlike in competence, since adults too use similar devices to negotiate identities and manage interactions.

Another way to look at Piaget's notion of egocentrism is to see it as a tendency for children to assume that a shared 'here and now' provides sufficient context for the hearer. The amount of specification of topic, participants, etc, required in any speech event is a function of the degree of shared knowledge that the speaker and hearer can assume at a given moment. As suggested in chapter 3, there are a number of devices available for topic specification and elaboration, such as modifiers (e.g. *red house, this boy, a girl*, etc.), prepositional phrases (e.g. *the book under the table*), relative clauses (e.g. *the boy who lives next door*), etc. Definite articles and demonstratives aid the listener in locating the referent by indicating that the listener already knows of its existence. Thus new information tends to be presented by indefinite articles, while old information is presented by definite articles (cf. Hawkins 1978).

The acquisition of definiteness and indefiniteness by English-speaking children has been studied extensively (cf. Maratsos 1976). It has been reported that children as young as three are able to make correct use of the definite article to mark referents that are uniquely given in previous discourse. It is not clear, however, that the children were reacting only to this dimension of the use of the articles. Karmiloff-Smith (1979a), for example, argues that the only reliable use of the article by three- to four-year-old children is the use of the indefinite article for naming, and the definite article for deixis, often accompanied by pointing. She stresses the fact that determiners are multi-functional, and that full control over all the functions is not achieved until age ten. The non-specific function is, in her opinion, not acquired until relatively late.

It can be seen that there is a great deal of variability among primary school children in the extent to which explicit reference rather than context is relied upon in specifying and elaborating topic. In my study of Edinburgh schoolchildren I elicited narratives in response to questions about television programmes, films, games, etc. (cf. chapter 2), in which we can see some of the ways in which children of different ages manage topics and introduce referents into discourse. I have already discussed the use of relative clauses and passives in relation to some of these discourse functions in chapter 3.

In one task I asked children to tell me where they lived and how they got from school to home, or vice versa. A six-year-old girl described her route as follows (all noun phrases are in italics):

> Well, sometimes I go down *the wee lane* instead of going up *the other way*. I go straight up and I cut up. I'm nearly there. I go along from *the bingo,* cross *the road* and I go along. I turn round *a bend,* where *the football* is, where they have *a match.* I just go along there. Then there's *this wee sweet shop.* After that, I go to *the shoe shop* and I turn round *the bend* and then I go into *my stair.*

It is clear that the naive listener would have few cues to aid him in following these directions. The first NP (and indeed, most of the NPs) is/ are introduced in a specific and definite sense, i.e. as if the listener knew which *wee lane* the child intended. Since this NP is contrasted with *the other way,* and assuming the school is the point of origin for orienting the listener, the child apparently assumes the listener is as familiar with the layout of the school as she is and would therefore know that there were several possible routes one could take. The next point of reference is indicated by the deictic *there.* It is cataphoric rather than anaphoric, i.e. pointing towards some NP still to come, but it is unclear what the referent is. It may be one of the other NPs like *my stair,* or *the bingo,* or an unmentioned NP like *the top of the wee lane.* Clark (1973) states that deictic contrasts between *this/that* and *here/there* in certain contexts are often not discernible in four year olds. The other use of *there* appears to be anaphoric, i.e. it refers to something in the previous discourse; in this case, the bend which has just been mentioned. Similarly, the use of the demonstrative *that* is also anaphoric, referring back to the clause 'after I passed the sweet shop'. Although the use of adjectival modifiers like *wee, sweet, shoe, my,* etc. specify the reference to their nouns further, the child introduces the NPs as if they had been previously mentioned. There is, however, one instance of an NP with the indefinite article, which is then followed by two locative relative clauses, i.e. *a bend, where the football is, where they have a match.* (Cf. Hickmann, forthcoming for further discussion of the development of reference in discourse.)

As I showed in chapter 3, relative clauses represent a highly explicit, but also fairly complex, syntactic means of specifying a referent. Developmental studies indicate that they are among the syntactic structures acquired late. McNew (1975) found that three-year-old children described referents almost exclusively with demonstratives, e.g. *this one.* If listeners expressed confusion, the child elaborated the reference either prosodically (e.g. by stress or intonation), or gesturally (i.e. by pointing to the object). These strategies were used even by eight-year-old children in my study. One girl, for example, when asked where she lived, got up and pointed from a window. She said, 'Just down the road, see, see, where that back green is down there'. Here the context of the utterance together with the deictic *that* followed by a relative clause make the reference unambiguous (cf. also Wales 1979 and de Villiers and de Villiers 1974).

Four-year-old children in McNew's study described referents almost exclusively with adjectives and prepositional phrases. Only the five to six year olds began to use relative clauses. He concluded that the various types of topic-specifying modifiers were acquired in a sequence of increasing explicitness, with the most syntactically difficult appearing latest, i.e. relative clauses. As noted in chapter 3, there tends to be a gradual movement away from context-bound strategies to morpho-syntactic ones with increasing age. In the following description of a television programme, we can see how a 12-year-old boy relies on various morpho-syntactic possibilities to specify referents and develop the topic in such a way so as take the listener's needs into account. He says: 'I like *Love Thy Neighbour. It's* about *two families. One's a darkie family* and *the other ones* are white. And *they* always call *the one* who's white, calls *the darkie* a Sambo and all that. *The one* that's black call *the white one* snowdrops.' This particular text does not rely on context for its meaning. There are no cases where pronouns are used where the the antecedent cannot be recovered. For example, *it's* refers to the programme previously named, *one* and *the other ones* refer anaphorically to the *two families*. The NP *a darkie family* is introduced as new information. This particular instance is interesting because the boy self-initiates a repair after he has said 'they always call' by using a relative clause, *the one who's white,* to disambiguate the potentially unclear reference of *they*. He also uses another relative clause, *the one that's black*.

It is important to emphasize, however, that multiple strategies exist at any stage for these children as well as for adults (cf. chapter 3). Ullmer-Ehrich (1981) observes that even 12-year-old children have difficulty in organizing room descriptions in a manner clearly comprehensible to the listener (cf. Weissenborn 1983 on the development of skills in spatial orientation). Unless we want to argue that adult speech is egocentric too, or conversely childlike, we need to recognize that the extent to which speakers rely on morphosyntactic vs. other strategies is not only situation-specific, but also language-specific (cf. Keenan 1974 on Malagasy). Bernstein, whose work will be discussed in later chapters, believes that the morphosyntactic stragegy of making referents explicit is more character-istic of middle-class children and adults, while greater reliance on context is more typical of the working class. All of the children in my Edinburgh sample came from working-class backgrounds, but there was a great deal of variability in the use of strategies for topic elaboration, not all of which can be accounted for by age. This appears to indicate that children are not unaware of the functions of these devices or unfamiliar with these structures, but rather that they make different assumptions about the kind of information the hearer requires. The reasons why some children might make these assumptions is a matter I will deal with in chapters 6 and 7.

5.2 *Children's narrative skills*

The multiple strategies which I looked at in the last section are also in evidence in the narratives which children tell, either spontaneously or in response to questions. Although there has been a great deal of discussion of narrative, as both a literary and a spoken genre, there is probably no set of definitional criteria which would be accepted unanimously by those working on narrative skills. Nevertheless, since relating narratives is common in everday life and many children are encouraged to produce written and spoken narratives by adults, particularly teachers (cf. chapter 6), I would like to look specifically at the development of spoken narrative skills outside the classroom setting.

I will begin by taking Labov's (1972b: 359–60) definition of narrative. He characterizes a minimal narrative as a sequence of two clauses which are temporally ordered, e.g. 'I got knocked over last Wednesday. This car came along and this one car stopped for me and I crossed and I never seen the other car coming and I got knocked down.' This narrative told by a ten-year-old Edinburgh girl is more than a minimal narrative by Labov's definition since it contains more than two temporally ordered cluases. It has the following sequence of actions:

1 this car came along
2 and this one car stopped for me
3 and I crossed
   and I never seen the other car coming
4 and I got knocked down.

In this case the order of the clauses matches the temporal ordering of the events in real (as opposed to narrative) time. There are, however, other ways to structure a narrative, which can be thought of in more general terms as a recapitulation of past events. Temporal ordering is just one device available to the narrator; another has to do with syntax, or in other words the syntactic means which are available for the 'transformation of experience in narrative syntax', as Labov puts it. Here the speaker simply connects a series of independent clauses with the co-ordinating conjunction *and.* Another way in which the speaker might have presented the 'same' narrative would be as follows:

1 I got knocked down last Wednesday
2 when I crossed the road
3 there were two cars coming
4 one stopped
5 and I didn't see the other one coming.

In this version the temporal ordering is reversed and the connections between the clauses are expressed somewhat differently. For example, 1 and 2 are joined by the subordinator *when*.

Narratives can range from very simple recountings like this one to highly skilled dramatic performances. In the later case, the narrative may almost be what Goffman (1981) calls a 'replaying', or what Wolfson (1982) calls a 'performed narrative'. Narratives can vary in the extent to which the speaker structures the recapitulation of past events in such a way so as to allow his own view and subjective evaluation to come through. An example of a more dramatic narrative told by another ten-year-old Edinburgh girl follows:[5]

		Can I tell you about Julie and Mark?
abstract	(a)	Yesterday there was a fight. [aside] And you know what they call it?
		An agro. A right bash-in.
sub-narrative	(i)	I says, I says to Julie [aside] cause I never heard it, I says, 'What's an agro?'
	(ii)	And she started laughing.
repetition	(iii)	And I says, 'What's an agro?'
elaboration	(iv)	And she says, 'Do you not ken what an agro is?'
	(v)	I says, 'No, I dinna ken.'
	(vi)	A right bash-in.
	(b)	And Julie . . . Mark got a hold of Julie's hair
	(c)	and he swinged it right down
	(d)	and Julie battered him.
	(e)	She kicked him in the ribs and in the back.
evaluation		She really battered him.
		He was greetin'.
	(f)	She kicked him in the eye too.
	(g)	Well, Mark says, 'I could batter you anyday' to Julie.
	(h)	And Julie says, 'Right, I'll fight you after school.' So everybody was saying, 'There's going to be an agro.'
	(i)	And the fight started.
coda	(j)	And Julie won in the end.

repetition   (k)   She really kicked him and punched him and thumped him
              (l)   and punched him in the nose.
              (m)   She got him crying.
evaluation   (n)   I wouldnae like to be in this school cause they really could batter you.

Let us look at the performative aspects of this narrative first before examining its structure in more detail. The narrative is an excellent example of Wolfson's performed narrative, as can be seen by a number of features which she cites (1982: 25) as characteristic of this type of narrative, e.g. direct speech, asides, repetition, expressive noises and sound effects, motions and gestures. Most of these features of performed narrative are found here, even though the speaker herself was not one of the main characters. Wolfson found that for adults at any rate, narratives were more likely to be performed if the speaker was the central figure (i.e. the one narrating and the one about whom the narrative is told — (cf. Goffman's distinction between the speaker as animator, author and principal).

At this stage it is instructive to contrast this girl's account with two others, one of which is told by Mark, one of the principal characters in the narrative. First, look at a ten-year-old boy's account, which was told as an aside in his own narrative about a fight he was involved in.

That was like Julie and Mark yesterday. The two of them were fighting. Julie got him by the hair and was kicking him in the back about six times and then he went away home greetin' — crying.

Next, examine Mark's version:

Well, Julie started calling me names and after school we had a fight. She started kicking me, so I got her back and somebody said she kicked me in the face and she did kick me in the face. Then she pulled my hair and dragged me along the ground. I couldn't see cause she kicked me right in the eye there. I couldn't see. Then she ran away . . . Well, I kicked her and I pulled her hair cause if I'd have kicked her in the face everybody would have butted in and started fighting. M would have stopped the fighting. That was the end of it.

Neither of these recountings of the 'same events' is as elaborated as that of the young girl — not even Mark's, although he was one of the main characters. In fact, I had to elicit the end to Mark's tale; the spontaneous bit of his narrative ended with the remark, 'Then she ran away.' I have quoted these three versions to show the variability in the way in which the same narrative can be presented in strikingly different ways from the perspective of three different speakers who have more or less the same linguistic system at their disposal. I propose, however, to focus on the way in which the girl constructs her narrative.

The child presents an 'eye-witness' account, whose vividness derives partly from the fact that a number of events are reported in direct speech. She quotes herself and others directly as she shifts back and forth changing scenes and perspectives in adopting the role of various participants, e.g. I says, she says, etc. The use of what Wolfson and others call the conversational historical present (CHP), i.e. the use of the present tense to refer to past events, marks these changes in scene and allows the girl to present the narrative as a performance. There are also kinesic markers, i.e. motions and gestures, which accompany the story, as well as asides and repetitions.

Wolfson observed that performed (as opposed to non-performed) narratives rarely occurred in the typical linguistic interviews conducted by Labov with adult informants (cf. the discussion in chapter 2). Their infrequent occurrence is in Wolfson's view due to constraints imposed by the interview as a speech event. That is, given the ground rules for interaction which govern an interview between two strangers, narratives occur largely in response to interviewers' questions and are not introduced spontaneously as they would be in everyday conversation. Wolfson also found that narratives were more likely to be performed when the speaker perceived that the listener shared his background, i.e. was of a similar age, status, ethnicity, sex, etc. The right to perform is evidently affected strongly by status relations so that it is generally inappropriate for a subordinate to perform a narrative to a superior. Thus the performance of this girl's narrative in such an asymmetrical situation, where the interviewer and child share almost nothing in common is almost unexpected.

Nevertheless, since there were other performed narratives in my data (both solicited and unsolicited), there are at least two possible reasons why the norms for performance, such as Wolfson defines them, were apparently 'violated'. One explanation would be that young children are not aware of the appropriateness conditions for the genre, i.e. they do not take the status relations between participants into account. This would mean then that perhaps the significance of this dimension of the speech events is learned later.

However, the way in which the child introduces the narratives would indicate that she *is* aware of the constraints since she *asks* permission to perform. This suggests that she is aware that she does not have the right to introduce and perform an unsolicited narrative to someone she doesn't know. Another possible explanation is that the occurrence of the performed narrative is indicative of an interview which has been successful in creating a context for the occurrence of spontaneous speech. I suspect that both of these factors are at work here. While the child is aware of the inappropriateness of a spontaneous narrative, she decided to ask permission to tell one because she perceived that the interviewer would be a sympathetic listener. Apart from the use of features like CHP and direct speech, etc., the narrative is performed largely in a 'vernacular style', as evidenced by the use of vernacular verb forms like *ken* − 'know', *greet* − 'cry', *wouldnae* − 'wouldn't, etc., and non-standard phonology. Some of the speaker's repetitions can be thought of as code-switches between casual and non-casual speech styles; for example, when she says, 'He was greetin',', as opposed to 'She got him crying,' and variously refers to the fight as an 'agro' and a 'bash-in'. Another possibility is simply that Wolfson is wrong in her assessment of the social significance of performed (as opposed to unperformed) narratives. There may be crucial differences between adults and children in this respect. It may be the case that there is nothing particularly skilful involved in performing a narrative per se as opposed to relating it. Performance may be a simplifying device for some speakers in that it allows them to avoid some of the more problematic aspects of narrative structure, e.g. anaphora. Hickmann (forthcoming) shows how children may use performance in this sense as a means of avoiding the problems of anaphora in discourse. This suggests that the notion of complexity as far as narrative structure is concerned must take into account both linguistic and social factors.

As for the structural and temporal organization, as well as content of the narrative, it would certainly count as complex, at least according to Labov's criteria. Since it contains considerably more than the minimal two-clause structure, it is really an extended narrative, which contains a number of sub-components. Labov (1972b: 363) says that a fully formed narrative has the following elements:

1 abstract
2 orientation
3 complicating action
4 evaluation
5 result or resolution
6 coda

A complete narrative is one which begins with an orientation, moves on to complicating action, is suspended at the focus of evaluation before the resolution, concludes with a resolution, and then brings the listener back to the present in the coda. We have already seen how the narrative clauses which present the complicating action may not occur in strict temporal order. This also applies to the speaker's evaluation, which according to Labov (1972b: 369) forms a secondary structure, penetrating the narrative in waves. Only the complicating action is required for the story to count as a narrative.

Let us look at how the components are structured into a narrative. The function of the abstract is to summarize the story. This speaker begins with 'Yesterday there was this fight' (and the previously discussed narrative begins with 'I got knocked over last Wednesday.' Since the abstract covers the same ground as the narrative in a more condensed form, it is not necessary. It is a stylistic frill in much the same way as 'once upon a time' serves the structural and stylistic function of marking what follows as a narrative. In a study of the narratives of personal experience told by girls between the ages of seven and fourteen, Kernan (1977: 93) found that there was a tendency for older girls (ten to fourteen) to use abstracts. However, since most of his narratives were elicited within an interview, it may be that some speakers 'count' the question as an abstract.

The orientation identifies the time, place, person, etc., or situates the activity. The speaker has already located her narrative in time by using the word *yesterday* in her abstract. Apart from this, there are no clauses devoted solely to introducing participants and locating the scene of the action. We learn later that it took place after school, but not precisely where. Labov (1972b: 364–5) observes that while it is theoretically possible for all the orientation clauses to be placed at the beginning of the narrative, in practice it often occurs at strategic points later on. Narrative clauses may of course be multi-functional, as indicated earlier; they may fuse an evaluation with a report of an event, or as in this case an abstract may provide some orientation. Much of the orientation, however, occurs in other places throughout the narrative and is established during the course of narration. When we examine the narrative as a whole from the perspective of the order of events in real time, we could restructure it in the following way: Begin first with clause (g), where Mark threatens Julie and she replies in (h) that she accepts the challenge. The next events in real time begin with the statement (which does not advance the actual events of the story): 'So everybody was saying, "There's going to be an agro".' The clauses which I have labelled as a sub-narrative, i.e. (i)–(vi), serve as an interesting metalinguistic orientation, which precedes in real time the fighting, which is the topic of the narrative proper. Clause (i) of the main narrative which marks the onset of the fight, and the next event in real time, comes near the end of the narrative.

In the sub-narrative the speaker explains the term *agro* with asides and evaluations, which indicate her awareness that since she didn't know the term herself the listener might need this bit of information to make sense out of the main narrative. Instead of just glossing the term for me, however, she performs or recapitulates the events which led to her own understanding of the term. In this sub-narrative she introduces Julie, who is to be the 'heroine' of the main events. The clauses (b)–(f) constitute the rest of the narrative proper, which follow in real time the events of clauses (g), (h), (i) and (i)–(vi). The clauses (b)–(f) shift back and forth between the actions of the two main characters, Julie and Mark. Clauses (k), (l) and

(m) repeat the main action and (j) concludes it. It simply states the result, which the reader can infer anyway from clauses (d), (e) and (f). Clause (j) functions as a coda. It bridges the gap between the moment of time at the end of the narrative proper and brings the listener back to the point of entry. After a coda, there is no point in asking, 'What happened next?' We can see that there are no new events which follow after this, either in real or narrative time. The last clause of the narrative proper may function simultaneously as a coda and a statement of resolution. The codas of some literary narratives may be highly stylized, e.g. 'and they lived happily ever after.'

In this narrative the speaker sums up and repeats a bit of the main action after the coda, and then finishes with an evaluation. As we have seen already, evaluation may be spread throughout the narrative. To some extent, the sub-narrative is partly evaluative. Places where the speaker makes an aside or repeats an action to emphasize it are also evaluative in that they select certain things which from the narrator's perspective are worth commenting on or saying again (cf. Keenan 1977 on the use of repetition in children's discourse). The function of the evaluation is to present the speaker's point of view, and, as indicated earlier, narratives may differ greatly in the extent to which the speaker's viewpoint is conveyed. Speakers may differ too in the devices they use to present their evaluation, and to tell their listeners why they are telling the story, what effect it had on them, etc. The child makes use of CHP as an internal evaluation device; or in other words the way in which it is presented conveys information to the listener about how the speaker feels. The listener is not simply 'told' but also 'shown'.

In some narratives there may be no external evaluation at all. That is, the speaker may not step outside the bounds of the narrative proper to make remarks like, 'What happened next was funny,' or 'This scared me because I'm scared of fights,' or 'I wondered what I'd do next.' By contrast, therapeutic narratives (e.g. between a psychiatrist and a patient) may serve as a framework for evaluation; the patient's reactions to the event are of greater significance than the events themselves. The therapist is more likely to ask, 'How did you feel about that?', rather than, 'What happened next?'

Labov (1972b: 372–3) distinguishes different degrees of embedding the evaluation into the narrative. One method is by quotation of the speaker's own thoughts, e.g. 'I says, "What's an agro?" ' It is clear by implication that if the speaker asks this question, she does not know the word; but before she asks, she makes the remark, 'cause I never heard it', to explain the reason for the question she is about to ask. Addressing remarks to the listener outside the narrative is, according to Labov, a more sophisticated type of evaluation, and one which is used frequently by middle-class adult speakers.

Another degree of embedding is achieved by quoting another person, who evaluates the narrative. In this girl's narrative her quotation of her friend's characterization of an agro as a 'right bash-in' is an evaluative device, which by its choice of words implies that the event is worth telling about. That is, it is not just an ordinary fight, but one which is well worth reporting (an opinion which receives independent support from the fact that this particular fight is reported by other children in their narratives about fighting). Labov (1972b: 373) observes: 'it should be emphasized that this technique [embedded evaluation comment] is used only by older, highly skilled narrators from traditional working class backgrounds. Middle class speakers are less likely to embed their evaluative comments so deeply in the narrative and are in fact most likely to use external evaluation.'

While I do not accept Labov's generalizations about the age and social class distribution of evaluation devices in narrative (cf. further in chapter 6), I would say that this child's use of evaluation is skilful and sophisticated. The connection between narrative styles and social class is discussed in more detail in the next chapter. Labov recognizes an even greater degree of embedding of evaluation in telling what people *did* rather than what they *said*. Although this girl relies heavily on direct quotation, she also cites her friend's reaction to her question about the word *agro*, i.e. 'she started laughing.' She could have omitted this and merely reported her friend's reply, 'Do you not ken what an agro is?', where the fact that her friend asks implies that she cannot believe the speaker doesn't know.

These differences in evaluation have to do with whether the speaker fills in the narrative or leaves the hearer to read between the lines on the one hand, and with the devices he has available for doing so on the other. Tannen's work (1982) on oral vs. literate styles indicates that the extent to which evaluation is external is an important stylistic variable cross-culturally. The implications of this will be discussed in the next chapter when we look at how children display their narrative skills at school and how they are evaluated by teachers. In his study Kernan (1977: 101) found that there was a development of evaluative devices with increasing age. The youngest speakers (seven to eight) more often implied their feelings and never used quotations, while the oldest groups (ten to eleven, and thirteen to fourteen) relied increasingly less on implications and more on quotation and explicit statements of their feelings (cf. also Goffman 1981 for discussion of these devices in adult conversation).

I would like now to look more specifically at the structure of the narrative in order to see what linguistic devices are used to link the clauses to one another to form a cohesive text. In doing so I will rely heavily on the framework developed by Halliday and Hasan (1976) for describing text structure, and Halliday's view (1975a) that in acquiring language children are essentially developing semantic-pragmatic systems. From this perspective syntax is seen as a system of choices which realize different kinds of meaning. I have already talked in this chapter about the way in which one part of the semantic system is mapped onto syntactic structure when discussing the way in which reference to participants, events and objects is achieved by means of the use of definite and indefinite articles. And in chapter 3 I looked specifically at the use of two complex syntactic structures, relatives and passives. In a developmental study of narrative Martin (1983) found that there was a tendency for older children (ten to eleven years old) to approximate more closely to the kind of self-contextualization associated with narrative genre in western culture. In other words, the move away from context dependency tends to increase with age.

One important way in which meaning is built up by syntactic structure is through what Halliday and Hasan (1976) call 'cohesion', i.e. the semantic system used by speakers to connect clauses to one another and to relate them to the context of discourse. They recognize a number of types of connectives or clause relations: additive, temporal, causal, adversative and conditional. Additive relations are primarily realized in the conjunctions *and* and *or*. Temporal connectives like *then, after, before,* etc. relate clauses in terms of succession or simultaneity. Connectives which mark relations of causality include *so, because* and *therefore*. Adversative contrasts may be indicated by *but, although, however*. Conditionality may be expressed by markers such as *if/then*. These connectives can be used in narratives to make explicit certain relations between clauses. When they are absent, these relations must be inferred.

For example, if I have the following two propositions, and order them in a narrative without any connectives, the hearer will infer a temporal sequence in which the event expressed in proposition 1 is assumed to take place before the event in proposition 2 (cf. the discussion of the 'order of mention' principle in chapter 3):

1 The boy turned off the light
2 He went upstairs

Simple juxtaposition represents one of the possible syntactic choices for realizing the meaning of these two propositions; namely, as two independent sentences with no explicit marking of the connections between them. The ordering of the clauses in discourse matches the sequence of events in real time (i.e. assuming 1 did take place before 2), and is therefore iconic. If they were to appear in reverse order, i.e. 2, then 1, the tendency would be for the hearer to infer that 2 took place before 1, at least in the absence of any other clues to indicate the order of events.

Another way of presenting the same information would be to join the two propositions by means of an additive or other connective, as in the following sentences:

(i)   The boy turned off the light and (he) went upstairs
(ii)   The boy turned off the light and then he went upstairs

In these two cases the meaning of the two independent propositions is encoded syntactically in one sentence with two independent clauses. In the first alternative the hearer will still infer, however, that proposition 2, which is realized by the second clause, *and he went upstairs,* took place after the boy turned off the light. In the second version this interpretation is marked explicitly by means of the connective *then,* as well as implicitly by the iconic ordering of the clauses in the sentence.

Yet another way of conveying the same propositional content exists in alternative (iii):

(iii)   When he had turned off the light, the boy went upstairs
        After he had turned off the light, the boy went upstairs.

In this case the two propositions are condensed into one sentence consisting of one main and one subordinate clause introduced by the connective *when/after,* which indicates explicitly the order of events. In a sense the use of explicit marking is redundant since the interpretation is supported by the context, clause ordering and tense sequencing of the verbs in the two clauses.

A more complex way to realize the content of these two propositions in narrative syntax would be to order them non-iconically within one sentence containing one subordinate and one main clause. Thus,

(iv)   The boy went upstairs after he turned off the light
(v)   Before he went upstairs, the boy turned off the light

By non-iconic ordering, I mean that the order of the clauses in discourse does not match the order in which the events expressed in the propositions occurred in real time. In alternatives (iv) and (v) the event which took place first appears second; in one case it is encoded by a subordinate clause headed by *after,* which explicitly lexicalizes the temporal relation between the two, while in the other it is encoded in a main clause, preceded by a subordinate clause introduced by *before.* In both cases the hearer has to know the meaning of the connectives *before* and *after* since the context is not sufficient to support the correct temporal interpretation. Indeed, one might say that the explicit relations marked by the syntax are in a sense at odds with the meaning which would be inferred from the discourse context.

There is evidence which indicates that young children have difficulty in interpreting sentences in which syntax and context are at variance with one another. Some of these complex constructions, like the passive sentences discussed in chapter 3, may not be mastered until the child learns formal writing styles which are highly context-independent. Clark (1973), for example, found that young children relied on what she calls an 'order of mention contract' in producing and understanding complex sentences. The 'order of mention contract' specifies that two events will be mentioned in the order in which they occurred and that constructions which follow this principle will be produced and comprehended earlier and more easily than those which do not. She observed that at an early stage children tended to describe events in their order of occurrence with a separate sentence for each event, or a series of clauses joined by *and* or *and then*. This principle gives way later to one in which main clauses appear first, and then finally children learn to produce subordinate clauses introduced by adverbials like *when* in first postition.

Clark also found that when children were asked to act out a series of two events with toys, they treated the first clause in the sentence as if it described the main and first event. When the order of mention coincided with the order of occurrence, e.g. *The boy patted the dog before he kicked the rock,* young children responded correctly 93 per cent of the time. When the order of mention did not correspond to the order of occurrence, their rate of correct response was only 18 per cent. Older children were able to pay attention to the conjunctions and by the age of five or six most of them could understand the order of events correctly. This pattern of acquisition appeared to hold for each new conjunction the children acquired. Ervin-Tripp (1978b: 361) argues that the order of development in the acquisition of conjunctions reflects the cognitive difficulty of the semantic relationship lexicalized by them. This would of course follow more generally from the view that complexity is indicative of cognitive difficulty.

Table 5.1 Number of connectives in an Edinburgh girl's narrative

	implicit	and	because	well	so
N	20	13	2	1	1
%	54	35	5	3	3

With these findings in mind, let us look more specifically at the syntax of the narrative examined earlier. I have simply listed in table 5.1 the frequency of occurrence of different connectives which appear in the 37 clauses of this narrative. It can be seen that the most frequent means of connecting narrative clauses is direct sequencing with no explicit marking by a connective such as *and*. The use of narrative features like CHP, however, contributes to the overall architecture of the story by indicating shifts in persona, scenes, etc. The next more frequent method of clause connection is by use of the additive connective *and,* which is used almost one-third of the time. The use of other connectives is marginal.

How do these findings relate to the development of narrative syntax and discourse skills? Kernan (1977), who looked at the clause linkage of girls' narratives, found that the youngest children (seven to eight) used additive and temporal connectives much more frequently than the oldest group (thirteen to fourteen). Although the oldest group used *and* and *then*, they also used markers of consequent or causal relations more frequently, e.g. *so, so then*. He does not mention, however, to what extent relations were indicated implicitly, i.e. were not overtly marked. Martin (1983) observed a general trend towards greater explicitness in the marking of non-additive clause relations with increasing age. The younger group (six to seven) marked clause relations significantly less often than older children (eight to nine, nine to ten). He concluded that one way in which children adapt their language to the demands of narrative structure is in making increasingly explicit the relations between clauses.

Martin also found that the extent of explicitness in marking was a function of genre. He collected narratives from three age groups of children in three different task situations: one in which the child had to verbalize a story from a series of pictures on index cards; a second in which the child had to retell the story without the aid of the cards; and a third in which the child had to retell a fable read to him by an adult. The two older groups of children tended to produce more context-independent stories in these tasks than the younger ones, which indicated a different orientation to the task. Overall there was less marking of explicit additive relations in the first task since the additive meaning is inherent in the turning over of the cards. Task three had the smallest number of additive and greatest number of causal and temporal connectives. Martin's explanation for this finding is that the story in the third task depends more on relations of consequence and comparison than does a simple narrative of vicarious experience. The oldest children relied less on *and* as a clause connective and more on other connectives which expressed simpler semantic relations.

We can compare these findings with those of Labov, who stresses the fact that 'the narrative clause is one of the simplest grammatical paterns in connected speech' (1972b: 375). He notes that the fundamental simplicity of narrative syntax is not confined to the stories of pre-adolescents; narratives told by adults show the same pattern. Syntactic complexity is thus generally a rare feature in oral narratives. Labov found that there was a tendency for adults to produce narratives which were on average three times longer than those of pre-adolescents (ten to twelve), as measured in terms of the number of independent clauses. Kernan, however, in his study (1977), did not find a clear indication that length of narrative increased with age. Labov observed a developmental progression in the use of evaluative devices from pre-adolescents to adults, particularly with regard to the use of what he calls correlatives and explicatives. Correlatives serve to combine two events into a single independent clause; they are equivalent to what I have been referring to here as the syntactic processes of conjunction and subordination. Labov says that correlation is an operation requiring complex syntax and is therefore beyond the range of young narrators. Explicatives include some of the more complex connectives I discussed earlier, such as those which mark causality, temporality, etc. These too appear to be outside the repertoires and linguistic capacities of pre-adolescents. Adults, by comparison, have developed the ability to evaluate their representation of experience with more complex linguistic devices. A further interesting point emerged from Labov's comparison of black and white speakers' narratives. There was evidence to suggest that black narrators were more advanced than their white age mates in terms of their use of evaluative syntax. This adds further support to the view that black vernacular culture is rich in verbal skills (cf. the discussion in the next chapter).

Both Labov and Martin raise the question of whether these kinds of differences in syntactic structure are indicative of underlying variability in communicative ability and cognitive development. This would be one way to intepret the finding that given the same task or situation and drawing on the 'same' linguistic resources, children produce systematically different types of texts depending on their age. The linguistic system is the 'same' to the extent that children of the age of six and older are able, for example, to use definite and indefinite articles to present given and new information, and they can use and comprehend additive, temporal and causal connectives. Martin stresses, however, that differences in what he calls 'coding orientation' do not necessarily imply differences in communicative abilities. The coding orientation of younger children's texts is more context-dependent. What matters nonetheless from the point of view of most educators is *how* things are said and done. Within the classroom, as we shall see in the next few chapters, the coding orientation which is considered most prestigious and considered to be connected with success is a context-independent one.

6

Influences on children's language: family, school and peer group

Language is transmitted and acquired through culture-specific socialization and interaction with others in various contexts. In this chapter I will examine the role which home and family, peer group and school play in the child's acquisition of communicative competence.

Bernstein (1981: 334) has used the term 'discourse reproducing agency' in talking about the contexts of transmission of language in society. The three domains of social interaction which I will discuss in this chapter can be thought of as serving the function of primary discourse-reproducing (and also discourse-creating) agencies. As we shall see, the family, peer group and school provide some of the most important characteristic settings in which very different types of discourse and strategies for interaction can be developed, maintained and reproduced.[1]

6.1 *Language at home and in the family*

Children do not acquire language all by themselves. They learn to talk by conversing with others. It is generally taken for granted that the child's primary conversational partners are his parents, in particular, mothers. This is not universally so. I will use the term 'care-taker' or 'care-giver' to refer to those who have the main responsibility for the child's socialization. In some cultures, e.g. Luo, Koya and Samoa, older siblings are responsible for most of the care-giving. Although a great deal more research needs to be done on cross-cultural variability in child-rearing practices and their relation to language learning, it now seems clear that the type and quality of language and conversation to which the child is exposed is a crucial variable which can no longer be neglected. It was not until the late 1960s that descriptions of mothers' speech to children began to counteract the prevailing view that language acquisition was largely innate and occurred independently of the child's social environment. Now much more attention is being paid to the role of adults and other care-givers in shaping the child's linguistic development.

Wells (1979: 17) claims that conversation is the most important context for child language development. The term 'conversation' is used to refer to a speech event which is characterized by an interchange between at least two persons who alternate between speaking and hearing. It is above all a collaborative activity in which each participant conveys his intention and takes account of the informational needs and expectations of the hearer. The successful management of conversation requires a number of skills, e.g. turn-taking, topic introduction and control, interruption, etc.

The developmental history of conversation-like behaviour begins with pre-linguistic infants. At this stage establishing the process of communication is the job of the care-taker, who provides all of the conversation, since children are not yet producing verbal language. The earliest exchanges between child and care-taker are to some extent non-verbal. Routines like dressing and feeding the child may be accompanied by care-taker vocalization. Snow (1977) observes that mothers respond to any kind of sound or facial expression as if it were a conversational remark. Trevarthen (1979) refers to these early exchanges as 'proto-conversations'. The mother's contribution to these ritualistic interactions provides the child with an opportunity to learn about the structure of conversation, so that long before the emergence of true speech the child has learned to take part in conversational exchanges in which notions like turn-taking are observed. Although Piaget would have rejected the idea that children as young as three months could participate in a social interaction, Halliday (1975a) has argued that the child's earliest proto-language utterances are primarily interpersonal (cf. Stern 1977 for some experimental data). They are concerned with the initiation and maintenance of social interaction and develop even before linguistic structure emerges in the two-word stage. Weeks (1979: 45) says that in participating in conversation children demonstrated a knowledge of *when* to say something, even if they had nothing to say. In the extracts below the child's 'ah' functions as a conversational place-holder. The child used this utterance between the ages of 1.3 and 2.3.

Adult: Would you like to tell me about this book? You like this one don't you?
Child: Ah.
Adult: What's that?
Child: Ah.
Adult: Would you like to turn the page of the book?
Child: Ah.

Adult: Why don't you talk to Mummy on the telephone?
Child: (picking up toy telephone) Ah, ah, ah, ah.

Weeks found that other children had different place-holders, e.g. *is it*. The place-holders used by children are primarily of interactional rather than referential significance. They are used to sustain an interaction with others, even though the child at this stage cannot add new material to the adult-initiated topic. Corsaro (1977) and others have found that children develop a number of different routines for engaging adults and others in talk, e.g. *Know what?* Asking a question is a frequently employed strategy for opening conversations since a question creates a discourse obligation to respond, even for young children.

The development of conversational competence should not be seen as a purely cognitive activity which unfolds in a pre-programmed way. Adults provide crucial contextual support and input, as we have seen; but what evidence is there to indicate that adult interaction is necessary or responsible for more rapid psycholinguistic development? One of Chomsky's main arguments for the nativist position is based on the view that adult speech is mostly ungrammatical and full of false starts, hesitations, etc. If input is so degenerate, how can the child learn the relatively abstract structures of a specific language? Chomsky's answer is that input must play a very small role.

There are several ways in which one could counter Chomsky's claim that language must be largely innate and that its development is largely independent of the child's sociolinguistic environment. For one thing, the ungrammaticality of everyday speech appears to be a myth with little basis in actual fact. This observation comes from Labov (1970b: 42), who after having examined samples of everyday speech concluded that about 75 per cent of the utterances were well formed. He says, 'when rules of ellipsis are applied and certain universal editing rules to take care of stammering and false starts, the proportion of truly ungrammatical and ill-formed sentences falls to less than two per cent.' Newport et al. (1977) found that only one out of 1500 of observed utterances used by mothers to their children was disfluent. Secondly, there is increasing evidence that the child is not confronted with highly 'abstract' data. (It is generally not made clear in arguments of the type what is meant by 'abstract'.) Mothers introduce forms and meanings in a principled way and so organize the child's input. The evidence from this comes from a number of studies which have investigated 'motherese' or 'baby talk', as it has been variously referred to (cf. the papers in Snow and Ferguson 1977).

These studies have identified a number of characteristics of mothers' speech to young children. Not only does it tend to be highly fluent, it is also redundant, simple and produced with a higher pitch. Snow (1977: 47) says that the semantic content of mothers' speech is largely limited to constructions the child has already learned. The MLU (mean length of utterance) of mothers' utterances is closely associated with the child's rate of psycholinguistic development (cf. Cross 1977: 166). It is difficult to argue, however, that the mother's input is syntactically simple, at least when measured by the usual yardstick of derivational complexity or history. Mothers also use a wide range of sentence types in talking to their children. The only sense in which baby talk is simpler is that utterances are shorter. Each sentence tends to encode one proposition at a time. It is this semantic limitation which produces the ostensible grammatical simplicity. Mothers tend to use co-ordinate or subordinate clauses in addressing children. This means that MLU is measuring something quite different from syntactic complexity and that syntactic complexity is not isomorphic with propositional complexity (this is a point I will return to later in the discussion of syntactic complexity in section 6.2). MLU reflects semantic more than syntactic complexity. Virtually the same amount of semantic information can be conveyed in one proposition as opposed to two. How semantic information is conveyed in surface syntax depends on the options available at a particular stage within a linguistic system and to a learner for encoding it (cf. chapter 3).

There are at least two main objections one could raise to Brown's (1977: 20) conclusions about the significance of baby talk in the child's development. He says that research overwhelmingly refutes:

> the rather offhand assertions of Chomsky and his followers that the pre-school child could not learn language from the complex but syntactically degenerate sample his parents provide without the aid of an elaborate innate component. But it has turned out that parental speech is well formed and finely tuned to the child's psycholinguistic capacity. The corollary would seem to be that there is less need for an elaborate innate component than there at first seemed to be.[2]

The first objection that can be raised is that, just by demonstrating the special characteristics of mothers' speech to children, one does not prove that it is better for the language learner. There are no universal design features which delimit this type of speech from all others and make it unique. Ferguson (1977) points out that baby talk shares some characteristics with foreigner talk (i.e. the speech addressed to foreigners) and pidgins (i.e. languages which develop for purposes of intergroup communication among people who have no language in common). Some of the features such as repetition, short MLU, etc. shared by baby talk derive from the attempt to converse with conversational partners who are in some respects inadequate. In other words, the style emerges in the form it does not because mothers are in any sense aware of what is simple or best for language learning, but out of this exigencies of communicating with a naive conversational partner. Whatever constructional simplifications occur, do so by dint of interactional constraints.

Newport et al. (1977) think that the effects of baby talk on children's language development have been somewhat exaggerated. Their objections are mainly methodological, and they attempt to establish the baseline from which the child starts in relation to where it eventually ends up. They maintain (1977: 131) that certain highly delimited aspects of motherese have an effect on limited aspects of learning. It is very interesting that they found the mother's speech style exerts its greatest influence on language-specific structures. In other words, certain language-specific aspects of morphology and syntax which vary cross-linguistically are influenced quite strikingly in their rate of growth. Newport et al. (1977: 133) found that the English-speaking child's growth rate for noun inflection correlated highly with the mother's tendency to use imperatives. What is universal, or common to all languages, appears largely unaffected by what the mother does. For example, the use of complex sentences is unaffected by the mother's speech. Their emergence seems to be purely a function of age, and dependent therefore on cognitive and linguistic maturity. The authors conclude (1977: 147) that 'the mother has little latitude to teach her child about the nature of language, but she can at least improve his English'.

The second objection one could raise to the claims made for the effects of baby talk on children's language development is based on cross-cultural evidence. Ferguson (1977: 233) observes that, given the wide variation in the linguistic details of baby talk from one community to another, it seems highly unlikely that it is a crucial element in the acquisition process. He furthermore suggests (1977: 209) that baby-talk register types are probably universal and that all speech communities have special ways of talking to young children which differ more or less systematically from the forms customarily used with adults. Ferguson's remarks need a great deal more investigation. Nevertheless, from the relatively few cross-cultural studies of language acquisition which exist, it is obvious that children can and do learn language without the benefit of the characteristics of baby talk.

There are great cultural and subcultural differences in what is believed about and expected of children. Although some researchers like Ferguson have suggested that features of baby-talk register are universal, the most that should be said is that it is probably found cross-culturally in societies in which the child is seen as a legitimate participant in interaction. It is certainly widespread in the middle-class 'Anglo' society in which most of the research on child acquisition has been conducted. In this particular sub-culture, care-givers expand utterances and remodel the child's meanings in terms of the adult system of syntax. The child's utterances are seen as imperfect renditions of what the care-giver assumes the child intends to say. Adults treat the child's language as merely an immature and imperfect form of their own.

The extent to which caretakers attend and respond to children's babblings and other vocalization varies a great deal. Among many sectors of English-speaking communities it is widely believed that children who talk early must be bright, and that those who speak late are 'delayed'. Chaga-speaking[3] parents boast of their children's linguistic accomplishments and report their every word. Weeks (1979: 40) notes that the Ottawa believed that the cries of infants were meaningful and had specialists to interpret them. The Mohave and Tlingit also consider young infants to be capable of understanding speech.

By contrast, in other cultures such as Japan, parents do not believe the baby understands anything and tend not to encourage speech production. They imitate the baby's sounds but do not converse with him. In discussing child-rearing practice in Western Samoa, Ochs (1982: 83) says that the Samoan care-giver 'sees the unclear utterance as nothing like adult language' and therefore does not expand it. The child's imperfect output is ridiculed (if it is attended to at all) and treated literally as if it were a foreign language. By comparison, the Kaluli society of Papua New Guinea studied by Schieffelin (1979) is one in which care-givers assume the role of language teacher; Samoan care-givers do not. Scollon and Scollon (1979: 133) report that Chipewyan parents assume that children do not speak until they are five. This is the 'normal' process of growing up respectfully and is not interpreted as a sign of 'delayed' acquisition. Korean parents similarly stress silence as a part of good behaviour. Chipewyan adults furthermore assume that good grammatical performance is expected only of older people. It is generally believed that Chipewyan takes a lifetime to learn because it is so difficult. Blount (1977: 299) notes that in Luo and Koya society care-givers were not responsive to the language mistakes made by children; however, they did pay attention to and gave explicit instructions for the social appropriateness of speech.

Cultural definitions of the social positions which children occupy are a major component in the process of linguistic socialization. Ochs (1982), for instance, says that the process of acquisition for Samoan children is strongly shaped by the social norms for using language and cultural attitudes and beliefs about communication between care-givers and children. These can be seen to affect the form and content of the child's grammar and the order of acquisition. In Samoan households there are a number of care-givers who differ in age and status, but it is the lowest-ranking persons who bear the responsibility of satisfying children's needs. She found that Samoan children acquired ergative case marking fairly late (i.e. after four years) by comparison with the Kaluli children studied by Schieffelin (1979) and (1981), who acquire it quite early (i.e. 2.2 years). Bickerton (1981) has recently cited the Kaluli child's early acquisition as support for his theory that the semantic distinction encoded in ergativity (i.e. causative vs. non-causative) is biologically basic and therefore pre-programmed and innate. He predicts that since the syntactic marking of ergativity is salient and uniform (in that it consists of a causative suffix applied to agentive nouns), it is acquired early. If Bickerton is right, then Samoan children should acquire ergative case marking no less early since it is encoded in an equally transparent manner in their language too. This is in effect the view endorsed by Slobin, (forthcoming) as discussed in chapter 4, Slobin (1980) and Brown and Hanlon (1970). In Ochs's view (1982: 78), however, the reason for this 'delayed acquisition' is social. Ergative case marking is not distributed equally throughout the community. It is more typical of men's rather than women's speech. Furthermore, it rarely appears in the speech of family members within the household, where women and older siblings are the child's primary socializing agents.

Ochs's findings certainly have far-reaching ramifications for developmental psycholinguistic studies which attempt to explain the order of acquisition of various structures in terms of purely cognitive and innate principles. Many of those who have argued for a link between complexity and order of emergence have not taken account of the fact that social context is an important mediator in this process. While cognitive development may be a pace-setter for the syntactic categories available to the learner, the semantics of these categories is often specific to a particular language and it is simplistic to argue that developmental theories of cognition and syntax/semantics are order-isomorphic (cf. chapter 4).

The beliefs and perceptions of care-givers with regard to the linguistic competence expected of a child shape the nature of interaction between child and caregiver. Snow (1977: 37) says that even prelingual children in some societies elicit simplified speech from adults who believe that children are to be treated as participants (albeit deficient ones in some respects) in an interaction, but not from those who do not.

One need not go to the South Pacific for examples of 'exotic' cultures, where beliefs and expectations have an effect on the care-taker register and the child's input. Heath (1983) presents a striking comparison of the differences in the norms of linguistic socialization between white middle-class communities and lower-class black and white ones in the Southern United States.

Heath says that one white working-class community (referred to as Roadville) is one which teaches its children how to talk, while in another working-class black community (referred to as Trackton), children learn how to talk. Trackton children are not incorporated into the adult talk around them until they have learned to demonstrate appropriate conversational skills. During the child's babbling stage adults do not treat the child's 'noises' as communicative attempts. Although adults are literate and read a great variety of material, they do not generally have reading materials for their children, nor do they observe a bedtime ritual of reading to their children as parents in Roadville do. When Trackton children are at a more advanced stage of syntactic development, they imitate adult utterances and make up bits of conversation. They are not attended to by the adult unless they get so noisy that they interfere with adult conversation. Only at a later stage do they participate in conversations.

In Roadville the child is exposed to what Heath calls 'literacy-based stimuli' from the time it is born. Adults point to objects in the environment, decorations on the wall, pictures in books, etc. They recite nursery ryhmes, and expand children's utterances. Before they can talk, children are introduced to visitors and prompted to perform politeness routines and greetings. Children have books from an early age and are frequently read to at bedtime.

Children in Roadville not only participate in adult conversational interactions, but they also participate in reading. That is, when read to, children are asked to provide labels for pictures, point to pictures, make animal sounds and relate the events of a story to real-life objects and events. Bedtime story episodes orient Roadville children to the written word at an early age. Children socialized in this type of environment develop what Heath and others have called 'pre-school literacy skills'. Scollon and Scollon (1981: 62) observed that their two-year-old daughter had learned to 'write' stories on a page by making marks from left to right and to 'read' them with a prosody which was distinct from conversation prosody. The child had acquired a good understanding of the relationship between the written symbol and the read text even though being years away from being able to decode it. Heath found that young Roadville children often sat on their own with books repeating chunks which they had memorized, turning the pages and making eye movements as they went.

The significance of different modes of socialization has received much discussion in various quarters for a least 30 years or so, particularly in relation to their alleged connection with educational success. A crucial question is the extent to which school socialization and experience are discontinuous with respect to that of the home. Undoubtedly, learning to participate in the discourse of the classroom is a major step in the development of communicative competence since it is there that the child adds the linguistic skills of reading and writing to his repertoire.

6.2. Language in the school

By the time children enter school they are capable of constructing most of the sentence types of their language and of encoding complex semantic relationships. In school they are probably not going to encounter an overwhelming number of syntactic constructions or phonological units which are unfamiliar. However, this is not intended to under-emphasize the amount of language learning which the child still has to do. In the communicative situation of the home the child develops the ability to communicate and interpret meaning within a system where there is already an assumed basis of shared knowledge. In school, however, communication does not always proceed against a background of shared assumptions. Children must learn to appreciate what part of their assumed communicative knowledge must be expressed explicitly in any particular situation.

In the transition from home to school the relationship between language and context is one aspect of the child's experience which changes quite dramatically. Given the enormous variability in language socialization which children may receive at home, it would be a mistake to talk about the notion 'language of the home' as if it were a homogeneous and monolithic entity and to compare it with 'school language'. It is generally true, however, that most of the talk and learning which goes on at home arises out of the context of practical activity. Often these activities are initiated by the child. The school, however, is more often mainly an adult-structured setting. Classroom talk is largely teacher-initiated, and the contexts in which learning is designed to take place are often unfamiliar to the child and are abstract. To the extent that the contexts for interaction and learning differ between school and home, children may experience difficulty. Strategies for interpreting, using and learning language at home may turn out to be ineffective and even unproductive at school.

A great deal of the work on the causes of educational success and failure has identified language as the key factor. While language is undoubtedly at the heart of learning, Rosen (1972) says that language has now replaced IQ as an explanation for social and education disadvantage. Much of the work on the study of language in relation to social class and school failure has claimed that the difference between home and school language is responsible. The majority of the discussion has been carried out in the absence of any systematic comparison of the uses of language in these two settings. Two notable exceptions are the work of Heath in the US and Wells in Britain.

One of the earliest and most influential theories about the connection between language and success or failure in school is that of Bernstein. I do not intend to attempt to discuss fully Bernstein's views here. These have been variously formulated over the past 25 years or so and have been discussed and criticized by others (some of the best discussions and summaries of Bernstein's ideas can be found in Stubbs 1976, Rosen 1972, Gordon 1981). In his early work of the late 1950s Bernstein distinguishes between a 'public language' used mainly by the working class and a 'formal language' of the middle class. These are later referred to as 'restricted' and 'elaborated' codes respectively. The codes have different linguistic properties; the elaborated code, for example, has a greater syntactic complexity, as evidenced by a high proportion of subordinate clauses, conjunctions, etc., and complex modification structures, e.g. adjective and adverb phrases. The elaborated code makes meaning linguistically explicit; one does not have to be in the situation to understand what is going on. The meaning is in the text and not in the context. A code can be thought of as a strategy for using language to realize meaning. The distribution of these codes in society is considered by Bernstein to be a major cause of social inequality and educational failure. The codes are acquired by socialization into particular kinds of family structures and social class background and through exposure to different speech models.

For many, the implication of Bernstein's work was that speakers of underprivileged groups would be able to succeed in school if they had access to the elaborated code. This led to many versions of what has been called 'deficit' theory in which the claim is made that children who come to school without having been socialized in the uses and kinds of language which lead to school success have been deprived and are deficient. The notion of deprivation and deficit has not been well defined. It refers sometimes to material deprivation, such as in the case of children who come from overcrowded homes and/or are under-nourished. Others have referred more specifically to linguistic deprivation (which may not be exclusively a feature of materially disadvantaged homes). Deutsch et al., for example, devised (1970) an index of cultural deprivation based on questions like how often children eat dinner with their parents, how frequently they go to museums, etc. The index is based on a concept of a 'good home' which is culture- and often class-specific. The style of child-rearing favoured by white middle-class mothers in the US and Britain is not the only way to produce children with well-developed linguistic skills. It is therefore over-simplified to say certain 'deficiencies' on the part of certain, mainly working-class, mothers and their children explain the child's failure at school. What is 'deficiency' in one culture is the norm elsewhere, as we have seen in section 6.1.

Nevertheless, it has been demonstrated repeatedly that children from working-class homes on the whole do less well at school than those from middle-class homes. In Britain, for example, it has been found that the chances of an unskilled manual worker's child being a poor reader at age seven are six times greater than those of a professional worker's child, and that an unskilled worker's child has at the same age a fifteen-times greater chance of being a 'non-reader'. On the basis of 'facts' such as these and a 'theory' of language deficit, programmes of compensatory education were launched in the US and elsewhere to provide 'deprived' pre-school children with compensating experience and exposure to middle-class culture so that when these children came to school they could start on an equal footing with middle-class children. Between 1965 and 1970 ten billion dollars was spent on this type of education for poor and minority groups in the US; the best known of these programmes was Project Headstart.

When the results of these programmes became available and they were found to have only negligible effects, many people, especially sociolinguists like Labov, began to criticize the logic of compensatory education and deprivation theory.[4] Labov (1969) argued that the concept of cultural deprivation was a myth and he attacked Bernstein severely for contributing to this view. It is not at all clear, however, to what extent Bernstein has held this view of deprivation or even whether his work implies it. Bernstein in fact published an article in 1970 attacking the concept of compensatory education. Nevertheless, many people have assumed that Bernstein's theory is one which supports the notion of linguistic deprivation.

Extreme versions of deficit theory have been put forward by Bereiter and Engelman (1966) and Deutsch et al. (1970), who claimed that children did not have 'enough' language and that the job of the teacher was to teach 'a language'. One result of this was the adoption of methods of foreign-language teaching for native speakers of English. When programmes of this type did not prove successful either, some argued that intervention had come too late. Some said it was mothers who needed compensatory education because they were not socializing their children into the kind of environment which would lead to school success. Obviously if this sort of argumentation is pushed to its extreme, we are no longer talking about environmental differences, but genetic ones (the nature/nurture controversy once again); and indeed some did argue this (Jensen 1969).

Labov's counter-argument to deficit theories has since come to be known as the 'difference' hypothesis or theory: different groups have different ways of using language but no one's language is deficient. Labov argued his case most forcefully in a paper (1969) which examined the differences between Black English Vernacular and standard English. His case against verbal deficit is based on three types of evidence which have emerged from sociolinguistic research. The first of these I have discussed in chapter 2 in relation to methodology and will return to again in my discussion of testing procedures in chapter 8. Children may not perform well in situations which they perceive as threatening. Labov compares the behaviour of a young black boy when interviewed by a white interviewer and a young black interviewer. In the former situation the child is judged as non-verbal, while in the latter he is very talkative. The second piece of evidence is discussed in section 6.3 and comes from studies of peer groups' influences on language, in particular the role of these groups in enforcing the norms of non-standard speech and patterns of behaviour which are directly opposed to those required for school success. Labov also points out that native black culture is very rich in verbal skills.

The third bit of evidence comes from linguistic studies of the features of Black English Vernacular. Labov argues that non-standard dialects are just as structurally complex, rule-governed and capable of expressing logical arguments as standard English. It is due to the fact that the prestige of non-standard speech is low that it is considered inappropriate for school use. Labov compares a sample of speech from a black teenager in Harlem with that of an upper-middle-class college-educated black speaker to show that the syntax used by both is capable of presenting a logical argument. Moreover he is critical of the educated speaker who uses elaborate qualifications and repeats some of the same information as being too verbose.

There are a number of fallacies behind the assumption made in deficit theory. Perhaps the most dangerous is the idea that logicality is linked specifically with the use of particular linguistic means of expression and that since it is middle-class children who do better in school these speech habits are essential to learning. Greater attention is now being paid to the role of social function and not just syntactic complexity, which is a superficial characteristic. And it has become increasingly evident that differing styles of interaction do not correlate neatly with social class.

I will look next at some of the studies on classroom discourse and teacher talk to see whether they lend any support to the idea that school experience is to some extent discontinuous with that of the home. Learning to participate in classroom discourse is essential if children are to benefit from teaching activities. If we look at the overall context of the classroom as a setting for learning as opposed to that of the home, there are a number of obvious differences. For one thing, maintenance of order in a large group-interactional setting like the classroom presents a substantial management problem. I am using 'order' in a physical as well as a linguistic sense. The teacher cannot carry out his/her goals if all the children speak at once or move freely about the classroom doing what they like. Great emphasis is placed on order in both these senses in the classroom. Desks and materials must be kept in order and so must discourse. Although all the children have developed discourse skills and know some interactional routines, they are not necessarily equipped to participate in the interaction which occurs in the classroom. The child may be presented with a more limited set of conversational options than he has encountered at home. The distribution of rights to speak, question and introduce topics is asymmetrical. The teacher decides who speaks and when and what contributions count as appropriate and right. The school day is organized into a number of sub-events such as story-telling, reading, lessons, show and tell, etc., each of which is governed by certain (often implicit) rules. The classroom need not of course be structured in this way, but by tradition it very often is. The structure of classroom discourse and teacher talk have received extensive discussion (cf. Sinclair and Coulthard 1975 and Heath 1978).

To what extent does teacher talk possess special properties which delimit it from other kinds of discourse the child may have experienced? Mehan (1974) examined how teachers framed questions and how pupils answered them. In one lesson he observed the teacher was trying to teach children to talk about spatial relations such as *behind, under,* etc. by getting them to describe the location of certain objects in pictures. When the children did not respond to the teacher's satisfaction, sometimes she just said, 'Can you say that in a sentence?' and gave a model for imitation such as 'The seed is under the grass.' Having an example of the teacher's idea of a complete and correct response does provide the child with more information, but the features which make a sentence more correct by comparison with other possible answers such as 'under the grass' are not made clear. The teacher does not say why certain answers are correct and why others are incorrect, even though they may not be factually wrong, but only inappropriate in terms of the teacher's unstated expectations. She differentially counts some answers as right and others wrong. When the child produced a correct answer, the teacher did not say, 'That's the kind of answer I want – from now on answer like that'. The teacher is more concerned to correct what she perceives as matters of good grammatical usage rather than fact and she has decided that of all the possible formulations the one which states the facts in a complete sentence is the only correct one. Presumably the teacher is merely acting on the grammatical ideology taught to her in which a sentence is a unit expressing a complete thought. These and other definitions can be easily found in prescriptive grammars, which try to make a connection between the expression of logical thought and certain features of surface syntax. This is a connection which is made in grammar books but which has no objective linguistic basis. It is due to the sanctioning of certain modes of grammatical expression by society that complete sentences are regarded as better than incomplete ones.

Dannequin (1977) observes similar classroom practices by French teachers with regard to notions of correctness. She emphasizes that the pupils do not have the 'right' to make mistakes, but must instead conform to teachers' standards. Often these are implicit. One teacher said to a child (Hardy et al. 1977: 26). 'Parle plus lentement: tu parles trop vite. Parle lentement et fais moi des phrases bien correctes. Tu veux parler trop vite et tu ne parles pas bien français. Reflechissez pour parler bien comme il faut, pour ne pas dire n'importe quoi'. ('Speak more slowly. You speak too quickly. Speak slowly and in correct sentences. You speak too quickly and you're not speaking good French. Think about what you're going to say so that you speak well in the way one is supposed to and so that you don't just say anything.')

Another example from Dannequin (1977: 94–5) shows a teacher trying to elicit a complete sentence from children and using repetition drills which are similar to those used to teach foreign-language learners.

T: Avec quoi prend-on la température?
     What does one take a temperature with?

P: Un thermomètre.
      A thermometer.
T: Une petite phrase. Avec quoi prend-on la température? Véronique,
      une phrase.
      A short sentence. What does one take a temperature with? Veronica, a
      sentence.
V: Un thermomètre.
      A thermometer.
T: Tu me réponds par un mot. Je veux une phrase.
      You've given me a word. I want a sentence.
V: Avec un thermomètre.
      With a thermometer.
T: Ce n'est toujours pas une phrase. Tu me réponds par un autre mot. Je
      voudrais une phrase − Myriam.
      That's still not a sentence. You've just given me another word. I want a
      sentence − Myriam.
M: Maman/prend/la température/avec un thermomètre [utterance is
      syllable-timed with each chunk forming a separate tone group].
      Mother takes a temperature with a thermometer.
T: Voilà. Répète Véronique.
      There. Repeat, Veronica.

We can see that French teachers have many of the same ideas about
what counts as 'good French' as English teachers have about 'good
English'. Children are told to speak slowly and clearly and to use 'correct'
(i.e. complete) sentences. In correcting the contributions of students the
teacher uses a variety of evaluative devices such as 'That's not very nice,'
or 'Can one say that better?', but very little explicit guidance as to what is
required. The teacher also considers 'planned contributions' better than
'unplanned ones', although she does not say explicitly how the children are
supposed to reflect on or plan ahead the contributions that they will offer
in response to the teachers' questions. The distinction between 'planned
and unplanned' discourse is drawn by Ochs (1979). Discourse which is
planned is often very formal and less spontaneous than unplanned
discourse. The more planned uses of languages draw upon knowledge
transmitted through formal education. This includes, according to Ochs
(1979: 54), the use of complex syntactic structures (e.g. complementation,
cleft constructions, certain types of relative clauses, passives) and more
formal discourse devices (e.g. use of textual cohesion and transitional
terms such as *for example, that is, furthermore,* and the use of topic
sentences to open paragraphs in written discourse). Before coming to
school many children may be exposed primarily to spontaneous unplanned
discourse, which is probably the most frequent mode in interpersonal
interaction. In spontaneous speech speakers rely less heavily on syntax to

articulate semantic relations between referents or propositions. We have already seen some of these differences in looking at children's narrative syntax in chapter 5.

There is also the issue of metalinguistic awareness, i.e. one's notions of the ability to talk about language as having an objective existence. We have observed how some children may have a great deal of pre-literacy experience and come to school with some idea of words, paragraphs, etc. Teachers sometimes assume that children understand their grammatical formulations and ask questions like 'What does this letter say?' in teaching children to read. Weeks (1979: 29) reports the story of a child who thought she was deaf because she was unable to hear the letters whispering. She later discovered that letters do not really say anything. Shuy reports a similar story of a boy who did not understand the teacher's distinction between 'long e' and 'short e' when asked to say them, and he produced the sound /i/ one short and one longer, i.e. [i] and [i:]. The teacher was referring to the difference in quality and quantity between the sounds in *bed* and *seed*. Another aspect of the problem of metalinguistic vocabulary in the earlier example of the French teacher is the fact that French makes no distinction between what in English is referred to as 'phrase' or 'sentence'. The word *phrase* could be translated as either, and is therefore ambiguous. It is also interesting in the French example that the teacher treats both replies 'un thermomètre' and 'avec un thermomètre' as equivalent, referring to both of them as an example of an answer which employs a 'mot' rather than a 'phrase'. It is not therefore obvious from anything the teacher explicitly says that the kind of answer she wants is a complete sentence, but it becomes clear when she accepts Myriam's version and asks Véronique to repeat it.

Since much of the teacher's strategy is based on question–answer exchanges, one possible source of difference between home and school may lie in the use of questions. Heath (1982a) conducted a comparative study in a community in the southeastern US. She examined questioning strategies in a working-class black community,[5] the classrooms attended by children from the community and the homes of teachers from these classrooms. Previous studies of questions reveal that they are used for training children to interact verbally with their caretakers and to direct their attention to things. Snow (1977), for example, found that a large percentage of utterances used by middle-class mothers with their children are questions (to which they often provide the answers for the child). Heath points out, however, that the specific characteristics of questions and their uses in socializing young children are dependent on the network of those who ask questions. The classroom teachers used questions at home with their children for a number of purposes. The most frequent type was a question to elicit an answer which the questioner already knew (the so-called 'known answer' question), e.g. 'What colour is that?' Questions of this type accounted for nearly half the data. Another type asked for answers which the addressee knew, e.g. 'What do you want?' Others were rhetorical questions or directives, e.g. 'I wonder why he's there?' 'Would you like to set the table?' In the teachers' homes, questions were used to talk with children as conversational partners and to talk about things out of context.

In the other homes, children were asked questions but generally they were not of the type for which adults already had the answers. Children were not asked 'What's that?' but more often 'What's that like?' Children were not requested to name objects or events but to compare events, objects and persons. One grandmother commented to Heath (1982a: 24), 'We don't talk to our children like you folks do; we don't ask them about colours, names and things.'

Questions about things figure prominently not only in the teachers' homes but also in their classrooms. And one of the complaints of the teachers was that some children did not seem able to answer the simplest questions. Some of the children appeared aware of the difference in the questions they were asked at home and school. Heath (1982a: 1) cites classroom incidents in which a teacher persisted in asking questions about a story the children had just read, e.g. 'Who is it the story talks about?' (note the use of the metaphor of a story 'talking'), 'Who is the main character?', etc. One child replied: 'Ain't nobody can talk about things being about themselves.' The boy was reacting to the fact that the teachers' questions were so often about events and things in isolation of their context. Another example came from a four year old whom Heath observed acting out conversations in front of a mirror. When Heath asked her who she was, she said she was playing at talking like Mr Griffin, who was an insurance salesman. The child was imitating the type of questions he asked ('What's your name?') and she knew he asked questions in ways different from members of the community. Yet another child on the way home from nursery school, where he had spent a few weeks, asked Heath a series of questions about a fire truck that passed, e.g. 'What colour dat truck? What colour dat coat? What colour dat car?' When she expressed surprise at being asked questions to which they both knew the answer, the boy began laughing. He had been imitating the questions the teacher had asked at school.

In comparing the classroom with the homes, Heath (1982a: 36) comments that the communicative competence acquired by children in responding to questions in their own community had little positive transfer to the classroom. She identified three major characteristics of school questions which children had not learned: (1) They had not learned how to respond to utterances which were interrogative in form, but directive in pragmatic function. (2) Questions of the type which expected students to feed back information known to the teachers were outside their general experience.

(3) They had little or no experience with questions which asked for a display of specific skills and content information acquired primarily from a familiarity with books and ways of talking about them. One of the main contexts for this type of experience is the bedtime story discussed in section 6.1.

Heath reports the progress of one boy when he began nursery school, which was his first experience in an institutional setting away from the family. During school activities which focused on giving labels to things and discussing the attributes of objects, the child did not participate and showed no interest in looking at books. However, in those learning tasks in which the teacher showed children how to do things rather than talked about them, he was enthusiastic. He was more familiar with a style of learning which took place by showing rather than telling (cf. the Scollons' 1981 discussion of these styles among native Alaskans).

Heath's study is also a good example of the value of ethnographic work. By feeding back her findings to the classroom teachers, they became aware of the need to teach children how to verbalize the characteristics of things in and of themselves. Teachers openly discussed with students the different kinds of questions used in the classroom and the kinds of answers required. Teachers also used some of the questioning strategies which the children were familiar with, e.g. 'What's this like?', 'What's happening here?' The children responded and became involved in lessons when they knew how to answer.

Heath's work illustrates the invisible barriers which can arise from the fact that what appears to be superficially the same linguistic form, i.e. questions, can be embedded in particular communication and interpersonal contexts. To the extent that strategies of questioning at home and school are carried out in different ways to accomplish different goals, children's access to the participation structure of the classroom is impeded.[6] There has been some discussion of what psychologists have called 'cognitive styles' in teaching and learning. One type, 'field independent', is characteristic of learners who work independently, are competitive, seek individual recognition and prefer distance rather than physical contact with the teacher. Another type, 'field sensitive', is characteristic of children who prefer working with others and seek a personal relationship with their teachers. These styles should not be seen as absolutes; individual learners may, however, tend more towards one style of learning than others. Discontinuities between teacher and student styles of interaction in the teaching/learning process can cause a number of problems for members of various minority groups (e.g. native Americans, Afro-Americans, Hawaiian Americans, rural Appalachians and some working-class white groups in the US and Britain).

Gumperz (1981: 19) shows how differences in the norms for interpretation of communicative strategies can lead to the stereotyping of children as slow or uncooperative learners. In one classroom he observed situations in which black children responded to the teacher's requests by saying 'I don't know,' 'I can't do this', etc. These replies were interpreted by white teachers as unwillingness to co-operate. Black listeners, however, agreed that the meaning which the black children conveyed to them was that they did not want to be alone in performing activities such as reading or writing.

Philips (1974) found that American Indian children participated more enthusiastically and performed more effectively in classroom activities which minimized the obligation on the part of the students to perform publicly as individuals and in settings where the teacher did not control performance styles and correct 'errors'. The fact that students performed better in these circumstances was attributable to the similarity between these contexts and the kinds of relationships children were accustomed to on the reservation. These lateral networks of children in groups were much more important than hierarchical role-differentiated networks of adults and children.

I pointed out in my introduction to this section that one of the reasons why school has such an important influence in shaping a child's language development is that it creates a context in which new uses of language occur. Probably the most significant of the new linguistic skills a child learns in school are reading and writing. I have already mentioned too that certain kinds of activities in the home such as the reading of bedtime stories can prepare children for acquiring literacy. A number of classroom activities build on the pre-literacy skills which some children bring with them to school. Michaels (1981) shows how one such classroom event, 'sharing time', in which children relate a narrative of personal experience, can either provide or deny access to key literacy-related experience depending on the extent to which the teacher and child bring to the activity a shared set of discourse conventions and interpretative strategies. When the child's discourse style matches the teacher's own literate style and expectations, collaboration is rhythmically synchronized and allows the child to develop and reinforce a literate discourse style.

Sharing time can be thought of as a speech event whose rules are defined by the teacher. It is opened by a request such as 'Who has something important, special or exciting to share?' In asking the children to tell about 'important' things, we can see again that some implicit and tacit assumptions are being made by the teacher about what is important and what is not, just as in the earlier example I cited of a French teacher who urged children to think carefully about what they were going to say. As Michaels (1981: 434) says: 'Simply reminding the children to talk about important events did not provide them with the criteria for either topic selection or discourse style. Telling about important things was, in effect a gloss for topic centred accounting. It made sense only if one had a topic centred schema to begin with.' From the remarks some children made it was evident that they did not have a clear idea what the teacher meant by 'important'. Michaels cites one exchange where the teacher asked: 'Is this very, *very* important because we don't have much time this morning?' The child replied: 'I don't know if it is or not but I want to say it anyway.'

Through Michaels's careful ethnographic monitoring of sharing time it emerged that what the teacher wanted was for the children to tell about one thing and to do so in a literate style which made the topic sound important. In other words, certain topics of discourse were not inherently trivial or uninteresting (and therefore categorized as 'unimportant'), but often some of the children used rhetorical styles which made it seem (to the teacher at any rate) that there was no topic whatsoever. The teacher's schema for sharing had something in common with the everyday notions of narrative structure and logical temporal sequencing I discussed in chapter 5, but in many respects her criteria were far more restrictive. Her view was that an important account should take the form of a simple statement and resolution centring on a single topic. Michaels (1981: 427–8) summarizes her schema as follows:

1 Objects were to be named and described, even when in plain sight.
2 Talk was to be explicitly grounded temporally and spatially.
3 Minimal shared background or contextual knowledge was to be assumed on the part of the audience.
4 Thematic ties needed to be lexicalized if topic shifts were to be seen as motivated and relevant.

If we applied these criteria of evaluation to everyday conversationally embedded narratives of the type we looked at in chapter 5, we can see that the school narratives expected by the teacher are book-like in that details have to be fully lexicalized and explicit and are in certain respects far removed from the narratives of everyday life. It is important to point out that the difference between ordinary narratives like the one told by a ten-year-old Edinburgh girl and the ones required in the classroom lies not in any notion of absolute complexity. I have demonstrated the complexity in narrative structure which the girl manages to achieve, even though she relies on fairly simple syntactic structures and clause/sentence connection. This teacher expects much less complexity of organization, but greater syntactic complexity. It is not the case that one mode of expression is any less logical than the other, but rather that one is judged to be better, largely because standards of correctness are based on the norms of the written language.

Michaels also observed that when children used the style of narration the teacher expected, she was more successful in picking up on the child's topic and expanding it through her questions and comments. Both the teacher and the child have a shared sense of what the topic is and collaborate in rhythmically synchronized exchanges, developing together a high degree of cohesion within and across turns. When the teacher can do this she plays a crucial role in structuring the child's discourse and can help the child learn the kind of discourse she considers appropriate in the classroom. Unfortunately, however, since many of her criteria are implicit, she can do this most successfully with children who already have the rudiments of this style of narration. Michaels contrasts what happens when some of the children presented narratives in different discourse styles. The black children in the classroom tended to use what Michaels (1981: 429) calls a 'topic-associating' style in which a series of implicitly associated personal anecdotes is related. The topic-associating style had few explicitly lexicalized connectives and no general statement of theme, and topic shifts were signalled prosodically. This kind of discourse was difficult for the teacher to follow, who expected thematic focusing on a single topic. In terms of the teacher's notions of sharing, these children seemed to ramble on and their narratives seemed to have no beginnings, middles or ends. The 'thematic focus' was never overtly stated but had to be inferred from the series of anecdotes rather than through tightly structured linear description.

It is worth examining in detail how the teacher reacts to these two different styles and what the consequences of her differential success are. The following is a condensed version of a narrative told in the topic-associating style. The contributions labelled D are those of the child and T those of the teacher.[7]

T: I want you to share some one thing that's very important.
D: In the summer, I mean, when I go back to school in September, I'm gonna have a new coat and I already got it and it's got a lot of brown in it and when I got it yesterday and when I saw it, my brother was going somewhere. When I saw it on the couch and I showed my sister and I was reading something out on the bag and my big sister said: Deena you have to keep that away from Keisha cause that's my baby sister and I said 'no' and I said the plastic bag because when she was with me my cousin and her –
T: Wait a minute. You stick with your coat now. I said you could tell one thing.
D: This was about my –
T: OK. All right, go on.
D: And yesterday when I got my coat my cousin ran outside and he tried to get him and when he got in my house he layed on the floor and I told him to get up because he was crying.
T: What's that have to do with your coat?
D: Because he wanted to go outside.
T: Why?

D: Cause my mother wanted us to stay in the house.
T: What does that have to do with your coat?
D: Because . . . I don't know.
T: OK. Thank you very much, Deena.

At the points where the teacher interrupts, she tries to bring the child back to develop what she believes to be the important thing or topic, namely the coat. She is looking for an explicit thematic connection but what she gets is a narrative listing of temporally related events, i.e. they all happened 'yesterday'. The teacher continues to urge the child for an explicit thematic link until the child finally sits down.

Michaels interviewed the child afterwards about the narrative to see if there was some semantic connection between the topics which had failed to be made explicit. The child explained the link between her cousin and her new coat by saying that she was trying to keep him from putting his dirty hands on it. The other topic had to do with her baby sister and the plastic bag. Michaels argues that for the child there was a link between these two topics in that in the one case she was protecting a young child from the coat and in the other the coat from a messy child. It is not of course possible to say whether the child could or would have verbalized these links had she been able to go on with her narrative. Michaels stresses, however, that what is important is the failure of the teacher and the child to develop the topic collaboratively. Part of the reason why the teacher does not help the child to produce the kind of narrative she wants is that she cannot see her way in; she cannot follow the transition between topics. During Michaels's interview with the child it emerged that she had felt frustrated and interpreted the teacher's interruptions as a sign of her lack of interest. She remarked: 'She was always stopping me, saying "That's not important enough" and I hadn't hardly started talking' (Michaels 1981: 439).

The next extract is from a child who uses a topic-centred style, which the teacher builds on (Michaels 1981: 431–2): M refers to the child and T to the teacher.

M: When I was in day camp, we made these candles.
T: You made them?
M: I tried it with different colors with both of them but one just
      came out. This one just came out blue and I don't know what this
      color is.
T: That's neat-o. Tell the kids how you do it from the very start. Pretend
      we don't know a thing about candles. OK. What did you do first?
      What did you use? Flour?
M: There's some hot wax, some real hot wax that you just take a string
      tie a knot in it and dip the string in the wax.
T: What makes it have a shape?

M: You just shape it.
T: Oh you shaped it with your hands.
M: But you have first you have to stick it into the wax and then water and then keep doing that until it gets to the size you want it.

The teacher and the child are in synchrony in this narrative. The teacher waits until she pauses and then asks questions which give the child some guidelines about how to proceed and what information is 'important'. When she asks the child to 'pretend we don't know anything about candles', she is instructing her to assume no knowledge and to be explicit. When the child does not go on, she prompts her by asking what she did first and then gives an example of the type of response she wants. The child picks up her clue and builds on the teacher's contribution. Michaels (1981: 433) points out that the child's discourse in response to the teacher's questions and comments is far more complex than the spontaneous utterances produced without the teacher's help. Moreover the teacher's attempts to help were not perceived as interruptions because they occurred at the prosodically appropriate moments. Michaels concludes (1981: 440) that the teacher's differential treatment of the children arises from a mismatch in their communicative styles and that over a long term it affects the children's progress in the acquisition of literacy skills.

From Heath's work it is clear that children are aided in their transition from home to school ways of speaking, not solely via the exposure to 'story-telling', but by the form, content and functions which stories are assumed to have. She (1983) contrasts two styles of story-telling in Trackton (the working-class black community) and Roadville (the working-class white community). In Roadville stories stick to the truth and are factual. They maintain strict chronicity, end with a summary statement or moral, and serve the function of maintaining values and reaffirming group membership. Any fictionalized account is a lie. Trackton stories, on the other hand, are hardly ever serious. The best stories are 'junk'; and the best story-tellers are those who can 'talk the best junk', i.e. make the most wildly exaggerated comparisons and tell outlandish fictive narratives.

Heath (1983: 189) draws the acute contrast between community norms in observing that:

in Trackton there is only the 'true story', which would be to a Roadville resident anything but true. In contrast, neither Roadville's factual accounts nor tales from the Bible would be termed stories in Trackton. Since Trackton parents do not read books with their children and do not include these in their gifts to pre-schoolers, they have no occasion to talk of the stories in books. In short, for Roadville, Trackton's stories would be lies; for Trackton, Roadville's stories would not even count as stories.

Both Roadville and Trackton have a variety of oral and literate traditions which represent ways of negotiating meaning: and people in both communities spend a lot of time telling stories. However, neither community's ways with the spoken or written word prepare its children for school. Roadville and Trackton ways of speaking and using language are in contrast with those of the mainstream townspeople, who socialize their children early in the uses of language they will learn in school. For the Roadville and Trackton children, school is the first place where they meet the mainstream way of using oral and written language. There they encounter very different notions of truth, style and language appropriate to a 'story' from those they have known at home. They must learn not how to 'tell stories', but new definitions of stories, and know when a story is meant to be true, when to stick to the facts, and when to use their imaginations. Neither group has had the experience of helping negotiate with an adult the meaning of a story. The townspeople's children, however, find continuity in their home pattern of language use when they go to school.

Heath (1983: 293–4) recounts an incident in which two Roadville girls expressed their understanding of the different conventions and moral values which were attached to stories by home and school. On the school bus Wendy regaled her friend Sally with a tale about how she was going to bring her dog to a school party. The following exchange took place (W refers to Wendy and S to Sally):

S: That story, you just told, you know that ain't so.
W: I'm not tellin' no story, uh-er-ah, no. I'm tellin' the kind Miss Wash [her teacher] talks about.
S: Mamma won't let you get away with that kinda excuse. You know better.
W: What are you so, uh, excited about. We got one kinda story Mamma knows about and a whole 'nother one we do at school. They're different and you know it.
S: You better hope Mamma knows it, if she catches you making up stuff like that.

The girls' remarks demonstrate a metalinguistic awareness of the differences between 'story-telling', an event which is accepted and promoted in school, and 'telling' a story', an event equated with lying and exaggerating at home. Heath remarks that the close personal network which gives stories their context and meaning at home finds no counterpart in the event which goes by a similar name at school.

As I will show in the next chapter, teachers' ideas about communicative styles in classroom discourse are based heavily on the norms of the written language. This is illustrated by an extract from a lesson in a French classroom in which the teacher is trying to get the children to describe a picture on the wall. She has asked what the dog, Bobi, is doing, and she is not satisfied when a child replies that he is running (Dannequin 1977: 79– 80):

P: I les chiens sautent.
     They (the dogs) leap.
T: Oui, ils courent en sautant. Mais, à la place de courent qu'est-ce qu'on pourrait mettre encore?
     Yes, they run while leaping about. But instead of 'run', what would it be better to say?
P: Bobi joue.
     Bobi is playing.
T: Il joue, mais –
     Yes, he is playing, but –
P: Bobi marche.
     Bobi's walking.
T: À la place de court courir.
     Instead of 'runs', 'to run'.
P: Marche.
     Walks.
T: Marche, saute. Les petites souris comment font elles?
     Walks, leaps. Little mice, what do they do?

The teacher is trying to get the children to say, 'Bobi trotte', which is the answer prescribed by the authors of the teaching manual she is following. It is not surprising that the children have difficulty in coming up with this answer since the collocation of *chien* and *trotter* is not a frequent one in the spoken language. The teacher does not give an indication why one answer is to be preferred over another.

6.3 Peer influence on language

We have already seen how the transition from home to school brings children into a wider sphere of social activity and involves learning new styles of speaking and writing to cope with new communicative tasks and functions. At this stage the child's main input may have come mostly from adult family members with whom he has developed a way of speaking which is effective for intra-group communication. In playing with other children and forming friendships the child learns other ways of speaking and various routines, e.g. games, boating, teasing, arguing, etc. I mentioned earlier that it was not necessarily true cross-culturally that children learn language from adults; children learn language from whomever they come into contact with. In Samoan society early socialization is less bound by the constraints of single families. Care-taking is spread among a circle of individuals, kin and non-kin and older siblings. Blount (1977: 303) observed that the Luo child from 18 months onwards spends most of his time in the company and care of children. When a Luo boy reaches the age of three he is no longer allowed to eat meals with his mother and younger children. He eats with his father and older brothers; and from his older brothers he learns to use deferential and respectful speech. Older children in many societies function as both models and monitors.

Even in the so-called 'mainstream' middle-class white societies which have been so extensively studied, it is the case that in a child's adolescent years other adolescents become more important than adults in providing models. An increasing amount of sociolinguistic research on the structure of intra-group communication has revealed that one of the most important influences in the development of communicative competence is the style of speaking used in peer group interaction and the continuous monitoring from peers to which members are subjected. Studies of peer group language provide us not only with data on the learning of new speech styles but also with important information on how a child may restructure certain aspects of speech in conformity with peer group pressures.

The process of peer group formation has been of interest to sociologists as well as linguists, although the latter have a special interest in the role which language plays in maintaining group cohesiveness and solidarity. I have already discussed in chapter 2 how sociolinguists have used group recording sessions in an effort to overcome the Observer's Paradox. This is based on the belief that obligations to one's peers override constraints on speaking formally to an unknown interviewer. Milroy (1980: 60–1) gives a very dramatic illustration of the effect of peer group pressure on speech. She recorded one boy in front of his friends, who shifted his style of speech to suit the interview situation and was laughed at by the others. On the next occasion, he shifted his speech style markedly in the direction of the vernacular. Obligations to the group were powerful enough to override the influence of the recording equipment and the outsider–interviewer.

From a very early age children form and participate in various groups. There are a number of ways in which one may define a group; for the moment I will use Sherif and Sherif's definition of it (1973: 144) as: 'a social unit which consists of a number of individuals who stand in (more or less) definite status and role relationships to one another and which possesses a set of values or norms of its own, regulating the behaviour of individual members at least in matters of consequence to the group'. Morrison and McIntyre (1973: 134) in talking about the kinds of social groups formed by schoolchildren say that membership of such groups is voluntary and involves shared acceptance of certain ways of behaviour.

Notwithstanding the importance of individual choice in the process of group formation and membership, it would be wrong not to recognize that the choices are more or less constrained. One may belong to a group and deny membership of it and therefore avoid all behaviours associated with it. Conversely, one may wish to join a particular group and be denied access to it. Furthermore, some group structures have a greater capacity for norm enforcement than others. The price for attempting to leave some teenage street gangs or even adult 'underworld' networks such as the Mafia can be death. Some groups have explicit canons of behaviour and exact penalties for violation. In one secondary school where I made some recordings, there was a group of boys who operated a system of fines for co-operating with school teachers in the classroom lessons.

Le Page (1978), who has formulated a sociolinguistic theory based on the notion of identity, attaches great significance to the process by which the individual creates patterns of linguistic behaviour so as to resemble those of the groups with which he wishes to identify (and by implication, those with which he does not wish to be identified). The individual is, however, constrained by the extent to which:

1 he can identify the groups,
2 he has sufficient access to them and the capacity to analyse their systems,
3 his motivation is positive or negative, taking into account the feedback he receives from them of the chances of his being allowed to join them,
4 he is still able to modify his behaviour.

Most school-age children are able to identify the members of the group(s) they see themselves as belonging to. Although most children belong to one or more groups during their school years (i.e. roughly between the ages of five and sixteen) some children are more susceptible than others. Important factors seem to be age and sex. Berenda (1950), for example, states that children tended to become less conforming to peer influence as they increased in age. And in his work with black peer groups in Harlem Labov (1972b: 246) found that membership was a function of age: boys aged eight to nine were non-members. Membership was strongest in the 13–15-year-old range and fell off rapidly in the later teens. A few 18–19-year-old boys acted as senior members in the group, especially if younger brothers served as group officers. Labov estimates that 50–60 per cent of the boys in the age range ten to sixteen were participants of the street culture in the neighbourhood where he worked.

In her work among peer groups in Reading, Cheshire (1982a: 22–3) also found age to be a significant factor in membership. She recorded two groups of girls and one group of boys. The age range tended to be smaller for the girls (nine to thirteen), compared with a range of eleven to seventeen for the boys. Most of the girls were 12 and the older ones took little part in group activities: they were more interested in boy friends. This brings us to another important point about peer group structure: children's peer groups are generally single sex and boys groups tend to be more tightly structured than those of girls. In asking Edinburgh children about their friends, I found that the girls tended to name one or two close friends they played with regularly, while boys tended to name a larger network – usually ones they played football with. To some extent the size of groups may be a function of the different types of games and activities played by the boys and girls at different ages, e.g. it only takes three girls to skip rope, but usually more boys to have a game of football. When asked whether they played with members of the other sex, most said no. There were some games played by mixed groups on the playground, but these very often ended in fights.

Socialization and extensive interaction in single-sex peer groups is no doubt a crucial source of some of the sex-specific uses of language found among adults and in the development of the kinds of sociolinguistic patterns of sex differentiation discussed in chapter 4. The process of acquiring gender-specific speech and other sex-linked behaviour patterns involves more than the simple copying or assimilation of adult genderlects by pre-school and school-age children. The 'assimilation' model discussed in chapter 4 fails to explain some of the patterns of sex differentiation I found among schoolchildren in Edinburgh, where differences between boys' and girls' use of certain linguistic features were greatest in the youngest group. Children may learn gender-specific cultures from their age-mates and sex-specific patterns of behaviour may emerge due to the differing social organization of boys' and girls' groups and the types of activities they engage in (cf. Meditch 1975).

Sociologists and linguists have paid much less attention to female peer groups than male ones, and there is some doubt whether peer networks are as important to girls as they seem to be to boys and whether girls have their own distinct sub-culture. Maltz and Borker (1982), however, outline a number of ways in which the uses of language differ in male and female groups. They say (1982: 205) that girls learn to accomplish three things with language: (1) to create and maintain relationships of closeness and equality; (2) to criticize others in acceptable ways; and (3) to interpret accurately the speech of other girls. These uses of language are connected with ways of behaving and playing in groups. Girls' activities are generally co-operative and non-competitive. Differentiation between girls is not made in terms of power; groups are non-hierarchical. Friendship for girls involves intimacy, loyalty and commitment. When conflicts arise, the group breaks up. Disputes tend not to be solved by appeals to individual power. Goodwin (1980) found that girls tended to use inclusive forms such as *let's, we're gonna, we could* in getting others to do things. Bossiness tended not to be tolerated and girls talked negatively about using commands with equals. When arguing, girls tended to phrase their arguments in terms of group needs and situational requirements rather than in terms of personal directives and orders.

Boys on the other hand tend to have more hierarchically organized groups than girls, and status in the hierarchy is paramount. Labov (1972b: 281–2) describes the social organization of the teenage 'clubs' such as the Jets and Thunderbirds as a tightly knit one, which has persisted for years with extraordinary stability. Grammar is just one of the elements of the social pattern which is transmitted. By examining the terms used to refer to others and common ways of speaking, Labov was able to uncover the social structure of the group (cf. also T. Labov 1982). Members referred to each other as guys, boys or dudes, but not brother. These and other features of language delimit the group. Although members of the group may overtly deny that there is a leader, Labov says that the group is hierarchically structured with some members having more prestige and status than others. Some boys are less well integrated into the core activities of the group and are only peripheral members.

Maltz and Borker (1982: 207) cite three ways in which speech is used in boys' groups: to assert one's position of dominance; to attract and maintain an audience; and to assert oneself when others have the floor. They maintain that the expression of dominance is the most straightforward and best documented pattern in boys' peer groups. Social success among boys is based on knowing how and when to use words to express power. Certain kinds of stylized speech events and routines are highly valued and cultivated in boys' peer groups, e.g. story-telling, joke-telling and other narrative performance events. A boy has to learn how to get the floor to perform, maintain his audience and get to the end of the story.

Some of the most extensive sociolinguistic work on the verbal skills of male peer groups has been done in black communities in the US and the West Indies (e.g. Smith 1972, Kochman 1972 and Labov 1972b). Labov describes a number of the competitive speech events in which peer group members participate. One of these is called sounding, or playing the dozens, in which insults (usually about mothers or relatives) are exchanged. Some of these are in the form of rhymed couplets and some are more like taunts or challenges, e.g. 'Your mother wears high-heeled sneakers to church' (Labov 1972b: 311). Others involve similes or comparisons, e.g. 'Your mother so low, she can play Chinese handball off the kerb' (Labov 1972b: 312). The winner in these contests is the boy with the largest store of sounds, the best memory and the best delivery (cf. also Mitchell-Kernan 1972).

Another example of the kind of verbal duelling is found among Turkish boys aged eight to fourteen, as discussed by Dundes et al. (1972). As in the case of sounding, the stylistic structure and content of the verbal duels is important and similar rules apply to Turkish ones too. The goal of the duel is to insult one's opponent and place him in a female, passive role; very often the challenges are more sexual in nature. The one who receives the insult must defend his virility and his reply must end-rhyme with the initial insult. Again memory is an important factor in success, since there is a great store of traditional retorts to specific insults. The function of these duels amongst Turkish and black American boys is similar: they are used to manage challenges, to assert one's dominance and status, and also to vent hostility in sanctioned ways so as to avoid physical confrontation.

Maltz and Borker (1982) emphasize the continuity between these adolescent ways of speaking and management of social interaction and later adult sex-specific patterns of language behaviour. Women's conversation tends to be mainly interactional. They tend to use personal and inclusive pronouns such as 'you', 'we'. They send out and look for signs of agreement and engagement and they also tend to link what they say to the discourse of others. Maltz and Borker identify common elements in the speech style of men and boys; namely, story-telling, verbal posturing and arguing. Men tend to challenge one another rather than give statements of support. Women on the other hand do not value aggressiveness. This evidence indicates that socialization in sex-specific peer groups leads to the development of particular styles of speaking which prevail in adulthood and offers less support for the view that children gradually assimilate male and female norms of interaction from adult role models.

Some peer groups exert powerful influences to conform to group norms which are at odds with those expressed by family and school. Labov (1972b) says that the parents of the boys he studied disapproved of their choice of friends and membership in the group. The group's influence even extended to school-related areas such as level of acceptable academic achievement and reading ability. Labov (1972b) found a regular relationship between peer group membership and status and reading failure. When he compared the levels of reading ability for group and non-group members, he found that the group members on the whole had lower scores. The majority were three or four years below the level expected for their age. Labov emphasizes the fact that the lowest scores of the group members do not reflect a deficiency in verbal skills, since these are the same boys who gain their prestige and status in the group by displaying their prowess at sounding and narratives. Neither does he believe that the depressed reading scores are indicative of structural interference between Black English Vernacular and the standard English of the school. Labov's explanation is that the school and peer group embody conflicting sets of values and ideology. What makes one successful in school, e.g. reading, is irrelevant to prestige within the group. The focal concerns of the peer group are toughness, smartness, trouble, excitement, autonomy, and fate. Those who were the most integrated into the peer group and street culture rejected the ethic of the school and the values of white middle-class society. Other black students who were outside the street culture (either because they reject it or are rejected by it) accept the norms of the school, but at the expense of becoming 'lames'. Labov uses the term 'lame' to describe a boy who does not know the rules for participating in street culture. The lames not only did better in school (as measured in terms of the school's criteria) but also did not show the same degree of use of the linguistic features of Black English Vernacular, e.g. copula deletion. Labov (1972b: 255) concludes that 'the consistency of certain grammatical rules is a fine grained index of membership in the street culture and that patterns of social interaction may influence grammar in subtle and unsuspected ways'.

The behaviour of these black teenagers is typical of a number of minority groups in British and American society. Blacks in particular seem deliberately to have adopted communicative strategies developed in opposition to the dominant white majority. The newly emergent varieties of West Indian speech in Britain, e.g. 'talking Jamaican', represent what Halliday (1978) has called an 'anti-language'. It is a symbol of a black identity which mainstream society stigmatizes (cf. Sebba and Le Page 1983, Edwards 1979 and Hewitt 1982). These groups develop alternative routes to survival and success, e.g. hustling rather than 'Uncle Tomming' partly because they are denied access to the mainstream system. A group of this type has great power to exert pressure towards conformity and also to resist external linguistic and social pressures.

Le Page (1978) argues that a linguistic norm can be seen as a natural product of the process of focusing. He believes that the same kinds of social processes can operate on speakers from different cultures and statuses. In British society, for example, social conditions have favoured the emergence and maintenance of two highly focused language varieties at the highest and lowest strata of society, i.e. standard and non-standard English. The speech characteristics of those who have attended public schools can be seen as a product of a closed network just as much as Black English Vernacular can be thought of as the product of a highly focused set of vernacular norms. In the latter case these norms symbolize solidarity and loyalty to a set of values of the non-institutional kind.

Cheshire (1982a) found a similar set of vernacular forms in use by white teenage peer groups in Reading. She devised a vernacular culture index based on activities which were considered prestigious for the male and female peer groups respectively. She noted that certain linguistic variables (discussed in chapter 4) could be grouped into categories according to the extent to which they functioned as markers of vernacular loyalty. Her results were similar to those of Labov: those most firmly integrated into the peer group displayed the greatest linguistic allegiance to it. Cheshire also discovered significant sex differentiation. It was not the case, however, that girls were more influenced by the overt prestige of the standard norms and therefore used non-standard forms less frequently than boys, but rather that 'linguistic features serve as markers of vernacular loyalty for girls, but not for boys and vice versa' (Cheshire 1982a: 197–8). For the Reading teenagers, however, adherence to vernacular culture may be just a temporary phase in the linguistic development of the members of the peer group. We have already discussed this increased use of non-standard language cited by Labov (1970a) as a hallmark of the age-grading cycle. Even though it may ultimately 'disappear', i.e. not contribute to an overall restructuring of adult norms or lead to the emergence of a new variety of speech in the community's repertoire, it is no less an important symbol of identification for those who use it. The speech of many white urban working-class adolescents may be a good example of what Giles and Smith (1979) have called 'downward convergence', i.e. a style of speaking which is deliberately adopted for group identification (cf. also Labov 1980). Some of the marked forms may also exist in the adult community (but with a different meaning), e.g. the vernacular verbs, while others do not. Adelman (1976: 86) in discussing teenage argot cites the following example:

(1) I had a little *bother* (e.g. starting the car)
    I had a little *bovver* (i.e. involved in a fight)

The vernacular verbs identified by Cheshire are favourable sites for the occurrence of certain non-standard morphosyntactic features such as the use of -*s* in present tense non-third person singular forms like 'I goes'.

   The pressure towards conformity is not always focused in the direction of the vernacular, however, as the previous examples would appear to suggest. Dannequin (1977: 145) reports a conversation among three French schoolgirls, in which two of the girls correct the third for using a non-standard pronunciation of *oui:*

Girl 1:   Moi, j'ai un oncle qui s'appelle Gérard.
          I've got an uncle called Gérard.
Girl 2:   Ah, bon.
          Oh, really.
Girl 1:   Ouais.
          Yes [with non-standard pronunciation].
Girl 3:   On dit pas 'ouais'. On dit 'oui'.
          One doesn't say 'yes' [with non-standard pronunciation]. One says 'yes' [with standard pronunciation].
Girl 1:   Moi, j' sais dire les deux.
          But I know how to say both.
Girl 3:   Ici, on dit 'oui'.
          Here we say 'yes' [with standard pronunciation].

This example can be taken as another instance in which women exhibit strong normative tendencies towards the standard (cf. chapter 4).

Cheshire also compared peer group style with a school style (i.e. with recordings made at school) for some of the children, but some of the differences which she obtained were not related to the degree of adherence to vernacular culture. One boy who was not very closely integrated into the peer group nevertheless used a large number of non-standard variants in school – much more than he normally did. Cheshire's explanation is based on Giles's speech-accommodation theory. The boy was very much opposed to school and his teacher and so exploited the resources of the vernacular to express his antagonism towards the school.

We have seen then a lot of evidence to suggest that a great deal of language learning and socialization is carred out in various peer groups that children belong to. Many theories of language acquisition and change are based on the idea that the process of transmission of language patterns goes from parent to child. Halle (1962), for example, argues that on the basis of the input from the parent the child constructs a grammar of his own by restructuring and simplifying the rules of the parent's grammar. He furthermore says that rules can be freely added to and incorporated into the child's grammar up to the age of puberty (13–14 years), but that after that no major restructuring takes place. Thus only children have the ability to restructure or alter their grammar in major ways. However, Halle's model does not take into account the fact that for many children the major source of input may not come from adults during school years. This raises the question of the extent to which children can reconstruct or remodel their grammars on the basis of the patterns of speech they hear from their peers. A particularly interesting example is what happens when children move to new dialect areas. Do they retain the speech of the home and parents, or do they learn how to speak like their new friends? If so, what sort of things do they learn from them?

Payne (1980) conducted a study of children whose families had moved into the Philadelphia area from elsewhere to see what types of rules they were capable of learning and whether there were any social factors which appeared to accelerate or hinder acquisition of the new dialect. She calculated the rate of overall success for each child by looking at the extent to which he/she had fully, partially or not at all acquired the local norms for five phonetic variables. Payne found that with the exception of one variable, these tended to show a high rate of success in acquisition; each variable was acquired by 50 per cent or more of the children and there were very few children who failed to acquire the new pattern. This finding is consistent with the belief that low-level phonetic rules which do not entail restructuring can be added to the grammar; in other words, the variables involve allophonic variations in surface phonetics and do not entail a reorganizing of deep phonological rules. For example, one of the variables involves the centralization of the diphthong /ai/ to /əi/ as in *fight*. For a speaker to produce the centralized vowel, he could add a realization rule to the grammar which would apply to all cases of /ai/ to convert them to /əi/. Wells (1973) reports that Jamaican immigrant children in Britain were relatively unsuccessful in their acquisition of London English phonology when phonological restructuring (as opposed to phonetic modification) was involved. It is not clear whether similar findings would obtain for the acquisition of new regional syntactic variants.

Payne found that the age at which the children moved to the new dialect area had an effect on learning ability. She identified the age of eight as the critical turning-point in the child's learning. Those who were born and raised in the new area or who moved there by age four and lived there between the ages of four and sixteen years and those who moved between the ages of five and eight and lived there for eight to sixteen years had more or less the same degree of success in learning the phonetic rules of the local dialect.

The results obtained for a more complex variable, short /a/, were quite different. Unlike the phonetic variables which can be learned by adding a fairly simple low-level realization rule, the short /a/ pattern involves intricate lexical and phonological conditioning. The rule is responsible for the raising and tensing of short /a/ in words like *cat, man,* etc. in a number of American (and also British) English dialects. The rule differs somewhat from region to region; in New York City, for example, the rule applies before front nasals (e.g. *Ann*), voiceless fricatives (e.g. *pass*) and voiced stops (e.g. *bad*). In the Philadelphia dialect area which Payne studied, however, the rule is less generalized and more complex because it affects a subset of the environments specified in the New York rule. A child has to learn not only the phonetic conditioning of the rule, but also grammatical conditioning (e.g. *ran, swam, began* and *wan* − the latter the past tense of *won* − are exceptions to the front nasal environment), and lexical conditioning (e.g. *glad, mad, bad* are exceptions to the voiced stop environment). The acquisition of this rule would involve reorganizing the phonology since there is no way to add one simple rule which will produce all the correct realizations.

Payne found that the children showed varying degrees of acquisition which depended partly on age, length of residence and the dialect area from which they had moved. Apart from two children, most have been unsuccessful in learning this rule. Indeed some children had learned practically nothing, including three children who were born and raised in the area but whose parents were not native to the community. This is quite a surprising finding and indicates the need for a great deal of research in this area. It raises a number of fundamental questions for sociolinguistic methodology. Labov (1966), for example, in his study of New York City speech assumed that anyone who had resided in the city since the age of eight qualified as a native speaker. Payne's results raise the question of what the criteria for native-speaker status are. What is the minimal period of residence and length of exposure to what kind of rules necessary to acquire productive control over them? And what is the nature and extent of interaction between family and peer group as models?

Some answers to these questions are found in a study of the development of some aspects of the prosodic system of a Japanese child who has been exposed to two regional dialects, Tokyo and Kyoto. The child's parents speak the Tokyo dialect, but have moved to another part of Japan. Neither has acquired the new local Kyoto dialect. At age two to three the child developed a Tokyo type accentual system on the basis of her parents' (mainly her mother's) model. The Tokyo system constitutes the primary linguistic input for the construction of her system at this stage, even though she is raised in a locality where that accentuation is different. At this stage the child's interaction with her parents at home is the centre of her communicative activity: interaction with peers is very limited, socially and linguistically. She shows only minimal traces of variant accentuation and local copula forms. Up until age eight the influence of the Kyoto model is negligible, but thereafter the child acquired the local system through mixing with her peers. The results add further support to the view that children restructure their system in certain ways. This particular study demonstrates that the acquisition of accentuation rules takes place at a fairly early stage of development (cf. Pike's 1952 study of her own children's 'relearning' of English prosody). It is 'complete' by age three, which predates the completion of the acquisition of segmental phonology. Even so, it is potentially open to restructuring through peer interaction. The child did not, however, completely abandon the old rules of her parent's system. She developed competence in using two different systems and switched between her parent's and peer's codes on appropriate occasions (cf. Kobayashi 1981 for details of the study).

It is known the non-segmental systems, e.g. intonation and tone, exhibit regional and social differences similar to those found in phonology and syntax, but much less work has been done in this area. Local (1982) has documented the process by which pitch movements are redistributed in time over different syntactic structures in the speech of children who are in various stages of acquiring particular kinds of localized intonational systems. But much remains to be done in order to integrate work of this kind into the substantial amount of research on sociolinguistic patterns in other areas of the language system.

From the studies available so far it appears that the constraints on learning are partly linguistic and partly social. That is, given a certain model to which one has access, assimilation of it is constrained by linguistic, biological and social factors. Among the relevant linguistic factors would be the extent of alteration required to one's own pattern of linguistic behaviour. Where only minimal moderations are required learning is likely to be successful. One can positively transfer knowledge already possessed to a new situation. Wolfram's (1973) study of black and Puerto Rican peer groups in Harlem provides an illustration of this type of case. He found that Puerto Ricans in New York City deleted final t/d more often than black speakers: the question is whether this difference can be attributed to the influence of the surrounding Spanish-speaking Puerto Rican community or whether it is due mainly to the influence of the black community, who are the main source of non-Puerto-Rican contact. Wolfram examined the rate of deletion for three groups of speakers, blacks, Puerto Ricans and Puerto Ricans who socialized in black peer groups. He concluded that it is the convergence of influence from Spanish and Black English Vernacular speakers that accounts for the higher incidence of deletion among Puerto Ricans than blacks. Those who had the highest rate of deletion were the Puerto Ricans with black friends. Wolfram says this is due to the fact that a pattern of t/d deletion already existing in Puerto Rican English due to Spanish influence is being reinforced by a similar tendency in the language of the group they are in contact with. Thus linguistic influence operates additively in this case. Assimilation is aided by the fact that there is some common linguistic ground between the two groups.

There is, however, also evidence that assimilation can take place in the absence of great linguistic similarity, providing motivation is strong and access to the new pattern is available. Labov (1966) found that the English spoken by second-generation Italian speakers showed little retention of substratum influence from their parents' speech. They were well integrated into the local norms of New York City speech and participated in the rule of short /a/ raising unlike their parents who kept their native [a] in the class of English words with [æ]. Labov explained this as another manifestation of *hypercorrection* in which speakers aspiring to native status were seeking to remove themselves as far as possible from the low prestige pattern of their parents. For Italians, unlike other ethnic groups, this process of assimilation involved not only abandoning the parent's native language but adopting the vernacular norms of New York City speech.

Another illustration of this type of assimilation is provided by Agnihotri (1979), who looked at the speech of Panjabi-speaking Sikh children in Leeds. There was a tendency for this younger generation of Panjabi speakers to use English and a mixed code drawing on elements of Panjabi and English as a language of intra-group communication. Language behaviour in situations like these is often a crucial index of group identity or solidarity and the degree of assimilation or acculturation. Agnihotri (1979: 234) discusses the case of one of his informants who had a great deal of contact with the host community in Leeds and negative attitudes towards the Sikh community. This social distance was reflected in her linguistic behaviour; she not only showed greater use of local Leeds English phonological variables, but also retained fewer native features than the other children. The variety of English to which these children are exposed is a very localized working-class Leeds English. Agnihotri found that Sikh children were modelling their English on the casual speech of native working-class Leeds speakers and that their ambitions were in line with those of the local working class. New varieties of English are presently emerging in many urban areas among minority groups via a refocusing of norms away from standard English.

Yet another example comes from Trudgill's (1983) study of the modifications which British pop singers make in order to make their pronunciation sound more American. Some of these alterations, e.g. insertion of post-vocalic /r/ in words like *cart*, are stereotypically associated by British speakers with American pronunciation. Trudgill observes (1983: 148), however, that singers often over-generalize and hypercorrect by inserting /r/s where they do not belong; and of course all American accents are not rhotic (cf. chapter 4 for discussion of this variable in British and American English). In this respect, then, one might say that the extent to which speakers can successfully imitate American speech is constrained by the extent to which they have sufficient access to the model and sufficient analytical skills to work out the rules. Punk rock singers, however, use a number of the phonological and grammatical features associated with low-status southern English speech in an attempt to identify with British working-class youth. This motivation has not completely replaced the desire to imitate American accents and thus conflicting tendencies occur. This leads to the emergence of a new style of singing in which stereotypically American pronunciations combine with stereotypically working-class English forms. Trudgill (1983: 158–9) says that this way of singing represents an attempt to find a balance between the conflicting pressures of 'how to behave like a genuine pop singer' and 'how to behave like a British urban working-class youth'.

All of these examples provide further support for Le Page's view that speech is an act of identity and that speakers bring into play the variable linguistic resources available to them in a community as a means of identifying with different groups, subject to certain constraints. This process of assimilation and continuing realignment of norms proceeds into adulthood and is an ongoing source of change in individual and community ways of speaking. Milroy (1980), for example, has found that identification with various social and cultural groups and interaction in different types of networks are just as important a source for adults in working-class communities in Belfast as for teenagers in Reading and Harlem. When codes and variables lose their symbolic function as markers of various social identities the way for linguistic change is paved. Dense network structures can function powerfully to maintain intact a highly focused set of non-standard linguistic forms. Other speakers, however, whose networks are more open and broadly based (e.g. the lames in Harlem, women in Belfast), i.e. those whose members are socially and geographically more mobile, are in Le Page's terms more diffuse with regard to patterns of language behaviour. The papers in Romaine (1982b) discuss this model in relation to other societies.

7

The acquisition of literacy and its role in communicative competence

Hymes does not specifically mention the role of literacy in the development of communicative competence; however, given the high social premium placed on literate modes of expression in modern societies, it follows that skills in reading and writing comprise an important component of communicative ability.

Although the literature on educational psychology is full of 'theories' of reading, not a great deal has been said about the acquisition of reading and writing as social skills. It is the sociolinguistic aspects of literacy which I will consider in this chapter. In the previous chapter I argued that one of the most important new registers of language which children acquire in school is the written language. The development of reading and writing skills is crucial to successful participation and progress in school. Although all children learn to speak and hear without formal instruction, this is not true for reading and writing. There are a number of problems children face in learning to transform the language system they have developed for speaking and use largely in interpersonal interaction into a written language used mainly for writing essays. While there are registers which are common to both speech and writing, such as personal narratives of everyday life, there are significant differences in the mode and context of production of these, which make the skills required as a speaker/hearer difficult to transfer to those required of a good reader/writer. In reading and writing the child is no longer involved in a face-to-face interaction where the meaning is jointly created and negotiated between participants. A child must develop a text alone – whether he is writing for a reader who is distanced and unknown or reading a text which someone else, often unknown to him, has produced at some other point in time. This is just a way of saying that writing establishes autonomous discourse, i.e. discourse which exists apart from the person and context which produced it.

7.1 *The difference between speech and writing*

Stubbs (1980: 15) maintains that a coherent theory of literacy must be founded on a sophisticated account of the relation between spoken and written language and on recognition of the fact that this relation differs for different writing systems and for different cultures. When I spoke above of 'transforming' and 'transferring' skills from one medium to another, I was to some extent using misleading terms. If writing is seen as a secondary system, i.e. a visual representation of spoken language, then learning to read does not involve learning a new communicative system, but merely transferring a skill already acquired from one medium to another. This is a controversial issue. The debate still continues between linguists who believe that written language is principally dependent on spoken language and those who maintain that writing is essentially distinct. I will take the position here that written language and spoken language exist in complementary distribution by virtue of being used, by and large, for different purposes in different situations. Hence, each must be studied in its own right. The recognition of speech and writing as coexistent, autonomous systems is based on the distinction between language as an abstract system (or form) and medium as physical realization of language (or substance). However, it is not hard to see why the idea has been fostered that speech is an imperfect reflection of (written) language. Ontogenetically and phylogenetically, the primacy of speech over writing cannot be disputed. Only a minority of the world's languages today exist in written form. As Stubbs points out, it is often the case that from a social point of view, writing is primary. In most literate communities the written language has social priority over speech because it has prestige, and often official recognition (but more on the reasons for this in the next chapter).

Great claims have been made for the cognitive effects of literacy from historical studies of cultural and social changes associated with the advent of widespread literacy. It has been argued, for example, that writing represents a unique way of constructing reality and that different mentalities emerge in oral as opposed to literate cultures.

Greenfield (1968: 148) states: 'There is a form of human competence uniquely associated with development of a high degree of literacy that takes years of schooling to develop'. Luria (1976) found that literates and illiterates in Central Asia differed in terms of their use of concrete, situation-bound and abstract, decontextualized thought. Pre-literates were not able to decontextualize. (Recall Bernstein's views (1973) on restricted vs. elaborated codes discussed in the last chapter.) It has been argued that non-literate and literate modes of thought can be distinguished by differential experience with the production and the exposure to various types of writing.

Some evidence for this can be derived from the different strategies used by literates and illiterates in coping with syllogisms, as in (1).[1]

(1) All people who own houses pay a house tax
   Boima does not pay a house tax
   Does Boima own a house?

Luria (1976) and Scribner and Cole (1981) found that many pre-literate adults had difficulty solving this kind of problem. Those who could, often were unable to explain how they arrived at the answer. The use of syllogistic reasoning is often assessed on intelligence tests and it is often assumed to be a universal mode of thought. But this kind of schema is evidently acquired primarily through schooling in particular kinds of literacy. We can see how this might happen if we examine the structure of the syllogism more carefully. The first statement is one which establishes general premises; the second states a specific fact; and the third requires a conclusion to be drawn about a specific case from the general premises. Great importance has been attached to this deductive mode of inference by western philosophers and logicians, and by philosphers of science in their discussion of scientific method. The syllogism is self-contained in that conclusions are to be derived only by reference to the premise and not by reference to anything outside it. Pre-literate persons, however, who were not familiar with this schema tended to give answers which were contextualized and related to events and people in the real world. Some said, for example, that Boima had no money to pay a house tax, therefore he would not have had the money to buy a house. Solving syllogisms requires decontextualization and knowledge that there is an 'internal' logic and truth in sentences themselves.[2]

By looking even more carefully at the logical structure of syllogisms, we can see that the following equations are set up between referents in each of the three statements.

All men are mortal
$a = b$
Socrates is a man
$c = a$
Socrates is mortal
$c = b$

The mathematical argument is thus: if $a = b$ and $c = b$, then c must also equal a. This does hold true within certain branches of finite mathematics. In mathematical equations, however, the numbers do not represent anything beyond values in a closed system. In language the items we deal with, i.e. words, do have referential meaning and expressive value which extends beyond the closed system of logic. We can see this if we substitute the following:

Nothing is better than heaven
a = b
Anything is better than nothing
c = a
Anything is better than heaven
c = b

In this case the sense relations and meanings of the lexical items representing a, b and c render the syllogism paradoxical.

I pointed out in chapter 3 that children have more difficulty with reversible than irreversible passives because they appear to rely on context more than form in the early stages of acquisition. Children are thus in Erikson's terms (1980) 'sociocentric' (rather than egocentric as Piaget suggests); they tend to ignore logic and truth conditions in processing sentences. Donaldson and Lloyd (1974), for example, report that when children are asked to make truth judgements about a sentence like:

(2) All the cars are in the garages

they judged it to be true if presented with a state of affairs in which a whole row of garages was full. They did not pay attention to the number of cars relative to the number of garages. In the early stages children map sentences onto a perceived world; in school they are asked to map sentences into sentences. The more readily children can acquire the ability to process language in terms of the grammatical–logical relations between sentences, the more successful they will be in coping with the demands made on them by tests and reading/writing tasks. What goes by the name of 'logic' when applied to grammar is not inherent or innate in language, but an acquired way of talking and thinking about language which is largely made possible by literacy. The illusion that logic is a closed system has been encouraged by writing. Similarly, what leads linguists as well as laymen to believe that language or grammar can be so structured as to be perfectly logical or consistent with itself is due to the possibility of representing a language in its written form. Teachers often apply algebraic logic in correcting their pupils for using multiple negation. The argument is that because in the logical system which makes the solution of algebraic equations possible, two negatives make a positive, so it must be when two negatives appear in the same sentence. Thus, it is argued that a sentence like:

(3) I don't have no money

must logically mean 'I have some money.' Languages do not obey logical rules of this type. There are no doubt universal constraints on logical form, but this cannot be one of them. Many languages require multiple negation; and earlier in the history of English multiple negation was customary. It has, however, become a social convention that in standard English such sentence types are no longer acceptable.

There are many schemas which derive their mode of interpretation from literate uses of language which children must acquire. Take, for example, the type of test or quiz in which children are asked to say whether a statement is true or false. When given a sentence like:

(4) Henry VIII had two wives. True or false?

why is it that the only correct answer is 'false'? Henry had more than two wives, which means that he had at least two, but the conventional interpretation of this question type is: 'Henry VIII had *only* two wives' (cf. Stubbs 1983: 208). There is nothing in the linguistic form of the statement to indicate that the conventional interpretation is what it is.

7.2 *Literacy in a historical and cross-cultural perspective*

In order to understand why such significance is attached to literacy, we have to examine the historical context in which various kinds of literacies have developed. One factor which emerges is that literacy is always connected with power; reading and writing were the prerogative of a select, specially trained group. In seventeeth-century England, for example, literacy was class-stratified; only those in certain positions wrote. Margaret Paston, who was herself a prolific letter writer, complains in one of her letters to her husband of a family steward who was unwilling to write the family accounts. At that time it was expected that a man occupying such a position would be able to keep written records. Different people and different societies are conscious of themselves as language-users in different ways. Conversation was once the most inportant form of communication; even after literacy in England became more widespread, etiquette books stressed the necessity for well-brought up ladies to acquire the art of polite conversation. In the western European countries it was the educated, literate classes who imposed their norms of language use on society as a whole.

The use of language to exercise power is not confined solely to literate speech communities. I pointed out that verbal skills are important in gaining status in black peer groups (cf. section 6.3). In pre-colonial Papua New Guinea, the village 'big-men' possessed extraordinary linguistic resources based on rhetorical skills and bilingualism (cf. Sankoff 1980). The difference between so-called oral and literate cultures cannot be explained by reference to cognitive dichotomies or in simplistic evolutionary terms, but rather in terms of social organization. Due to the increase in information and communication technology, discourse conventions and uses of language have arisen which must be learned through special schooling. Societies distribute their communicative resources differently and individuals develop skills in the context of the societal resources to which they have access. The way in which varieties of the written and spoken language function in relation to class structure depends on how transmission is controlled. In most post-industrial societies educational systems have taken the role of primary socializing agents and exclusive selectors for economic opportunity and social advancement. The alleged effects of literacy are intimately connected with those of schooling. Transmission of certain codes is controlled by the school. Even in a highly literate society like Britain, the development of elaborate vocabulary, the ability to vary structure and presentation according to the needs of different audiences, the cultivation of 'original style', are probably beyond the capacity of all but a few highly educated persons.

Scribner and Coles' (1981) work among the Vai people of Africa is particularly valuable because the acquisition of Vai literacy does not take place within the context of formal schooling. This means that it is possible to separate and study independently the effects of literacy from those of schooling. They found that the cognitive skills of traditional Vai people have been shaped by the range and functions of language use, especially their literacy practices. The skills associated with different literacies available to members of the community (i.e. Vai, Arabic and English) were highly differentiated so that the acquisition of Arabic and Vai literacy, for example, did not lead to the development of the same complex of skills. Nor did they singly or in combination substitute for English literacy as predictors of cognitive performance. Furthermore, neither served as a surrogate for schooling, nor did they produce the range of cognitive effects that schooling does. (Cf. however, the discussion of the effects of literacy on methods of memorizing in Yates 1966, who documents the loss of certain methods of training memory with the advent of printing.) Their findings emphasize the fallacy in assuming that the social and psychological consequences of literacy are always and everywhere the same. Moreover, they seriously undermine the idea that there can be a universal definition or standard of literacy. Skills of reading and writing have no inherent disposition to produce independent thinking.

In the light of Scribner and Cole's research, the far-reaching claims made about what must now be recognized as a highly culture-specific type of literacy are in need of modification. The original development of writing systems centuries ago and the production of particular kinds of text may have laid the basis historically for the emergence of new modes of intellectual representation; however, over time they may have lost their connection with the written word. As far as the present is concerned, there does not appear to be a necessary connection between the medium in which new forms of discourse come into being and the medium in which they are perpetuated and transmitted. The rise of the kind of literacy associated with western modes of thought is not inevitable; nor is it a prerequisite of social and economic development.

If the special effects of literacy appear to be less sweeping than some have supposed, this means that greater attention must be paid to the way in which different kinds of literacies function in a society. I have already talked about Heath's (1983) comparison of a black and white community in the southeastern United States, where strikingly different ideas about language and the way in which children figure in language events prevail. One community oriented its children to literate ways of talking and thinking about language before the children went to school. Heath also observed differences in the reading practices of adults in the two communities. In the white community reading a book by oneself was considered a legitimate activity; children often observed adults engaged in solitary reading. In the black community, however, reading was generally a group activity. Written messages were read aloud by someone with acknowledged ability and interpretation was arrived at by group consultation.

A number of literary scholars and linguists have now recognized that one can no longer associate literate modes of expression solely with writing. This narrow view of literacy has been increasingly rejected in favour of the notion that there is an oral–literate continuum (cf. Tannen 1982). For most cultures both oral and literate traditions exist. That they do not coincide exactly with speech and writing can be seen from the examples of a lecture (delivered orally, but in the literate mode, with little assumption of shared knowledge and high focus on thematic progressions) and many personal letters (delivered in written form, but focusing on interpersonal relationships and shared knowledge). Literate modes centre on decontextualized, non-participant presentation of material, whereas oral modes of expression whether spoken or written, focus on contextualized participant interaction.

Just because there is no evidence that one must personally engage in writing to develop literate modes of thought does not diminish the great social value placed on reading and writing as social skills. While some of the functions of speech and writing overlap, writing usually develops specific codes in a language, which are different from oral codes in the 'same' language. The personal diary, for example, is a genre which owes its existence and is exclusive to the written language. The use of so-called *style indirecte libre* (free indirect speech) as a literary device for reporting the speech (and internal thoughts) of characters is made possible by the written language (cf. Banfield 1982). Compare, for example (5) and (6) (both are taken from Doris Lessing, *The Four-Gated City,* cited in Traugott and Pratt 1980: 300):

(5) Who would have thought that coming to this house meant having her nose rubbed in it. Why was she here at all?   (free indirect speech)
(6) She wondered whether anyone would have thought that going to that

house was to mean that she would be subjected to humiliation . . . She asked herself why she was there at all   (indirect speech)

The first of these illustrates free indirect speech and the second indirect speech. The stylistic difference between the two is often referred to as 'point of view'. In direct speech the author undertakes to report exactly what the characters say, as in example (7); whereas in indirect speech the time and place in which the saying and reporting occur are different, as in (8):

(7) She said 'I'll meet you tomorrow'
(8) She said that she would meet him the following day

The effect of the change from direct to indirect speech is to remove or shift all those features directly related to the embedded speech situation; thus, *I* becomes *she,* and *tomorrow* becomes *the following day.* Or in the earlier example (5) of free indirect speech, it is as if the author has removed herself and left the characters to reveal their thoughts. The fact that events are seen from the perspective of the main character, Martha Quest, is indicated linguistically by the choice of *coming, this house* and *here,* all of which are features which take into account the location of the speaker. In the other example (6), *going, that, house* and *here* appear. There is a certain freeness about the way in which events are reported in that the author does not commit herself to a reproduction of actual speech. The author can be relatively distant or remote from her characters and readers depending upon the narrative perspective she takes. Personal diaries generally are characterized by first person narration, but third person narration is probably more frequently employed in texts which children read in school.

Not all users of English become skilled in all the uses of language which are made possible by writing. Probably the great majority of people manage primarily on the spoken language in their everyday lives. It is probably also true that most people tend to read more than they write. In the next section I will examine the extent to which discontinuities exist between speech and writing which pose problems for children learning to read and write.

7.3 *From spoken to written language*

There are 'mismatches' of various types and degrees between the ways in which oral and written language are put together, which pose problems for all learners. For example, all children must learn the sound–symbol correspondences required to decode the printed word. This may be more of a problem in some languages than others; it depends on how consistently a writing system represents these correspondences. The English spelling system is notorious for its alleged irregularity, e.g. ‹gh› may be used to represent the sounds of /g/ initially, as in *ghost,* or /f/ finally, as in *tough,* or nothing, as in *through.*

Despite these seemingly erratic correspondences between sound and symbol, Stubbs (1980: 54) argues that there are some important regularities. His analysis of George Bernard Shaw's proposal that *fish* should be spelled *ghoti* reveals a number of interesting facts about English spelling:

> no English word is ever spelled in such a way that it gives no information about pronunciation. Even orthographic units such as *gh* are quite restricted in their possible pronunciations. It is only possible to pronounce *gh* as /f/ at the end of morphemes, e.g. *tough.* In word initial position it is always /g/. Interestingly enough, it was Caxton who introduced the Dutch convention of spelling words with *gh,* which formerly had been spelled with *g.* Most of the words which retain *gh* today have pejorative connotations, e.g. *ghost, ghetto, ghastly.*

There are thus features of English spelling which appear irregular only when one attempts to account for the whole system in terms of inviolable letter–sound correspondences. English spelling is not only phonemic but morphophonemic, since the symbols convey lexical and syntactic information. In isolation almost every English orthographic symbol can represent more than one phoneme and every phoneme can be represented by more than one orthographic symbol.

While reading does not consist of pronouncing isolated letters, there is growing evidence to suggest that the processing of sound–symbol correspondences is most important for the reader in the beginning stages of learning to read; but they become less important as syntax/semantics become more crucial. The diagram in figure 7.1 (Shuy 1979: 78) shows how different levels of language take on prominence at different stages in the acquisition of reading. Children begin by decoding from letters to sounds and end up decoding at the level of larger units like morphemes, words, phrases, etc. This emphasis on isolated sound correspondences is in sharp contrast to the way in which the child has automatically become proficient in processing the spoken language, where chunks of information structured in prosodic units are taken in.

One implication of this finding for the teaching of reading is that in the early stages of acquisition greater interference is to be expected in sound–symbol decoding, while at a later stage an increase in syntactic/semantic differences may be found. Because English spelling is not consistently phonemic and since not all children come to school speaking the same variety of language, most children will experience some difficulties in relating the printed symbols to sounds. However, different groups of

Letter–sound
correspondences

Syllables

Affixes

Whole words

Syntax

Semantic
meaning

Functional
meaning

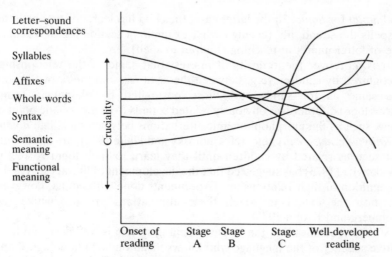

Onset of   Stage Stage   Stage   Well-developed
reading   A   B   C   reading

Figure 7.1   The acquisition of reading
Source: Shuy 1979

learners will have different problems. For example, the child who does not distinguish in his speech between *thin* and *tin* may have more difficulty than another who does make the distinction. However, since the written language does not stand in a one-to-one relationship with any spoken variety, the errors which are likely to be made by an individual child cannot be predicted without knowing something about the spoken variety the child brings to school. Those who have attempted to introduce children to the printed language by means of simplified and regularized alphabets such as the ITA (Initial Teaching Alphabet) have not always appreciated this point. And in any case, at some stage children must learn to cope with the standard spelling system. It is important that teachers should be aware of the potential areas of conflict between the child's spoken language and the written language. Otherwise they may count as 'errors' pronunciations which reflect normal regional and social variation, but have no consequences for the understanding of a text.[3]

Read (1980) has examined the strategies behind the creative spellings and spelling 'errors' used by young children learning to write. He conducted a series of perception experiments which showed that children grouped sounds for spelling purposes according to consistent patterns of phonetic naturalness. He argues that some seemingly non-standard spellings are actually 'advanced' in that they rely on a recognition of phonetic relationships among sounds. A child who spells *clobbered* as *ckloberd,* for example, knows that *ck* is one way to represent the sound /k/, but he has not yet learned that it is restricted to morpheme final position, e.g. *truck*. Read also found evidence of 'letter-name' spelling, e.g. *r* for *are* and *Santu* for *Santa*. In the latter case, the child has learned that the letter *u* spells the sound 'uh' (cf. my earlier example in section 6.2 of teachers' use of letter names in teaching children to spell).

It is moreover theoretically of interest that some of the relationships recognized by children (e.g. between the /i/ of *feet* and the /i/ of *fish*) are the same as (or similar to) those postulated by phoneticians and phonologists. Other less obviously related sounds from a phonetic point of view, such as the morphophonemic alternations between pairs like *divine/divinity, serene/serenity*, etc. (cf. Chomsky and Halle 1968), are apparently not seen as related by children until they learn to spell them correctly. Moskowitz (1973) has suggested that the development of literacy drives the recognition of their relationship. Experiments done with adults, however, question the extent to which these alternations are productive (cf. Steinberg and Krohn 1975).

Stubbs concludes that the English spelling system is well designed for a native speaker of the language who knows its automatic phonological and morphological rules. It is best suited then to adult fluent readers rather than children or foreign learners. It follows that in learning how to read and write English, one ends up knowing quite a bit about the phonological and morphological organization of the language. It is impossible to read English correctly without knowledge of the rules of stress placement, allophonic alternations, morpheme boundaries, etc. (cf. also O'Neil 1980). These facts suggest some sociolinguistic reasons why English spelling has been so resistant to various campaigns designed to reform it; namely, people have invested considerable effort in learning to write and read a complex morphophonemic system and are therefore unwilling to abandon it. Being able to spell correctly is a sign of good education in the English-speaking world.

I have given some examples in chapter 6 which indicate that children have not developed a metalinguistic awareness of some aspects of language; this may pose problems for children in trying to make sense out of the way in which teachers talk about language. By the age of four children apparently have an intuitive knowledge of English phonological structure and can make judgements about whether certain sound sequences are possible English words (cf. Elliot 1981: 75–7). Words and phonemes, however, have only a tenuous reality for schoolchildren. Pre-school children have difficulty in segmenting speech into a sequence of words. They tend to base their segmentation on semantic considerations or features which have to do with the rhythm of a sentence. When asked to identify the number of words in a sentence, they frequently did not count function words; for example, *the men, to go, a lot* would count as one word, and so would items like *man runs,* which form a coherent semantic and grammatical unit. When children were asked to say what word was left when a letter was left out, e.g. *snail* minus /n/ = *sail,* or *feel* minus /f/ = *eel,* only those with a mental age of seven could do this. In the initial stages when a child learns how to read he is faced with a realization of language which is quite different from his experience of language as a spoken medium. Instead of hearing language in a more or less continuous flow of speech with prosodic structuring, he has to acquire a perceptual skill involving eye-span and recognition of shapes and contend with written words separated from each other. This experience will vary somewhat and depend on the kind of written language the child acquires. In acquiring Vai literacy, for example, the child will not have to learn to segment language into words because there are no spaces between them in Vai script; decoding a Vai text successfully when reading aloud may require several trials until the reader is able to impose a prosodic structure on the sequence of symbols. Different languages may set different limits on the extent of metalinguistic awareness. There may be some aspects of language which the native speaker has no ability to describe; and similarly there may be some aspects of language which can be made available to conscious manipulation only when the language exists in a written form. Silverstein (1981) proposes a scale of metapragmatic transparency of forms which ranges from those which are below the level of conscious awareness to those which can be the subject of evaluation. Units such as the word are not categories recognized intuitively by speakers of all languages.

Rozin and Gleitman (1977) believe that one of the major cognitive problems in reading can be viewed as a subpart of the more general problem of metalinguistic awareness. (Cf. Saywitz and Wilkinson 1982, Hakes 1982 and Tunner et al. 1984 for further details of the development of metalinguistic awareness.) The lower the level of the language feature that must be attended to, the later in his development a child is able to perform tasks which rely on it. They found that the greatest difficulty for children was the segmentation of words into syllables. As we have seen, this is precisely the skill required at initial stages of reading, when phonological decoding skills are at the crux of learning to read. This is particularly true when children learn alphabetic writing systems; this is why I said earlier that attempts to introduce children to reading English by means of alternative alphabets such as ITA merely vary the task, but do not simplify it in any appreciable sense. Rozin and Gleitman taught Philadelphia schoolchildren to read by means of a syllabary and logographic script and found that both were easier to acquire than alphabetic script. The logographic was also easier than the syllabic. This is a very interesting finding when seen in historical perspective since alphabetic writing systems are relatively late developments in the history of writing. It suggests that there may be substantial differences in acquisitional rate and the level of attainment in writing which are correlated with the type of writing system.

As far as the syntax of the written language is concerned, children who come to school using some of the non-standard grammatical features discussed in chapter 3, e.g. sentences such as (9) and (10), will not come across these in written texts.

(9) I ain't seen nobody
(10) We was there yesterday

It has been argued that the existence of constructions like these in the spoken language may lead to interference in reading and writing. Whiteman (1981: 153) cites the following example from a 13 year old's essay:

(11) Mickey was TV star and everyone love him
Mickey have so many friend and they want to be like him

There are three features here which are characteristic of BEV and other non-standard varieties of English. The first is the omission of -ed in the verb *love*, where the past tense seems to be indicated. The second is either a case of non-standard subject/verb concord, i.e. the use of *have* for *has* or a failure to mark the past tense by using standard English *had*. The third is the omission of the plural marker -s in *friend*. Whiteman, who analysed essays and the speech produced by working-class black and white students aged 13–14, found that dialect influence was responsible for some of the occurrences of non-standard features in writing, but that not all cases in which non-standard usage occurred could be traced to transfer from the spoken language. Her analysis showed, for example, that plural -s was absent in the writing of white students about 13 per cent of the time even though it was absent only 4 per cent of the time in their speech. A comparison of her results for four features in the speech and writing of black students is given in table 7.1 (Whiteman 1981: 161). It is striking that

Table 7.1 Absence rates (per cent) of four inflectional suffixes in speech and writing

	Speech	Writing
Verbal -s	up to 71.4	37
Plural -s	up to 5.8	31.3
Possessive -s	up to 26.8	44.4
Consonant cluster -ed	up to 76	25.9

there is no regular relationship between absence rates in speech and writing. The absence rates for all the features in writing are similar; in speech, they are not. Furthermore, two of the features, plural -s and possessive- s, actually are more frequently absent in writing than in speech. Whiteman (1981: 161) argues that since these features are all inflectional suffixes it must be this characteristic which is at least partly responsible for their deletion in writing. Thus it cannot be solely due to influence from the spoken language. This finding is further support for the autonomy of speech and writing.

Whiteman also found a pattern of age-grading in the absence rates in writing of verbal -s, plural -s and consonant cluster -ed for blacks and whites. Nine year olds have higher rates of deletion than thirteen year olds and blacks more so than whites in each age group. This supports the interpretation that the omission of inflectional suffixes in writing is partly a developmental or acquisitional phenomenon. In other words, unskilled writers appear to use a reduction strategy which eliminates inflectional suffixes in order to cope with learning a new code. These same suffixes are also frequently omitted by first- and second-language learners of spoken English. Whiteman (1981: 165) also noted that non-standard phonological features rarely occurred in writing, even when they were extremely frequent in the writer's spoken language. That is, features like post-vocalic /r/ were not omitted; nor were there occurrences of non-standard grammatical features like *ain't* and multiple negation, which do not involve suffixes. This could of course reflect partly the fact that these may be more socially stigmatized so that there is greater resistance to transferring them to writing.

It is not just non-standard syntax and grammar, however, which may pose problems for children in reading and writing. In some cases children may find constructions in early reading materials which they have not encountered before in the spoken language. Wolfram et al. (1979: 2) cite the following examples from children's readers:

(12) Over and over rolled the ball
(13) Up the hill they ran
(14) The boy has a boat. The boat is red

Some of these may actually be so artificial that they lead children to misread or make 'forced errors'. The first two of these examples involve the use of a constituent other than the subject, topic or direct object in sentence initial position. In the first case the phrase 'Over and over' is part of a phrasal verb 'to roll over', and in the second, the constituent 'Up the hill' is a prepositional phrase. We have already seen in chapter 3 that in the spoken language there is a very high tendency for the first item to be taken as the subject/topic; this is one reason why children do not learn the passive until relatively late. The occurrence of a direct object NP in subject position violates discourse expectancies. In (12) 'Over and over' is neither a subject nor an object and the word is VS, a very unusual one in English. In (13) the canonical SVO word order is maintained, but the first constituent is not the subject or topic. Milroy (1981) has noted that in colloquial Belfast English prepositional phrases may serve as the subject/topic of a sentence, as in:

(15) Over the road is nice

It would be interesting to find out if children in Belfast who were familiar with this construction have difficulty with the type in which the prepositional phrase appeared first but in a non-subject/topic role. The third example is sterotypical of children's readers. Short sentences are used in which there is little anaphora by pronominalization. Other alternatives would be:

(16) The boy has a red boat
(17) The boy has a boat. It is red

In this case the choice to repeat a referent which has already been established in the discourse makes the text artificial.

Not only do children find different construction types in the texts which they learn to read, but they will also not find some of the constructions they habitually use in spoken discourse. Readers do not contain sentences like:

(18) My sister, she looks like me, she's got a new bike

The repetition of the topic in pronomial form is quite common in spoken language, but is not accepted in written texts (cf. section 3.2). Indeed this structure is widely condemned and children are often corrected for using it in speech. Dannequin (1977: 74–6) observes that French-speaking children are corrected for using similar constructions. If anything, the divergence between the written and the spoken norms in French with regard to topicalization is even greater than in English (cf. Harris forthcoming, for a more detailed discussion of the history of word order in French). Simply speaking, however, French allows a topic to occur sentence initially and finally:

(19) Ils se promènent, les garçons
    they are going for a walk, the boys
(20) Les garçons ils se promènent
    The boys, they are going for a walk

The English equivalents are also grammatical, although my guess is that topic initial position is preferred over topic final. Spoken French also allows sentences like (21), which would be largely unacceptable in the written language, where (22) is the more usual equivalent:

(21) Paris, nous, on y va
    Paris, us, we're going there
(22) Nous allons à Paris
    We are going to Paris

Dannequin (1977: 4–5) cites the following extract from a lesson in which the teacher does not accept a topic chain from a child. P refers to pupil and T to the teacher.

P₁: I s'promène(n)t les oies.
   They're taking a walk, the geese.
T: Oui, alors tu me dis, 'i s'promène(n)t les oies.' Il faut mieux dire.
   Yes, well, you've told me 'They're taking a walk, the geese'.
   You have to say that better.
P₂: Les oies se promènent.
   The geese are going for a walk.

The teacher does not say why the second pupil's answer is the better one. When Dannequin (1977: 79) asked the children if they understood what the teacher meant in correcting them, they said that they did not. As it happens, the teachers use the spoken language forms themselves in addressing questions to the children. One teacher said (Dannequin 1977: 76): 'Les très longues dents du loup qui s'accrochent dans les habits, dans la peau, on les appelle comment:' ('These very long teeth of the wolf, that get hold of clothes, and skin, they are called what?'). When given this as a model it is not surprising that a child would be confused when corrected for using the same construction. It has been observed in a number of cases that teachers often enforce norms they do not use themselves. In many cases they are probably not aware of it. The influence of the written language is so pervasive that it is hard to have intuitions about speech independently of notions of correctness and prestige attached to the standard written form of the language. Dannequin found that in general French teachers were correcting 'errors' which were features of ordinary spoken discourse. In effect, then, the lessons used in the school did not allow children to use and build on the grammatical constructions learned in responding to spontaneous speech situations.

Another related example which Dannequin (1977: 84–5) cites concerns an instance in which the teacher is trying to get a child to be explicit. In this extract she is asking the child (P) about a story which has been read.

T: Que fait le papa de Daniel?
   What's Daniel's father doing?
P: Il promène la chèvre.
   He's walking the goat.
T: Bon, alors elle rèpond: 'i promène la chèvre'. Qui est-ce *il*?
   Good, well, she's answered: 'he's walking the goat. Who is this he?
T: Elle m'a dit 'il'. Moi, je sais pas qui c'est *il*.
   She told me 'he'. I don't know who this he *is.*
P: Promène la chèvre le −
   Walks the goat the −

T: Qui?
    Who?
P: Le fermier.
    The farmer.
T: Alors je repose ma question: 'Que fait le papa de Daniel?'
    *Now I'm going to ask my question again. What's Daniel's father
    doing?*
P: Le fermier promène la chèvre.
    The farmer is walking the goat.
T: Oui. Est-ce que, je t'ai demandè ce que fait le fermier? J'ai demandè
    ça? J'ai demandè ça les petites filles?
    *Did I ask you what the farmer's doing? Did I ask that? Did I ask that,
    girls?*

The answer the teacher wants is 'Le papa de Daniel promène la chèvre,'
but fails to elicit it. She rejects various answers. Firstly, when the child fails
to make the subject explicit, using instead the pronoun 'il' to refer to the
referent 'le papa de Daniel' in the teacher's question, she tries to get her to
repeat the referent by saying that she does not know who the pronoun
refers to. The teacher prompts again before the child tries another answer.
When the child finally does give a noun which is semantically coreferential
with 'le papa de Daniel', the teacher rejects it too without saying why and
then repeats her original question. The pupil interprets this as a prompt to
produce a complete sentence, but this still does not satisfy the teacher.

It is not clear why only an absolutely coreferential NP, i.e. an NP which
is not just semantically equivalent but also formally identical to the
referent, is the right answer. Both *le fermier* and *il* accomplish the same
thing and there is little chance that either would be mistaken for a new
topic in the discourse. In replying to the teacher's original question, the
pupil is merely using a means of cohesion which is quite acceptable in both
the spoken and written language; namely a referent known by speaker and
hearer can be referred to as 'he' on subsequent mentions. One could even
argue that the pupil's reply shows a good knowledge of topic development
and cohesion in that the anaphora occurs between conversational turns.
That is, she takes the referent introduced into the discourse by the teacher
and elaborates it. Imagine that this discourse took place between the
teacher and a friend in her home. Consider the likely reaction if the friend
was asked this question and replied as the child did. The friend would
certainly think the teacher did not know how to carry on a conversation if
after the reply to the question the teacher then said that she did not know
who *il* referred to. Only in the classroom could such an 'abnormal' case of
language use count as a legitimate exchange. By 'abnormal' in this case I
mean that, although there is nothing ungrammatical, the exchange violates
the rules governing communicative competence in face-to-face interactions

The basic problem here is that the teacher is trying to impose on the child a language which is too explicit within the context of the situation − one which is a calque of the written language − without explaining why it is necessary or 'better' to do so.

In these last examples it is not just differences between the spoken and written language at the level of syntax which are responsible for the difficulties, but also semantics and pragmatics. Conflicts in these latter areas arise when the way of getting at the meaning of a text is not the same in written and in oral language.

We saw in chapter 5 that the order in which utterances appear creates certain expectancies and inferences about the relationship between them. These relations, which have to do with cohesion, can be explicitly or implicitly conveyed. When a series of sentences occurs in succession the natural tendency for the reader or hearer is to infer some sort of temporal or causal connection to them, e.g. first mentioned, first occurred. The following example is taken from a children's reader, *Examples from America*, Macdonald's Starters (1972: 8):[4]

(23) These animals are in the everglades
     The everglades are hot and wet
     Plants grow very quickly

This bit of text appears on a page with an illustration of plants and animals in the Florida everglades. There are no explicit connectives here; yet through the juxtatposition of the sentences with one another and the illustration, a causal connection is inferred. That is, *Plants grow very quickly* is taken to be the result of the fact that *The everglades are hot and wet*. Furthermore it is assumed that the plants in question are the ones that grow in the everglades and not somewhere else, although the text does not say this.

In the next example (1972: 9), these three sentences occur together, again without any lexicalized connectives.

(24) There are hot, dry deserts in Texas
     It snows in the Rockies
     Sometimes hurricanes blow along the west coast

This time, however, there is no illustration and no previous mention of Texas or the Rockies. Furthermore, there is no connection at all between these statements; yet a child could reasonably infer that the Rockies and hurricanes are in Texas. The text is simple from a syntactic point of view but the processing is made difficult because the connections are not made explicit. There are no instructions which tell the reader that on one page there *is* a causal relationship to be inferred but that on the next page there is not.

An even more problematic example occurs later (1972: 19):

(25) These astronauts are on the moon
They take photographs
They drive around in a special moon car
One day astronauts may have moon cars like this

This text occurs on a page with a photograph of astronauts on the moon with cameras and moon cars. Again, there are no connections between sentences. From the first sentence, however, a link is made between the photograph and the discourse. The *astronauts* are referred to as *these astronauts*; the use of *these* signals the introduction of a known referent. The referent is known from the context of the illustration in which the text is embedded. Similarly, the two *theys* of the second and third sentence are coreferential with *these astronauts*, who have been established as referents in the illustration. The final sentence however is a non-sequitur in terms of the text expectations which have been set up by the text and the picture. To an adult it will be clear that *astronauts* does not refer to the same astronauts who have been referred to previously. Even though the lexical items are the same, the people referred to are not. There is a sudden shift from the 'make believe' world set up by the picture and text in which astronauts are seen driving mooncars to the real world, where such events are merely hypothetical. Nothing in the text indicates that a shift in scene has taken place, which in effect invalidates the presupposition that there is a chain of coreference connecting the four sentences with each other and with the illustration: i.e. *these astronauts*$_1$ = *they*$_1$ = *they*$_2$ = *astronauts*$_2$. In this example, syntactic simplicity is traded off against pragmatic/semantic complexity. The reader bears the burden of uncovering meaning which the writer could have alleviated by taking the perspective of the reader.

Another way in which access to the meaning of a text may be blocked is through the use of unfamiliar vocabulary. Although there have been extensive studies of syntactic complexity and the processing problems it entails, much less is known about the connection between lexis and semantic complexity. Some recent work, however, has been done in this area by Corson, who proposes a *lexical bar theory*. Corson's claim (1983: 213) is that there is a 'semantic barrier in the English lexicon which hinders the users of some social dialects from access to knowledge categories of the school curriculum in their oral and written language'. He believes that the existence of this barrier is a principal cause of school failure for some social dialect users.

Corson compared the use of words of Graeco-Latin origin in the speech and writing of 12- and 15-year-old children in Britain and Australia. He found that at age 12 there were no differences in the oral use of Graeco-Latin lexis which could be correlated with social class background, but by the age of 15 there were massive differences. Working-class children revealed little significant developmental change in oral or written use of Graeco-Latin words.

The use of Graeco-Latin words is not an indication of cognitive superiority, nor is their absence a sign of deficit. Nevertheless, children who have a good active and passive control over this part of the English lexicon have easier access to the semantic fields and genres in which they predominate. Historians of English have documented the periods of intensive borrowing of foreign words, which began in early Middle English. They have commented on the boundary between ordinary everyday words, which are primarily Anglo-Saxon in origin and the more formal, technical and abstract stratum of words, which are of foreign provenance. Corson (1983) estimates that words of Graeco-Latin origin comprise 65–100 per cent of the total specialist vocabularies of knowledge categories in the school curriculum; there is almost a total absence of Anglo-Saxon words within the technical vocabularies of the most abstract knowledge categories, e.g. philosophy. There is also a progressive increase in the use of Graeco-Latin words in school texts. This means that children need to acquire an increasingly specialized lexical competence in order to participate in the semantic milieu of the school.

Familiarity with this part of the English lexicon is acquired late and largely through exposure to the written language and discussion of texts containing them in the classroom. Outside the classroom they tend to be infrequently used; in fact they may be avoided altogether by many speakers in their active spoken vocabularies. They differ not only in length, but require knowledge of a different set of morphophonemic alterations than is required to use native English words. For example, the relationship between *electric* and *electricity* and *profound* and *profundity* involves alterations in vowel quality (e.g. /au/→/ ʌ /), consonants (e.g. /k/→/s/), and stress shift.

The use of Graeco-Latin words not only allows access to the more technical and abstract areas of the curriculum, but it is a badge of education and social status. Children who can impress teachers with their language have an advantage over those who cannot, since important evaluations of language ability are based on how well language is displayed. As children get older, increasing demands are made on their reading and writing. There is a greater emphasis on expository prose and essays, which involve the use of language to explain things and ideas. In the earlier years the demands made on children focus more on personal narratives. Corson also (1982) compared the use of Graeco-Latin words in two oral tasks, one descriptive and one explanatory. He found that language produced in the descriptive task relied much less on Graeco-Latin vocabulary. The explanatory task placed greater demands on lexical resources.

Corson's research demonstrates that it is important for children not only to increase their vocabulary, but to expand it in particular semantic fields, where Graeco-Latin words predominate. His approach is a much needed improvement on typical vocabulary measures which have been generally based on simple word counts. This procedure has obvious weaknesses since it does not measure what range of meanings a child has for a word, nor the relationship among them.

7.4 *The role of literacy in communicative competence*

Most of what I have said about literacy so far has concerned the acquisition of reading. During the years spent in school a great deal of time is taken up by writing narratives, reports and essays. One of the main functions of writing in the classroom is to serve as a means of recording information and demonstrating what has been learned. The ability to write well is generally acknowledged to be a worthwhile achievement in its own right and writing tasks are often assigned as exercises for their own sake. In many cases no explanations are given to students why writing is important, and many see no relevance in it. Corbett (1981: 49) states that when students are exercised in writing literary essays to the exclusion of more utilitarian kinds of writing, e.g. writing a letter of complaint or condolence, they are being scandalously short-changed. While the importance of reading appears to require no justification, the function of traditional writing tasks in the school curriculum has been seriously questioned by educators and linguists.

Martin and Rothery (1980: 4) say that teachers with whom they spoke were unable to give explicit criteria for evaluation of their students' essays. When asked what constituted good writing they mentioned factors like 'good ideas' and 'good expression'. Upon closer examination of essays which the teachers had marked they found that proficiency in writing was evaluated in terms of correct grammar, accurate spelling and pronunciation as signs of literacy. Thus their criteria had little to do with content and coherence.

In looking at the kinds of corrections which teachers made on students' writing assignments, I found much the same as Martin and Rothery. It is instructive to examine some of these in detail. The following is an extract from a 13-year-old girl's attempt to write a 'character sketch'.

> *A character sketch of Rurth*
> . . . I also think that she is mature and responsible of Borina and
>   even *thoug* Jan is part of the family she takes good care and bes
>   *reisponsible* of the children. And she is *intellegent*.

There are three spelling errors here, which I have italicized. The teacher corrected only the first and last of these. Inconsistent marking of spelling errors occurs throughout the child's writing exercise book, which spans a period of three years. This must be very confusing to the writer; sometimes the girl misspells the same word in the same exercise and the teacher marks only one instance as incorrect. Teachers are apparently told that it is better not to correct all the errors a child makes for fear that children will get discouraged if they see too many red marks on their work. There is one grammatical error, *bes*, which the teacher changes to *is*. The form *bes* is not typical of this girl's writing in general, although it is a feature which is often characteristic of younger children. The teacher has also inserted *not* between *is* and *part* in the second line since this is what the child intended. The negative has apparently just been left out. There is one more correction the teacher makes, and that is to cross out the word *of* after *responsible* in the first line. She writes above it the words *by looking after*. She does not, however, alter the third and fourth line where the child uses the same collocation, *responsible of*, again. This inconsistency must also be confusing for the writer. Furthermore, the teacher's correction of the first instance does not appear to solve the problem. The sentence now reads:

(26) I also think that she is mature and responsible by looking after Borina

This seems to me just as awkward as the original. What the girl seems to have in mind is the construction *to take care of someone*, which is what she uses in the third line; because she has used a co-ordinate structure *takes good care and bes responsible of*, she has not taken account of the fact that different prepositions are required for *to take care* and *to be responsible*. Other ways in which these sentences could be repaired are:

(27) She is mature and has responsibility for Borina
     She is mature and takes responsibility for Borina
     She is mature and is responsible towards Borina

the teacher evidently wants the child to replace the phrase *responsible of* by *looking after*; that is,

(28) She is mature and looks after Borina
     She is mature because she looks after Borina
     She is mature and takes responsibility by looking after Borina

At the end of the character sketch, the teacher wrote: 'You should try to explain *why* your opinion of her is so high – what made you choose some of these words?' It is not clear what the import of this directive is, or in what way the child should build on what she has already written in order to satisfy the teacher. In my view, the girl has explained why she thinks Rurth is mature; namely, because she behaves responsibly as far as the children are concerned. This in effect serves as an explanation or a definition of maturity. Perhaps the teacher wants to see the connections explicitly lexicalized; for example, Rurth is mature *because* she takes good care of the children and is responsible for them. The teacher is no doubt also looking for a clarification of the child's choice of *intelligent* in describing Rurth. Although nothing is explicitly said in the text, one could infer that it is a conclusion the child has drawn from what has already been said explicitly; namely, responsibility and maturity are signs of intelligence.

This one extract reveals a number of problems in the way that teachers correct children's writing. Perhaps the most fundamental ones are failure to be consistent and failure to give explicit guidance in terms which children can understand. In addition to spelling and punctuation errors, the teacher also singles out for attention cases in which children fail to write in complete sentences. There are a number of corrections of this type in this young girl's exercise book. In on assignment the teacher has asked the children to list five reasons for studying English. The child has written:

Five reasons for studying English
(1) Writing application's for jobs
(2) You learn to put words together
(3) It is the language of our country
(4) It gives us knowleage
(5) Easy to learn and understand

The teacher made two corrections on this passage. One was a punctuation error, i.e. *applications,* and the other a spelling error, i.e. *knowledge.* At the end the teacher wrote: 'Write in sentences, please.' She does not, however, point out to the child which, if any, of her five statements count as sentences (e.g. 2, 3, 4) and can be used as models in rewriting the ones which are not. Elsewhere in her exercise book the child has copied down the teacher's definition of a sentence as: 'A sentence is a complete thought. It must tell us something.' One of the writing exercises the teacher gave earlier in the year was to write a long sentence. The girl wrote the following:

Sentence
Susan and I went into the shop and brought some sweets but Susan lost her money down the drain so we looked down the drain but it rolled down along so we went into the next shop and brought apples, pears bananas and we went home.

The teacher has not made any corrections on the actual passage. She has not queried the child's use of *brought,* where presumably *bought* is intended. Nor has she marked any punctuation errors, even though elsewhere in the girl's exercise book she has made a number of corrections in the child's punctuation of phrases like *apples, pears, bananas.* At the end of the passage, however, she has written: 'Yes I suppose this is a sentence but it is unsatisfactory because you repeat joining words.' The teacher appears to be objecting to the repeated use of *and* and *so* as clause connectives, which she refers to as 'joining words', but she does not give an example of how some of the phrases could be rewritten without them. As I pointed out in chapter 5, this type of loose paratactic connection is characteristic of spoken narratives told by children and adults. It must also be confusing to the child that the teacher is not really sure if this passage counts as a sentence or not. In terms of the teacher's criteria, it does tell something and it is complete. But how does one decide what counts as one thought or two? There are several events in this passage, but do they count as separate, complete thoughts? The teacher is not even sure how to apply her own criteria, let alone how to provide explicit guidance to the child which will enable her to rewrite the text in the way she judges to be correct.

I have already commented on the way in which the grammatical ideology which pervades the school's teaching of language skills adds up to a vague theory about the primacy of sentences, their structure and their logic. It is not just the teacher's views about language, which are encouraged to a large extent by literacy and the written language; Chomsky's theory of generative grammar also takes the sentence as a primary unit of linguistic structure. A major part of grammatical competence for Chomsky is knowing whether or not sentences are grammatical.

It is interesting to see what views teachers and children have about the value and purpose of writing. The teacher I referred to above gave her class a set of statements about writing, which were to be sorted under the headings of 'agree', 'disagree' and 'don't know'. A comparison of the answers the teacher expected and those given by the young girl mentioned above provide some insight into the assumptions which both parties make.

The girl's list was as follows:

Agree
i. Teachers don't teach you to write. They just tell you to do it.
ii. Handwriting matters a great deal.
iii. A story with many spelling mistakes cannot be good.
iv. If you can't punctuate, you can't write.
v. Poor punctuation and spelling spoil a good story.
vi. Either you can write or you can't. That's all there is to it.
vii. A story needs a beginning, a middle and an end.
viii. Its important to know what you're going to write before you begin.

Disagree
i. Good writing can be boring.
ii. Writing is the most important thing you can learn in school.

Don't know
i.   You can be a good writer but a poor speller.
ii.   Its important to write about things that matter to you.
iii.   You can't write the way you talk.
iv.   People who can't write get along O.K.

Let us look first at the statements with which the girl has agreed. It is evident that the girl has perceived the importance of the superficial form or mechanics of the writing task. In other words, she and the teacher share the view that spelling, punctuation, handwriting and organization are more important than the content of the text itself. A story cannot be good if it does not 'look good'; this is essentially the message the teacher conveys when she pays more attention to these features than to the content of the text itself. There are, however, two statements which the child agrees with, but which the teacher does not. The girl believes that writing is an ability one comes by naturally rather than learns by practice and explicit teaching. She agrees that either you can write or you can't, and that teachers don't teach writing. It is not surprising that she holds this view since the teacher offers little in the way of practical guidance or models. Most schools require writing but few teach it. The teacher, however, thinks otherwise; thus there is a crucial mismatch between the teacher and pupil with regard to the process of how one acquires writing skills. Someone who thinks that either you can write or you can't, that spelling and punctuation are more important than a good story, and is corrected for these kinds of 'errors' frequently, will come to accept that there is no point in doing anything because he/she is just a poor writer by 'nature'. The teacher may create these beliefs by her own attitude and reinforce them in her marking practices.

The issue of whether one can separate form from content is not quite as clear-cut as I have made it appear, at least from the child's point of view. Although she seems to share the teacher's opinion that form is more important than content, she is unsure whether you can still be a good writer even if you are a bad speller. The teacher, however, believes that good spelling is a prerequisite for good writing. Another one of the statements raises the question to what extent one can/should evaluate a piece of work in terms of two sets of criteria, one relating to form and the other to content. In her list of statements with which she disagrees, the child has included the one which states that good writing can be boring. The teacher also disagreed with this one. Her reasoning seems to be that if a story is written with correct spelling, punctuation, grammar and well organized, then it counts as good and therefore is not boring. In other words the packaging of a text guarantees its worth. We have seen a similar view on the part of the classroom teacher observed by Michaels who considered any topic interesting and important as long as it was rendered in a particular discourse style. While I do not deny that there is an important relationship between form and content, I would still want to recognize that a story which was well written (not just in the terms of the teacher's superficial features) could be evaluated as boring by some readers. Conversely, a great many texts present interesting material, but are not very skilfully written. What makes a piece of writing good is the ability to use the linguistic means at one's disposal in a creative way. What characterizes bad writing is inappropriateness and incoherence; writing which fails to satisfy the requirements of a genre, such as the examples we looked at earlier from a child's reader, is bad. Appropriate style depends on the interaction of setting and participants. Criteria for competence vary according to the writing task. Styles differ lexically, syntactically, semantically and pragmatically in terms of what one chooses to say explicitly, how it is said, and what is conveyed by implicature. Knowledge about these matters is essential to being a successful and skilful user of the spoken language too. Many children are skilful users of the spoken language when they come to school. When teachers correct children for the use of some of the oral discourse strategies in writing, they deprive children of some of their main text-generating resources. I pointed out in chapter 3, for instance, that one of the main devices children use for thematization in oral narratives is the *get* passive. Martin and Rothery (1981: 42), however, found that teachers corrected these and insisted that children use the BE passive instead.

This brings us to the questions of the value and purpose of writing. I have already mentioned the criticism which claims that school writing assignments generate products that meet teacher demands and academic requirements but apparently do not serve any other instrumental ends. To return to the young girl's list of statements about writing, we can observe that she does not know whether it's important to write about things that matter to you. Although the teacher thinks this is important, her assignments do not really reflect this. Children may find it hard to see why a character sketch should matter to them, or indeed what the point is of writing a sentence as an assignment. Similarly, the girl is uncertain what the value of writing is within the classroom and beyond it. She disagrees with the statement that writing is probably the most important thing you can learn in school. She is not sure, however, whether people who can't write can get along OK.

Heath (1982b) advocates the use of ethnography to find out what writing functions are essential to and valued by a community. One needs to investigate the context and content of literacy events, i.e. what is read, who reads it and how it is read, e.g. publicly or privately. She found that in one community where children were given writing assignments which reflected the community's literacy patterns, they learned to write in a range of styles for these functions.

Is writing the most important thing learned at school then? There are at least two very different perspectives one can take in trying to answer this question. As it is presently defined and understood in many classrooms, writing does not necessarily provide one with literacy skills which are useful or required for the functions literacy serves outside schools. Many children therefore see little point in writing. Regardless of whether the school explicitly gives the acquisition of school-type literacy top priority, its supremacy is implicitly recognized in the school's assessment procedures for both writing and speech. It is interesting that the young child referred to above says she does not know whether you can write the way you talk. This indicates her uncertainty about the relationships between speech and writing. It would have been even more interesting to know how the teachers and pupils would respond to the statement: You can't talk the way you write. I have given a number of examples in the previous two chapters to illustrate the fact that the school tries to impose on its students a style of spoken and written discourse which relies heavily on a form of literacy, which is erroneously regarded as the inevitable form that literacy must take. With the growth of mass communication and the need to communicate with people of diverse backgrounds, often unknown to the speaker/writer, a socially distant and seeming neutral style of speaking has evolved for use in teaching, and public speaking, etc., which has taken on many of the characteristics of essayist prose.

Many have been critical of this particular style of writing, among them lay and professional critics. Tibbitts and Tibbitts (1978: 22) single out what they call 'preposition piling' as a 'fairly good sign of imminent breakdown in thought'. By preposition piling, they mean the use of too many prepositions, as in the example they cite:

(29) English teachers everywhere agree that personal ownership and use of a good desk dictionary is a prime necessity for every student in obtaining the maximum results from the study of English

This 'overuse' of prepositions derives partly from the use of what some linguists (cf. Williams 1981) have referred to as 'nominal' as opposed to 'verbal' style. Compare, for example, the following sentence pairs.

(30) The fact that you performed so well in the examination impressed us favourably
It surprised us that he came so quickly   (verbal style)
(31) Your good peformance in the examination made a favourable impression on us
His coming so quickly surprised us   (nominal style)

Williams (1981: 154–8) observes that it is virtually impossible to write on a very general or abstract level without using nominalizations separated from their accidental subjects and objects. This kind of writing is ordinarily associated with 'advanced' societies, i.e. post-industrialized ones, having the leisure to pursue philosophical thought. Once verbs are converted into noun-like constructions, a writer is able to manoeuvre them into various positions in the sentence. With abstract nominalization the underlying objects and subjects of the original verb can be deleted. The following 'transformation' can be written to convert verbal sentences into nominal ones:

Subject + verb + direct object → subject + verbal noun + $\begin{cases} \text{prepositional} \\ \text{object} \\ \text{complement} \end{cases}$

The subject of the underlying verb can appear in a variety of positions: e.g. as a possessive before a noun,

The man's death (cf. The man died)

in a prepositional phrase,

The departure of the train (cf. The train departed)
Misbehaviour on the part of the students (cf. The students misbehaved)

as a compound noun,

student misbehaviour

as adjective + noun,

a French invention (cf. The French invented something)

Brown and Levinson (1978) have claimed that there is an important stylistic difference between the types of sentences I have called nominal and verbal, which relates to level of formality, degrees of politeness and extent of social distance. The degrees of politeness and formality go hand in hand with what Ross (1969) has called 'nouniness'. Compare the following sentences:

(32) I am surprised that you failed to reply
       I am surprised at your failing to reply
       I am surprised at your failure to reply
       The failure to reply was a surprise

These sentences appear to illustrate a hierarchy of formality which is also related to their likelihood of being spoken or written. The first sentence seems to be the least formal and is much more likely to be spoken than written. By contrast, the last sentence displays the greatest degree of nouniness and would most likely appear in a formal written business letter. It is the most 'nouny' and the subject and object have been deleted; we no longer know who failed to reply and who was surprised. When passivization is coupled with nominalization the depersonalization of language is at its maximum; compare:

(33) We regret that we cannot assume responsibility if customers lose personal belongings
It is regretted that no responsibility can be assumed for lost personal belongings

The more nouny an expression is, the more removed the agent is from doing or feeling something. Instead of the predicate being something attributed to the agent, the action becomes an attribute of the agent, e.g. I regret → it is my regret. With the progressive removal of the active part of a sentence, the more formal and distant it becomes.

In commenting on the historical source of the nominal style in English, Williams (1981: 160) notes that it lies in contact with Latin and French in the Anglo-Norman and later Middle English period when most serious writing was done in Latin and French. I have already noted in connection with my discussion of Corson's work on lexical bar theory that English borrowed extensively. In the meantime it was losing some of its native resources of word formation. Early Anglo-Saxon authors compounded native words like *mod* ('mind or spirit') + *cearo* ('sorrow') instead of borrowing *anxietas* ('anxiety') from Latin. Since late Latin style was often nominal, the noun was borrowed into the language before the verb.

Nominal style has spread in particular in academic disiplines. Williams (1981: 154) writes:

It is no exaggeration to say that this particular grammatical structure, the abstract nominalization, has become centrally important in the style of much modern English prose. In conjunction with words borrowed from Latin and French, with the passive, and with the constructions that combine two or more general words where a single specific word would do, it has come to characterise what is know as burocratese, educationalese, medicalese − the worst kind of super-literate writing in our society.

Students are expected to acquire a style similar to this in their own writing and are often told explicitly not to use 'I' or any indications of first person reference under the assumption that third person reference and passivization are more objective. Students are expected to write 'one', 'we,' or 'this author' in referring to themselves. The use of these circumlocutions is still common in much academic writing. Nominal style is evidently highly valued by Swedish teachers too, judging from the studies which have been done on the written language of Swedish school pupils (cf. especially Larsson 1979). Gustavsson (1979), who looked at the use of nouns and verbs in schoolchildren's essays, found that the teacher gave higher marks to those children whose essays had a higher number of nouns. Larsson (1979) found that students who used more passives also got higher marks. Gustavsson says that Swedish teachers view the nominal style as better and more complex. Both Gustavsson and Larsson looked for evidence of social class, sex and stylistic differentiation in the students' essays. They found that sex, age and type of essay were more important than social class background in the use of nominal style. Contrary to what has been widely believed about female superiority in verbal skills (but erroneously so, according to Macaulay 1978b) at least in the United States, boys did better than girls. Their essays were marked higher due to greater control of the nominal style. They also used more compound nouns and passives with increasing age than girls. The children were asked to write two types of essays, one a personal narrative and the other a more explanatory account. The second task produced a higher proportion of written language rather than everyday language forms and a greater degree of nominal style.

The differences between the language of conversation and expository prose are more or less arbitrary; they are a matter of convention. Chafe (1982) regards them as two extremes of the oral/literate continuum; and he notes specifically that nominalizations, relative clauses and passives are more frequent in written than spoken language. The kind of expository prose we have looked at here must be seen as the product of a particular sociohistorical context and the outcome of a certain type of literacy. The sociolinguistic relations between speech and writing may, however, change. The relationship between the author and the reading public is not self-evident and different conventions have held at different times. English essayist literacy encodes only some of the possible relationships. Different cultures have different expectations about these relationships and about the allocation of particular functions to particular channels. The Scollons (1981) maintain that learning the discourse patterns of English literacy is tantamount to acquiring a new identity, at least for some ethnic groups.

In order for an Athabaskan Indian to produce a written English essay, he must put on a major display, which is viewed as totally inappropriate behaviour. This sort of display would be appropriate only if the individual were in a position of dominance in relation to his audience. But both the audience and author are fictionalized in typical essayist prose. The author is not necessarily known to his reader and he usually is writing not to a specific individual but to a more general audience. I have already mentioned that even in cases where it is clear and obvious to the child that the teacher is the main audience for his spoken and written discourse, he is asked to pretend that the teacher does not know him or have any background knowledge against which shared assumptions can proceed.

When participants are not known, the dominance relations are obscured. And in interactions where relationships between individuals are not known, the Athabaskan prefers to be silent. The paradox of literacy for Athabaskans is that their native set of discourse patterns is mutually exclusive with those of English essayist prose. In order to read and write they must adopt discourse patterns that are identical with those of English speakers. Writing in English for distinctly native purposes presents a critical dilemma. In fact, the Scollons claim that an Athabaskan cannot as an Athabaskan write about Athabaskan things. There is a conflict between the things that have to be communicated and the ways and means of communicating them, which are available (i.e. in this case) by way of English discourse patterns.

This example suggests that if literacy is related as closely to discourse patterns and ethnic identity as it seems to be, then other ethnic groups (or indeed any group) which have quite obviously different discourse patterns can be expected to relate in different ways to literacy. This is not a problem just for multi-cultural education; there is evidence from studies of urban working-class speech in Britain which complements Heath's work in the United States in suggesting that the written channel is evaluated quite differently from the spoken (cf. Milroy 1980). In section 6.1 I showed how black students may reject the school's instruction in reading due to the influence of peers. Wick (1980) coins the term 'superliterates' to refer to young black Americans who sport illiteracy as a badge of hostility to white values. To express black power and solidarity in certain situations one must use black vernacular; in order to adopt the values associated with the group one must express views in its way of speaking.

Traugott (1981) discusses the obstacles faced by writers who wish to write in minority dialects. Generally speaking, the use of non-standard dialect indexes a social status which is socially or educationally inferior to that held by speakers of the standard. Standard English is the norm for written language; when dialect appears, it is usually to represent the speech of comic characters or for a local colour effect. Those who speak dialects in books are marked by their speech or somehow set off from the other characters with respect to the way their speech is represented. In everyday life, however, the use of non-standard speech frequently serves as a mark of intimacy and solidarity amongst those who interact regularly by means of it. (Remember Trudgill's informants, discussed in section 4.5, who said they would not want to speak posh.) To use standard English would set up a distant relationship between the speaker and hearer. Thus the problem for a speaker of non-standard English who wants to write in it is how to reverse the expectation that dialect within literary texts is a distancing (and often comic) device. Traugott notes a similar identity crisis faced by the black writer, who wants to use BEV as a marker of a particular cultural identity. If BEV comes to be a language suitable and acceptable for third person narratives then it will of necessity be at odds with itself as a minority dialect.

My purpose in drawing on a wide range of studies of literacy and its effects is to support my argument that the so-called writing or literacy crisis is a purely school-based problem as long as it neglects the uses/functions of speech and writing in the community. By narrowing definitions of literacy in this way, learning to read and write is made discontinuous with everyday experiences with language.

This brings us back to the issue of whether standards of literacy can be defined and maintained, and in addition whether there can be a developmental theory of communicative ability, which will allow us to evaluate some functions and uses of language as better or more advanced than others. I have already shown how educators have tended to assume that school standards of literacy have been represented as essential for developing the highest level of cognitive and linguistic functioning. I hope I have exposed the faulty and ethnocentric logic which underlies this view. This does not, however, stop these ideas from being influential. Some recent work in the field of bilingualism and multi-cultural education has taken for granted some of the mistaken notions I have discussed here and in previous chapters.

Cummins (1981) has proposed a model of language proficiency which is based on the view that there are two dimensions of language proficiency, CALP (cognitive–academic language proficiency) and BICS (basic inter-personal communicative skill). These are seen as separate components. CALP involves those aspects of language proficiency which are closely related to the development of literacy skills (in one's native as well as second or other language(s)), metalinguistic awareness, logic, vocabulary-concept knowledge and knowing how to process decontextualized knowledge. Cummins (1981) says that CALP reflects the demands inherent in the educational system. He intends CALP to represent a universal, cross-linguistic aspect of competence, and believes that, once its features are learned, they are applicable to any language. His explanation for why some bi/multilingual children fail is that they have not had sufficient schooling in their mother tongue to enable them to acquire CALP. Therefore, he claims that children are not able to transfer the abilities for handling decontextualized language to a new language.

BICS, on the other hand, has to do with oral fluency, accent and certain aspects of sociological competence. BICS seems to be confirmed to fairly superficial features. According to Cummins, everyone acquires BICS; it represents a composite of basic skills, which everyone shares. He argues that BICS is unrelated to school success. In support of his assertion he cites Wells's (1979) work in which it was found that assessments of pre-schoolers' spontaneous language did not correlate highly with later reading tests taken in school. There were, however, high correlations between success in reading and interaction style with parents in the home. This serves to emphasize Heath's (1983) finding that certain types of interaction in the spoken language are a kind of communicative apprenticeship for the uses of language, both written and spoken, at school.

Edelsky et al. (1983) present an extensive critique of Cummins's ideas about CALP and BICS and their relation with school success. The claim that CALP is transferrable from one language to another is a very difficult hypothesis to test because the skills which comprise CALP are bound up with culture-specific types of literacy and experience with the written language; and, as I have pointed out, the effects of literacy are in turn connected with those of schooling.[5] The fact that literate Vai do not do better on CALP-type tests than non-literates should make the distinction between CALP and BICS suspect if both are seen as independent of rather than shaped by the language and context in which they are acquired and used. The cross-cultural research on the differential social and psychological effects of literacy which I discussed in section 7.1 and 7.2 should also warn us against lending too much credence to theories of competence developed by generative grammarians, which are based on the uniformity of an idealized underlying grammatical competence, which reflect cognitive organization and capacity. Hymes (1974) emphatically rejects the assumption of uniformity and equifunctionality of competence. In the next chapter I will look at the assumptions about competence and language which underlie the testing of language proficiency.

8

The measurement of communicative competence

There has been much discussion in both the popular press and academic professions of the problem of 'declining standards' in language proficiency. The cover story of *Newsweek* (8 December 1975) was entitled 'Why Johnny can't write'. Bolinger (1980) observes that English is probably the most analysed language on earth; moreover, there are probably no countries which compare with the Anglophone ones in terms of the amount of exposure its citizens have to the pronouncements of those he calls the 'language gurus' or 'shamans'. The latter are self-made language pundits, who have undertaken to make prescriptive grammar available to the masses in the form of handbooks like *Strictly Speaking* (Newman 1974).

A great many of these gurus have expressed alarm about the state of the language. What is it the shamans are trying to save us from? According to Tibbitts and Tibbitts (1978: 4), for example, sloppy grammar is 'destroying the ability to think in the peoples that used to speak that wonderfully expressive tongue [i.e. English SR]'. Like many other language gurus, Tibbitts and Tibbitts complain that English is 'slowly being crushed to death under the weight of a verbal conglomerate, a pseudo-speech at once pretentious and feeble, that is created daily by millions of blunders and inaccuracies in grammar, syntax, idiom, metaphor, logic and common sense'. They fear that 'illiteracy is catching.'

Standards change. This is true of language no less than other cultural products like fashions. People have complained about the decline of English since at least the fifteenth century. But in what sense can one speak of declining standards in the use of spoken and written language? In order to answer this question, we must look at the way in which standards are set and the procedures and instruments used to assess them. Current definitions of success in school rely on the measurement of reading and writing ability. A good reader is one who has the ability to perform well on reading achievement tests. Similarly, a good writer can do well on writing tasks, which involve knowledge of punctuation, spelling, etc. Children's success or failure is measured in terms of publicly sanctioned yardsticks like the *Scholastic Achievement Test* (SAT), which is required by most colleges in the United States as an entrance examination, or in Britain by O and A level examinations. I will argue in this chapter that the tests used in many schools are only indirectly related to common-sense notions of what it means to be a competent language-user. When notions like the 'ability to extract meaning' become operationalized as scores on reading tests, a child who fails is then labelled as one who is 'unable to extract meaning'. Similarly, when the 'cognitive aspects' of language are tested in terms of being able to produce synonyms, then the child who cannot is branded as 'lacking in the cognitive aspects of language development'. Once certain features, like the mastery of complex syntax, accurate spelling and punctuation, etc., become established measures of language proficiency, it is hardly questioned what is meant by language ability, and what role these features play in it.

It is a matter of objective fact, however, that whatever knowledge of language the school tests appear to be measuring is unevenly distributed amongst schoolchildren. Very often skills are stratified along social class and ethnic dimensions. When test scores are looked at nationally from a longitudinal perspective, concern has been expressed at the finding that, on the whole, today's school population appears to be performing less well on the traditional measures of verbal ability than the previous generation. In the United States, for example, many are alarmed by the fact that SAT scores have been declining for a number of years. There is, however, no reason to panic about this. When the SAT was normed, its population represented a small minority of white middle-class students: thus it tests the extent to which all who take it have acquired the skills possessed by the literate white upper-middle class. No wonder 'standards have declined' when the same set of norms is being used to measure what is now a much more diverse testing population, which includes more students from non-white middle-class backgrounds. It cannot be claimed that the dramatic failure of some children on standardized tests is mainly the fault of the communicative systems children have learned at home and from peers. Declining test scores are partly to be seen within the context of socioeconomic change, radically shifting functions of different kinds of literacies and a reliance on evaluation procedures, which do not take these factors into account. The kinds of tests children take at school are tailored to a special kind of consciousness about language, which is deeply conditioned by western modes of literacy. The crisis in language proficiency is in some respects an academic problem which arises because definitions of competence, literacy, etc., have been narrowed to such an extent that they make children's experience with language at school discontinuous with everyday communicative competence.

Indeed, the problem of 'declining standards' and the need for redefining them are no less severe amongst teachers than pupils, at least according to some accounts in the popular press. A recent article in *Newsweek* (16 January 1984) reports the test results and reactions of teachers to a requirement of some school districts in the United States that teachers must take basic tests in verbal and mathematical ability in order to qualify for promotion and higher salaries. When one of these tests was given to teachers last year, *Newsweek* reports that teachers began behaving like some of their students. They cheated, passed notes and talked amongst themselves. Nearly half (44 per cent) failed the reading test: 46 per cent failed mathematics and 26 per cent failed the writing test. Some complained of the subjective and arbitrary nature of the questions they were asked, particularly on the writing test. One of the questions asked for improvements to be made on the sentence 'Children like teachers who are easygoing, generous and who can be depended on.' The options given by the testers were all grammatical, but the correct answer according to the testers was 'Children like easygoing, generous and dependable teachers.' I have already cited similarly arbitrary examples in previous chapters, which have been applied in teaching children good style and grammar in writing tasks.

I will focus in this chapter on several issues which arise in connection with measuring communicative competence; namely, the notions of 'standard English' which underlie school tests, and the extent to which dialect interference may lead to bias in scoring. I will conclude by suggesting some guidelines, which I hope will lead to a more realistic assessment of prevailing ideas about language, literacy and the testing of language proficiency.

8.1 *Defining standard English*

I have operated up to this point with a more or less tacit definition of the notion of standard language, in particular the idea of a variety which I have referred to throughout the book as 'standard English', which exists in opposition to non-standard varieties of English. Although it may seem strange and somewhat out of place to postpone defining these notions explicitly until nearly the end of the book, I have done so in order to be able to draw more fully on the discussion of literacy in previous chapters.

The process of language standardization has received a great deal of discussion within the context of the theory of language planning (cf. especially Haugen 1966 and Fishman 1971). A simple definition of a standard language is that it is a highly codified variety of a language, which has been developed and elaborated for use across a broad range of functions. English is perhaps an extreme example of this type of language since it serves an international community, which includes both native and non-native speakers (cf. Trudgill and Hannah 1982 on standard English as a world language). The process of standardization converts one variety of language into a standard by fixing and regulating its spelling, grammar, etc., in dictionaries and grammars, which serve as authorities in prescriptive teaching of native speakers as well as foreign learners. It is extremely important to stress the fact that standardization is not an inherent but rather an acquired or deliberately imposed characteristic. Standard languages do not arise via a 'natural' course of linguistic evolution or suddenly spring into existence. They are created by dint of conscious and deliberate planning. It is useful to make an analogy between the process of language standardization and that of the standardization of coinage, weights and measures, etc. In all these cases the aim is to remove variation and establish one system to serve as a uniform currency.

Most of the present-day standard languages of western Europe emerged within a climate of intense political nationalism. They were developed in part out of the need to create prominent ideological symbols of shared purpose, nationhood, etc. The models selected for codification were those current in capitals like Copenhagen, Paris, London − seats of the court, centres of trade and finance, and breeding places of the aristocracy and bureaucracy. The spread of these 'new' languages was made successful by the printing press, and the rise of the newly literate middle classes who adopted them eagerly as a means of social advancement and mobility.

In some countries there are special institutions, like the Académie Française, which have responsibility for and control over these matters. It defines what counts as 'good or correct French'. It is not sufficient for a language to have what Hymes, Stewart and others refer to as de-facto norms (cf. Stewart's 1968 typology of types of language based on social function).

Probably all communities evaluate instances of language as good or bad relative to some communal consensus (cf. Bloomfield 1927). Neither is it sufficient to have dictionaries and/or grammars. Jamaican creole has both, but these are linguists' grammars and have no official recognition. Standard British English is the only variety approved for use in school.

When a language is written, linguistic matters can be subject to regulation in a way they cannot be when a language exists in spoken form only. The creation of a written standard language gives one particular variety a power far exceeding any spoken variety. Haugen (1966) uses the term *grapholect* to refer to a standard written language. No other variety has the resources and prestige of the grapholect. The fact that it exists in one sense as an autonomous object described in grammars, etc., engenders the notion that it is somehow the 'real' language or the language as it 'should be' and that other varieties are degenerate or corrupt versions of it. There is usually a great deal of resistance to changes in it. And over time the differences between it and spoken varieties may become quite considerable due to the conservatism of the written form. The existence of a highly codified written language also tends to reinforce the idea that linguistic matters can be judged as right or wrong. The possibility of prescribing the use of certain constructions as right (and conversely, proscribing others) presupposes the existence of a means of recording language so that the way in which it is put together can be inspected. The idea that certain ways of transmitting language can be incorrect and that there are right and wrong ways to use words goes back to medieval grammatical tradition. In actual fact, however, what goes by the name of correct or standard English represents nothing more than the development of a variety which was once a regional dialect associated within the southeastern part of Britain. Standard written English is not anyone's 'mother tongue'; it is furthermore the product of a particular kind of literacy which a child learns via schooling (cf. Heath 1980 and Shaklee 1980 for further discussion of standard English). This variety of English has no more claim to correctness than any other, but the fact that many people believe it does plays an important role in the attitudes the public have towards language and the way in which language skills are assessed.

8.2 The use of standardized tests as a measure of communicative competence

There appears to be an inverse relationship between what can be easily measured and assessed quantitatively and its importance in effective communicative skills. It is easier for instance to measure accuracy in pronunciation and spelling than meaning. Shuy (1977: 78) illustrates the dilemma in a diagram (figure 8.1) which depicts an iceberg with the visible features above the water line, but the more critical ones below. Shuy observes that the more visible and highly recurring features are measured and quantitified throughout a child's school career without regard for their interrelationship with other levels of linguistic organization. These features tend to be the ones that are measured because we know what they are and because their inventory is easier to delimit more than because of what they tell us of language learning and development. When these features are measured by the answers to test questions, it is assumed that by knowing the answers one has acquired the skill the tests claim to be measuring. Often children's progress is assessed longitudinally by comparing scores obtained on the same or similar tests from year to year. This practice asumes that because a feature measures something meaningful at one

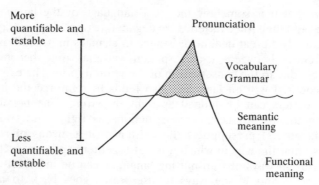

Figure 8.1 Visible evaluation points of language
Source: Shuy 1977

stage, it continues to do so. I demonstrated in chapter 6, however, that different levels of language take on significance at different stages in the process of learning to read; pronunciation is less important at a later stage. This means that there is not much point in measuring decoding ability at the phonological level in the advanced stages of reading.

Shuy and Staton (1982: 181) observe that people tend to make judgements about the ability, intelligence and even the personality of speakers on the basis of linguistic features which have no particular bearing on those areas of development, e.g. pronunciation and grammar. In other words, most standardized assessment procedures measure the surface aspects of language. Schools often have screening procedures for identifying children with 'language problems' and on the basis of these children may then be diagnosed as having difficulty in certain areas and sent for therapy. Tests used by speech therapists do not always take into account local dialect differences and children who do not use the standard forms against which the test is scored and normed may be judged to have disorders. This means that successful and normal language acquisition is equated with the learning of middle-class mainstream varieties of English, or in other words, standard English.

Wolfram and Christian (1976: 134–7), for example, examined the ITPA (Illinois Test of Psycholinguistic Abilities), which is a widely used test in the United States for assessing cognitive ability and grammatical development. It is mainly a diagnostic tool in which specific abilities and disabilities may be spotted for remedial work. All of the responses must be in standard English to be scored correct. They found that 25 out of 33 (76 per cent) of the items on one subject, grammatical closure, were dialect-dependent. According to the grammatical rules of one variety of English they studied, i.e. Appalachian English, these 25 items would have different answers. Similar results obtain for speakers of BEV who are given this test. This is one example of a dialect-dependent question.

(1) This boy is writing something. This is what he *write/has written/did write*

The possibilities in Appalachian English are *writed/writ/has wrote,* none of which appears as an alternative. A child who answered these and other questions concerning the grammatical inflection of verbs incorrectly might be judged not to understand the concept of 'past tense'. Similarly, there are items such as (2), which test the use of plural nouns:

(2) Here is a dress. Here are two *dresses*

Speakers of BEV who mark only variably plurals and past tense forms with the correct endings may be judged deficient. Wolfram and Christian (1976: 135–6) observe that if a ten-year-old speaker of Appalachian English applied the rules of his own variety and these were scored as incorrect, his abilities would be assessed as equivalent to those of a child of 4.5. And even if the child answered only half of the questions in accordance with his own dialect, his score would still be three years below his actual age. Such a score would be sufficient to recommend a child for remedial language training. They say that with a test like this one it is possible to 'misdiagnose a child's language abilities and penalise him for having learned the language of his community'. The problem with tests of this type is that they conflate the distinction between conceptual or logical form and the linguistic means for expressing it.

From my own work in Scotland I found that there was a great deal of confusion about *speech therapy* and *speech training.* Certain socially unacceptable forms of speech were condemned as slovenly and inarticulate and children were sent to speech therapy sessions for the correction of their everyday norms of pronunciation and habitual articulation. The doctrine of MacAllister's *A Year's Course in Speech Training* (1963) appears to have dominated teacher training colleges' instruction in the spoken language in central Scotland for quite some time. Most teachers with whom I spoke were quite familiar with her work and spoke highly of it. Although MacAllister is willing to accept certain local features of Scots, e.g. /ɪ/, she condemns others as 'crude' (1963: 155), e.g. the use of dark instead of clear /l/. In a series of broadcasts and workbooks for the Scottish schools entitled *Speech Training for Juniors* (1938–9), she gives the following advice to pupils aged seven to nine about the pronunciation of /l/:

The new sound we are going to practise today is a lovely one when it is made correctly. Try to sing it *clearly* [emphasis MacAllister's].
Listen listen!
Listen well,
Tinkle goes
a tiny bell.

The Scots norm is a velar /l/ in almost all phonetic contexts; some, however, do have dental (rather than alveolar/velar) allophones in consonant clusters ending in /t/ or /d/.

In other tests children may be asked to discriminate in their production sounds in word pairs which are homophones in some dialects, e.g. *pin* and *pen*. For some Americans both are realized as /pIn/. In various kinds of articulation tests dialect bias is very apparent; the production of consonant clusters in words like *nest* or dental fricatives in words like *thin* or *both* are often treated as diagnostic in determining articulatory development. The processes of consonant cluster simplification are widespread in many dialects of English as we have seen in chapter 4, and each of these (and other) items would have different realizations in different dialects. For example, in one articulation test which Wolfram and Fasold (1974: 209–13) studied, over 70 of 176 items (i.e. 40 per cent) could potentially have realizations which differed from those counted as correct by the test designers.

It does not necessarily follow that children (or indeed adults) should be able to perceive differences in sound which they do not habitually make. As it happens, there seem to be a number of striking asymmetries between production and perception, which are not well understood. For example, in his study of mergers (e.g. *fool/full, cot/caught*) in American and British English, Labov found that people were capable of producing differences in sound which they and others could not distinguish auditorily. In his study of Italian and American children in Boston, Biondi (1975: 65) found that overall children showed a no better than chance level of 'correct' perception of the contrast between pairs like *thank/tank, boat/both*, etc. This correlates almost exactly with their level of production. Although on average perception mirrors production in this case, as we saw in chapter 4 there were some interesting differences which correlated with age, sex and ethnicity.

The repetition or shadow test has also been used in assessing the grammatical competence of young children. The assumption behind this technique is that children's reproduction is limited by their productive capability. When a child can repeat the adult version, he is assumed to have the productive as well as the receptive competence. In general, there is evidence which suggests that receptive competence outstrips active production skills, e.g. children will not accept adults' imitations of their production errors. Bever (1975: 2) quotes the following exchange between a father and child:

Child:　Mommy goed to the store.
Father:　Mommy goed to the store?
Child:　No, Daddy, I say it that way, not you!
Father:　Mommy wented to the store?
Child:　No.

Father: Mommy went to the store.
Child: That's right. Mommy wen. . goed to the store.

The repetition technique has been widely used in psycholinguistics and in a number of studies on social dialects (cf. e.g. the discussion in Wolfram and Fasold 1974: 65, and Slobin and Welsh 1973). In the latter case it has been demonstrated that children who speak non-standard dialects often have receptive competence of standard English, as evidenced by their dialect paraphrases of standard English stimulus items.[1] The converse does not necessarily hold, however (cf. Baratz and Shuy 1969). Those who speak standard English generally do not have receptive competence in many areas of the non-standard grammar (cf. also Wolfram and Fasold 1974: 60–5 on elicitation techniques).

There are further criticisms of so-called standardized language tests of the type I have been discussing. These tests are referred to in the literature on testing as *discrete point tests* (cf. Oller 1979: 37). They attempt to focus attention on one point of grammar, e.g. phonology, or assess only one skill, e.g. listening. Testing formats of this type are highly decontextualized since there is no ordinary naturally occuring discourse situation in which one's attention would be involved in placing appropriate suffixes on verb stems or distinguishing and producing minimal pairs. The discrete point method of testing also has led to the development of discrete point teaching methods, e.g. drills which require students to imitate or repeat sentences or paradigms. Discrete point tests and teaching methods are based on the assumption that it is possible to separate analytically different aspects of language competence without reference to the context of usage. This is a highly questionable assumption. Oller (1979: 423–56) states that the data from first language acquisition studies do not support the view that competence is divisible into isolated components, but rather that the factorial structure of language proficiency is unitary.

Although I have talked about a number of aspects of communicative competence and tried to outline the components which comprise it, I have also emphasized throughout that language proficiency cannot be neatly compartmentalized in this way. Hymes has continually stressed that knowledge and use of grammar cannot be separated.

It is worth adding to this that a number of theoretical linguists would endorse the view that one cannot assume 'separation of levels' in grammar, so that the lexicon, for example, is not really distinct from syntax. Nor can one easily draw boundaries between syntax and phonology, syntax and semantics and semantics and pragmatics.[2] Theories of language should not only influence but also inform language testing procedures. I will return to this question in more detail later in this chapter.

Many of the discrete point tests we have looked at allow only dichotomous scoring, i.e. correct or incorrect responses. This procedure is based on the implicit assumption that language differences are either right or wrong rather than merely indicative of regional or social differences in speech. Characteristic ways of speaking may form an important part of one's identity and integrative constraints may outweigh whatever instrumental motives there may be for performing in the standard.[3] Lambert (1972) for instance concludes that attitudinal factors are more significant in affecting one's level of proficiency in a second language than cognitive factors. Those who are favourably disposed towards the ways of speaking and culture of a second-language group often show better ability than those who do not have an integrative motivation. I will look at the question of attitudes in more detail later in this chapter.

Oller (1979: 38) contrasts what he refers to as pragmatic tests with discrete point tests by defining the former as integrative tasks which cause the learner to process sequences of elements in a way which conforms to the normal contextual constraints of that language. This approach to testing recognizes the crucial nature of discourse as a central unit of communicative competence. Nevertheless, they are not free of bias; the key here is what is understood as being 'normal'. Through research relying on ethnographic methods we are beginning to understand some of the ways in which the meanings attached to texts and comprehension tasks may vary cross-culturally and within the 'same' language group. A number of sociolinguists have commented on the remarkable differences between the sorts of things children say, the uses they put language to and the language of books they are expected to learn to read from and the uses of language which are tested. Some examples were given in previous chapters. In criticizing the concentration of most work on social dialect at the superficial level of phonology and syntax, Halliday says (1975b: 27): 'Until we face up to the question: Are there or can there be differences between social dialects at the semantic level? (which Labov does not ask), we cannot embed the work on social dialect into a wider perspective of language and learning.'

Horvath (1977: 15–16) gives some examples of the cultural bias which can appear in tests in which pupils must draw inferences, or evaluate the author's purpose, or assess the intentions of fictionalized characters. It appears that there may often be more than one 'right' answer, depending on one's socialization, although this is not taken into account by the test designers. She cites the following case from the PAT Reading Comprehension test used in New Zealand:

Yellow Cat had something to eat in her dish. Just then her kitten, Jumper, walked by. 'What is in your dish?', asked Jumper.
What will Yellow Cat probably do next?
1. Run away from Jumper
2. Let Jumper see the dish
3. Have a party for Jumper

The test designer sees the second alternative as the right outcome. Upon questioning children who gave the first choice, Horvath found one child who said that number 1 was the right answer because Yellow Cat does not want Jumper to have any of the food. Horvath points out that running away does not mean that Jumper will not eat her mother's food, but it is the only answer which allows the child to express his/her belief that Yellow Cat does not want to be nice to Jumper. She is right in saying that we cannot rule this out as a possible outcome in the real world, although in the world of children's stories, where everyone is always nice, it may not be the usual outcome.

In another test item discussed by Horvath, pupils are questioned about the author's purpose in writing a story (1977: 16)

Mr. Brown liked animals. He had a duck, a pig, and a bear.
They liked Mr. Brown. He was kind to them.
Why was this story written?
1. to tell about someone
2. to tell something funny
3. to tell how to do something

The best answer according to the test designers is the first one. However, children who chose the 'wrong' answers were able to give reasonable accounts of their choices. One child who chose the third answer explained that if you had one of those pets, Mr. Brown told you how to take care of them by being kind. Another child, who said that it told something funny, said that it would be funny to have a duck, pig and a bear together as pets in a house (some other examples can be found in Wolfram et al. 1979: 17–18). Some of the variation is due to age, e.g. the difference between the way a child sees the world by comparison with an adult (cf. Donaldson 1978). Some of the variability is due, however, to cultural differences.[4] In the last chapter I showed how syllogistic reasoning is a culture-specific mode of cognitive processiong conditioned in part by exposure to and acquisition of different types of literacy. It involves a way of thinking about language which has to be taught explicitly. The greater the similarity between the test designer and the test population, the easier it is to match expectations and answers. There is no neurolinguistic evidence which indicates that all normal adults do not control the same basic cognitive functions; there is, however, a large body of anthropological research to suggest that what differs cross-culturally are habitual ways of perceiving relationships and conventions governing how language is used. The value of the increasing number of studies of the ethnography of speaking lies in the challenge they present to generalizations about the functions and kinds of language which tend to be derived from investigations of a single society.

This brings us to an even more serious criticism of language tests;

namely, that for any student whose native language variety is different from the one used in school, many tests (and interactions between teacher and student) may be primarily tests of the ability to use language in different and new functions. Tests may be assessing responses to a situation more than language abilities. The reliance on tests and classroom settings as the primary basis of assessment will reveal a lop-sided view of a child's competence, part of which involves using language appropriately across a range of settings, not just one or two. Edelsky et al. (1983: 14) argue that scores on school tests demonstrate 'school test-wiseness'. This involves knowledge of written etiquette, conscious knowledge of school grammar and willingness to perform for the sake of performance. They observe further (1983: 37–8) that another aspect of middle-class priming may be the reinforcement of adult rather than peer definitions of what constitutes a good successful child. Children who are used to using language on the command of adults, for the sake of performing, and to looking to adults rather than to other children for approval may find school activities more familar at the interactional level. It is obvious too from Heath's work that some children come to school with a good understanding of the relationship between the written symbol and text even though they are years away from being able to decode it. There is a great deal of variability in the amount of pre-school familiarity children have with the modes of thought and language required for success at school.

Tests represent a particular type of text and world of discourse, whose rules have to be learned by experience. I have already given a number of examples which demonstrate that the type of literacy and language ability required for success in school is known to be highly dependent on decontextualization. Information must be processed by attending to the internal cohesion of the text; in other words, the text itself provides the context. The relationship of the text to the world of action is subordinated to its internal arrangement. This characteristic of writing (as opposed to speech) helps to explain one of the examples cited earlier, where a child said it would be funny for someone to have a duck, a pig and a bear as pets. This child had not learned that in interpreting the written text, objects which would never occur together naturally in the real world may appear juxtaposed in writing, where there is a greater emphasis on logical relations which are explicitly marked and on truth value rather than on common-sense everyday logic.

The reasoning of the test makers in deciding which of the answers is to count as the correct one is by contrast, a 'superimposed' logic made possible by virtue of arranging items in print. It is a similar type of logic which is used by prescriptive grammarians in their campaign against so-called 'dangling modifiers', as in example (3).

(3) Lincoln wrote the Gettysburg address while riding in a train on the back of an envelope

Bolinger (1980: 53), from whose book this example is taken, says that children are told by teachers that this means that the train is on an envelope and is therefore incorrect. They are taught to alter this sentence in order not to 'confuse' all those people who do not know that a train is bigger than an envelope. He furthermore observes that 'we learn a great many more important solutions for which there are no problems.'

8.3 Displaying competence: who decides what counts and how?

We have already had several illustrations of the way in which assessment of competence in school is based largely on the premise that children must display publicly what they know. These displays are not, however, always synchronized with the procedures and criteria for their display officially sanctioned by those with the power to assess. In chapter 6 I showed how some narratives told by children during 'sharing time' did not 'count' as contributions because they were not told in the 'right' way. In this particular case it was not so much the knowledge or content that was at fault, but the 'packaging'. Mehan (1979: 12) strikes a distinction between interactional form and academic content. As an example of content without form he says that in classrooms which he observed it often happened that students knew the correct answers to the teachers' questions, but did not always employ the correct procedures for gaining the floor, e.g. raising their hands, speaking in complete sentences, etc. Failure to distinguish between content and form in assessment procedures can lead to biased estimates of what children know. Although a great many of the routine classroom events, such as sharing time, are not labelled as official 'assessments' in a way that, for example, a spelling or a reading test might be, they nevertheless count as public displays. Teachers build up a composite image of their pupils based on their knowledge of the child's performance in everyday events. Negative evaluations from the teacher on these occasions may lead to stereotyping a child as a poor performer.

Much of Erikson's work (1982) is devoted to demonstrating the kinds of things which can go wrong in gate-keeping encounters, e.g. counselling interviews, screening procedures, etc., when the participants are not in synchrony. He reports (1980) what happens in a screening test given to a five-year-old kindergarten child by a special education teacher to determine whether the child had handicaps which required remedial training. Since the child had been at school only a few days and had no previous experience with tests, it is not surprising that there were some fundamental difficulties in defining the situation, role status, communcative rights and obligations of the participants as far as the child was concerned. These were never fully resolved; but most important, however, was the failure of the child and tester to synchronize their questions and answers. At one point in the testing the child provided the right answer to the tester's question, but she said the answer at the wrong time, e.g. before the tester had completed the question or when the tester had gone on to another one. The role played by timing in organizing the successive question and answer slots was so crucial that the tester did not take account of right answers given at the 'wrong' time. Since the tester literally did not hear these mistimed answers she wrote down referentially wrong answers as the 'official' answers. Erikson observes that it appears to be the social rightness of the temporal placement of the answer relative to the end of the tester's questions that is salient for the tester. The tester hears the answer that is given in the right time, even though the answer may be referentially wrong. In a similar way, the teacher observed by Michaels could not perceive any structure in a narrative that was not told in the topic-centred style she expected.

Mehan (1983) shows how different assessments of students' performances are at a higher level transformed into an official judgement about a student's competence, which may then form the basis for a referral to a remedial or special education programme. In examining the nature of this decision-making process he found that while different members of the assessing committee often had quite different views of particular students at the outset, any discrepancies between 'lay opinions' (e.g. those of the mother and the classroom teacher) as opposed to 'professional reports' (e.g. those of the school psychologist and nurse) were finally resolved by accepting the professional version as the 'official' version of the student. The lay and the professional view represent alternative perspectives and are based on different types of experience and access to different kinds of knowledge obtained in very different settings. The mother for instance knows the child at home, and has known him the longest and most intimately. The classroom teacher knows him in the classroom. The school psychologist, however, has discussed the child with the mother and teacher, administered formal tests and observed him in the classroom. It is part of the job of the psychologist to collect these individual reports and present them in one official report, which is then displayed to a higher committee. Thus the knowledge base of lay professional reports is very different in shape and nature. The lay reports are grounded largely in everyday, personal and first-hand observations; the professional report is based on this information, plus qualitatively different data obtained from tests. The composite profile drawn up by the psychologist constitutes the child's 'case'.

In addition to the difference in knowledge source, there is also the issue of the manner in which the lay and professional reports were presented to the committee. The psychologist's report was presented officially in a standard format to the committee in one single uninterrupted delivery. The mother's and teacher's reports, however, were elicited by interrogation. Their turns at talks were delimited by the committee members. This differential treatment reflects the stratification and rank of the participants in this institutional setting. As a professional, the psychologist is deemed to have the most authority and what the psychologist says is accordingly given more weight. Mehan (1983: 200) notes that the most technical information is made available by the most highly trained people, while the personal observations were made available by the participants with the least amount of technical expertise.

The language in which the lay as opposed to the professional report is presented plays an important role in establishing their authority. The report by the psychologist is accepted without question and interruption and is presented in a highly technical clinical style − a sign of the psychologist's right to authority by virtue of specialized training. The mother and teacher by contrast are asked to clarify what they mean, provide more details, etc.

The outcome of meetings such as these at which students' cases are presented is that one version of the student, namely, that provided by the representatives of the central school district, prevails. Their purpose is, as Mehan (1983: 202) says, to 'solve the student's problem . . . by altering or modifying the internal states of the student'. In his monitoring of classroom activities he found that teachers do not perceive students' behaviour directly. Their judgements about which students to refer are mediated by culturally and experientially derived categories that bear little relation to students' actual behaviour. As they stand, his remarks appear to be a rather severe indictment on the educational profession. It should be emphasized, however, that what Mehan says is true for *all* persons. That is, no one ever perceives anyone's behaviour (or, for that matter, any phenomenon) directly. The context relativity of all observation was discussed in chapter 2. We all interpret behaviour in line with certain individual and socioculturally based schemas; otherwise, the plethora of observational data we take in would not make 'sense'. Rommetveit (1980) gives a dramatic example of the strikingly different interpretations placed by different passers-by on a man mowing his lawn. One, for instance, sees him as a good citizen keeping up appearances and property values in the neighbourhood, while another sees him engaging in an inconsiderate activity at an unsociable hour. It is not the case that any particular interpretation is *the* 'correct' one, but rather that individuals bring different conceptional frames, background knowledge and assumptions to the same setting and arrive at an interpretation which is consistent with the alternatives available to them.

And so it is in the case of the reports laid before the referral committee. The mother's report of her son is contextualized, personalized and grounded in sociohistorical particulars. The professional reports are stripped of these contextual features and result in what Mehan (1983: 205) calls a context-free view of disability, i.e. the cause of the student's problem is in himself. The student is to blame for failing. The crucial point of Mehan's research, however, lies in the fact that while alternative views exist at the onset of the meeting, by the end they have given way to one official one, usually the professional one established by the school psychologist, who speaks for the institution. Contrary to what one might expect from reading the sociological and political literature on the process of decision-making, in this case Mehan says that there is no negotiation or debate. Instead, a decision is presented; and it is the professional point of view which wins out because its authority resides in the very mode of its presentation rather than from its superior value or inherent claim to objectivity.

It is much the same with language ability that is displayed in the right place, at the right time and in the right way. A number of educators and linguists in fact now see the main difficulty which 'interferes' in learning to be the school's (and by implication, society's) attitudes towards language rather than actual language differences between the home and school. Sociopsychological research has demonstrated that subjective reactions to different accents and dialects are not aesthetic evaluations of inherent qualities or virtues in different ways of speaking, but rather stereotypes of the groups and individuals who speak this way (cf. Lambert 1960). To someone who does not speak English at all, there is little difference between standard English spoken with an RP accent and more local varieties, e.g. Birmingham or Glasgow English; a native speaker of British English, however, will quickly reject both these kinds of English as incorrect, sloppy and unpleasant, etc.

In what is now perhaps the most famous of the experiments on evaluative reactions to spoken language, Lambert (1960) had French/English bilinguals read a spoken text in French and English. Then he played these tapes to French and English speakers asking them to evaluate the personality of the person who was speaking in terms of dimensions such as good/bad, friendly/unfriendly, educated/uneducated, etc. What the judges did not know, however, was that they were evaluating the same speaker twice in 'matched guises', i.e. one when the person spoke French and one when the person spoke English. The reactions to the same person were different depending on the language used.

The English-speaking judges gave the English guises more favourable ratings on most traits, while the French guises received less favourable ones. Thus the *same* person was thought to be less friendly, less intelligent, less well educated, etc., when speaking French than when speaking English. What was perhaps unexpected was the French judges also perceived the English guises more favourably than they did the French ones. This, however, is a common finding in research of this type: namely, the minority often 'accept' the stigma attached to their way of speaking by the socially dominant majority.

For example, West Indians have reacted negatively to West Indian speech. In one case the same girl was judged more favourably when speaking with a working-class white accent than a West Indian one. Experiments like this one have since been carried out in a number of languages, dialects and accents with similar results. Evaluations of spoken language tell us more about the social context in which, for example, French and English exist in Canada than they do about French and English as languages. We can say then that stigmatized features are stigmatized because the people who use them are socially stigmatized. Linguistic features are just one symbol of a more generally stigmatized social identity.

The relatively arbitary nature of the features which come to have prestige (and by contrast those which do not) and the role of the socially and politically powerful in defining them is well illustrated by an incident related in Bolinger (1980: 45). During the administration of President Jimmy Carter a popular American television programme had a character representing a state department official, who spoke conspicuously like a Georgian. When a New Yorker next to him called attention to his Georgian accent he replied, 'We don't have an accent any more. You do.' What 'causes' a particular way of speaking to be perceived as superior is the fact that it is used by the powerful.

These attitudes and stereotypes which one group has of another can be a powerful factor in influencing educational performance. It is now well known that learners perform at least in part according to the expectations teachers have of them. Speech serves as one of the first clues to social identity we have when we meet a person. If we begin to behave according to our stereotyped views, attitudes can be translated into 'reality'.

In an experiment similar to the original matched guise, researchers used samples of children's work (drawings and compositions) and matched these with different speech samples and photographs to build up profiles of 'hypothetical children'. They had previously obtained separate ratings of each of the four items, i.e. speech sample, drawing, composition and photograph, before presenting these in various combinations to a group of judges. Thus a 'hypothetical child' might be created by combining a speech sample which was judged as sloppy with good photographs, drawings and composition, or vice versa. The results showed that the assessment of the student's likely success in school was linked most strongly to the speech sample. Those who had speech samples judged to be bad, even though they had drawings and compositions which were independently rated good, were stereotyped as under-achievers. Low expectations can tend to lead to low performance. This only serves to reinforce the preconceived stereotype and the cycle is perpetuated.

Le Page (1974) comments: 'Learning must now be seen to a large extent as a socially determined process. One's ability to learn to change the rules for one's behaviour is constrained by one's motivation to do so, one's motivation to do so is constrained by feedback from society as to the chances of attaining a particular goal.' Adoption of standard ways of speaking and writing acknowledges acceptance of the values and identity of those who use the standard language. The only way in which someone can be persuaded to change the way he/she speaks is if he/she is willing to identify with the group who speak in this particular way. Not surprisingly, the motivation of some speakers, such as the black teenagers discussed by Labov or West Indians in Britain, to identify with standard English is not great. Many feel they have little opportunity to use standard English outside school and would be ridiculed for doing so by family and friends. Constant correction and criticism of one's way of speech produce feelings of linguistic insecurity, and even antagonism towards standard English. It is for this reason that Trudgill (1974b) has observed that if motivation is not present, there is little the classroom teacher can do to 'make' children learn standard English. Isenbarger and Smith (1973) report the results of an experiment in which white college students were subjected to constant correction for not being able to produce utternaces in black English. The teacher found that students began to withdraw from classroom interaction and lost confidence.

8.4 *Some guidelines for assessment*

I have argued that the evidence from sociolinguistic research on urban dialects has shown that there is nothing about the phonological or syntactic characteristics of these varieties which will impede learning how to read and write. However, it is not just grammar as such in this sense which can 'interfere' with educational achievement. Studies of grammatical and phonological variability are not likely to yield insight into the way in which the use of language in new functions and in a new medium may create learning problems. There are some basic misconceptions about what language is, what constitutes ability in language and how competence is to be measured. I will conclude this chapter by recommending some guidelines for assessment.

The first recommendation is simply a plea for more information from sociolinguistic research about language. Bolinger (1980) observes that we cannot talk seriously about what ought to be until one understands what it is. Schools will never abandon formal testing completely as a means of assessment. This means that language assessment procedures should be firmly grounded in community-based norms; educators should have access to information about the language(s) spoken by the children they teach. It is up to sociolinguists and others interested in language to provide the necessary descriptive base. Labov (1970a: 297) states: 'The first task of the linguist in any speech community is a descriptive one. There is little to say about educational problems or motivation, or interference until one can give an account of the linguistic behaviour of the native speakers of the particular speech community in question.' I agree with Stubbs (1980: ×), who says that 'linguists have the responsibility of trying to present in a helpful way those parts of the subject which could be of use to others.' Bolinger recommends that linguists join forces with the 'language gurus' in order to focus attention on public attitudes towards language issues which really matter.

The language gurus and linguists have generally been at odds with one another because linguists have maintained a distinction between prescriptive and descriptive norms. The gurus, on the other hand, have seen grammar as a discipline related to propriety and socioeconomic advancement. Some have taken the view that the so-called scientific study of grammar advocated by linguists has led to a decline in the teaching of traditional grammar and fostered the idea that 'anything goes'. In some curricula traditional grammar teaching was not replaced by anything, or replaced by the 'new grammar', based on transformational generative grammar or what went by the name of structural or descriptive linguistics. During this transitional period, however, the standards of testing in public examinations changed little; and thus it appeared that language standards were falling. There was a great uproar when *Webster's Third International Dictionary* 1961 (cf. Sledd and Ebbitt 1962) appeared. Much of the furore was due to the fact that Webster's Third accepted as 'Standard English' words to which Webster's Second had attached 'warning' labels such as 'slang, incorrect, colloquial, erroneous, incorrect, illiterate, dialectal', etc.

For some, this seeming abdication of responsibility on the part of the dictionary makers not only to dictate but uphold standards was opening the door to anarchy. The American Bar Association said of Webster's Third: 'A serious blow has recently befallen the cause of good English . . . [it has] abdicated any role as judge of what is good English' (cited in Tibbitts and Tibbitts 1978: 111). In a discussion on American Public Television (reported in Bolinger 1980: 164), linguists were specifically blamed for appearing to advocate a laissez-faire attitude to language. The follow extract is revealing of public attitudes towards language and linguistics.

The idea that anything and everything goes, and what's behind it is these either disaffected or very esoteric or very sterile intellectuals in the academic . . . who have to have a profession, a profession that has not been in existence before, so things like sociology get invented . . . But finally they invent structural linguistics and descriptive linguistics, and this means you go out into the field and you find the obscurest and the most benighted group of speakers or non-speakers and record every one of their miserable grunts and introduce it in the next edition of the Webster's dictionary. So you have the *Webster's Third* where twenty pronunciations were listed as possible, any kind of solecism and ungrammatical usage is considered all right because somebody somewhere uses it, and the result is chaos. And then you get some joker who says, 'But look, here's Shakespeare who used English badly . . .' but poor Shakespeare, he did not have the benefit of these good dictionaries and these good grammars – grammars which we have since evolved. Now that we have these good grammars, for God's sake let us use them!

Linguists have argued that because standard English is not inherently superior in linguistic terms to other varieties of English, to maintain and enforce its norms while refusing to recognize the structural integrity and legitimacy of other ways of speaking is linguistic imperialism. Educators have perhaps been given the impression that linguists believe anything goes when they ask, as Labov (1969) has done, 'what's wrong with being wrong?' Labov, however, is not advocating that standard English be abandoned, but rather that it should be recognized for what it is. His main point is that errors which students make are not signs of illogicality and retarded cognitive development. Nevertheless, it is because standard English is such a prominent social symbol, which requires not just occasional display but near constant demonstration, that many believe that children should not only use it all the time but be able to recite its rules (cf. Heath 1980). Bolinger (1980: 168) observes that many of the distinctions made by the language gurus are very fragile and impractical; the price of maintaining them is too high, e.g. the *lie/lay* distinction. He adds, however, that this is exactly what makes these fine distinctions so useful as social passwords. 'Without the advantage of a proper background or proper schooling you fail. (And if it has cost you an effort and you have mastered it, you do not want to admit that you have wasted your time).'

Perhaps the question that should be asked is: what's worth knowing? If one of the aims of education is to turn out pupils who can use language effectively, rather than those who can discriminate phonemes, parse sentences and complete morphological paradigms, then there should be less concern with the superficial trappings of language. It is possible to talk nonsense fluently (i.e. fill up time with talk, in Fillmore's 1979 sense of fluency) or to have nothing much to say, but say it very well. Indeed, this is one point which Labov (1969) makes in his attack on the fluent middle-class speaker, Charles M., who presents a point of view in a much more verbose and literate but no less logical style than Larry, a teenage speaker of BEV. In attending to the form to the exclusion of content we run the risk of losing sight of the overall performance. Tests of grammar and pronunciation are not accurate predictions of how effectively a person can use language for particular purposes.

It is for this reason that the sociolinguistic approach to language has laid greater emphasis on assessing communicative competence or what Shuy (and others) call functional language. This entails testing register flexibility, appropriateness, etc.; in other words, knowing what utterances can be used to accomplish certain functions. For example, the terms in (4) can all function as commands (Shuy 1977: 80), even though only the first one appears in the grammatical form associated with the commanding function by traditional grammarians, i.e. imperative mood.

(4) Raise your hand, Mark
Would you raise your hand, Sophia?
In this class we raise our hands, Gene
I can't hear you because you didn't raise your hand

A student who knows that there is a sense in which these can all mean the same thing knows something about how language is used. Someone who can manipulate grammatical paradigms may know only facts about language (cf. also Cazden et al. 1977).

As long as society accepts the idea that children will not learn to speak properly unless they are taught grammar in the narrow sense, and that schools and teachers are the only institutions and agents dispensing grammar, knowledge of standard English will depend on successful passage through the educational system. As long as the school reinforces society's present definition of literacy and its standards and measures of language proficiency, it acts as a gatekeeper. My second recommendation therefore is that there should be a reassessment of the notion of language proficiency and the assumptions upon which evaluation is based.

This means recognizing that definitions of literacy and language proficiency must be seen in relation to the kinds of social organization which create the conditions for a variety of literacy activities. There is no universal standard of literacy. Literacy changes in line with changes in the way in which language is used. English literacy is currently undergoing a fundamental redefinition. McLuhan (1962) has claimed that writing is a vanishing and dispensable act. While I think that his view is extreme, I believe that the 'new literacy' will have to take into account exposure not only to mass media, e.g. radio and television, but also to computer technology. Part of what it means to be educated in the last decades of the twentieth century will include knowing how to use word processors, etc. Those who argue that television is undermining literacy are objecting to the threat it poses to the way in which literacy has been traditionally defined and disseminated by the middle class. Pattison (1982: 183–4) remarks that the so-called 'new illiteracy' is not a new phenomenon. The working class can read and write too, but they do not have exposure to the kinds of uses of literacy which allow them to do well in public examinations. Lower scores on these tests indicate that society is divided along fairly rigid class lines. The upper classes control the major social institutions and perpetuate their control by training their young in established patterns of literacy

If practically every test is a surreptitious test of language ability, it is not hard to understand why school success is highly correlated with so-called verbal skills. Oller (1979: 2) observes that even the measurement of motor abilities in children is related to a child's ability to respond in the appropriate way to language. He further states (1979: 456) that studies do not support the view that the factor of intelligence (as measured by IQ tests) is distinguishable from global language proficiency.

If tests rely on such a shaky foundation and problematic assumptions about what it means to know a language and that levels of proficiency and stages of acquisition of certain skills can be measured reliably, why are they used at all? Not surprisingly, educators have been unwilling to adopt novel testing methods or to abandon testing because of the need for 'objective' results and 'tangible proof' of knowledge acquired. Buros (1974: xvii) says that 'most standardized tests are poorly constructed, of questionable or unknown validity, pretentious in their claims, and likely to be misused more often than not.' In some cases standardized tests appear to substitute objective measures of the abilities of individuals for subjective judgements which are influenced by our attitudes towards groups who behave in a particular way.

Horvath (1977: 3) suggests that tests should be subjected to a socio-linguistic analysis of content validity, which would assess the following dimensions:

1 What aspect of the linguistic system does the test focus on? How much of that system is being tested?
2 What is the current state of our knowledge about that aspect of the system and its sequence of development?
3 Are these any reasons to suspect that that aspect of the linguistic system is subject to variability, particularly to social dialect or regional variation?
4 Are there other aspects of the test such as the language of the directions, social features of the population or aspects of the test situation itself to which our understanding of the social context of language use are relevant?

My third recommendation is for tolerance of variability and a change in attitudes towards language. This entails shifting the focus of research on language and education; instead of looking for deficits, why not look for abilities? I have tried throughout this book to take Hymes's view that a positive notion of competence underlines all instances of performance. One's knowledge of how to communicate is manifested in all speech events. This does not mean to say that all communication is successful or that all speakers are equal. In dealing with the question of whether some ways of using language are 'inherently problematic', one has to distinguish between the knowledge which is inherent to the individual and the way in which the use of it may become difficult because a society perceives certain complexes of skills as problematic or makes it somehow difficult or unacceptable for a speaker to use the skills he has. I showed how in some cases the language used in school lessons does not allow the child to use the grammatical constructions he has learned in responding to spontaneous speech situations. Teachers often correct 'errors' which are ordinary features of spoken language. Forms of discourse which were originally confined to written texts have come to be transmitted through teacher–pupil exchanges. Dannequin (1977) goes so far as to suggest that the school is an impoverished linguistic environment because at school the child is allowed to operate only with a fraction of his expressive potential. Schools therefore run the risk of blocking the linguistic development of the child.

She says (1977: 120):

dans la classe de langage traditionelle, l'enfant n'a pas réelement la possibilité d'exercer ses capacités linguistiques. On lui impose des contraintes non justifiées par la situation et, sous prétexte de simplicité, des énonces plus elaborés, (constructions avec présentatifs, passages à la subordination), que les élèves sont capables de produire, sont refusés.

In the traditional language lesson, the child does not actually have the possibility of using his linguistic potential. Constraints which are not justifiable in terms of the situation are imposed on him and, under the pretext of 'simplicity', more elaborate utterances (constructions with presentatives and subordinate clauses), which children are capable of producing, are rejected.

We need to look at the productive skills of speakers in terms of a strategic accomplishment in performance and not in terms of deficit or inadequacy in competence. It is impossible to define what constitutes the minimal competence one must have to be adequate except relative to the norms of a particular community. A number of studies on the effects of printing and learning to read and write challenge the view that literacy and formal schooling result in individual social mobility.

Heath (1983) states that no amount of books or public service programmes teaching parents how to help their children read would have made an appreciable difference in the community she refers to as Trackton. Although Trackton is a literate community, it does not value individual reading. Successful completion of a composition and advanced grammar classes in high school would not have secured better-paying jobs for its residents nor would improved scores on tests of reading comprehension or the SAT have given them access to more information for political decision-making than they had through news on television and radio. Cressey (1980: 189) comments that although in various times and places 'literacy unlocked a variety of doors, it did not necessarily secure admission.'

A change in public attitude towards language will also involve adopting an honest rationale for teaching standard English, which is not based on appeals to its alleged logicality, superiority, etc. It will mean at the same time recognizing students' rights to their own language. The National Council of Teachers of English in the United States adopted a resolution which guarantees this right. It states (1974):

> We affirm the students' right to their own patterns and varieties of language — the dialects of their nurture or whatever dialects in which they find their own identity and style. Language scholars long ago denied that the myth of a standard American dialect has any validity. The claim that anyone's dialect is unacceptable amounts to an attempt of one social group to exert its dominance over another . . . A nation proud of its diverse heritage and its cultural and racial variety will preserve its heritage of dialects. We affirm strongly that teachers must have the experience and training that will enable them to respect diversity and uphold the right of students to their own language.

It is possible to interpret some of the recommendations of the Bullock report *Language for Life* (1975) as equal opportunity statutes guaranteeing pupils the right to their own language. One of these states that: 'No child should be expected to cast off the language and welfare of the home as he crosses the school threshold and the curriculum should reflect those aspects of his life.' The legislation of language rights does not, however, guarantee them in any absolute sense. Many programmes and laws involving language (particularly ones concerning bilingual and multi-cultural education) are put into effect without much knowledge of the situation to be addressed. Political mobilization on the part of linguistic minorities and legislation prompted by Equality of Opportunity statutes have led to the development and funding of programmes which have had little in the way of precedent and lack basic linguistic research on which to draw. Courts have mandated tests of competence, proficiency and various kinds of language assessment, which no one had experience in devising. It is clear that litigation is preceding the technology necessary to carry it out.

In some cases courts have become battlegrounds for issues which, although not primarily linguistic, have had fundamental linguistic implications. The Ann Arbor decision on black English is an example of a case in which litigation was brought under the Equality of Opportunity legislation, which makes no mention of language rights. It guarantees that no one shall be denied equal educational opportunity on account of race, colour, sex or national origin through 'the failure by an educational agency to take appropriate action to overcome language barriers that impede equal participation by its students in its instructional programme (US code section 1703(f) of Title 20). The issue of language, in particular the autonomy of black English, became salient in this case because it was argued that a language group, i.e. speakers of BEV, coincided with a racial one. It is surely significant that the Ann Arbor case could not have occurred or led to the outcome it did without the research base that now exists on BEV. Without the studies done in the 1960s and 1970s the argument could not have been made that BEV was a rule-governed system which was different but not deficient with respect to standard English. With this knowledge parents could ask that their children's language be taken into account in the education process.

In the Ann Arbor case Judge Joiner ruled in favour of the black parents and their children. He made the point that BEV became a language barrier when teachers did not take it into account in teaching standard English. The inability to read at the level expected was acknowledged to impede children's equal participation in the educational programme of the school. The school was furthermore found to be negligent in not providing teachers with information which would have enabled them to help the children. The judge therefore ruled that the Ann Arbor school board failed to 'take appropriate action' to overcome the language barrier. Taking appropriate action was defined in terms of |the requirement that the school board submit to the court within 30 days a plan stating the action they proposed to take: (1) to help the teachers of the children to identify children who spoke BEV, and (2) to use that knowledge in teaching students how to read standard English.

The educational plan submitted by the school board focused primarily on in-service teaching training in general language and dialect concepts, in particular the contrasting features of BEV and standard English. On completion of the course it was expected that each participant should:

1 be able to recognize the basic features of a language system as they apply to dialect differences;
2 be able to describe the concept of dialect and dialect differences within English;

3 be sensitive to value judgements about dialect differences;
4 be able to describe the basic linguistic differences between BEV and standard English;
5 show appreciation for the history and background of BEV;
6 be able to recognize children and adults speaking black English;
7 be able to discuss knowledgeably the important linguistic issues of code-switching between BEV and standard English;
8 be able in the classroom to distinguish between a dialect shift and a decoding mistake when black students are reading orally from standard English;
9 to use a variety of possible instructional strategies to help BEV-speaking students to learn to read standard English.

The Ann Arbor case is clearly a precedent-setting one, and it is reasonable to expect other cases to follow; (the case of Larry P. vs. The State of California in 1979 appears to be the first). As I indicated earlier, these cases raise a number of questions about the responsibility of sociolinguists in affecting public language attitudes and policy. This brings me back to my first recommendation; namely, the need for more research and dissemination of information on the problem of language and education. The role of sociolinguistic testimony in guiding Judge Joiner's decision in the Ann Arbor case is perhaps a sign that linguists are coming to be credited as professionals whose jurisdiction properly involves matters of language use in much the same way as doctors and other professionals are recognized and relied on by the courts as experts in medical matters. The data brought to bear on the case by expert linguistic testimony obviously influenced the judge in his decision. It is significant that in his statement he acknowledges the autonomy of Black English. He states: 'The systematic nature of "Black English" has been shown to be a distinct definable version of English different from the standard English of the school and the general world of communications. It has definite language patterns, syntax, grammar and history.' (Cf. Labov's 1982 and Whiteman's 1980 discussion of the significance of the Ann Arbor case.)

Despite the fact, however, that the Ann Arbor case represents a landmark decision for black English and is witness to the efficacy of sociolinguists in entering into the arena where decisions concerning language use are made and influencing them in a crucial way, some basic assumptions remain unchallenged. The judge's decision does not really question the long-held assumption that middle-class language habits are seen as essential for learning and educational success. The plan of action submitted by the Ann Arbor school board makes it explicit that:

1 the school is not being required to teach students to speak black English;

2 the school system is not being directed to send professional staff into the plaintiff homes to diagnose children's language and dialect;
3 because the Order refers only to reading, the plan is limited to instruction in reading.

Thus the school board is not prepared to go beyond the 'letter of the law'. It still assumes that reading failure is symptomatic of language barriers and maintains a dichotomy between 'school language' and 'home language'. Standard English is the taught language of the school.

Neither the judge nor the school board question the school's criteria for success seen in terms of ability to read at grade level and measured by standardized tests. I have discussed the assumption made by test-makers that knowledge of language is assessed in terms of the extent to which one knows a particular variety of it, i.e. the standard. The test-makers also assume a fairly uniform order and rate of acquisition and language development. Too little in known about variability in this area which is related to dialect differences. Most acquisition studies are based on the development of white middle-class children and their mothers. Although the judge's decision says nothing about testing, it has the potential of forcing a resolution to some of the problems that arise when standardized language tests are used to assess children's linguistic ability. The school's proposal to 'identify' black English speakers will require some scrutiny of evaluation procedures. Test constructers will have to devise ways of determining whether children have acquired concepts like plurality, negation, causality, etc., independently of the specific surface forms that are used to mark these categories.

Beyond, this however, is the more far-reaching problem of how to encourage 'appropriate action' elsewhere without court order, and how to bring information about language to teachers and other professionals in an unthreatening way and in a format that is useful. At the moment the Ann Arbor case still points painfully to the gap between research and its application. The implementation of the judge's order to take 'appropriate action' relies on the provision of linguistic expertise in setting up teacher training programmes.

9

Child language acquisition and linguistic theory

I remarked in chapter 1 that there is an important interface between linguists' theories of grammar and child language acquisition. I contrasted briefly two approaches to the study of child language development. One, which relied on Chomsky's view of competence, assumed that children have a Language Acquisition Device (LAD). This consists of a set of principles of syntactic organization and is regarded as the major determinant of language development. Within this framework, children's acquisition is treated as a semi-autonomous unfolding of innate language capabilities. The other approach takes as its starting point the notion of communicative competence, and assumes that the grammar which the child internalizes is shaped in important ways through socialization into a particular speech community which uses language in culturally specific ways. In this chapter I will consider in more detail what the differences in these two approaches entail when seen in relation to child language acquisition.

9.1 Generative grammar as a theory of language acquisition

According to Chomsky, the grammar of a language represents a set of rules which speakers have internalized. It is a speaker's knowledge of these formal rules which underlies his competence. For those who have linked Chomsky's theory of grammar with the problem of child language acquisition, this means that the task of language learning for the child is essentially a problem of rule formulation. From a descriptive point of view, this meant that the child's language system was often modelled in terms of a formal grammar, which contained the rules needed to generate the structures observed at any one stage. The process of linguistic maturation seen in these terms involved progression through a series of more or less discrete stages, which represented increasingly closer approximations to the adult's grammar. This way of conceptualizing the child's linguistic development has led, among other things, to a tendency to see the child as a 'mini-linguist' or grammarian (cf. Gleitman et al. 1972). That is, children's grammars were sometimes regarded as merely lesser, under-developed and simpler forms of adult grammars.

Donaldson (1978), and others, have cautioned against the tendency to view the child as a 'mini-adult'. She argues that because children turn out to be in some respects closer to adults than has been supposed, we should not conclude that they are really just like them. There are some fundamental methodological problems with the 'child as mini-adult' perspective. If we assume, for example, that the child proceeds through a series of grammars, this raises the theoretical question of what status the child's grammar has at each stage. It is often claimed that the grammar the linguist produces for a particular language is a model of competence, and therefore psychologically real. This would mean then that the grammar ascribed to the child at each stage would represent the child's competence. In chapter 3 I noted some of the kinds of difficulties which arise from this assumption, e.g. how does one know when/if children operate with the same categories as adults, and when can we say that children have acquired substantially the same rules as adults?

White (1982: 53) has argued that the child's aim must be expressed in terms of the data he perceives, and not in terms of a teleological progression through a sequence of grammars towards the ultimate adult grammar. She claims that the child's grammar is optimal at all stages and correct in terms of the observed data. This means that the child proceeds through a series of optimal grammars, which are not to be regarded as a series of sub-grammars of the adult system. Children's grammars reflect data, rather than attempts to construct adult grammar.

As I suggested in chapter 3, this assumption that language learning takes place in discrete stages which must be seen independently of one another gives rise to the further methodological issue of how to describe the transition between them. Those who have viewed children's grammar in this fashion faced the same problem as historical linguists, who described the history of a language as a succession of grammars. In neither case were models of description available which could handle the kind of diversity and variability which is now seen as a prerequisite for change (cf. Weinreich et al. 1968 for discussion). Bailey (1973) has argued for a reconceptualization of language development so that it will include not only changes associated with early childhood, but also processes of historical change, pidginization, creolization, etc. He has tried to formulate general principles, which regulate the kinds of changes which take place in developing systems, e.g. rate and directionality (cf. Horvath 1983 for further discussion of Bailey's view in relation to child language acquisition).

While it may at first glance seem paradoxical that Chomsky ignores virtually all evidence from developing language systems, it is a misconception to think of his theory of grammar as a model of how acquisition proceeds in real time. He observes (1981a: 35) that 'one might hope to learn something from the extensive literature on cognitive development and language acquisition, but at the moment it is impossible.' Because Chomsky is interested in explaining the shape of mature grammars, he idealizes the actual process of language acquisition. He assumes that it takes place instantaneously. This allows him to ignore 'the intermediate states attained between the initial and steady state, the role of these intermediate states in determining what constitutes linguistic experience and other kinds of interactions that may be essential for the growth of language in the mind' (Chomsky 1981a: 34–5). Lightfoot (1982: 178) notes one reason why he thinks little is to be learned about the properties of grammar which are universal to the human species from studies of real-time acquisition. That is because utterances in the earliest stages of so-called 'two-word' speech, e.g. 'milk all-gone', 'Daddy bye-bye', etc., are 'irrelevant to most grammatical principles and it stretches normal usage to refer to this as language.'

This strikes me as a rather extreme view to take. There is evidence for the gradual development of the ability to communicate and for the existence of developmental stages in the emergence of grammars characterized by internal consistency. While it may seem to Lightfoot that there is little connection between the child's early utterances and the mature adult grammar, this is a result of narrowing the conception of 'language', so that it is seen largely in terms of formal syntactic structures. I argued in chapter 3 that at first glance it might seem that there was little affinity between relative clauses and passives, for example, but that this was a consequence of looking at the formal aspects of these structures in isolation of their communicative function. I showed that the two constructions shared important functional similarities at the level of discourse. I also claimed that there was ontogenetic and diachronic continuity between passives and relative clauses, and early topic/comment structures of the type noted above. Relative clauses can be thought of as the result of a process of grammaticalization of comment, while passives can be seen as the outcome of the grammaticalization of a chain of topicalization. The transition from pragmatically to syntactically motivated structure is evidenced in both child language and language history.

These kinds of facts are not, however, disputed by Chomsky and other generative grammarians; only their relevance to linguistic theory is questioned. In justifying their view of instantaneous language acquisition, Chomsky and Halle (1968: 331) write: 'We have been describing acquisition of language as if it were an instantaneous process. Obviously this is not true. A more realistic model of language acquisition would consider the order in which primary linguistic data are used by the child . . . this more realistic study is much too complex to be undertaken in any meaningful way today.' I discussed in chapter 6 some examples of how the way in which language is used by care-givers in different societies affects the kind of data which children receive as input. This may affect the order of emergence of certain grammatical constructions, e.g. ergative marking in Samoan. This suggests that social factors interact with the LAD in culturally specific ways.

Lightfoot (1982), however, draws a distinction between 'acquisition', which refers to the ideal system, and 'development', which refers to the real-time system. Following Chomsky's more recent attempts to strengthen the biological underpinnings of linguistic theory, Lightfoot (1982: 19) argues that it is inappropriate to speak of 'language learning'; one should talk instead of 'language emergence'. He and Chomsky compare the growth of the language faculty in the human mind to the growth of a physical organ in the body.

The generative concept of the idealized language learner with built-in propensities to acquire grammar does nonetheless discredit the possibility of arguing for the genetic inferiority of any particular group defined racially, ethnically or otherwise. All normal speakers share the innate disposition to acquire language, and therefore have competence in Chomsky's (1965) sense. I noted in my opening remarks in chapter 1 that all normal children learn to use at least one variety of a language made available by their care-takers and/or peers. In this respect then, all speakers are equal.

However, just as the actual process of acquisition is idealized, as far as Chomsky is concerned, so is the speaker's underlying competence. Chomsky's (1965: 3) characterization of the goal of linguistic theory in relation to this ideal competence is well known and has remained fundamental to generative grammar. Thus 'Linguistic theory is concerned primarily with an ideal speaker–listener, in a completely homogeneous speech community, who knows its language perfectly and is unaffected by such grammatically irrelevant conditions as memory limitations, distractions, shifts of attention and interest, and errors (random or characteristic) in applying his knowledge of the language in actual performance.'

9.2 Communicative competence as a theory of language acquisition

Hymes and others have drawn attention to the fact that within the generative view of competence there is no way to deal with differences in the way in which the potential of the underlying system is realized. There is no way to distinguish between the abilities of good and poor, and fluent and non-fluent speakers in a heterogeneous speech community. Such topics would come under the study of performance. Chomsky (1965: 15), however, relegates this area of research to the periphery of linguistic enquiry; studies of performance were, at least in the early days, seen as by-products of generative grammar. Performance was regarded as only an implementation of a model of grammatical competence. Hymes (1970: 10) has objected to the arbitrary restriction of the domain of the knowledge underlying language to what is grammatical. He argues that Chomsky's dichotomy between competence and performance obscures the fact that performance entails its own underlying competence. A speaker might know, for example, that a certain kind of language was appropriate in a given situation, but yet not be able to use that knowledge in actual performance, e.g. he may be nervous.

In later writings, Chomsky (1980) discusses the notion of pragmatic competence, which coexists (and possibly interacts) with grammatical competence. Pragmatic competence would underlie the actual use of language, and thus appear to satisfy one of Hymes's objections. However, Chomsky is still quite insistent that the study of grammatical competence must take precedence over that of pragmatic competence in order to make any progress in linguistic theory. Nevertheless, Hymes's basic criticism stands; that is, one must transcend the dichotomy between competence and performance and work instead towards an integrated theory of language in which competence is still a central concern, but in which the rules of use are not separate from the rules of grammar.

The goal of a theory of communicative competence would be to show the ways in which the systematically possible, the feasible and the appropriate are linked to produce actually occurring cultural behaviour. As far as the process of child language acquisition is concerned, this means that knowing what syntactic constructions a child is capable of at a certain age (i.e. are in his grammar) tells us nothing about how he can use them to get things done and in what context a child may or can use them. Hymes (1971, 1974) has emphasized the fundamental inequalities which exist with regard to language use, some of which have crucial implications when seen from an educational perspective. I discussed some of these in chapters 6, 7 and 8. Baetens-Beardsmore (1982: 90) ignores the qualitative differences in children's language skills when he says: 'the normally constituted monoglot child will, by puberty, attain the total range of linguistic abilities which will make him virtually indistinguishable from other monglots in the same speech community.'

The state of the art in research on the acquisition of communicative competence has not yet reached the point which has been attained in the developmental study of syntax, phonology, etc. Throughout this book I have drawn particular attention to the variable aspects of linguistic development which are socially and culturally conditioned. However, an important question which must be addressed in future work is whether there are universal stages in acquiring competence in the social use of language, and whether there are sociolinguistic universals of language use (cf. Brown and Levinson 1978 on the latter).

Another crucial area of concern will be to identify the extent to which certain aspects of communicative competence are largely maturational and the degree to which they can be taught. In chapter 5 I looked at children's acquisition of certain politeness routines, which are explicitly provided to children by care-takers' coaching. In chapters 6 and 7 I showed how the competence which the young child brings to school can be altered by various social factors, e.g. learning to read and write, becoming integrated into a peer group. A confrontation between different systems of communicative competence developed in the school and community shows how one system can affect another.

In conclusion, I would like to point out that there has been some confusion over the term 'communicative competence'; some have argued that it makes no sense to talk of a communicative competence. Those who object to it appear to have misunderstood what Hymes has in mind. A theory of communicative competence is not to be confused with a theory of performance in Chomsky's sense.[1] Perhaps the problem here is that the term 'communicative' implies the use of rules, and Chomsky is quite adamant that it makes no sense to think of the basic function of language as communication. I would agree that it does not make much sense to speak of 'applying' or 'using' the kind of underlying knowledge which Chomsky refers to as grammatical competence. The knowledge underlying the use of language involves not only knowledge of grammar, but also knowledge of many other things, as I said in chapter 1. Nevertheless, the point Hymes is making is that one cannot just tack on a theory which deals with communicative competence and performance to one which deals exclusively with grammatical knowledge.

As far as the relationship between a theory of communicative competence and language acquisition is concerned, I have argued in this book that the competence underlying language use emerges early. The data from which the child constructs his grammar is not divided into data for the construction of communicative rules and data for the construction of cognitive or grammatical rules. Children acquire language by using it. Communicative competence must be built into the very core of a theory of language because the way in which language is used affects our knowledge of it, and our knowledge shapes the way in which language is used.

Notes

2 Methodology for studying the language of children

1 Shuy and Staton's (1982: 186) Principle 4 is related to this: Oral language goes by so fast and is so multi-layered that it is not possible to assess it effectively or accurately without tape-recording it and studying it at length. They argue strongly, however, for recording speech only in naturalistic settings.

2 If they had not guessed it by my accent; interestingly six year olds were not able to do this, eight year olds varied in their ability and ten year olds were consistently accurate.

3 Wallace (1962: 2) is the first to use the term 'ethnographic monitoring'.

4 Spindler (1982: 2n) distinguishes between 'ethnography of schooling' and 'educational ethnography'. The former is the less narrow term of the two in that it refers to the study of educational and enculturative processes, whether school-related or not (cf. also Wilcox 1982).

3 The development of syntactic structure

1 Although it seems to be true that overall languages do not differ greatly in terms of ease of acquisition or processing (cf., however, Bickerton 1981), it appears that some systems of the grammar pose more difficulty than others. Slobin (forthcoming) offers some interesting cross-linguistic data on the rate of acquisition of relative clauses in Turkic and Indo-European languages which show that there are some substantial differences, in particular between English and Turkish. Not only are relative clauses used more frequently by English-speaking children (and adults) overall, but their development shows a much accelerated growth curve. A major spurt takes place at around 3.6 for English speakers, while the mastery of Turkish relative clauses takes place later than 4.8 Slobin attributes these differences to two general psycholinguistic processing problems which Turkish relative clauses present to the learner: they are not easily isolable as clauses; and they are not constructed in a uniform way across different types of relativization. They are thus less transparently encoded in the syntactic structure of Turkish.

2 I am not attempting a universalist definition of a relative clause, because it is difficult to give an inclusive and unique set of defining properties shared by all the constructions which syntacticians have discussed under the heading 'relative clause'. I have furthermore confirmed my discussion here to

restrictive relative clauses. In most treatments of English grammar (and many other languages) a distinction is often made between restrictive relative clauses, which have the function of restricting the reference of the head NP they modify, and non-restrictive relative clauses. The latter are often said to function as comments, adding only additional information to a head which is already independently identified, or is unique in its reference, and has no need of further modification to identify its referent. The distinction is nonetheless tenuous, both synchronically and diachronically in English (cf. Romaine 1982a) as well as developmentally. Tavakolian (1978: 70) says that there is no evidence that children interpret a restrictive relative clause as a restriction of the head noun rather than as a non-restrictive comment about it (cf. also note 16 below).

3 MacWhinney (1982: 111–6) predicts a similar hierarchy, but on the basis of a pragmatic rather than syntactic parallelism of function. Sentences of the SS type can be correctly interpreted or enacted without any change in perspective. SO sentences are the hardest because they require a double shift in perspective.

4 Hamburger and Crain (1982) have objected to the pragmatic artificiality of some of the sentences which have been used in such experiments. They observe that one reason for the variability in the results for OS and OO relatives may have to do with discrepancies between conceptual order and order of mention. In line with the view that relative clauses function as assertions or comments on topic/referents set up in discourse, both the OS and OO types of relative clauses would involve violations of the conceptually natural ordering: presupposition, assertion. What is presupposed may be assumed to have taken place already regardless of its order of mention. In a sentence such as the one below, there may be a tendency to act out only what is asserted.

The duck stands on the horse [that jumps over the pig]

Goodluck (1978) has shown that there are also semantic restrictions on the compatibility of certain matrix sentences with their relative clauses. For example, in the following sentence, the relative clause combines more readily from a semantic point of view with the object of the matrix sentence than with its subject (i.e. girls do not bite horses):

The girl pushed the cow [that bit the horse]

Selectional restrictions may have biased the responses and led to the finding that children have more difficulty with OS than with SS relatives. Children may not be responding to NPs such as cows, etc., as types, but as tokens with lexically and semantically specific content. This tendency may have inhibited the children's attempts to bind the referents correctly syntactically. Goodluck also found that children's performance improved sharply when the number of animals was reduced from three to two by using an intransitive verb in the relative clause, as in the example:

The dog kicks the horse [that jumps up and down]

5 Slobin (forthcoming) maintains that the on-line parsing strategies developed for English relative clauses may not be univerally valid. Turkish children cannot fully interpret some of the SO and SS types of relative clauses which English-speaking children can. Slobin suggests that parsing mechanisms are constructed ontogenetically in accordance with the typology of the input

language. Verb-final languages like Turkish require the listener to hold information until encountering clause-final verbs or postpositions. This means that the kind of sentence-processing heuristics proposed for SVO languages like English are not feasible for SOV ones. The reason why Turkish children have such difficulty in the early stages is consistent then with the view that the types of strategies required in Turkish are more demanding than those first attempted by children (cf. also Antinucci et al. 1979, who argue that the way in which a relative clause is constructed in an SOV language presents an obstacle to its effective perceptual processing and that this creates pressure for diachronic change).

6   The analysis used here (and elsewhere in chapters 3 and 4) is GLIM (generalized linear interactive modelling). Royal Statistical Society of London.

7   From a purely structural point of view, this type is similar to the indirect object relative in that prepositions are sometimes required for indirect objects, e.g. I gave *the man* the book / I gave the book *to the man*. One could say that these two sentences represent different syntactic encodings of the same semantic role of indirect object (cf. the discussion in Comrie 1981: 60–1).

8   Quirk et al. (1972: 863) note that in modern English when the head noun is non-personal there is some tendency to avoid *whose*, possibly because it is regarded as the genitive form belonging to *who* only, and not to *which*. The Scots form, *that's*, may not, strictly speaking, represent an instance in which an invariant relative marker (i.e. *that*) acquires case-coding, as I have suggested elsewhere (cf. Romaine 1982a). It may just be a morphophonologically condensed form of *that his*, which was reanalyzed and generalized. This would not be an inconsistent development, given the widespread use of *his* as a sign of the genitive, especially in the sixteen and seventeenth centuries. Wyld (1920: 314–15) cites examples such as *Seynt Dunstone his love* (1440), and suggests that they arose via a reinterpretation of the Old English genitive -*es* ending, which would have been homophonous with weak unstressed *his*.

9   The primacy of the WH strategy over the option of using *that* or Ø is also noted by Keenan and Comrie, although they intend the term *primary* in a more technical sense. They argue that WH is primary because all the positions in the case hierarchy are accessible to relativization by means of this strategy. However, we have already seen that since Scots has the option of relativizing genitive NPs by means of a strategy using *that*, we could easily argue for the primacy of *that*. Diachronically, *that* is primary since it is older than WH.

10 There has been considerable debate about the status of resumptive pronouns and the nature of the relationship between them and extracted constituents with respect to binding conditions (cf. especially Chomsky 1982, and Zaenen and Maling 1982). The terms copy, resumptive and shadow pronoun have also been used in a number of different, and sometimes overlapping, senses by syntacticians. Schachter (1973), for example, sees relativization as a syntactic process of copying and deletion, in which a copy of a constituent of an embedded sentence is inserted into a matrix sentence, where it replaces a dummy symbol. Within the embedded sentence the copied constituent is either replaced by a relative pronoun or deleted.

Following Ross's (1967) distinction between two types of movement rules, i.e. chopping rules, which obey island constraints and leave gaps, and copying rules, which leave pronouns and do not obey island constraints, I will use the term 'resumptive pronoun' in the sense in which it is used in the most recent versions of government and binding theory (cf. Chomsky 1982). In a sentence such as the following, *him* is a resumptive pronoun equivalent to *t* (i.e. the trace of *who*) and is a variable bound by *who*.

the man [who$_i$ John saw him$_i$]

It has generally been assumed that resumptive pronouns will occur where extraction with gaps is impossible. Copying rules are rare in standard English, but more common in other languages. In Swedish, for example, all unbounded dependencies (e.g. relatives and topicalized sentences) give rise to resumptive pronouns under certain conditions. Chomsky (1977) assumed that there was a basic difference in the binding relation between gaps and resumptive pronouns; namely, in the case of a gap, the binding relation is syntactic, whereas in the case of a resumptive pronoun the binding relation is anaphoric. Zaenen and Maling (1982), however, argue on the basis of the non-complementary distribution of resumptive pronouns and gaps in Swedish that they must have the same syntactic status. More recently, Chomsky (1982: 94–5n.) has suggested that relative-clause constructions with resumptive pronouns might be interpreted as involving an operation of predication with the relative clause being regarded as an open sentence predicated of the head. Since the possibility of island conditions is explicitly associated with the application of movement rules, this would mean then that the resumptive pronoun strategy would be generally immune to conditions following from bounding theory because the pronoun is base-generated rather than formed by movement.

11   There is some experimental evidence to support the argument that resumptive pronouns facilitate processing. Wall and Kaufman (1980) presented native speakers of English with sentences with and without resumptive pronouns. Recall was significantly better for the sentences with resumptive pronouns than for comparable sentences with gaps. Zaenen and Maling (1982: 228) query why it is commonly the case that resumptive pronouns cannot occur too close to their antecedents. They say that non-extraposed sentential subjects are more difficult to process than subordinate clauses which follow their main verbs. Resumptive pronouns can be used to make extractions out of relative clauses acceptable.

12   Zaenen and Maling (1982: 228) note that the structures in which resumptive pronouns are found are in themselves more difficult to process than those out of which extraction is possible with a gap. The fact that extraction out of some islands cannot be saved by resumptive pronouns suggests that a uniform account of island violations will not work. Some sentences are unacceptable for reasons unrelated to processing. Zaenen and Maling (1982: 224) distinguish two sources for island constraints: processing difficulties and functional deviance. That is, island violations involving processing difficulties can be saved by a resumptive pronoun, but violations which create functionally deviant sentences cannot.

13   Menyuk (1969) found that 87 per cent of children between the ages of three and seven used object relatives, while 46 per cent used subject relatives. Slobin (forthcoming) also found that for both English- and Turkish-speaking children and adults more relative clauses were formed overall on non-subject NPs. He concludes that if a language provides equivalent means for relativizing on various positions of the case hierarchy, the advantage to subject relativization is not demonstrated.

14   While Keenan and Comrie have emphasized the more formal syntactic implications of the case hierarchy, they do not deny that notions, like semantic

prominence may also be operative. Kuno (1976: 427) has argued that as far as relativization is concerned, the case hierarchy reflects accessibility to thematic interpretation. He proposes an analysis of relativization in Japanese in which relative clauses are derivatives of themes of embedded clauses rather than ordinary NPs. The derivational process is deletion, but in Kuno's view the syntactic constraints on relative-clauses formation are derivatives of constraints on what can qualify as a theme. Hakuta (1979) also presents evidence from Japanese that sentence configuration is a major variable influencing children's comprehension of relative clauses. This is to a large extent independent of direction of embedding (cf. also note 24).

15   There is support for this idea in Kroll (1977), who compared the use of co-ordinate and subordinate structures in samples of speech and writing. When people were asked to speak about an experience, they used 74 per cent co-ordinate structures) later, when writing about the same topic, they used only 57 per cent.

16   In some languages this type of construction may be the closest equivalent structure to the canonical embedded relative clause defined earlier (cf. Hale 1976 for a discussion of some Australian languages which use both the conjoined and embedded type construction, and Romaine 1983a for the discussion of the evolution of embedding strategies in Germanic). There has been considerable debate amongst syntacticians over the issue of whether relative clauses are best derived via conjuction or embedding (cf. Thompson 1971 for some arguments in favour of the conjunction anaylsis).

17   There has been some discussion of the task-dependence of the results of Chomsky's experiments. The salience of the blindfold may have biased responses towards the 'incorrect' sentence: 'The doll is hard to see.'

18   In some languages only demotion of an agent and no promotion takes place, i.e. Latin *curritur* – 'there was running'.

19   According to Kageyama (1975) the accessibility of indirect and oblique objects to relativization is a recent phenomenon in the history of English. Thus a parallel could be drawn between child acquisition and diachrony, in so far as in both strands of development the rule of passivization appears to have undergone an extension of scope in terms of the positions of the case hierarchy which are accessible to its application.

20   This general tendency has been discussed by a number of linguists. Cooper and Ross (1975), for example, refer to it as the 'me-first principle'. Silverstein (1976) proposes an agency hierarchy, which states that first person animate and human referents take precedence over third person agents and experiencers. The notion of a case role hierarchy for promotion to subject has been discussed by Zubin (1979), who suggests the following ranking: agent › experiencer › dative › instrument › patient › location. This hierarchy reflects a preference for animates over inanimates, and humans over non-humans in establishing the point of view of a sentence.

21   Another parallel can be drawn here between the child's development and diachrony (cf. note 19), if we attribute synchronic validity to Wasow's distinction between transformational and lexical passives. Namely, the transformationally derived type seems to emerge late in the history of English as well as in the child's acquisition. Wasow (1980), however, has revised his original distinction and refers to the transformational type as verbal and the lexical type as adjectival. Both are now lexically derived.

22   Notions of syntactic complexity are also furthermore not independent of the

model of grammar within which they are formulated. Langacker and Munro (1975) postulate a two-tier analysis of passives (as opposed to Chomsky's one-tier derivation). That is, Chomsky derives a passive from a single sentence, while Langacker and Munro claim that passives arise via the embedding of one sentence within another. There has been some dispute, however, amongst those who opt for the two-tier analysis over whether the embedded S is to be seen as an object or subject (Lakoff 1971) complement of the verb BE. Nevertheless, within either of these analyses passives would still count as more complex than their active counterparts, except that their complexity would derive from the process of embedding and the application of a rule which would raise a subject or object complement into the NP slot of the higher S, i.e. the subject of BE.

23 Maratsos and Abraovitch (1975) present results which contradict Horgan's claim about the separateness of development of the two constructions.

24 It has generally been found that young children tend to produce patients more frequently than agents. This ties in with my earlier remarks in section 3.2 about young children's more frequent relativization of object than subject NPs. This finding would follow from Givón's claim (discussed in section 3.3) that agents are high in presuppositionality. Therefore it is the category of patient which is less predictable and thus more often in need of further specification and elaboration.

25 Reflexives such as *John injured himself* do not passivize. There are also other semantic and lexical restrictions on passivization. For example, some verbs have no passive counterparts: e.g. *This hat fits me* cannot be passivized as *This hat is fitted by me*, or *I am fitted by this hat* (cf. Matthews 1981: 14). Conversely, there are passives with no active equivalents, e.g. *It was rumoured that John is ill*.

26 In discussing reflexive, beneficial and causative uses of the GET passives, Sussex (1982: 90) observes that the range of GET constructions is more extensive in American than in Australian and British English respectively.

27 This parallelism extends to certain BE passive constructions too, e.g. Spanish *se habla español* – 'Spanish is spoken'.

28 The innateness argument is based on Gruber's claim that the child had no model for these constructions in his parents' speech.

29 Research on topic/comment structures and related contrasts (e.g. theme/ rheme, given/new, background/forground, figure/ground, etc.) and notions such as presupposition and discourse perspective, has again become popular. Although these ideas have a long history in the linguistic theorizing of, for example, Prague School linguists (cf. communicative dynamism, functional sentence perspective, etc.), they have not been applied to the study of child language until recently (cf. Keenan and Schieffelin 1976).

30 Details of this chain of grammaticalization for Indo-European can be found in Lehmann (1976) and for Hittite in Justus (1976).

31 Weinberg's (1981) proposal that children initially hypothesize a rule which says 'Move patient', and that this is later restructured to one which states 'Move NP', is not inconsistent with the pragmatic perspective I have adopted here. That is, children operate first with semantic-pragmatic categories and then later switch to syntactic ones.

32 Two of the possible solutions which he rejects are:
1 a 'free order' phrase structure rule, S→NP S
2 S→S NP, followed by an optional transformational rule preposing NP

The first solution is rejected on the ground that this type of free-order rule never occurs in phrase structure grammars, and the second on the ground that a base-generated rather than transformational source for the topic/comment structure is more in line with the basicness of the child's grammar at this stage.

33   Within more recent models of generative grammar which prepose categories by adjunction to S or WH movement (cf. Chomsky 1977), we could generate topic/comment structures of the type illustrated in the tree diagram below, where what occupies topic position would bind a trace in subject position (cf. Koster 1978).

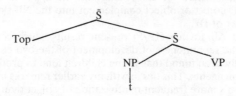

The element under Top could be a sentence, rather than just a free noun phrase. However, this analysis is somewhat problematic for similar reasons; namely, that superficially similar structures in child and adult language may not have the same underlying source (cf. also note 10).

4   *The acquisition and development of sociolinguistic patterns*

1   Cf. Guy 1975 and 1977 for further details.

2   The division between primary and secondary school pupils occurs at the age of 12–13 when children begin their higher study.

3   Trudgill's (1974a) study of phonological variation in Norwich revealed some 'irregular' patterns of stylistic variation. Hypercorrect behaviour was manifested by several different social class groups, among them the middle-working class and the upper-working class. Some of these differences reflect dissimilarities in the stratification of Norwich and New York City. However, it is not entirely satisfactory to explain the stylistic behaviour of groups who hypercorrect by appealing to the pressure to imitate socially prestigious speech (cf. Milroy 1980, Wolfson 1982, Coupland 1980 and Giles and Smith 1979 for alternative perspectives on style shifting).

4   There were no data for comparison for the first and fourth grades (Biondi 1975: 86)

5   Reid (1978: 165–6) suggests that the reason for the fall in scores in the playground style was due to a weakness in the design of the investigation. He was experimenting with the use of a radio microphone to record the boys while he was not present. The boys took the opportunity of using the situation to act out the role of radio commentator while their friends ran races, etc. The style of speech produced in this situation appeared to be not easily relatable to the other contexts since the boys imitated a number of features of TV commentators. Reid is however probably right in saying that these 'accidental' effects are suggestive of an even greater flexibility in speech styles than he was able to investigate.

6   The discussion session has been grouped with the card game in these tables

since there is not much difference between scores in these two situations

7 The reason for this pattern is essentially historical; Appalachian English and Scots English preserve historically older forms (cf. Romaine 1975 for further discussion of the history of this variable in Scots). The influence of spelling has been largely responsible for the introduction of the [ŋ] variant.

8 Some of these differences could of course be related to the fact that Macaulay and I used different scoring procedures for (a) and (au).

9 I have recalculated the figures in this table on the basis of the data reported in chapter 4 since Macaulay does not give data in a format which is directly comparable to mine.

10 The occurrence of the forms reflects the persistence of influence from older northern varieties of English, which had an -s suffix throughout the present tense paradigm. (cf. Cheshire, 1982a chapter 4 and Strang 1970: 146).

11 Robertson and Cassidy (1954: 141) discuss the historical development of subject–verb concord. Cf. also Milroy 1981 for discussion of this variable in Belfast, and Wolfram and Fasold 1974 in varieties of American English, and Feagin 1979).

12 Cf. also the discussion of this variable in Appalachian English by Wolfram and Christian (1976: 79–85).

13 Cheshire (1982b) gives an historical account of this variable.

14 This feature is not however confined exclusively to Scottish territory: its use extends beyond the border into Yorkshire.

15 Cf. also Cheshire 1982a: section 5.2, for a full treatment of this variable in Reading, which differs from Labov's in certain respects.

16 Cofer (1972), Hackenberg (1972) and Wolfram and Christian (1976) discuss the social distribution of relative markers in varieties of American English.

17 Further historical details of the use of zero marking can be found in Romaine (1981).

18 Todd (1975) reports a three-way system of deixis for Hiberno-English and cf. Wolfram and Christian (1976) on the use of yon in Appalachian English.

19 Grant and Murison (1941: II, 23) report some examples of double models from Scots. They also occur in BEV (cf. Labov. 1972b: 56–9).

20 Cf. also Labov (1972b: 59) on the quasi-modal status of liketa, sposta, (e.g. We sposta went to the gymnasium). Cf. also Feagin (1979: chapter 6).

21 Some of the values of the Edinburgh variables discussed earlier in this chapter are noted in this excerpt. The spelling tae indicates a 'dialect pronunciation' /te/.

22 A parallel example can be cited from Bausinger (1967) about a family who moved to Swabia (Germany) from an area where Bavarian dialect was spoken. When a tape-recording was made of the family by a researcher, the father asked his seven-year-old son to say something. The son replied: 'Soll i schwätze, soll i soge oder soll i spreche?' This remark indicates that the son is aware of the sociolinguistic relationships among the varieties he knows. The terms schwätzen, sagan (with regional pronunciation) and sprechen are all equivalent words for 'to speak, say, or tell', but each has somewhat different social and/or regional significance. The word sprechen is the standard.

23 The normative role of mothers is apparently not specific to the English-speaking world, and men also correct children. One of the creole-speaking children interviewed by Le Page (forthcoming) in his survey of Caribbean creoles reported being corrected by other parents for speaking in broad creole Spanish.

24 These are my translations from Swedish.

25   The findings of the Swedish survey are in contrast with those of Cremona and Bates (1977), who presented Italian working-class children with pairs of sentences in standard Italian and their own regional dialect for evaluation. By the time the children were of school age they selected the standard variant 80 per cent of the time as the one which was 'better'.

26   I am grateful to Gunnel Melchers for providing me with some of the preliminary results of her survey, which is part of her research project at Stockholm University on the Scandinavian Element in Shetland Dialect.

5   *The ontogenesis and development of children's speech events and discourse skills*

1   The findings for English-speaking children also receive support cross-linguistically in Turkish, Hungarian and Italian studies (cf. Ervin-Tripp 1977: 174–5).

2   T/V is used to symbolize a distinction made in the pronominal address system of a language in which politeness and/or social distance distinctions are marked in relation to the addressee (cf. French *tu/vous*).

3   Some of the schoolchildren I worked with in Edinburgh commented on how their mothers had taught them politeness formulas. One twelve-year-old boy said: 'When I was wee, she used to say, "Say please and say thank you." Everybody says that. When you don't want something and you just say "no", she tells you to say "no thank you".'

4   This learning strategy may in fact be more important than has been previously assumed. There may be other aspects of language which are first learned as low-level routines; and some learners may rely more on this strategy than others (cf. the discussion in Peters 1983). Clark (1974: 5), for instance, remarks that many sequences in young children's speech, which would be assumed to have internal syntactic structure if the utterances were produced by an adult, may instead be well-practised routines of which no part is substitutable.

5   I have followed the convention of labelling each successive clause, which advances the action with a, b, c, etc.

6   *Influences on children's language: family, school and peer group*

1   In adult society the workplace might be thought of as one of the major discourse-reproducing agencies.

2   This statement overlooks the fact that some of Chomsky's earliest arguments (e.g. in Chomsky 1965) are addressed to phonetic data, and therefore require no appeal to the alleged problem of the sloppiness of the primary linguistic data. Chomsky's main claim is based on the infiniteness of the possible hypotheses available to the child. This is why the Language Acquisition Device is needed; namely, so that the child is able to narrow down hypotheses. The sloppiness of the input is another complicating factor. This is an issue which the research on 'baby talk' does not address.

3   A Bantu language of Africa. Cf. Raum (1940).

4   The conclusion that the effects of these programmes are negligible is arguable. There are methodological problems associated in assessing the effects of treatment on outcomes, which were not properly controlled for in the

statistical analysis of the results. The main difficulty in interpreting the results is due to the fact that the lower social class groups started 'from behind' at the very outset of the experiment.

5   This is the community referred to as Trackton in section 6.1.

6   Although questioning strategies of the type discussed here are crucial to learning in mainstream English-speaking society, cross-cultural studies of the variable use of questions, particularly direct questions, raise doubts about the universality of the critical role of questions (Cf. Heath 1983: 378n, Eades 1982, and Goody 1978).

7   This extract is given in full in Michaels (1981: 435–6). I have condensed the narrative somewhat and normalized the transcription, so that prosody, false starts, overlapping, etc., have been edited out.

7   *The acquisition of literacy and its role in communicative competence*

1   This example is cited in Hudson (1980: 222) and taken from the work of Scribner (1977).

2   Henle (1962) reports some interesting results on the interpretation of 'real-life' syllogisms by New York City housewives. She found that 'errors' in deduction were the result of changing the premises of the situation rather than due to errors of inference.

3   Wolfram et al. (1979: 9) distinguish between dialect interferences and dialect influence. Only the former may inhibit comprehension. Dialect influence is of no semantic consequence.

4   I owe these examples to Malcolm Coulthard.

5   The social effects of schooling are discussed by Illich (1973).

8   *The measurement of communicative competence*

1   Labov (1973) and Trudgill (1982) report some interesting findings from their investigations of adults' passive knowledge of a range of variable syntactic constructions.

2   This runs counter, however, to Chomsky's views on the autonomy of syntax with respect to meaning.

3   Lambert (1972) makes a distinction between integrative and instrumental motivation in second-language learning and stresses the importance of the affective component of language use in studying proficiency and other language behaviour.

4   A similar example can be cited from experiments conducted by Gleitman et al. (1972), who asked children to say whether sentences were 'good' or 'silly'. Some suburbanite children rejected the sentence: *The men wait for the bus*, on the ground that only kids wait for buses.

9   *Child language acquisition and linguistic theory*

1   The theory of communicative competence developed by Habermas (1971) owes much to the ideas of Hymes, but is concerned to characterize what the nature of the conditions is for ideal communication amongst members of society.

Bibliography

Adelman, C. (1976) 'The language of teenage groups', in S. Rogers (ed.) *They Don't Speak Our Language*, London: Edward Arnold, pp. 80–105.

Agnihotri, R.K. (1970) Processes of assimilation: A sociolinguistic study of Sikh children in Leeds, D.Phil. dissertation, University of York.

The Ann Arbor Decision. Memorandum, Opinion and Order and the Education Plan, Washington DC: Centre for Applied Linguistics.

Aitchison, J. (1981) *Language Change: Progress or Decay?* London: Fontana.

Angiolillo, C.J. and Goldin-Meadow, S. (1982) 'Experimental evidence for agent–patient categories in child language', *Journal of Child Language* 9: 627–43.

Aniansson, E. (1979) 'Barnets språkliga identifikation: material och metoder', *FUMS Rapport*, No. 80, Uppsala.

Aniansson, E. (1981) 'Barns språkliga förmåga: Redogörelse för ett par test', *FUMS Rapport*, No. 84, Uppsala.

Aniansson, E. and Hammermo, O. (1981) 'Generationsmässig och situationell variation speglad i språket hos yngre eskilstunabor. Två delstudier från projektet Barnets språkliga identifikation', *FUMS Rapport* No. 99, Uppsala.

Antinucci, F., Duranti, A. and Gebert, L. (1979) 'Relative clause structure, relative clause perception and the change from SOV to SVO', *Cognition* 7: 145–76.

Asher, S.R. (1976) 'Children's ability to appraise their own and other person's communication performance', *Developmental Psychology* 12: 24–32.

Austin, J.L. (1962) *How to Do Things with Words*, London: Oxford University Press.

Baetens-Beardsmore, H. (1982) *Bilingualism: Basic Principles*, Clevedon, Aron,: Tieto Ltd.

Bailey, C.-J. (1973) *Variation and Linguistic Theory*, Washington, DC: Centre for Applied Linguistics.

Baldie, B. (1976) 'The acquisition of the passive voice', *Journal of Child Language*, 3: 331–48.

Banfield, A. (1982) *Unspeakable Sentences*, London: Routledge & Kegan Paul.

Baratz, J. and Shuy, R. (eds.) (1969) *Teaching Black Children to Read*, Washington, DC: Centre for Applied Linguistics.

Baron, N. (1977) *Language Acquisition and Historical Change*, Amsterdam: North Holland.

Bates, E. (1976a) *Language and Context: The Acquisition of Pragmatics*, New York: Academic Press.

Bates, E. (1976b) 'Pragmatics and sociolinguistics in child language', in A. and D. Morehead (eds), *Language Deficiency in Children*. Philadelphia: University Park Press.

Bates, E. and MacWhinney, B. (1979) 'A functionalist approach to the acquisition of grammar', in E. Ochs and B. Schieffelin (eds), *Developmental Pragmatics*, New York: Academic Press, pp. 167–211.

Bates, E. and MacWhinney, B. (1982)' Functionalist approaches to grammar', in E. Wanner and L. Gleitman (eds), *Language Acquisition: The State of the Art*, Cambridge: Cambridge University Press, pp. 173–219.

Bauman, R and Sherzer, J. (eds) (1974) *Explorations in the Ethnography of Speaking*, Cambridge: Cambridge University Press.

Bausinger, H. (1967) *Deutsch für Deutsche* Frankfurt am Main.

Beaken, M.A. (1971) 'A study of phonological development in a primary school population of London', PhD thesis, University of London.

Bellinger, D. (1979) 'Changes in the explicitness of mothers' directives as children age', *Journal of Child Language* 6: 443–58.

Bereiter, C. and Engelman, S. (1966) *Teaching Disadvantaged Children in the Pre-school*, Englewood Cliffs, NJ: Prentice-Hall.

Berenda, R.W. (1950) *The Influence of the Group on the Judgements of Children: An Experimental Investigation*, New York: Kings Crown Press.

Bergroth, H. (1924) *Svensk Uttalslära*, Helsingfors.

Berko, J. (1958) 'The child's learning of English morphology', *Word* 14: 150–77.

Berko-Gleason, J. and Weintraub S. (1976) 'The acquisition of routines in child language: "Trick or treat"', *Language in Society* 5: 129–37.

Berk-Seligson, S. (1981) 'Sources of variation in Spanish verb construction: the active, the dative and the reflexive passive', unpublished manuscript

Bernstein, B. (1970) 'A critique of the concepts of "compensatory" education', in D. Rubenstein and C. Stoneman (eds), *Education for Democracy*, Harmondsworth: Penguin, pp. 110–21.

Bernstein, B. (1973) *Class, Codes and Control*, II, London: Routledge & Kegan Paul.

Bernstein, B. (1981) 'Codes, modalities, and the process of cultural reproduction: A model', *Language in Society* 10:327–65.

Bever, T.G. (1970) 'The cognitive basis for linguistic structures', in J.R. Hayes (ed.), *Cognition and the Development of Language*, New York: Wiley.

Bever, T.G. (1975) 'Psychologically real grammar emerges because of its role in language acquisition', in D. Dato (ed.), *Developmental Psycholinguistics: Theory and Applications*, Washington, DC: Georgetown University Press.

Bickerton, D. (1975) *Dynamics of a Creole System*, Cambridge: Cambridge University Press.

Bickerton, D. (1977) *Change and Variation in Hawaiian English*, II: *Creole Syntax*, Social Sciences and Linguistics Institute, University of Hawaii.

Bickerton, D. (1981) *Roots of Language*, Ann Arbor: Karoma Press.

Biondi, L. (1975) *The Italian–American Child: His Sociolinguistic Acculturation*, Washington, DC: Georgetown University Press.

Bloch, B. (1947) 'English verb inflection', *Language* 23: 399–418.

Blom, J.–P. and Gumperz, J.J. (1972)'Social meaning in linguistic structure: code-switching in Norway', in J. Gumperz and D. Hymes (eds), *Directions in Sociolinguistics*, New York: Holt, Rinehart & Winston, pp. 407–34.

Bloomfield, L. (1927) 'Literate and illiterate speech', *American Speech* 2: 432–9.

Blount, B. (1977) 'Ethnography and caretaker–child interaction', in C. Snow and C. Ferguson (eds), *Talking to Children*, Cambridge: Cambridge University Press, pp. 297–309.

Bodine, A. (1975) 'Sex differentiation in language', in B. Thorne and N. Henley (eds), *Language and Sex: Difference and Dominance*, Rowley, Mass.: Newbury House, pp. 130–52.

Bolinger, D. (1980) *Language. The Loaded Weapon: The Use and Abuse of Language Today*, London: Longman.

Bowerman, M. (1973) 'Structural relationships in children's utterances: syntactic or semantic?', in T. Moore (ed.), *Cognitive Development and the Acquisition of Language*, New York: Academic Press.

Bowerman, M. (1979) 'The acquisition of complex sentences', in P. Fletcher and M. Garman (eds), *Studies in Language Acquisition*, Cambridge: Cambridge University Press, pp. 285–307.

Bowerman, M. (1981) 'Language development', in H. Triandis and A. Heron (eds), *Handbook of Cross-cultural Psychology*, Boston: Allyn & Bacon, pp. 93–185.

Boyd, S. and Guy, G. (1979) 'The acquisition of a morphological category', paper presented at the winter meeting of the LSA, Los Angeles.

Brazil, D. (1975) *Discourse Intonation*, University of Birmingham: English Language research.

Brenner, M. (ed.) (1980) *The Structure of Action*, Oxford: Blackwell.

Bresnan, J. (1976) 'On the form and functioning of transformations', *Linguistic Inquiry* 7: 3–40.

Brouwer, D., Gerritsen, M. and de Haan, D. (1979) 'Speech differences between women and men: on the wrong track?', *Language in Society* 8: 33–50.

Brown, K. (forthcoming) 'Relative clauses in a corpus of Scots speech', to appear in *English World Wide*.

Brown, K. and Millar, M. (1980) 'Auxiliary verbs in Edinburgh speech', *Transactions of the Philological Society* 1980: 81–133.

Brown, K. and Miller, J. (1975) 'Modal verbs in Scottish English', *Work in Progress* 8: 99–114, Department of Linguistics, University of Edinburgh.

Brown, P. and Levinson, S. (1978) 'Universals in language usage: politeness phenomena', in E. Goody (ed), *Questions and Politeness. Strategies in Social Interaction*, Cambridge: Cambridge University Press, pp. 56–311.

Brown, R. (1970) 'Three processes in the child's acquisition of syntax' in *Psycholinguistics: Selected Papers by Roger Brown*, New York: Free Press, pp. 75–100.

Brown, R. (1973) *A First Language: The Early Stages*, Cambridge, Mass.: Harvard University Press.

Brown, R. (1977) 'Introduction', in C.E. Snow and C. Ferguson (eds), *Talking to Children: Language Input and Acquisition*, Cambridge: Cambridge University Press.

Brown, R. and Hanlon, C. (1970) 'Derivational Complexity and order of acquisition in child speech', in J.R. Hayes (ed.), *Cognition and the Development of Language*, New York: Wiley.

Bullock (1975) *Language for Life*, Report of the Bullock Committee of Enquiry, London: HMSO.

Buros, O. (ed.) (1974) *Personality Tests and Reviews II: A Monograph Consisting of the Personality Sections of the Seventh Mental Measurements Yearbook 1972 and Tests in Print 1974*, Highland Park, NJ: Gryphon Press.

Butters, R. (1973) 'Acceptability judgements for double modals in Southern dialects', in C.J. Bailey and R. Shuy (eds), *New Ways of Analysing Variation in English*, Washington, DC: Georgetown University Press, pp. 276–86.

Bybee, J. and Slobin, D. (1982a) 'Why small children cannot change language on their own'. in A. Ahlquist (ed.), *Papers from the 5th International Conference on Historical Linguistics*, Amsterdam: John Benjamins, pp. 29–38.

Bybee, J.L. and Slobin, D. (1982b) 'Rules and schemas in the development and use of the English past', *Language* 58: 265–90.

Campbell, R. and Wales, R. (1970) 'The study of language acquisition', in J. Lyons (ed.), *New Horizons in Linguistics*, Harmondsworth: Penguin.

Carroll, J., Bever, T. and Pollack, C. (1981) 'The non-uniqueness of linguistic intuitions', *Language* 57: 368–82.

Cazden, C., Bond, J.T., Epstein, A.S., Matz, R.D. and Savignon, S. (1977) 'Language assessment: where, what and how', *Anthropology and Education Quarterly* 8(2): 83–91.

Chafe, W. (1982) 'Integration and involvement in speaking, writing and oral literature', in D. Tannen (ed.), *Spoken and Written Language: Exploring Orality and Literacy*, Norwood NJ: Ablex, pp. 35–55.

Chambers, J. and Trudgill, P. (1980) *Dialectology*, Cambridge: Cambridge University Press.

Chapman, R.S. (1978) 'Comprehension strategies in children', in J.F. Kavanagh and W. Strange (eds), *Implications of Basic Speech and Language Research for the School and Clinic*, Cambridge, Mass.: MIT Press.

Cheshire, J. (1982a) *Variation in an English Dialect*, Cambridge: Cambridge University Press.

Cheshire, J. (1982b) 'Variation in the use of *ain't* in an urban British English dialect', *Language in Society* 10: 365–81.

Cheshire, J. (forthcoming) 'Non-standard *never*', unpublished ms.

Cheyne, W. (1970) 'Stereotyped reactions to speakers with Scottish and English regional accents', *British Journal of Social and Clinical Psychology* 9: 779.

Chomsky, C. (1969) *The Acquisition of Syntax in Children from 5 to 10*, Cambridge, Mass.: MIT Press.

Chomsky, N. (1957) *Syntactic Structures*, The Hague: Mouton.

Chomsky, N. (1965) *Aspects of the Theory of Syntax*, Cambridge, Mass.: MIT Press.

Chomsky, N. (1977) 'On Wh movement', in P. Culivover, T. Wasow and A. Akmajian (eds), *Formal Syntax*, New York: Academic Press, pp. 71–133.

Chomsky, N. (1980) *Rules and Representations*, Oxford: Blackwell.

Chomsky, N. (1981a) 'Principles and parameters in syntactic theory', in N. Hornstein and D. Lightfoot (eds), *Explanation in Linguistics: The Logical Problem of Language Acquisition*, London: Longman, pp. 32–76.

Chomsky, N. (1981b) *Lectures on Government and Binding*, Dordrecht: Foris.

Chomsky, N. (1982) *Some Consequences of the Theory of Government and Binding*, Linguistic Inquiry Monograph 6, Cambridge, Mass.: MIT Press.

Chomsky, N. and Halle, M. (1968) *The Sound Pattern Of English*, New York: Harper.

Clark, E.V. (1973) 'How children describe time and order', in C.A. Ferguson and D. Slobin (eds), *Studies of Child Language Development*, New York: Holt, Rienhart & Winston, pp. 585–606.

Clark, R. (1974) 'Performing without competence', *Journal of Child Language* 1: 1–10.

Cofer, T. (1972) 'Linguistic variability in a Philadelphia speech community', PhD dissertation, University of Pennsylvania.

Comrie, B. (1981) *Language Universals and Linguistic Typology*, Oxford: Blackwell.

Cooper, W. and Ross, J.R. (1975) 'Word order', in R. Grossman, L. San and T. Vance (eds), *Papers from the Parasession on Functionalism*, Chicago: Chicago Linguistic Society, pp. 63–112.

Corbett, E. (1981) 'The status of writing in our society', in M.F. Whiteman (ed.), *Writing: The Nature, Development and Teaching of Written Communication*, I: *Variation in Writing*, Hillsdale, NJ: Lawrence Erlbaum, pp. 47–53.

Corsaro, W. (1977) 'The clarification request as a feature of adult interactive styles with young children', *Language in Society* 6: 183–207.

Corsaro, W. (1979) ' "We're friends, right?": Children's use of access rituals in a nursery school', *Language in Society* 8: 315–37.

Corsaro, W. (1981) 'Entering the child's world – research strategies for field entry and data collection in a pre-school setting', in J. Green and C. Wallat (eds), *Ethnography and Language in Educational Settings*, Norwood, NJ: Ablex, pp. 117–45.

Corson, D. (1982) 'The Graeco-Latin (G-L) Instrument: A new measure of semantic complexity in oral and written English', *Language and Speech* 25: 1–10.

Corson, D. (1983) 'Social dialect, the semantic barrier and access to curricular knowledge', *Language in Society*, 12: 213–23.

Coupland, N. (1980) 'Style shifting in a Cardiff work setting', *Language in Society* 9: 1–12.

Craig, D. (1971) 'Education and Creole English in the West Indies: some sociolinguistic factors', in D. Hymes (ed.), *Pidginization and Creolization of Languages*, Cambridge: Cambridge University Press, pp. 371–93.

Cremona, C. and Bates, E. (1977) 'The development of attitudes towards dialect in Italian children', *Journal of Psycholinguistic Research* 6: 223–32.

Cressey, D. (1980) *Literacy and Social Order: Reading and Writing in Tudor England*, Cambridge: Cambridge University Press.

Cross, T. (1977) 'Mother's speech and its association with rate of linguistic development in young children', in N. Waterson and C. Snow (eds), *The Development of Communication*, London: Wiley.

Cullum, J. (1981) 'Peer influence on the choice of some linguistic variants', MA thesis, University of Birmingham.

Cummins, J. (1981) *Bilingualism and Minority Language Children*, Ontario Institute for Studies in Education.

Dannequin, C. (1977) *Les Enfants Baillonnés*, Paris: CEDIC, Diffusion Nathan.

Deuchar, M. (1983) 'Relative clauses and linguistic inequality', paper given at the Linguistics Association of Great Britain Meeting, Newcastle-upon-Tyne, September.

Deutsch, M. et al. (1967) *The Disadvantaged Child*, New York: Basic Books.

de Villiers, P. and de Villiers, J. (1974) 'On this, that and the other, Non-egocentrism in very young children', *Journal of Experimental Child Psychology* 18: 438–77.

de Villiers, J.G., Flusberg, T., Hakuta, K. and Cohen, M. (1979 'Children's comprehension of relative clauses', *Journal of Psycholinguistic Research* 8: 449–518.

Donaldson, M. (1978) *Children's Minds*, Glasgow: Fontana.

Donaldson, M. and Lloyd, P. (1974) 'Sentences and situations: Children's judgements of match and mismatch', in F. Bresson (ed.), *Problèms actuels en psycholinguistique*, Paris: Centre de Recherche scientifique.

Douglas-Cowie, E. (1978) 'Linguistic code-switching in a Northern Irish village:

social interaction and social ambition', in P. Trudgill (ed.), *Sociolinguistic Patterns in British English*, London: Edward Arnold, pp. 37–52.

Dundes, A., Leach J. and Özkök, B. (1972) 'The Strategy of Turkish Boys' Verbal Duelling Rhymes', in J.J. Gumperz and D. Hymes (eds), *Directions in Sociolinguistics*, New York: Holt, Rinehart & Winston, pp. 130–61.

Eades, D. (1982) 'You gotta know how to talk: information-seeking in South-East Queensland Aboriginal society', *Australian Journal of Linguistics* 2: 61–83.

Edelsky, C. (1977) 'Acquisition of an aspect of communicative competence: learning what it means to talk like a lady', in S. Ervin-Tripp and C. Mitchell-Kernan (eds), *Child Discourse*, New York: Academic Press, pp. 225–43.

Edelsky, C., Hudelson, S., Flores, B., Barkin, F., Altwerger, B. and Jilbert, K. (1983) 'A language deficit theory for the 80s: CALP, BICS and semilingualism', *Applied Linguistics* 4: 1–22.

Edwards, V. (1979) *The West Indian Language Issue in British Schools*, London: Routledge & Kegan Paul.

Ehimovich, C. (1981) 'The intimacy of address: friendship markers in children's social play', *Language in Society* 10: 189–201.

Ellegård, A. (1978) *The Syntactic Structure of English Texts*, Gothenburg Studies in English 43, University of Gothenburg, Sweden.

Elliot, A. (1981) *Child Language*, Cambridge: Cambridge University Press.

Erikson, F. (1980) 'Timing and context in children's everyday discourse: implications for the study of referential and social meaning', *Working Papers in Sociolinguistics*, no. 67, Austin, Texas.

Erikson, F. (1982) *The Counselor as Gatekeeper: Social Interaction in Interviews*, New York: Academic Press.

Ervin-Tripp, S. (1971) 'Social backgrounds and verbal skills', in R. Huxley and E. Ingram (eds), Language Acquisition: Models and Methods, New York: Academic Press.

Ervin-Tripp, S. (1972) 'On sociolinguistic rules: alternation and co-occurrence', in J.J. Gumperz and D. Hymes (eds), *Directions in sociolinguistics*, New York: Holt, Rinehart & Winston, pp. 213–50.

Ervin-Tripp, S. (1976) 'Is Sybil there? The structure of American English directives', *Language in Society* 5: 25–67.

Ervin-Tripp, S. (1977) 'Wait for me, Roller Skate!', in S. Ervin-Tripp and C. Mitchell-Kernan (eds), *Child Discourse*, New York: Academic Press, pp. 165–88.

Ervin-Tripp, S. (1978a) 'Is second language learning like the first?', in E. Hatch (ed.), *Second Language Acquisition*, Rowley, Mass.: Newbury House.

Ervin-Tripp, S. (1978b) 'Some features of early child–adult dialogue', *Language in society* 7: 357–73.

Fasold, R. (1972) *Tense Marking in Black English*, Washington, DC: Centre for Applied Linguistics.

Feagin, C. (1979) *Variation and Change in Alabama English: A Sociolinguistic Study of the White Community*, Washington, DC: Georgetown University Press.

Ferguson, C. (1959) 'Diglossia', *Word* 15: 325–40.

Ferguson, C.F. (1977) 'Baby talk as a simplified register', in C.E. Snow and C.F. Ferguson (eds), *Talking to Children: Language Input and Acquisition*, Cambridge: Cambridge University Press.

Fillmore, C. (1979) 'On fluency', in C. Fillmore, D. Kempler and W. Wang (eds), *Individual Differences in Language Learning and Language Behaviour*, New

York: Academic Press, pp. 85–101.

Fillmore, C., Kempler, D. and Wang, W. (eds) (1979) *Individual Differences in Language Learning and Language Behaviour*, New York: Academic Press.

Fischer, J.L. (1958) 'Social influences on the choice of a linguistic variant', *Word* 14: 47–56.

Fischer, S. (1976) 'Child Language as a predictor of language change', *Working Papers in Linguistics*, 8.4: 71–104, Honolulu: University of Hawaii.

Fishman, J. (1971) *Advances in the Sociology of Language*, I, The Hague: Mouton.

Fodor, J. and Garrett, M. (1966) 'Some reflections on competence and performance', in J. Lyons, and R. Wales (eds), *Psycholinguistic Papers*, Edinburgh: Edinburgh University Press.

Fodor, J.A., Bever, T.G. and Garrett, M. (1974) *The Psychology of Language: an Introduction to Psycholinguistics and Generative Grammar*, New York: McGraw Hill.

Garvey, C. (1975) 'Requests and responses in children's speech', *Journal of Child Language* 2: 41–63.

Gauchat, L. (1905) 'L'unité phonétique dans le patois d'une commune', in *Aus romanischen Sprachen und Literatturen: Festschrift Heinrich Morf*, Halle: Max Niemeyer, pp. 175–232.

Geertz, C. (1976) 'From the native's point of view: On the nature of anthropological understanding', in K. Basso and H. Selby (eds), *Meaning in Anthropology*, Albuquerque, NM: University of New Mexico Press, pp. 221–37.

Giles, H. (1970) 'Evaluative reactions to accents', *Educational Review* 22: 211–27.

Giles, H. and Smith, P. (1979) 'Accommodation theory: Optimal levels of convergence', in H. Giles and R. St-Clair (eds), *Language and Social Psychology*, Oxford: Blackwell, pp. 45–65.

Gilmore, P. and Glatthorn, A. (eds) (1982) *Children In and Out of School: Ethnography and Education*, Washington, DC: Centre for Applied Linguistics.

Givón, T. (1979a) *On Understanding Grammar*, New York: Academic Press.

Givón, T. (1979b) 'From discourse to syntax: Grammar as a processing strategy', in T. Givón (ed.), *Discourse and Syntax*, XII: *Syntax and Semantics*, New York: Academic Press, pp. 81–109.

Gleason, J.B. (1973) 'Code switching in children's language', in T. Moore (ed.), *Cognitive Development and the Acquisition of Language*, New York: Academic Press.

Gleitman, L., Gleitman, H. and Shipley, E. (1972) 'The emergence of the child as grammarian', *Cognition* 1: 137–64.

Gleitman, L. and Rozin, P. (1973) 'Teaching reading by use of a syllabary', *Reading Research Quarterly* 8: 447–83.

Goffman, E. (1981) *Forms of Talk*, Philadelphia: University of Pennsylvania Press.

Goodluck, H. (1978) 'Linguistic principles in children's grammar of complement subject interpretation, PhD thesis, University of Massachusetts.

Goodwin, M. (1980) 'Directive response speech sequences in girls' and boys' task activities', in S. McConnell-Ginet, R. Borker and N. Furman (eds), *Women and Language in Literature and Society*, New York: Praeger.

Goody, E.N. (1978) 'Towards a theory of questions', in E.N. Goody (ed.), *Questions and Politeness: Strategies in Social Interaction*, Cambridge: Cambridge University Press, pp. 17–43.

Gordon, J.C.B. (1981) *Verbal Deficit: A Critique*, London: Croom Helm.

Grant, W. (1914) *The Pronunciation of English in Scotland*, Cambridge: Cambridge University Press.

Grant, W. and Murison, D. (1929–76) *The Scottish National Dictionary*, Edinburgh: University of Edinburgh Press.

Greenfield, P. (1968) 'Oral or written language; the consequences for cognitive development in Africa and the United States', paper presented at the Symposium on Cross-cultural Cognitive Studies, Chicago.

Grief, E.B. and Berko-Gleason, J. (1980) 'Hi, thanks and goodbye: More routine information', *Language in Society* 9: 159–67.

Grieve, R. and Wales, R. (1973) 'Passives and topicalization', *British Journal of Psychology* 64: 173–82.

Grimshaw, A. (1982) 'Comprehensive discourse analysis: An instance of professional peer interaction', *Language in Society* 11: 15–49.

Gruber, J. (1971) 'Topicalization in child language', in A. Bar-Adon and W. Leopold (eds), *Child Language: A Book of Readings*, Englewood Cliffs, NJ: Prentice-Hall, pp. 364–82.

Gumperz, J.J. (1976) 'The sociolinguistic significance of conversational code-switching', *Working Paper* 46, Language Behaviour Research Laboratory, Berkeley: University of California.

Gumperz, J.J. (1981) 'Conversational inference and classroom learning', in J. Green and C. Wallat (eds), *Ethnography and Language in Educational Settings*, Norwood, NJ: Ablex, pp. 3–25.

Gustavsson, G. (1979) 'Substantiv i skoluppsater', *FUMS Rapport*, No. 69, Uppsala.

Guy, G. (1975) 'The Cedergren-Sankoff variable rule program', in R. Fasold and R. Shuy (eds), *Analyzing Variation in Language*, Washington, DC: Georgetown University Press, pp. 59–70.

Guy, G. (1977) 'A new look at -t, -d deletion', in R. Fasold and R. Shuy (eds), *Studies in Language Variation*, Washington, DC: Georgetown University Press, pp. 1–12.

Guy, G. (1980) 'Variation in the group and individual: the case of final stop deletion', in W. Labov (ed.), *Locating Language in Time and Space*, New York: Academic Press, pp. 1–35.

Haas, A. (1979) 'The acquisition of genderlect', in J. Orasnu, M. Slater and L. Adler (eds), *Language, Sex and Gender*, Annals of the New York Academy of Sciences, 327: 101–13.

Haas, M. (1964) 'Men's and women's speech in Koasati', in D. Hymes (ed.), *Language in Culture and Society*, New York: Harper & Row, pp. 228–34.

Habermas, J. (1971) 'Vorbereitende Bemerkungen zur kommunikativen Kompetenz', in J. Habermas and N. Luhmann (eds), *Theorie der Gesellschaft oder sozialtechnologie – Was leistet die Systemforschung?*, Frankfurt, pp. 101–41.

Hackenberg, R. (1972) 'Appalachian English: A sociolinguistic study', PhD dissertation, Georgetown University.

Hakes, D. (1982) 'The development of metalinguistic abilities: what develops?', in S. Kuczaj (ed.), *Language development*, II: *Language, Thought and Culture*, Hillsdale, NJ: Lawrence Erlbaum, pp. 163–210.

Hakuta, H. (1979) 'Comprehension and production of simple and complex sentences by Japanese children', PhD dissertation, Harvard Univeristy.

Hale, K. (1976) 'The adjoined relative clause in Australia', in R. Dixon (ed.), *Grammatical Categories in Australian Languages*, Canberra: Institute of Aboriginal Studies, pp. 78–105.

Halle, M. (1962) 'Phonology in a generative grammar', *Word* 18: 54–72.

Hallencreutz, K. (1979) "*de-dem-dåmm* i svenskt elevspråk', *FUMS Rapport* No 71, Uppsala.

Halliday, M.A.K. (1975a) *Learning How to Mean: Explorations in the Development of Language*, London: Edward Arnold.

Halliday, M.A.K. (1975b) 'Talking one's way in. A sociolinguistic perspective on language and learning', in A. Davies (ed.), *Problems of Language and Learning*, London: Heinemann, pp. 8–28.

Halliday, M.A.K. (1976) *Explorations in the Functions of Language*, London: Edward Arnold.

Halliday, M.A.K. (1978) *Language as a Social Semiotic*, London: Edward Arnold.

Halliday, M.A.K. and Hasan, R. (1976) *Cohesion in English*, London: Longman.

Hamburger, H. and Crain, S. (1982) 'Relative acquisition', in S. Kuczaj (ed.), *Language Development*, I: *Syntax and Semantics*, Hillsdale, NJ: Lawrence Erlbaum, pp. 245–75.

Hammermo, O., Strömqvist, S. and Molin, R. (1981) 'Vi har inte lust att prata nån jäkla rikssvenska!', En dialektsociologisk enkätundersökning i bland götlandska gymnasieelever. *FUMS Rapport* No. 94, Uppsala.

Hardy, M., Platone, F. and Dannequin, C. (1977) 'Langage et classes sociales: quelques problèmes methodologiques', *Psychologie Française* 22: 37–46.

Harris, M. (forthcoming) 'The causes of word order change', to appear in *Lingua*.

Harwood, F. (1959) 'Quantitative study of the speech of Australian children', *Language and Speech* 2: 236–70.

Haugen, E. (1966) *Language Planning and Conflict: The Case for Modern Norwegian*, Cambridge, Mass.: Harvard University Press.

Hawkins, J. (1978) *Definiteness and Indefiniteness*, London: Croom Helm.

Heath, S.B. (1978) *Teacher Talk: Language in the Classroom*, Washington, DC: Centre for Applied Linguistics.

Heath, S.B. (1980) 'Standard English: biography of a symbol', in T. Shopen and M. Williams (eds), *Standards and Dialects in English*, Cambridge, Mass.: Winthrop Publishers, Inc., pp. 3–33.

Heath, S.B. (1982a) 'Questioning at home and school: A comparative study', in G. Spindler (ed.), *Doing the Ethnography of Schooling*, New York: The CBS Publishing Co., pp. 105–31.

Heath, S.B. (1982b) 'Protean shapes in literacy events: evershifting oral and literate traditions', in D. Tannen (ed.), *Spoken and Written Language*, Norwood, NJ: Ablex, pp. 91–117.

Heath, S.B. (1983) *Ways with Words*, Cambridge: Cambridge University Press.

Henle, M. (1962) 'On the relation between logic and thinking', *Psychological Review* 69: 366–78.

Hewitt, R. (1982) 'White adolescent creole users and the politics of friendship', *Journal of Multilingual and Multicultural Development* 3: 217–32.

Hickmann, M. (forthcoming) 'The implications of discourse skills in Vygotsky's Developmental Theory', to appear in J. Wertsch (ed.), *Culture, Communication and Cognition: Vygotskian Perspectives*, Cambridge: Cambridge University Press.

Hockett, C. (1950) 'Age-grading and linguistic continuity', *Language* 26: 449–57.

Hollos, M. (1977) 'Comprehension and use of social rules in pronoun selection by Hungarian children', in S. Ervin-Tripp and C. Mitchell-Kernan (eds), *Child Discourse*, New York: Academic Press.

Horgan, D. (1978) 'The development of the full passive', *Journal of Child*

Language 5: 65–80.
Hornstein, N. and Lightfoot, D. (eds), (1981) *Explanation in Linguistics: The Logical Problem of Language Acquisition*, London: Longman.
Horvath, B. (1977) 'Sociolinguistic assessements of standardized tests', unpublished paper given at the ANZAAS conference, Melbourne, Australia.
Horvath, B. (1983) 'Learning to talk in the new paradigm', *Australian Journal of Linguistics* 3: 217–41.
Huddleston, R. (1984) *An Introduction to English Grammar*, Cambridge: Cambridge University Press.
Hudson, R.A. (1980) *Sociolinguistics*, Cambridge: Cambridge University Press.
Hughes, A. and Trudgill, P. (1979) *English Accents and Dialects*, London: Edward Arnold.
Hymes, D. (1968) 'The ethnography of speaking', in J. Fishman (ed.), *Reading in The Sociology of Language*, The Hague: Mouton, pp. 99–139.
Hymes, D. (1971) 'Competence and performance in linguistic theory', in R. Huxley and E. Ingram (eds), *Language Acquisition Models and Methods*, New York: Academic Press.
Hymes, D. (1974) *Foundations in Sociolinguistics*, Philadelphia: University of Pennsylvania Press.
Hymes, D. (1979) 'Language in education: forward to fundamentals', in O. Garnica and M. King (eds). *Language, Children and Society. The Effects of Social Factors on Children Learning to Communicate*, Oxford: Pergamon Press, pp. 1–19.
Illich, I. (1973) *Deschooling Society*, Harmondsworth: Penguin.
Ingram, D. (1975) 'If and when transformations are acquired by children', in D.P. Dato (ed.), *Developmental Psycholinguistics. Theory and Application*, Washington, DC: Georgetown University Press, pp. 99-129.
Isenbarger, J. and Smith, V. (1973) 'How would you feel if you had to change *your* dialect?', *English Journal* 62: 994–7.
Janson, T. (1966) 'Reverse lexical diffusion and lexical split: loss of -D in Stockholm', in W. Wang (ed.), *The Lexicon in Phonological Change*, The Hague: Mouton.
Jensen, A. (1969) 'How much can we boost IQ and scholastic achievement?', *Harvard Educational Review* 39: 1–123.
Jespersen, O. (1924) *The Philosophy of Grammar*, London: Allen & Unwin.
Johnson, H.L. (1975) 'The meaning of *before* and *after* for preschool children', *Journal of Experimental Child Psychology* 19; 88–99.
Johnson-Laird, P. (1968a) 'The interpretation of the passive voice', *Quarterly Journal of Experimental Psychology* 20: 69–73.
Johnson-Laird, P. (1968b) 'The choice of the passive voice in a communicative task', *British Journal of Psychology* 59: 7–15.
Justus, C. (1976) 'Relativization and topicalization in Hittite', in C. Li (ed.), *Subject and Topic*, New York: Academic Press, pp. 213-247.
Kageyama, T. (1975) 'Relational grammar and the history of subject raising', *Glossa* 9: 165–81.
Kail, M. (1975) 'Étude génétique de la reproduction de phrases relatives', *Année Psychologique* 75: 109–26, 427–43.
Karmiloff-Smith, A. (1979a) *A Functional Approach to Child Language*, Cambridge: Cambridge University Press.
Karmiloff-Smith, A. (1979b) 'Language development after five', in P. Fletcher and M. Garman (eds), *Studies in Language Acquisition*, Cambridge: Cambridge

University Press, pp. 307–23.

Keenan, E.L. (1975) 'Some universals of passive in relational grammar', *Papers from the Eleventh Regional Meeting of the Chicago Linguistics Society*. University of Chicago.

Keenan, E.L. and Comrie, B. (1977) 'Noun phrase accessibility and universal grammar', *Linguistic Inquiry* 8: 63–99.

Keenan E.L. and Comrie, B. (1979) 'Data on the noun phrase accessibility hierarchy', *Language* 55: 332–52.

Keenan, E.O. (1974) 'Norm-makers, Norm breakers: uses of speech by men and women in a Malagasy community', in R. Bauman and J. Sherzer (eds), *Explorations in the Ethnography of Speaking*, Cambridge: Cambridge University Press, pp. 125–44.

Keenan E.O. (1977) 'Making it last: repetition in children's discourse', in S. Ervin-Tripp and C. Mitchell-Kernan (eds). *Child Discourse*, New York: Academic Press, pp. 125–39.

Keenan, E.O. and Schieffelin, B. (1976) 'Topic as a discourse notion: a study of topic in the conversation of children and adults', in C. Li (ed.), *Subject and Topic*, New York: Academic Press, pp. 335–85.

Kernan, K. (1977) 'Semantic and expressive elaboration in children's narratives', in S. Ervin-Tripp and C. Mitchell-Kernan (eds), *Child Discourse*, New York: Academic Press, pp. 91–102.

King, R.D. (1969) *Historical Linguistics and Generative Grammar*, Englewood Cliffs, NJ: Prentice-Hall.

Kirsner, R. (1976) 'On the subjectless "pseudo-passive" in Standard Dutch and the semantics of background agents', in C. Li (ed.), *Subject and Topic*, New York: Academic Press.

Kobayashi, C. (1981) 'Dialectal variation in child language', in P. Dale and D. Ingram (eds), *Child Language: An International Perspective*, Baltimore, University Park Press, pp. 5–29.

Kochman, T. (ed.) (1972) *Rappin' and Stylin' Out: Communication in Urban Black America*, Champaign: University of Illinois Press.

Koster, J. (1978) 'Why subject sentences don't exist', in S.J. Keyser (ed.), *Recent Transformational Studies in European Languages*, Linguistic Inquiry Monograph 3, Cambridge, Mass.: MIT Press.

Kroll, B. (1977) 'Combining ideas in written and spoken English: a look at subordination and coordination', in E. Keenan (ed.), *Discourse Across Time and Space*, SCOPIL No. 5, Department of Linguistics, University of Southern California.

Kuczaj, S. and Maratsos, M. (1975) 'What a child *can* say before he *will*', *Merrill-Palmer Quarterly* 21: 89–111.

Kuno, S. (1976) 'Subject, theme and speaker's empathy: a re-examination of relativization phenomena', in C. Li (ed.), *Subject and Topic*, New York: Academic Press, pp. 417–45.

Labov, T. (1982) 'Social structure and peer terminology in a black adolescent gang', *Language in Society* 11: 391–413.

Labov, W. (1963) 'The social motivation of a sound change', *Word* 19: 273–309.

Labov, W. (1966) *The Social Stratification of English in New York City*, Washington, DC: Centre for Applied Linguistics.

Labov, W. (1969) 'On the logic of non-standard English', *Georgetown Monographs on Language and Linguistics* 22. Washington, DC. Georgetown University Press.

Labov, W. (1970a) 'Stages in the acquisition of Standard English', in H. Hungerford, J. Robinson and J. Sledd (eds), *English Linguistics*, Glenview, Illinois: Scott Foresman, pp. 275–302.

Labov, W. (1970b) 'The study of language in its social context', *Studium Generale* 23: 30–87.

Labov, W. (1972a) *Sociolinguistic Patterns*, Philadelphia: University of Pennsylvania Press.

Labov, W. (1972b) *Language in the Inner City*, Philadelphia: University of Pennyslvania Press.

Labov, W. (1973) 'Where do grammars stop?' in R. Shuy (ed.), *Sociolinguistics: Current Trends and Prospects*, Washington, DC: Georgetown University Press, pp. 43–84.

Labov, W. (1980) 'The social origins of sound change', in W. Labov (ed.), *Locating Language in Time and Space*, New York: Academic Press, pp. 251–64.

Labov, W. (1981) 'Field methods of the project on linguistic change and variation', *Working Papers on Sociolinguistics* 81, Austin, Texas.

Labov, W. (1982) 'Objectivity and commitment in linguistic science: The case of the Black English trial in Ann Arbor', *Language in Society* 11: 165–203.

Labov, W., Cohen, P., Robins, C. and Lewis, J. (1968) *A Preliminary Study of the Structure of English Used by Negro and Puerto Rican Speakers in New York City*, Final report: Cooperative Research Project No. 3091, Washington, DC: Office of Education.

Labov, W., Yaeger, M. and Steiner, R. (1972) *A Quantitative Study of Sound Change in Progress*, 2 vols, Philadelphia: US Regional Survey.

Lakoff, R. (1971) 'Passive resistance', Papers from the Seventh Regional Meeting, Chicago Linguistic Society, pp. 149–63.

Lakoff, R. (1973) *Language and Women's Place*, New York: Harper & Row.

Lambert, W.E. (1960) 'Evaluational reactions to spoken languages', *Journal of Abnormal and Social Psychology*, 60: 44–51.

Lambert, W.E. (1972) *Language, Culture and Personality: Essays by W.E. Lambert*, ed. A.S. Dil, Stanford: Stanford University Press.

Langacker, R. and Munro, P. (1975) 'Passives and their meaning' *Language* 51: 789–831.

Larsson, K. (1979) 'Elevtexter: en material beskrivning från projektet. Textstruktur och språkfardigheit hos skoleleve', *FUMS Rapport* No. 66, Uppsala.

Lawson, C. (1967) 'Request patterns in a two year old', unpublished ms., Berkeley, California.

Leander, M. and Synnemark, M. (1970) 'Andelsevariation i neutrum bestamd form hos några gruppa Eskilstunabor', *FUMS Rapport* No. 9, Uppsala.

Lehmann, W.P. (1976) 'From topic to subject in Indo-European', in C. Li (ed.), *Subject and Topic*, New York: Academic Press, pp. 457–91.

Le Page, R.B. (1974) 'Processes of pidginization and creolization', *York Papers in Linguistics* 4: 41–69.

Le Page, R. B. (1978) 'Projection; focussing; diffusion: steps towards a socio-linguistic theory of language', Caribbean Linguistics Society Occasional Paper No. 9.

Le Page, R.B. (forthcoming) 'The need for a multidimensional model', to appear in G. Gilbert (ed.), *Pidgin and Creole Languages: Essays in Memory of John Reinecke*.

Levine, L. and Crockett, H.J. (1967) 'Speech variation in a Piedmont community:

postvocalic /r/', in S. Lieberson (ed.), *Explorations in Sociolinguistics*, Bloomington: Indiana University Press, pp. 76–98.

Levinson, S. (1983) *Pragmatics*, Cambridge: Cambridge University Press.

Li, C. and Thompson, S.A. (1976) 'Subject and topic: a new typology of language', in C. Li (ed.), *Subject and Topic*, New York: Academic Press, pp. 457–91.

Lightfoot, D. (1982) *The Language Lottery: Toward a Biology of Grammars*, Cambridge, Mass.: MIT Press.

Limber, J. (1973) 'The genesis of complex sentences', in T. Moore (ed.), *Cognitive Development and the Acquisition of Language*, New York: Academic Press.

Local, J. (1982) 'Modelling intonational variability in children's speech', in S. Romaine (ed.), *Sociolinguistic Variation in Speech Communities*, London: Edward Arnold, pp. 85–105.

Luria, A.R. (1976) *Cognitive Development: Its Cultural and Social Functions*, Cambridge, Mass.: Harvard University Press.

Lyons, J. (1968) *Introduction to Theoretical Linguistics*, Cambridge: Cambridge University Press.

Lyons, J. (1977) *Semantics*, 2 vols, Cambridge: Cambridge University Press.

MacAllister, A. (1938-9) *Speech Training for Juniors*, BBC Broadcasts to Scottish Schools.

MacAllister, A. (1963) *A Year's Course in Speech Training*, 9th edn, London: University of London Press.

Macaulay, R. (1975) 'Negative prestige, linguistic insecurity and linguistic self-hatred', *Lingua* 36: 147–61.

Macaulay, R. (1977) *Language, Social Class and Education: A Glasgow Study*, Edinburgh: University of Edinburgh Press.

Macaulay, R. (1978a) 'Variation and consistency in Glaswegian English', in P. Trudgill (ed.), *Sociolinguistic Patterns in British English*, London: Edward Arnold, pp. 132–44.

Macaulay, R. (1978b) 'The myth of female superiority in language', *Journal of Child Language* 5: 353–63.

Macaulay, R (forthcoming) 'The rise and fall of the vernacular', to appear in *Language in Society*.

Maccoby, E.E. and Jacklin, C.N. (1974) *The Psychology of Sex Differences*, Stanford: Stanford University Press.

Macdonald's Starters (1972) *Examples from America.*

McLuhan, M. (1962) *The Gutenberg Galaxy*, Toronto: University of Toronoto Press.

Maclure, M. and French, P. (1981) 'A comparison of talk at home and at school', in G. Wells (ed.), *Learning through Interaction*, Cambridge: Cambridge University Press.

McNew, S. (1975) 'Elicitation of identifying expressions in pre-school children', unpublished ms., University of Colorado.

MacWhinney, B. (1982) 'Basic syntactic processes', in S. Kuczaj (ed.), *Language Development*, I: *Syntax and Semantics*, Hillsdale, NJ: Lawrence Erlbaum, pp. 73-137.

Maltz, D. and Borker, R. (1982) 'A cultural approach to male–female miscommunication', in J. Gumperz (ed.), *Language and Social Identity*, Cambridge: Cambridge University Press, pp. 195–217.

Maratsos, M.P. (1976) *The Use of Definite and Indefinite Reference in Young Children*, Cambridge: Cambridge University Press.

Maratsos, M. (1978) 'New models in linguistics and language acquisition', in M.

Halle, J. Bresnan and G. Miller, (eds), *Linguistic Theory and Psychological Reality*, Cambridge, Mass.: MIT Press.

Maratsos, M. and Abraovitch, R. (1975) 'How children understand full, truncated and anomalous passives', *Journal of Verbal Learning and Verbal Behaviour* 14: 145–57.

Markey, T.L. and Fodale, P. (1983) 'Lexical diathesis, focal shifts and passivization: the creole voice', *English World Wide* 4: 69–85.

Martin, J.R. (1983) 'The development of register', in J. Fine and R. Freedle (eds), *Developmental Issues in Discourse*, Norwood, NJ: Ablex. pp. 1–40.

Martin, J.R. and Rothery, J. (1980) Writing Project Report No. 1, *Working Papers in Linguistics*, Linguistics Department, University of Sydney.

Martin, J.R. and Rothery, J. (1981) Writing Project Report No. 2, *Working Papers in Linguistics*, Linguistics Department, University of Sydney.

Matthews, P. (1979) *Generative Grammar and Linguistic Competence*, London: Allen & Unwin.

Matthews, P. (1981) *Syntax*, Cambridge: Cambridge University Press.

Mayer, K.D. (1955) *Class and Society*, New York: Random House.

Meditch, A. (1975) 'The development of sex specific speech patterns in young children', *Anthropological Linguistics* 17: 421–34.

Mees, I. (1977) 'Language and social class in Cardiff: a survey of the speech habits of school children', thesis, Dept. of English, Rijksuniversiteit te Leiden, Leiden, Holland.

Mehan, H. (1974) 'Accomplishing classroom lessons', in A. Cicourel et al., *Language Use and School Performance*, New York: Academic Press, pp. 76–143.

Mehan, H. (1979) 'The competent student', *Working Papers in Sociolinguistics* No. 61, Austin, Texas.

Mehan, H. (1983) 'The role of language and the language of role in institutional decision making', *Language in Society* 12: 187–213.

Menyuk, P. (1969) *Sentences Children Use*, Cambridge, Mass.: MIT Press.

Michaels, S. (1981) ' "Sharing time": children's narrative styles and differential access to literacy', *Language in Society* 10: 423–43.

Millar, M. and Brown, K. (1979) 'Tag questions in Edinburgh speech', *Linguistische Berichte* 66: 24–45.

Milroy, L. (1980) *Language and Social Networks*, Oxford: Blackwell.

Milroy, J. (1981) *Regional Accents of English: Belfast*, Belfast: Blackstaff.

Milroy, L. and Margrain, S. (1980) 'Vernacular language loyalty and social network', *Language in Society* 9: 43–70.

Milroy, L. and McClenaghan, P. (1977) 'Stereotyped reactions to four educated accents in Ulster', *Belfast Working Papers in Language and Linguistics* 2: 1–10.

Mitchell-Kernan, C. (1972) 'Signifying and marking: two Afro-American speech acts,' in J. Gumperz and D. Hymes (eds), *Directions in Sociolinguistics*, New York: Holt, Rinehart & Winston, pp. 161–80.

Mitchell-Kernan, C. and Kernan, K. (1977) 'Pragmatics of directive choice among children', in S. Ervin-Tripp and C. Mitchell-Kernan (eds), *Child Discourse*, New York: Academic Press, pp. 181–208.

Morrison, A. and MacIntyre, D.C. (1973) *Teachers and Teaching*, Harmondsworth: Penguin.

Moser, C.A. and Kalton, G. (1958) *Survey Methods in Social Investigation*, London: Heinemann.

Moskowitz, B.A. (1973) 'On the status of vowel shift in English', in T.E. Moore (ed.), *Cognitive Development and the Acquisition of Language*, New York: Academic Press, pp. 223–60.

Munro, J.K. and Wales, R.J. (1982) 'Changes in the child's comprehension of simultaneity and sequence', *Journal of Verbal Learning and Verbal Behaviour* 21: 175–86.

National Council of Teachers of English (1974) Conference on College Composition and Communication.

Newman, S.E. (1974) *Strictly Speaking: Will America be the death of English?*, Indianapolis: Bobbs-Merrill.

Newport, E., Gleitman, H. and Gleitman, L. (1977) 'Mother, I'd rather do it myself: some effects and non-effects of maternal speech style,' in C. Snow and C.F. Ferguson (eds), *Talking to Children*, Cambridge: Cambridge University Press, pp. 109–51.

Newsweek (1975) 'Why Johnny can't write', 8 December.

Newsweek (1984) 'Taking the test for teachers', 16 January.

Nordberg, B. (1969) 'The urban dialect of Eskilstuna, methods and problems', *FUMS Rapport* No. 4, Uppsala.

Nordberg, B. (1971) 'En undersökning av språket i Eskilstuna', *Språkvård* 3: 7–15.

Nordberg, B. (1972) 'Morfologiska variationsmonster i ett central svenskt stadsspråk', in B. Loman (ed.), *Språk och Samhalle*, Gleerups: Lund, pp. 14–44.

Nordberg, B. (1975) 'Contemporary social variation as a stage in long-term phonological change', in K.H. Dahlstedt (ed.), *The Nordic Languages and Modern Linguistics*, Stockholm: Almqvist & Wiksell International, pp. 587–608.

Nyholm, L. (1976) 'Formväxling i Helsingforssvenskan – En studie i intervjusprak', *FUMS Rapport* No. 44, Uppsala.

Ochs, E. (1979) 'Planned and unplanned discourse', in T. Givón (ed.), *Discourse and Syntax*, XII: *Syntax and Semantics*, New York: Academic Press, pp.51–78.

Ochs, E. (1982) 'Talking to children in Western Samoa', *Language in Society* 11: 77–105.

Ochs, E. and Schieffelin, B. (eds), (1979) *Developmental Pragmatics*, New York: Academic Press.

Ochs, E. and Schieffelin, B. (1983) *Acquiring Conversational Competence*. London: Routledge & Kegan Paul.

Oksaar, E. (1981) 'Linguistic and pragmatic awareness of monolingual and multilingual children', in P. Dale and D. Ingram (eds), *Child Language: An International Perspective*, Baltimore: University Park Press, pp. 273–87.

Oller, J. (1979) *Language Tests at School: A Pragmatic Approach*, London: Longman.

O'Neil, W. (1980) 'English orthography', in T. Shopen, and J. Williams (eds), *Standards and Dialects of English*, Cambridge, Mass.: Winthrop, pp. 63–84.

Opie, I. and Opie, P. (1959) *The Lore and Language of Schoolchildren*, London: Oxford University Press.

Pattison, R. (1982) *On Literacy: the Politics of the Word from Homer to the Age of Rock*, Oxford: Oxford University Press.

Payne, A. (1980) 'Factors controlling the acquisition of the Philadelphia dialect by out-of-state children', in W. Labov (ed.), *Locating Language in Time and Space*, New York: Academic Press, pp. 143–77.

Pedersen, K.M. (1977) 'Dialekt, regionalsprog, rigssprog – en analyse af borns skolesprog', Abenraa, unpublished ms.

Peters, A. (1983) *The Units of Language Acquisition*, Cambridge: Cambridge University Press.

Pfaff, C. (1980) 'Lexicalization in Black English', in R. Day (ed.), *Issues in English Creoles*, Heidelberg: Julius Gross Verlag, pp. 163–81.

Philips, S. (1974) 'Warm Springs "Indian Time": How the regulation of participation affects the progression of events', in R. Bauman and J. Sherzer (eds), *Explorations in the Ethnography of Speaking*, Cambridge: Cambridge University Press, pp. 92–110.

Piaget, J. (1926) *The Language and Thought of the Child*, New York: Harcourt Brace.

Pike, E. (1952) 'Controlled human infant intonation', *Language Learning* 2: 1–21.

Portz, R. (1979) 'Another look at stages in the acquisition of standard English', Paper given at the Ninth International Congress of Phonetic Sciences, Copenhagen.

Quirk, R. (1957) 'Relative clauses in educated spoken English', *English Studies* 38: 97–109.

Quirk, R., Greenbaum, S., Leech, G. and Svartvik, J. (1972) *A Grammar of Contemporary English*, London: Longman.

Raittila, M. (1969) 'Variation i preteritum av svaga verb i Stockholms språket', unpublished ms.

Raum, O. (1940) *Chaga Childhood*, London: Oxford University Press.

Read, B. and Cherry, L.J. (1978) 'Preschool children's production of directive forms', *Discourse Processes* I: 233–45.

Read, C. (1980) 'Creative spelling by young children,' in T. Shopen and J. Williams (eds), *Standards and Dialects of English*, Cambridge, Mass.: Winthrop, pp. 106–37.

Reid, E. (1976) 'Social and stylistic variation in the Speech of some Edinburgh schoolchildren', MLitt thesis, University of Edinburgh.

Reid, E. (1978) 'Social and stylistic variation in the speech of children: some evidence from Edinburgh', in P. Trudgill (ed.), *Sociolinguistic Patterns in British English*, London: Edward Arnold, pp. 158–73.

Reuter, O. (1934) *On the Development of English Verbs from Latin and French Past Participles*, Societies Scientarum Fennica. Commentationes Humanarum Litterarum 6, Helsinki.

Ritchie, J.T.R. (1964) *The Singing Street*, London: Oliver & Boyd.

Robertson, S. and Cassidy, F.G. (1954) *The Development of Modern English*, Englewood Cliffs, NJ: Prentice-Hall.

Romaine, S. (1975) 'Linguistic variability in the speech of some Edinburgh schoolchildren', MLitt thesis, University of Edinburgh.

Romaine, S. (1978) 'Post-vocalic /r/ in Scottish English: sound change in progress?', in P. Trudgill (ed.), *Sociolinguistic Patterns in British English*, London: Edward Arnold, pp. 144–58.

Romaine, S. (1979) 'The Language of Edinburgh schoolchildren: the acquisition of sociolinguistic competence', *Scottish Literary Journal* (Language supplement) 9: 55–61.

Romaine, S. (1980a) 'Stylistic variation and evaluation reactions to speech', *Language and Speech* 23: 213–32.

Romaine, S. (1980b) 'The relative clause marker in Scots English: diffusion, complexity and style as dimensions of syntactic change', *Language in Society* 9: 221–49.

Romaine, S. (1980c) 'A critical overview of the methodology of urban British sociolinguistics', *English World Wide* 1: 163–98.

Romaine, S. (1981) 'Syntactic complexity, relativization and stylistic levels in Middle Scots', *Folia Linguistica Historica* 2: 56–77.

Romaine, S. (1982a) *Socio-historical Linguistics: Its Status and Methodology*, Cambridge: Cambridge University Press.

Romaine, S. (1982b) *Sociolinguistic Variation in Speech Communities*, London: Edward Arnold.

Romaine, S. (1982c) 'Introduction', in S. Romaine (ed.), *Sociolinguistic Variation in Speech Communities*, London: Edward Arnold, pp. 1–13.

Romaine, S. (1983a) 'Towards a typology of relative clause formation strategies in Germanic', in J. Fisiak (ed.), *Historical Syntax*, The Hague: Mouton.

Romaine, S. (1983b) 'The problem of short /a/ in Scotland', in *Focus on Scotland*, special issue of *English World Wide*, ed. M. Görlach, Heidelberg: Julius Groos Verlag.

Romaine, S. (1984) 'The sociolinguistic history of t/d deletion', *Folia Linguistica Historica* 5: 221–57.

Romaine, S. and Dorian, N. (1981) 'Scotland as a linguistic area', *Scottish Literary Journal* 14: 1–24.

Romaine, S. and Traugott, E.C. (1981) 'The problem of style in sociolinguistics', paper presented at the Linguistic Society of America Winter Meeting, December 1981, New York City.

Rommetveit, R. (1980) 'On "meanings " of acts and what is meant and made known by what is said in a pluralistic social world', in M. Brenner (ed.), *The Structure of Action*, Oxford: Blackwell, pp. 108–49.

Rosen, H. (1972) *Language and Class: a Critical Look at the Theories of Basil Bernstein*, Bristol: Falling Wall Press.

Rosenthal, M. (1973) 'Children's perception of social variation in English', PhD thesis, Georgetown University.

Ross, J.R. (1967) 'Constraints on variables in syntax', PhD dissertation, MIT.

Ross, J.R. (1969) 'Adjectives as noun phrases', in D. Reibel and S.R. Schane (eds), *Modern Studies in English*, Englewood Cliffs, NJ: Prentice-Hall, pp. 352–60.

Rozin, P. and Gleitman, L. (1977) 'The structure and acquisition of reading 1', in A. Reber and D. Scarborough (eds), *Towards a Psychology of Reading*, Hillsdale, NJ: Lawrence Erlbaum.

Rubin, D.L. and Nelson, M.W. (1984) 'Multiple determinants of a stigmatized speech style: women's language, powerless language or everyone's language?', *Language and Speech* 26: 273–91.

Russell, J. (1982) 'Networks and sociolinguistic variation in an African urban setting', in S. Romaine (ed.), *Sociolinguistic Variation in Speech Communities*, London: Edward Arnold, pp. 125–41.

Sachs, J. and Devin, J. (1976) 'Young children's use of age-appropriate speech styles in social interaction and role-playing', *Journal of Child Language* 3: 81–98.

Sandred, K.I. (1983) *Good or Bad Scots? Attitudes to Optional Lexical and Grammatical Usages in Edinburgh*, Studia Anglistica Upsaliensa 48, Stockholm: Almquist & Wiksell International.

Sankoff, G. (1980) 'Political power and linguistic inequality in Papua New Guinea', in G. Sankoff, *The Social Life of Language*, Philadelphia: University of Pennsylvania Press, pp. 5–29.

Sankoff, G. and Brown, P. (1976) 'The origins of syntax in discourse: the case of Tok Pisin relatives', *Language* 52: 631–66.

Saunders, G. (1982) *Bilingual Children: Guidance for the family*, Clevedon, Avon: Multilingual Matters.

Saville-Troike, M. (1982) *The Ethnography of Communication: An Introduction*, Oxford: Blackwell.

Saywitz, K. and Wilkinson, L. (1982)'Age related differences in metalinguistic awareness', in S. Kuczaj (ed.), *Language Development*, II: *Language, Thought and Culture*, Hillsdale, NJ: Lawrence Erlbaum, pp. 229–50.

Schachter, P. (1973) 'Focus and relativization', *Language* 49: 19–46.

Schieffelin, B. (1979) 'How Kaluli children learn what to say, what to do, and how to feel: an ethnographic study of the development of communcative competence', PhD dissertation, Columbia University.

Schieffelin, B. (1981) 'A developmental study of pragmatic appropriateness of word order and case marking in Kaluli', in W. Deutsch (ed.), *The Child's Construction of Language*, New York: Academic Press, pp. 105–20.

Scollon, R. and Scollon, S. (1979) *Linguistic Convergence: An Ethnography of Speaking at Fort Chipewyan, Alberta*, New York: Academic Press.

Scollon, R. and Scollon, S. (1981) *Narrative Literacy and Face in Inter-ethnic Communication*, Norwood, NJ: Ablex.

Scribner, S. (1977) 'Modes of thinking and ways of speaking: culture and logic reconsidered', in P. Johnson-Laird and P.C. Wason (eds), *Thinking Readings in Cognitive Science*, Cambridge: Cambridge University Press, pp. 483–519.

Scribner, S. and Cole, M. (1981) *The Psychology of Literacy*, Cambridge, Mass.: Harvard University Press.

Sebba, M. and Le Page, R.B. (1983) 'Sociolinguistics of London Jamaican English: Report on the pilot project (1981–2)', University of York, Department of Language.

Shaklee, M. (1980) 'The rise of standard English', in T. Shopen and J. Williams (eds), *Dialects and Standards of English*, Cambridge, Mass.: Winthrop, pp. 33–63.

Shatz, M. (1978) 'Children's comprehension of their mother's question directives', *Journal of Child Language* 5: 31–46.

Shatz, M. and Gelman, R. (1973) 'The development of communication skills: modifications in the speech of young children as a function of the listener', *Monographs for Social Research on Child Development* 38.5.

Sheldon, A. (1974) 'The role of parallel function in the acquisition of relative clauses in English', *Journal of Verbal Learning and Verbal Behaviour*, 13: 272–81.

Sherif, M. and Sherif, C.W. (1973) *An Outline of Social Psychology*. New York: Harper.

Shuy, R. (1977) 'Quantitative language data: a case for and some warning against', *Anthropology and Educational Quarterly* 1(2): 78–82.

Shuy, R. (1978) 'What children's functional language can tell us about reading or how Joanna got himself invited to dinner', in R. Beach (ed.), *Perspectives on Literacy: Proceedings of the 1977 Perspectives on literacy conference*, Minneapolis: University of Minnesota.

Shuy, R. (1979) 'The mismatch of child language and school language: implications of beginning reading instruction', in L.B. Resmich and P.A. Weaver (eds), *Theory and Practices of Early Learning*, I, Hillsdale, NJ: Lawrence Erlbaum, pp. 187–207.

Shuy, R. and Staton, J. (1982) 'Assessing oral language ability in children', in L. Feagans and D. Farran (eds), *The Language of Children Reared in Poverty*, New York: Academic Press, pp. 181–95.

Shuy, R., Wolfram, W. and Riley, W.K. (1968) *Field Techniques in an Urban Language Study*, Washington, DC: Centre for Applied Linguistics.

Silverstein, M. (1976) 'Hierarchy of features and ergativity', in R. Dixon (ed.), *Grammatical Categories in Australian Language*, Canberra: Australian Institute of Aboriginal Studies, pp. 112–72.

Silverstein, M. (1981) 'The limits of awareness', *Working Papers in Sociolinguistics* No. 84. Austin, Texas.

Sinclair, H. and Bronckhart, J.P. (1972) 'S.V.O. a linguistic universal? A study in developmental psycholinguistics', *Journal of Experimental Child Psychology* 14: 329–48.

Sinclair, H. and Ferreiro, E. (1970) 'Production et repetition des phrases au mode passsif', *Archives de Psychologie* 40: 1–42.

Sinclair, J. and Coulthard, M. (1975) *Towards an Analysis of Discourse*, London: Oxford University Press.

Sledd, J. and Ebbitt, W. (eds) (1962) *Dictionaries and THAT Dictionary*, Glenview, Ill.: Scott Foresman.

Slobin, D. (1968) 'Recall of full and truncated passive sentences in connected discourse', *Journal of Verbal Learning and Verbal Behaviour* 7: 876–81.

Slobin, D. (1973) 'Cognitive prerequisites for the development of grammar', in C. Ferguson and D. Slobin (eds), *Studies of Child Language Development*, New York: Holt, Rinehart & Winston.

Slobin, D. (1977) 'Language change in childhood and history', in C. Ferguson and D. Slobin (eds), *Studies of Child Language Development*, New York: Holt, Rinehart & Winston, pp. 175–208.

Slobin, D. (1980) 'The repeated path between transparency and opacity in language', in U. Belugi and M. Studdert-Kennedy (eds), *Signed and spoken Language: Biological Constraints on Linguistic Form*, Berlin: Verlag Chemie, pp. 229–43.

Slobin, D. (1981) 'The origins of grammatical encoding of events', in W. Deutsch (ed.), *The Child's Construction of Language*, London: Academic Press, pp. 185–99.

Slobin, D. (forthcoming) 'The acquisition and use of relative clauses in Turkic and Indo-European languages', to appear in K. Zimmer and D. Slobin (eds), *Studies in Turkish Linguistics*.

Slobin, D. and Welsh, C.A. (1973) 'Elicited imitation as a research tool in developmental psycholinguistics', in C.A. Ferguson and D. Slobin (eds), *Studies of Child Language Development*, New York: Holt, Rinehart & Winston.

Smith, A. (ed.) (1972) *Language Communication and Rhetoric in Black America*, New York: Harper & Row.

Smith, N. (1973) *The Acquisition of Phonology*, Cambridge: Cambridge University Press.

Smith, N. and Wilson,. D. (1979) *Modern Linguistics: The Results of Chomsky's Revolution*, Harmondsworth: Penguin.

Smith, P. (1979) 'Sex markers in speech', in H. Giles and K. Sherer (eds), *Social Markers in Speech*, Cambridge: Cambridge University Press, pp. 109–37.

Snow, C.E. (1977) 'Mothers' speech research: from input to interaction', in C.E. Snow and C. Ferguson (eds), *Talking to Children: Language Input and*

Acquisition, Cambridge: Cambridge University Press.

Snow, C.E. and Ferguson, C. (eds) (1977) *Talking to Children: Language Input and Acquisition*, Cambridge: Cambridge University Press.

Speitel, H. (1975) 'Dialect', in A. Davies (ed.), *Problems of Language and Learning*, London: Heinemann, pp. 34–53.

Spindler, G. (ed.) (1982) *Doing the Ethnography of Schooling*, New York: CBS Publishing.

Stein, G. (1979) *Studies in the Function of the Passive*, Tübinger Beiträge zur Linguistik 97, Tübinger: Gunther Narr.

Steinberg, D. and Krohn, R. (1975) 'The psychological validity of Chomsky and Halle's vowel shift rule', in K. Koerner (ed.), *The Transformational Generative Paradigm and Modern Linguistic Theory*, Amsterdam: Benjamins, pp. 233–59.

Stern, D. (1971) 'A micro-analysis of mother–infant interaction', *Journal of the American Academy of Child Psychiatry* 10: 501–17.

Stern, D. (1977) *The First Relationship: Infant and Mother*, Cambridge, Mass.: Harvard University Press.

Stewart, W. (1968) 'A sociolinguistic theory for describing national multilingualism', in J. Fishman (ed.), *Readings in the Sociology of Language*, The Hague: Mouton, pp. 531–45.

Strang, B. (1970) *A History of English*, London: Methuen.

Strohmer, H. and Nelson, K. (1974) 'The young child's development of sentence comprehension: influence of events probability, non-vebal context, syntactic form and strategies', *Child Development* 45: 567–76.

Stubbs, M. (1976) *Language, Schools and Classrooms*, London: Methuen.

Stubbs, M (1980) *Language and Literacy: The Sociolinguistics of Reading and Writing*, London: Routledge & Kegan Paul.

Stubbs, M. (1983) *Discourse Analysis*, Oxford: Blackwell.

Sussex, R. (1982) 'A note on the *get*-passive construction', *Australian Journal of Linguistics* 2: 83–93.

Sutcliffe, D. (1982) *British Black English*, Oxford: Blackwell.

Svartvik, J. (1966) *On Voice in the English Verb*, The Hague: Mouton.

Sweet, H. (1900) *A New English Grammar: Logical and Historical*, Oxford: Clarendon Press.

Tannen, D. (1982) 'Oral and literate strategies in spoken and written narrative', *Language* 58: 1–21.

Tavakolian, S. (1977) 'Structural Principles in the Acquisition of Complex Sentences', PhD Dissertation, University of Massachusetts.

Tavakolian, S. (1978) 'The conjoined-clause analysis of relative clauses and other structures', In H. Goodluck and L. Solan (eds), *Papers in the Structure and Development of Child Language*, University of Massachusetts Occasional Papers, vol. 4, Linguistics Department, University of Massachusetts, Amherst.

Thelander, M. (1982) 'A qualitative approach to the quantitative data of speech variation', in S. Romaine (ed.), *Sociolinguistic Variation in Speech Communities*, London: Edward Arnold, pp. 65–85.

Thompson, S.A. (1971) 'The deep structure of relative clauses', in C. Fillmore and D.T. Langendoen (eds), *Studies in Linguistic Semantics*, New York: Holt, Rinehart and Winston, pp. 79–97.

Tibbitts, A. and Tibbitts, C. (1978) *What's Happening to American English?* New York: Charles Scribner's Sons.

Tingbrand, B. (1973) 'Norge ha vi förresten *vart* ganska mycke i å *åke*, tittat' Om verbböjning i Eskilstunaspråket', *FUMS Report* No. 29, Uppsala.

Todd, L. (1975) 'Base form and substratum: two case studies of English in contact', PhD thesis, Leeds Univeristy.

Traugott, E.C. (1981) 'The sociolinguistics of minority dialect in literary prose', *Proceedings of the Seventh Annual Meeting of the Berkeley Linguistic Society*, University of California, Berkeley.

Traugott, E.C. and Pratt, M. (1980) *Linguistics for Students of Literature*, New York: Harcourt, Brace, Jovanovich.

Traugott, E.C. and Romaine, S. (1983) 'The problem of style in socio-historical linguistics', paper given at the Workshop on Socio-historical Linguistics in Poznan, to appear in J. Fisiak (ed.), *Proceedings of the Sixth International Conference on Historical Linguistics*, Amsterdam: Benjamins.

Trevarthen, C. (1979) 'Communication and co-operation in early infancy: a description of primary intersubjectivity', in M. Bullowa, (ed.), *Before Speech: The Beginning of Interpersonal Communication*, Cambridge: Cambridge University Press.

Trudgill, P. (1972) 'Sex, covert prestige and linguistic change in the urban British English of Norwich, *Language in Society* 1: 179–96.

Trudgill, P. (1974a) *The Social Differentiation of English in Norwich*, Cambridge: Cambridge University Press.

Trudgill, P. (1974b) *Sociolinguistics*, Harmondsworth: Penguin.

Trudgill, P. (1982) 'On the limits of passive competence: sociolinguistics and the polylectal grammar controversy', in D. Crystal (ed.), *Linguistic Controversies: Essays in Linguistic Theory and Practice in Honour of F.R. Palmer*, London: Edward Arnold, pp. 172–92.

Trudgill, P. (1983) 'Acts of conflicting identity', in *On Dialect Social and Geographical Perspectives*, Oxford: Blackwell, pp. 141–60.

Trudgill, P. and Hannah, J. (1982) *International English: A Guide to Varieties of Standard English*, London: Edward Arnold.

Tunner, W.E., Pratt, C. and Herriman, M.L. (eds), (1984) *Metalinguistic Awareness in Children: Theory, Research and Implications*, Berlin: Springer.

Turner, E. and Rommetveit, R. (1967) 'Experimental manipulation of the production of active and passive voice in children', *Language and Speech* 10: 169–80.

Turner, E. and Rommetveit, R. (1968) 'Focus of attention in recall of active and passive sentences as a function of subject or object focus', *Journal of Verbal Learning and Verbal Behaviour* 7: 246–50.

Ullmer-Ehrich, V. (1981) 'L'usage des prépositions indexicales dans un discours descriptif – la perspective déictique et la perspective inhérente', in C. Schwarze (ed.), *Analyses des prépositions*, Tübingen: Niemeyer, pp. 224–50.

Van den Broeck, J. (1977) 'Class differences in syntactic complexity in the Flemish town of Maaseik', *Language in Society* 6: 149–83.

van der Geest, T. (1975) *Some Aspects of Communicative Competence and their Implications for Language Acquisition*, Amsterdam: Van Gorcum.

Vygotsky, L.S. (1966) 'Play and its role in the mental development of the child', *Soviet Psychology* 12: 62–76.

Wald, B. (1982) 'Syntacticization in language development: clause status variation', paper given at NWAVE XI, Georgetown University, Washington DC.

Wales, R.J. (1979) 'Deixis', in P. Fletcher and M. Garman (eds), *Studies in Language Acquisition*, Cambridge: Cambridge University Press.

Wall, S. and Kaufman, L. (1980) 'The processing of resumptive pronouns', unpublished ms., Brandeis University.

Wallace, A.F.C. (1961) *Culture and Personality*, New York: Random House.

Wanner, E. and Gleitman, L. (eds) (1982) *Language Acquisition: The State of the Art*, Cambridge: Cambridge University Press.

Wasow, T. (1977) 'Transformations and the lexicon', in P. Culicover, T. Wasow and A. Akmajian (eds), *Formal Syntax*, New York: Academic Press, pp. 327–61.

Wasow, T. (1980) 'Major and minor rules in lexical grammar', *Glot-lexical Grammar* (1980) 285–312.

Watt, W. (1970) 'On two hypotheses concerning psycholinguistics', in J.R. Hayes (ed.), *Cognition and the Development of Language*, New York: Wiley.

Weber, M. (1964) *The Theory of Social and Economic Organisation*, Glencoe, Ill.: Free Press.

Weeks, T. (1979 *Born to Talk*, Rowley, Mass.: Newbury House.

Weinberg, A. (1981) 'Passive and the projection problem', paper presented at GLOW conference, Göttingen.

Weiner, E.J. and Labov, W. (1983) 'Constraints on the agentless passive', *Journal of Linguistics* 19: 29–59.

Weinreich, U., Labov, W. and Herzog, M. (1968) 'Empirical foundations for a theory of language change', in W.P. Lehmann and Y. Malkiel (eds), *Directions in Historical Linguistics*, Austin, Texas: University of Texas Press.

Weissenborn, J. (1983) 'Ich weiss ja nicht von hier aus; wie weit es von dahinten aus ist', Makroräume in der kognitiven and sprachlichen Entwicklung des Kindes', in H. Schweizer (ed.), *Sprache und Raum*, Stuttgart: Metzeler.

Wells, C.G. (1978) 'What makes for successful language development', in R. Campbell and P. Smith (eds), *Advances in the Psychology of Language*, II, New York: Plenum.

Wells, C.G. (1979) 'Describing children's learning: development at home and at school', *British Educational Research Journal* 5: 75–89.

Wells, J.C. (1973) *Jamaican Pronunciation in London*, Oxford: Blackwell.

Wells, J.C. (1982) *Accents of English*, 3 vols, Cambridge: Cambridge University Press.

Wessén, E. (1965) *Svensk Språkhistoria*, Stockholm: Almquist & Wiksell International.

Wexler, K. and Culicover, P. (1980) *Formal Principles of Language Acquisition*, Cambridge, Mass.: MIT Press.

White, L. (1982) *Grammatical Theory and Language Acquisition*, Dordrecht: Foris Publications.

Whitehurst, G., Ironsmith, M. and Goldfein, M. (1974) 'Selective imitation of the passive construction through modelling', *Journal of Experimental Child psychology* 17: 288–302.

Whiteman, M.F. (ed.) (1980) *Reactions to Ann Arbor: Vernacular Black English and Education*, Washington, DC: Centre for Applied Linguistics.

Whiteman, M.F. (1981) 'Dialect influence in writing', in M.F. Whiteman (ed.), *Writing: The Nature, Development and Teaching of Written Communication*, I: *Variation in Writing: Functional and Linguistic – Cultural Perspectives*, Hillsdale, NJ: Lawrence Erlbaum, pp. 153–66.

Wick, T. (1980) 'The pursuit of universal literacy', *Journal of Communication* 30: 107–12.

Widmark, G. (1970a) 'Generationsskillnaderna i språket', *Språkvård* 2: 3–10.

Widmark, G. (1970b) 'Stildifferentiering i Gyllenborgs Komedi Swenska Sprätt-hoken', *Nysvenska Studier* 49: 5–77.

Widmark, G. (1977) 'Lokatt och rikspråkligt en undersökning av Uppsalaspråk', in C. Elert, S. Eliasson, S. Fries and S. Ureland, *Dialectology and Sociolinguistics: Essays in Honor of Karl-Hampus Dahlstedt*, Umeå, pp. 246–62.

Wilcox, K. (1982) 'Ethnography as a methodology and its applications to the study of schooling, a review', in G. Spindler (ed.), *Doing the Ethnography of Schooling*, New York: CBS Publishing, pp. 456–88.

Wilkinson, A. (1965) 'Spoken English', *Educational Review*, supplement to 17(2) Occasional Publication.

Williams, J. (1981) 'Literary style: the personal voice', in T. Shopen and J. Williams (eds), *Style and Variables in English*, Cambridge, Mass.: Winthrop, pp. 115–217.

Wilson, J. (1926) *The Dialect of the Southern Countries of Scotland*, London: Oxford University Press.

Woehr, R., Barson, J. and Valadez, G. (1974) *Español esencial: un repaso*, Corte Madera: Holt, Rinehart & Winston.

Wolfram, W. (1969) *A Sociolinguistic Description of Detroit Negro Speech*, Washington, DC: Centre for Applied Linguistics.

Wolfram, W. (1973) *Sociolinguistic Aspects of Assimilation: Puerto Rican English in New York City*, Washington, DC: Centre for Applied Linguistics.

Wolfram, W. and Christian, D. (1976) *Appalachian Speech*, Washington, DC: Centre for Applied Linguistics.

Wolfram, W. and Fasold, R. (1974) *The Study of Social Dialects in American English*, Englewood Cliffs, NJ: Prentice-Hall.

Wolfram, W., Potter, L., Yanofsky, N. and Shuy, R. (1979) *Reading and Dialect Differences*, Washington, DC: Centre for Applied Linguistics.

Wolfson, N. (1976) 'Speech events and natural speech: some implications for sociolinguistic methodology', *Language in Society* 5: 189–211.

Wolfson, N. (1982) *CHP: The Conversational Historical Present in American English Narrative*, Dordrecht: Foris.

Wright, F. (forthcoming) 'Some aspects of the development of passives in the Jamaican post-creole continuum', PhD thesis, University of Birmingham.

Wright, J. (1905) *The English Dialect Grammar*, London: Henry Frowde.

Wyld, H.C. (1920) *A History of Modern Colloquial English*, Oxford: Blackwell.

Yates, F. (1966) *The Art of Memory*, Harmondsworth: Penguin.

Yngve, V. (1972) 'The depth hypothesis', in F. Householder (ed.), *Syntactic Theory*, I: *Structuralist*, Harmondsworth: Penguin, pp. 115–24.

Zaenen, A. and Maling, J. (1982) 'The status of resumptive pronouns in Swedish', in E. Engdahl and E. Ejerhed (eds), *Reading on Unbounded Dependencies in Scandinavian Languages*, pp. 223–30.

Zengel, M. (1968) 'Literacy as a factor in language change', in J. Fishman (ed.), *Reading in the Sociology of Language*, The Hague: Mouton, pp. 296–305.

Zubin, D. (1979) 'Discourse function of morphology: the focus system in German', in Givón (ed.), *Discourse and Syntax*, New York: Academic Press, pp. 469–501.

Index